Hedgehogs

Hedgehogs

Nigel Reeve

*Illustrated by
Ruth Lindsay*

T & A D
POYSER
NATURAL
HISTORY

© T & A D Poyser Ltd

First published in 1994 by T & A D Poyser Ltd
24–28 Oval Road, London NW1 7DX

Typeset by Paston Press Ltd, Loddon, Norfolk
Printed and bound in Great Britain by
the University Press, Cambridge

A catalogue record for this book
is available from the British Library

ISBN 0-05661-081-X

Contents

The colour plate section can be found between pages 148 and 149.

List of Colour Plates

1. The European hedgehog (*Erinaceus europaeus*). Note the alert stance of an undisturbed, active animal.
2. Hedgehogs are able swimmers but may be unable to escape from steep-sided garden ponds. Photo: Pat Morris.
3. A 'blond' European hedgehog from Britain. Unlike an albino, it has normally coloured eyes but pink skin on the nose and paws. The pale coloration makes it easy to see how dirty some hedgehogs can get!
4. A female central African hedgehog (*Atelerix albiventris*) from Kenya, with her litter of four (aged around 12 days). Photo: Martin Gregory.
5. Long-eared hedgehog (*Hemiechinus* spp.). Photo: Pat Morris.
6. The bristling spines of a European hedgehog (*Erinaceus europaeus*). Note how they interlock and point in all directions.
7. The first line of defence is to crouch and draw down the spines to cover the face and limbs. This European hedgehog is normally coloured except for its pink nose and paws.
8. Sharp sounds, such as the click of a camera shutter, trigger a very fast reflexive flinch which has blurred this photograph of a central African hedgehog (*Atelerix albiventris*). Photo: Martin Gregory.
9. A loosely rolled-up European hedgehog turned on its back. The spiny skin of the forehead and rump is tightly clamped together to encase the animal completely if it is threatened.
10. If left undisturbed the hedgehog soon unrolls. This partially unrolled European hedgehog is lying in a 'bowl' of spiny skin, the rim formed by the *orbicularis* muscle.
11. A fresh hedgehog dropping.
12. The author locates a young European hedgehog tagged with a radio transmitter. Photo: Pat Morris.
13. European hedgehog nests are typically made of broad leaves tucked under brambles or other ground vegetation. This one was concealed under a disused trailer overgrown with grass.

Acknowledgements

I am pleased to have the opportunity to thank the many people who have, in many ways, helped me to write *Hedgehogs*. Firstly, I must thank Ernest Neal for inviting me to write this book, but the work would have been impossible without the help and friendship of many others.

In Britain, since the 1960s, Dr. Pat Morris has carried out, supervised or collaborated in virtually all research into the natural history of hedgehogs—including my own. Our current knowledge of the hedgehog in Britain has depended greatly upon his continuing dedication. I thank him for the chances he gave me, his academic guidance (he must have despaired many times) and his support in establishing my academic career. He made valuable criticisms of the original manuscript of this book and allowed reference to his unpublished Ph.D. thesis and the use of his photographs (Plates 2, 5 and 12).

I would like to thank: Dr. Andy Wroot, who allowed free access to his Ph.D. thesis and supplied the data for Fig. 3.2; Michael Sealey (MRCVS) for his invaluable veterinary advice during the preparation of Appendix 1; also Dr. A. Jones and Dr. L. M. Gibbons of the International Institute of Parasitology (St. Albans, UK) who advised me on the taxonomy and nomenclature of cestodes, nematodes and acanthocephala (Chapter 9). I am greatly indebted to Dr. Martin Gregory who gave me vital early encouragement, and trusted me with his reprint collection, specimens and photographs of the central African hedgehog (Plates 4, 8, 15 and 19). Thanks also to Ian Condon (Plate 17). All other photographs are my own.

I am grateful to the Roehampton Institute, who granted me a vital period of sabbatical leave, and the stalwart colleagues who covered for my absence. Dr. Clive Bullock willingly read and perceptively commented on every one of my draft manuscripts. His friendship, encouragement and tuition have been invaluable. There are so many who have contributed in many ways that they cannot all be named. However, I would like to thank the library staff at the Science Reference Library (Aldwych) and Roehampton Institute, especially Mandy King who (in her spare time) helped me to compile my literature database (Daphne Mathews and Jaqui Hammond also helped), and Jenny Paul who dealt with most of my inter-library loan requests. I would also like to thank Peter Drobinski and Samantha Bentley, and my father, James Reeve, for bringing valuable source material to my attention.

In dealing with the many foreign language sources, I would have been lost were it not for my mother, Maria Reeve. I am especially grateful for her translations of numerous German and Dutch sources. For help with various other languages, I would also like to thank Stephanie Whittle, Britt O'Neil, Paola Capel-Williams, Juliusz Chrzastowski, Qudsia Sharief, Ann MacLarnon, Jennifer Ide and Jean Hunt.

Last but not least, I would like to say a big thank you for the support and love of my long-suffering wife Kati and our daughters Alexandra and Elizabeth.

Thanks also to Kati Reeve for the photograph of the author on the inside back cover.

Preface

There have been many popular books and booklets about hedgehogs, but most deal almost exclusively with the western European species and few do more than briefly mention the 13 or more other hedgehog species. An exception is the German work *Igel* by Konrad Herter in 1963, which was abridged and published in English in 1965 as *Hedgehogs: a comprehensive study*. Since then, some excellent popular books about the European hedgehog in Britain have been produced. *The Hedgehog* by Maurice Burton (1969), the informative, superbly readable (and much translated) volume *Hedgehogs* by Pat Morris (1983) and *The Complete Hedgehog* by Les Stocker (1987) are just a few of the works that have provided for the apparently insatiable desire of the British and European public to know more about hedgehogs.

With such a prolific popular literature, I have tried to offer readers a more critical and in-depth approach that provides a gateway to the extensive international research literature. Nevertheless, such a broad work as this cannot hope to be definitive, especially as our scanty knowledge of many hedgehogs leaves the relatively well-studied European genus *Erinaceus* to dominate many areas of this book. I have used the classification proposed by Corbet (1988) which is simplifying, logical and without unnecessary or unsupported taxonomic subdivisions. Although further revision is inevitable, Corbet's robust synthesis is a long-overdue standardization that should endure for some years.

I hope this book will be a useful, authoritative and enjoyable text for wildlife enthusiasts. I hope that it will entice non-specialists into topics they may previously have found inaccessible and that it will provide good introductory reading for further studies of hedgehogs wherever they occur.

Nigel Reeve (February 1993)

CHAPTER 1

An Introduction to Hedgehogs

HEDGEHOGS are one of the most distinctive and familiar groups of mammals, and are widely distributed throughout the Old World. In most places where they occur, especially in Europe, hedgehogs are common nocturnal visitors to farms, horticultural areas, parks and domestic gardens, even in densely populated suburbs. The ability to thrive amongst human habitation, together with its benign behaviour, may account for the hedgehog's great popular appeal and for the extensive folklore and mythology surrounding these animals. Hedgehogs feature widely in children's stories, as cuddly toys and puppets, and as designs for ornaments, jewellery, cakes, brushes, greetings cards, postage stamps, company logos and so on. They are a common subject for jokes and attract a good deal of attention from the popular press (Chapter 10).

Nevertheless, despite all the paraphernalia surrounding the image of the hedgehog in society, the nocturnal and often secretive habits of the *real* animals mean that much remains undiscovered about the biology of hedgehogs in the wild. Even today, our knowledge of the natural history of many species of hedgehog is based almost as much on informal observations and hear-say, as on biological research, and virtually nothing is known about some species.

EVOLUTION AND TAXONOMY

It is thought that the earliest placental mammals to have evolved were nocturnal and insectivorous, but the old idea that the order Insectivora represents a group of primitive mammals which is ancestral to the other eutherian (placental) orders, has been largely abandoned (Butler 1988). The insectivores do not really represent a proper taxonomic unit, but are a 'rag-

1

bag' group containing a miscellany of families which have only been included among the insectivores for want of a better place to put them. More logically, the living insectivores divide into three orders, the Scandentia (tree shrews), Macroscelidea (elephant shrews) and the Lipotyphla—which embraces the hedgehogs and moonrats, solenodons, shrews, moles and desmans, golden moles, tenrecs and otter shrews (Fig. 1.1).

With almost 350 living species, the Lipotyphla are far from a relict order; rather they represent a major group (the fifth largest order) of eutherian mammals with more species and genera than the primates (Butler 1988). The classification of insectivores (living and extinct) is a matter of continuing technical debate, which need not concern us now. Since the Lipotyphla contains most of the living insectivores, I shall risk upsetting some purists by informally referring to hedgehogs as belonging to the insectivores, a term still in general use and more widely understood than the alternatives.

The insectivores had evolved by the end of the Cretaceous period, but although the fossil record (of the lipotyphlans) extends back to the Palaeocene (60–70 million years ago), most of these early specimens are only teeth and jaw fragments. Many of the hedgehog-like animals of the past are now extinct but the family Erinaceidae today survives as a discrete group without close living relatives (Corbet 1988). The family seem to have originated in Asia during the Eocene (38–54 million years ago), and then colonized Africa and North America during the Miocene (7–26 million years ago), although none now survives in the New World.

The two surviving subfamilies of the Erinaceidae are the Galericinae (the so-called 'hairy hedgehogs') and the Erinaceinae (the spiny hedgehogs) which were already distinct in the Oligocene (26–38 million years ago) (Butler 1948, 1988). Modern forms of these two subfamilies have been around since the Miocene. The detailed features of the skull and dentition of many fossil and living erinaceids are well covered in several papers by Butler (1948–1988). The biggest of the fossil erinaceids was a species of the genus *Deinogalerix* (a hairy hedgehog)—first described by Freudenthal in 1972, who found it in a late Miocene deposit on the Gargano peninsula (Italy). A detailed interpretation by Butler (1980) of the fossils found so far suggested it was a spectacularly large animal that probably looked much like a giant version of the moonrat (*Echinosorex*, see below) and probably ate fish, frogs, crayfish or other similarly sized prey, rather than small insects. The largest found (not yet fully grown) had a 200-mm-long skull, a head and body length of 560 mm (plus a

FIG. 1.1   *A summary chart of the living insectivore groups. The phylogeny of the insectivores remains a matter of debate (see text). This summary provides a guide to the groups rather than a definitive classification. Previously, the three orders have been crudely grouped as the Order Insectivora but this was rejected by Butler (1988). Tenrecomorph grouping is after Eisenberg (1981), species numbers are from Vaughan (1986), Macdonald (1984) and Corbet (1988). The drawings are not to scale.*

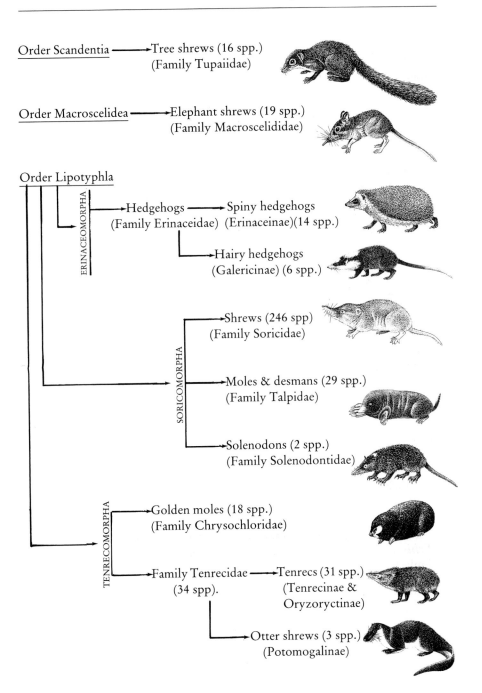

Order Scandentia ——→ Tree shrews (16 spp.)
(Family Tupaiidae)

Order Macroscelidea ——→ Elephant shrews (19 spp.)
(Family Macroscelididae)

Order Lipotyphla

ERINACEOMORPHA

→ Hedgehogs ——→ Spiny hedgehogs
(Family Erinaceidae) (Erinaceinae)(14 spp.)

→ Hairy hedgehogs
(Galericinae) (6 spp.)

SORICOMORPHA

→ Shrews (246 spp)
(Family Soricidae)

→ Moles & desmans (29 spp.)
(Family Talpidae)

→ Solenodons (2 spp.)
(Family Solenodontidae)

TENRECOMORPHA

→ Golden moles (18 spp.)
(Family Chrysochloridae)

→ Family Tenrecidae ——→ Tenrecs (31 spp.)
(34 spp). (Tenrecinae &
Oryzoryctinae)

→ Otter shrews (3 spp.)
(Potomogalinae)

TABLE 1.1　*Some typical characters useful in distinguishing the hairy hedgehogs (subfamily Galericinae) from the spiny hedgehogs (subfamily Erinaceinae).*

Character	Erinaceinae	Galericinae
Spines on back and crown of head	Yes	No
Short rostrum and muzzle	Yes	No
Well-developed anal glands	No	Yes
Number of pairs of mammae	4–5	2–4
Lachrymal foramen opens inside orbit	No	Yes
Posterior of zygomatic arch elevated	Yes	No
Palate with large fenestrations	Yes	No
Palate grooved	No	Yes
Hemispherical or V-shaped hollow (pit) in the basiphenoid bone	Yes	No
Tympanic bone broad, periotic bone reduced	Yes	No
Tympanic wing of the alisphenoid bone reaches the post-glenoid process	No	Yes
Condylar foramen emarginated, forming bi-lobed occipital condyle	No	Yes
Number of lower incisors	2	3
Number of lingual roots of teeth P^4–M^3	1	2
Pd_3[a] and adult P_3 present	No	Yes

[a] d denotes milk dentition.

Some features are illustrated in Fig. 1.6.

N.B. Tooth numbering reflects the basic full dentition of the Family Erinaceidae; the first premolar is absent in the Erinaceinae. Numbers in superscript and subscript, respectively, represent upper and lower jaw locations.

Source: Butler (1948) and Corbet (1988).

tail roughly 225 mm long), and probably weighed about 5·4 kg. The full adult head and body length was probably almost 0·75 m and it would have weighed about 9 kg.

During the Miocene the hairy hedgehogs were found in the same fossil beds as the first European representatives of the modern spiny hedgehogs (Viret 1938), but today the Galericinae have a limited distribution in South-East Asia, where no spiny hedgehogs are found (see below). The anatomical features that can be used to distinguish the two surviving hedgehog subfamilies are considered in detail by Butler (1948) and Corbet (1988); these are summarized in Table 1.1. but will not be considered further in this book.

The hairy hedgehogs (subfamily Galericinae)

Today's hairy hedgehogs, the gymnures and moonrats, are generally found in the high forests of South-East Asia. According to Corbet (1988) there are six species in five genera *Hylomys*, *Neohylomys*, *Neotetracus*, *Echinosorex* and *Podogymnura* (two species). Many authors (eg. Butler 1948, Herter 1968,

Eisenberg 1981, Wroot 1984b) have referred to this group as the subfamily Echinosoricinae, but Corbet (1988) rejected this name as incorrect. The Galericinae are generally considered to be the more primitive of the two living subfamilies, retaining certain features lost by the Erinaceinae (Butler 1948, Eisenberg 1981). As their common name suggests they are furry with no spines (although *P. aureospinula* has rather stiff guard hairs) and have relatively long, sparsely haired rat-like tails. Their noses are long and mobile, and extend well beyond the mouth. Like spiny hedgehogs, they are nocturnal and feed principally on a wide range of invertebrates, but may also eat small vertebrates: fish in the case of the moonrat (Lim Boo Liat 1967). They have up to 44 teeth and a usual dental formula of:

$$I\frac{3}{3} \quad C\frac{1}{1} \quad P\frac{3\text{--}4}{3\text{--}4} \quad M\frac{3}{3}$$

where I, C, P and M refer to the incisors, canines, premolars and molars, respectively. *Neotetracus* may have two to four upper premolars (Corbet 1988).

These hairy hedgehogs vary considerably in size, the largest being the greater moonrat (*Echinosorex gymnurus*), an animal with piebald fur, weighing up to 1·4 kg, around 300 mm long (sometimes up to 445 mm: Herter 1968), plus a tail of 200 mm or more (Fig. 1.2). This species is widely distributed in Malaya, in the fringes of lowland forest, rubber estates and mangrove forest (Lim Boo Liat 1967). The hairy hedgehogs have a pair of odour-producing glands by the anus. These seem to be particularly large and malodorous in the greater moonrat, which is reported to smell of garlic, sweat or rotten onions (Lim Boo Liat 1967, Herter 1968)!

The other species are smaller, around 100–200 mm long (plus 12–70-mm tails), and rather shrew-like in appearance, with shorter tails than the moonrat

FIG. 1.2 *The greater moonrat* (Echinosorex gymnurus), *one of the hairy hedgehogs from South-East Asia.*

(Butler 1948, Herter 1968, Corbet 1988). Little is known about the ecology and status of the hairy hedgehogs, but they are increasingly threatened by the severe deforestation resulting from shifting cultivation and logging for timber in many parts of South-East Asia. The Mindanao moonrat (*Podogymnura truei*) from the Philippine island of Mindanao, and the Hainan moonrat (*Neohylomys hainanensis*) are both vulnerable species (Burton & Pearson 1987).

The spiny hedgehogs (*subfamily* Erinaceinae)

The rest of this book is devoted to the spiny hedgehogs. As previously mentioned, several types of modern-form hedgehogs appeared during the Miocene period, including the surviving genera. Today, about 14 species of hedgehog are found throughout much of the old world, but are absent from South-East Asia and Australasia, although European hedgehogs have been introduced into New Zealand. Hedgehogs are easily recognized by their general appearance (Fig. 1.3 and Plate 1) and the distinctive coat of stout spines which covers the back and crown of the head. No hairs grow among the spines, but along the flanks there is a border of dense, long fur, rather reminiscent of the 'skirt' of a hovercraft!

In most respects the hedgehog body-plan is unspecialized and, apart from a very short neck and tail, there is no particular adaptation of the vertebrae with regard to rolling-up (Chapter 2). The limbs and their girdles are also of a general-purpose design (Fig. 1.4), similar to that of the earliest mammals. Nevertheless, they perform well and during constant speed locomotion, hedgehogs (and tenrecs) have a mechanical power output, per unit of body weight, similar to that of some much larger mammals with more specialized limbs, such as the dog (Heglund 1980). There are five strongly clawed toes on each foot, except in the case of one African species with 4-toed hind feet. The legs are not as short as they often appear in the live animal, which usually

FIG. 1.3   *General view of a European hedgehog (*Erinaceus europaeus*) showing a body form typical of all true hedgehogs. The spines are confined to the dorsal surface and bordered by dense fur along the flanks. When the animal is relaxed, the spines lie sleekly pointing backwards The legs are of medium length and there is a short tail.*

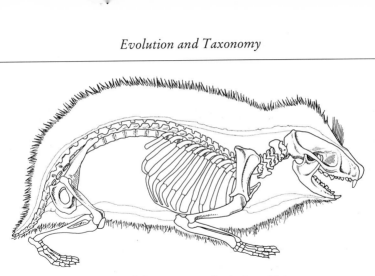

FIG. 1.4   *The skeleton of the European hedgehog* (Erinaceus europaeus), *showing a generalized body structure and unspecialized limb girdles. Note the short neck. The body outline is also indicated.*

crouches as one approaches. When an undisturbed animal is walking and running about, it has a more 'leggy' appearance and the belly is raised clear of the ground. Heglund recorded hedgehogs running (really a form of very rapid walking) at speeds of up to 9 km h^{-1} (150 m min^{-1}); see also Chapter 4. At each step the entire sole of the foot contacts the ground (plantigrade locomotion), although the somewhat lengthened heel of the hind foot may be raised up to increase the stride and power delivery during running, and to gain leverage when pushing the body forward into tight spaces. The elongated hind feet leave distinctively longer tracks than do the fore feet (Fig. 1.5).

Hedgehogs are good all-round performers, able to climb chain link fences or ivy-clad walls. Edwards (1957) noted that they could climb a six-foot-tall wire netting fence in a few seconds. Hedgehogs can dig quite powerfully with their front limbs, which are braced by a well-developed clavicle, and several species are known to dig nest burrows (Chapter 5). All hedgehogs are competent swimmers, even African species from arid regions (Burton 1969, Herter 1971, Morris 1988a). One account by Potter (1987) in Britain described how a hedgehog swam powerfully across a stream transformed into a 'roaring torrent' by heavy rains: 'on reaching the other side it shook itself like a dog and went on its way'. (See Plate 2.)

The skull (Fig. 1.6) is broad and blunt-nosed, with wide and well-developed zygomatic arches (cheek bones). Anomalies in tooth number have been frequently recorded in hedgehogs (*Erinaceus* spp.) in Europe and China, and especially in New Zealand (Brockie 1964, Poduschka & Poduschka 1986a). These include the absence of incisors (usually the lower second pair), extra incisors and abnormal eruptions. The second premolar in the upper jaw is variable in shape and occurrence. Poduschka & Poduschka (1986a) reported a forked first lower incisor in the Mongolian species of long-eared hedgehog (*Hemiechinus dauuricus*). In the central African hedgehog (*Atelerix albiven-*

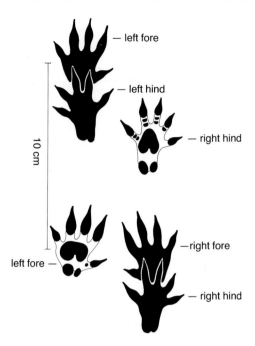

FIG. 1.5 *Typical five-toed tracks left by an adult European hedgehog (Erinaceus europaeus). Note the overlapping foot prints of a typical trail and the distinctively longer print of the hind foot. On the two non-overlapping foot marks the position of the pads are marked. Stride length = 10 cm. Source based on Lawrence & Brown (1973).*

tris) Harrison & Bates (1985) reported the absence of the second upper premolars and abnormally erupted third upper premolars. Nevertheless, all today's spiny hedgehogs normally have 36 teeth with a formula of:

$$I\frac{3}{3} \quad C\frac{1}{1} \quad P\frac{3}{2} \quad M\frac{3}{3}$$

Molars are absent in deciduous (milk) dentition.

The first upper incisors are long, widely spaced and project slightly forward (Fig. 1.6a and c), the canines are small and the molars have well-developed cusps (for crushing insects). In all living erinaceids the first upper premolar, in occlusal view, has a characteristically four-sided appearance (Fig. 1.7). In the Erinaceinae the roots on the lingual side of the tooth (under the hypocone and protocone) are fused to form a distinctive single laterally flattened ridge but the roots under the metacone and paracone remain separate.

The third upper premolar (because of a reduction in tooth number, this is equivalent to the fourth upper premolar (P^4) of erinaceids generally) shears against the first lower molar (M_1), a feature which shows some resemblance to the carnassial tooth form of carnivores. The jaw musculature has attachments

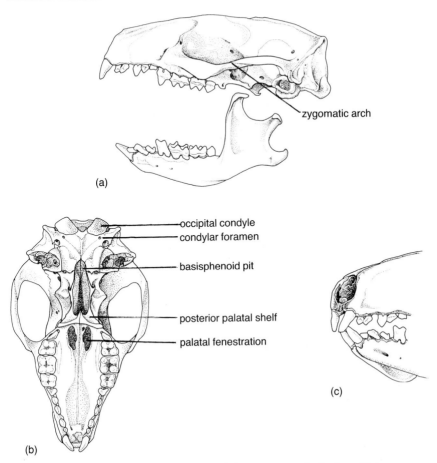

zygomatic arch

(a)

occipital condyle
condylar foramen
basisphenoid pit
posterior palatal shelf
palatal fenestration

(c)

(b)

FIG. 1.6   *The skull and lower jaw of the European hedgehog (Erinaceus
europaeus), showing selected general features of hedgehog cranial anatomy
as referred to in the text (scale bar = 10 mm). (a) Side view of skull and lower
jaw. Note the relatively blunt nose, forward-projecting incisors and the
upward curve of the rear portion of the zygomatic arch. (b) Ventral view of
the skull. Note its breadth across the region of the zygomatic arch. (c) Three-
quarter view of the snout region showing the widely spaced front incisors of
the upper jaw. Note how the lower incisors bite upwards into the gap
between them.*

well-forward on the zygomatic arch, applying more force to these shearing
teeth and, following this emphasis, the third molars are reduced, another
trend paralleled in the carnivores. The emphasis on the P^4-M_1 shear, and other
detailed aspects of the dentition are important features used to characterize
and define the erinaceids (Butler 1948).

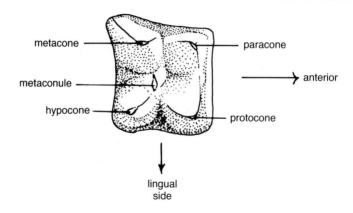

FIG. 1.7 *Occlusal view of the first upper right molar of the European hedgehog (*Erinaceus spp.*). In all living erinaceid genera the pattern of M^1 is essentially the same, four-sided, but the corner bearing the metacone is variously elongated. The metacone is separated from the paracone by a deep valley but a crest (in some genera bearing a small protoconule) joins the paracone and protocone. The hypocone is as large as the protocone, and the metaconule occupies a roughly central position. Labelling after Butler (1948). Illustration by the author.*

Hedgehogs and many other insectivores are often described as 'primitive', which really means that they possess a set of so-called conservative (plesiomorph) features of their morphology, physiology and behaviour (Eisenberg 1980). Modern hedgehogs inhabit a niche apparently very similar to that of their ancestors, and indeed similar to that of ancestral mammals which existed at the end of the Cretaceous period. They are nocturnal, terrestrial and principally insectivorous, and they build nests. Their dominant senses are olfaction and hearing; the olfactory lobes of the brain are well developed (Fig. 1.8).

Hedgehogs, like many other conservative mammals, tend to have rather small brains for their body size, but cross-species analyses of relative brain size suffer from many statistical problems and there is much to confound attempts to relate such data to the animals' behaviour and ecology. In simple terms adult European hedgehogs (*Erinaceus europaeus*) have a brain weighing around 3·5 g, equivalent to 0·39–0·54% of their bodyweight (Bauchot & Stephan 1966, Mace *et al.* 1981). Mace *et al.* gave a brain weight of 2·24 g for a central African hedgehog (*Atelerix albiventris*)—0·8% of its 280 g bodyweight. But for a valid comparative review of brain size, more detailed statistical analyses are needed to overcome the problems of scaling. The encephalization index used by Bauchot & Stephan (1966) for insectivores showed hedgehogs to be only slightly over the level of the most basic unspecialized insectivore (well below the average for the group), and Mace *et*

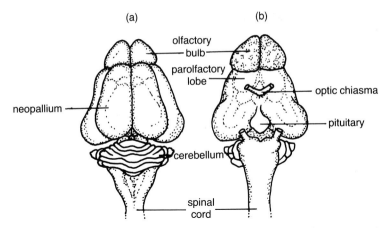

FIG. 1.8 *The hedgehog brain: (a) dorsal view, (b) ventral view. Note the well-developed olfactory regions, reflecting the hedgehog's dependence on its sense of smell and the smooth relatively undeveloped neopallium. Source: based on Herter (1965b). Illustration by the author.*

al. (1981) noted a much greater 'comparative brain size' in the specialized moles and golden moles than in the shrews and hedgehogs.

Although hedgehogs are not very 'brainy' and are typically conservative in many ways, they also show many 'derived' features (specializations), such as their highly specialized spines and the extraordinary development of the *panniculus carnosus* and the *orbicularis*, the main muscles used in rolling-up (Chapter 2). This forms a very effective anti-predator mechanism which, intriguingly, is convergent with that of the so-called 'hedgehog' tenrecs, the genera *Setifer* and *Echinops* (see below). Hedgehogs show well-developed maternal care of the young, often said to be minimal in conservative mammals. It is also somewhat unusual that a single genus (*Erinaceus*) of such a conservative mammal should have been able to colonize such a wide range of temperate and arid habitat types (Eisenberg 1980). Some workers have argued that hedgehogs have a primitive temperature-regulation physiology, but this view is open to question (Chapter 6).

Other spiny mammals

Although hedgehogs are spiny mammals *par excellence*, they are by no means the only mammals to have spines. Spines are modified hairs and have evolved independently in a variety of other mammals, none of which is closely related to the hedgehogs. Most other spiny mammals look nothing like hedgehogs, but the exceptions are the hedgehog-tenrecs which deserve a special mention. They belong to the insectivore family Tenrecidae (order Lipotyphla). Gould & Eisenberg (1966) and Herter (1968) described how hedgehog-tenrecs look amazingly like the true spiny hedgehogs (Erinaceinae), can erect their sharp spines and roll-up in defence (though their musculature is less specialized than that of a true hedgehog), can hibernate and inhabit a similar ecological niche.

These tenrecs are naturally confined to Madagascar and the nearby Comoro Islands (also introduced to Mauritius and Reunion) where no true hedgehogs occur, so one is unlikely to confuse them in the field. Tenrecs lack a jugal bone (part of the zygomatic arch), have well-developed canines and the short front incisors do not protrude as in the hedgehogs. Hedgehog-tenrecs weigh at most around 200 g and are much smaller than most true hedgehogs. Unlike the sparsely haired tail of hedgehogs, the short conical tail of the tenrec bears spines (Herter 1968).

The large hedgehog-tenrec (*Setifer setosus*) has very closely spaced, short (15 mm), thin spines; the young have soft fur interspersed among their spines, a feature not shown in the adult and never in true hedgehogs. The lesser hedgehog-tenrec (*Echinops telfairi*) has sparser, longer spines and, as it rolls-up, it clasps its hind and fore-paws together. Erectable spines are also interspersed amongst the bristly hair of the common 'tail-less' tenrec (*Tenrec (=Centetes) ecaudatus*) and the banded tenrecs (*Hemicentetes* spp.). Specialized spines on the back are vibrated together to produce a rasping noise (stridulation) (Gould & Eisenberg 1966).

No other spiny mammal looks anything like a hedgehog. Echidnas, genera *Zaglossus* and *Tachyglossus*, are monotremes (egg-laying mammals) from Australasia. Porcupines are hystricomorph rodents from the New World (family Erethizontidae) and Old World (family Hystricidae). All have stout spines, variably mixed with fur. Other spiny rodents include the African and Asian spiny mice (Muridae), the spiny dormice (Platacanthomyidae) from southern India, cane rats (Thryonomyidae) from Africa, and the so-called spiny 'rats' (family Echimyidae) and 'mice' (Cricetidae) from the New World (Vincent & Owers 1986). In all these species the spines are slender, sometimes little more than stiff bristles, and are interspersed among fur.

HEDGEHOGS OF THE WORLD

The literature about hedgehogs has always suffered from serious taxonomic confusion. The hedgehogs have been placed into between one and five genera and different authors have presented various interpretations of the number and naming of species and subspecies. A typical example is the central African (or white-bellied) hedgehog *Atelerix albiventris*, which has been named *Atelerix spinifex*, *Atelerix pruneri*, *Erinaceus albiventris*, *Erinaceus pruneri* and about eight other less commonly used aliases! This has been (and still is) very confusing, but Corbet (1988) produced an authoritative taxonomic review of the entire family, which eliminated the genus *Aethechinus* (Thomas, 1918) by including its members within the genus *Atelerix*, and simplified the classification into four genera (Table 1.2 and Fig. 1.9). The decision to merge these two genera has since been supported by comparisons of their karyo-

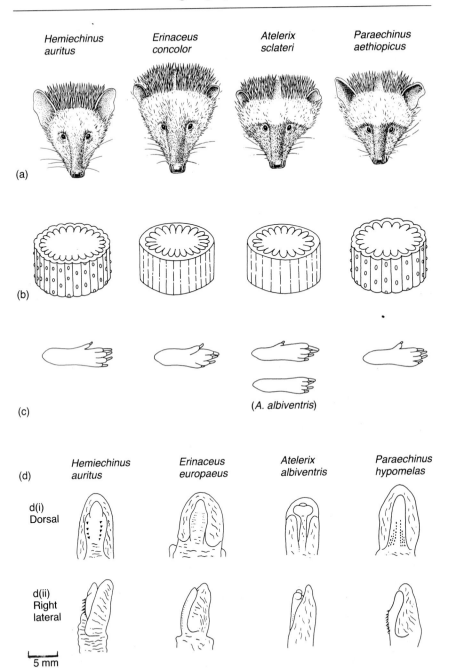

FIG. 1.9 *Some external characteristics of the four hedgehog genera. (a) Head showing naked centre-parting of spines on scalp and pattern of pigmentation, (b) section of spine, (c) hind left foot with hallux, (d) form of glans penis (see text). Source: based on Corbet (1988).*

TABLE 1.2 *A summary of the four genera and 14 species of hedgehog.*

Hemiechinus	Atelerix	Paraechinus	Erinaceus
H. auritus	A. albiventris	P. aethiopicus	E. amurensis
H. collaris	A. algirus	P. hypomelas	E. concolor
H. dauuricus	A. frontalis	P. micropus	E. europaeus
H. hughi	A. sclateri		

Source: Corbet (1988).

types (chromosome characteristics), which showed important similarities (Hübner *et al.* 1991). All the genera have the same diploid number of chromosomes ($2n = 48$) and in the species for which reliable information is available the number of autosomal arms has turned out to have a very limited range (88–92) (Geisler & Gropp 1967, Giagia & Ondrias 1980, Searle & Erskine 1985, Yongshan & Ficin 1987, Corbet 1988). Although some taxonomic revision may well occur in future, especially with regard to subspecific relationships, I have adopted Corbet's clarifying classification throughout this book and for consistency I have 'translated' the species names used by other authors, whenever possible. The species distributions given below are also based primarily on Corbet (1988), but additional data are used as indicated. In the following review I have used only a selection of the anatomical characteristics of the hedgehog genera and species, for more detail I refer the reader to Corbet (1988).

Genus Erinaceus

This widely distributed genus (Fig. 1.10) contains the most well-known of the hedgehogs, the European hedgehog (*Erinaceus europaeus*) (Fig. 1.3, Plate 1), sometimes called the western European hedgehog or the brown-breasted hedgehog. This species is found in Ireland, Britain, southern Scandinavia and the rest of western Europe. To the east of approximately longitude 15°E, *E. europaeus* is replaced by the white-breasted, or eastern European hedgehog (*Erinaceus concolor*) (Fig. 1.11)—often referred to by the specific or subspecific name *roumanicus* (= *rumanicus*). The ranges of the two European species do overlap somewhat (see below), especially in the Czech Republic. *Erinaceus concolor* extends as far south as Israel and, north of the Caspian, as far east as the province around Novosibirsk (roughly 80°E). Much further east the genus crops up again in the form of *Erinaceus amurensis*, which is found in eastern Manchuria (China), the Korean peninsula, and parts of the rest of China east of about 110°E and north of 29°N, but not in Japan (Corbet 1988).

All three species in this genus are characterized by a faintly visible centre-parting of the spines on the crown of the head, smooth spines lacking papillae, and a very well-developed big toe (hallux) on the hind foot. Although there are no data for *E. amurensis*, in the other two species the glans of the penis has

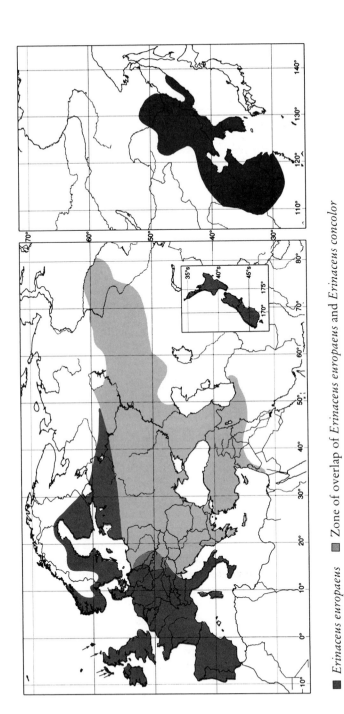

■ *Erinaceus europaeus* ■ Zone of overlap of *Erinaceus europaeus* and *Erinaceus concolor*

□ *Erinaceus concolor* ■ *Erinaceus amurensis*

FIG. 1.10 *Distribution map of the genus* Erinaceus. *Source: Kristiansson (1981b); Corbet (1988). Records for Scottish Isles: South Uist, Sexton (1989); Lewis and Harris, N. Giles (pers. comm.).*

(a)   (b)

FIG. 1.11   *(a) The eastern European (white-breasted) hedgehog (*Erinaceus concolor*). Note the generally dark fur, and the distinctive white patch of fur extending across the chest (inset b).*

no lateral expansions and bears only small keratinous papillae (not spines) on the dorsal surface (Corbet 1988). The ears are short (20–30 mm) and are mostly concealed by the rather coarse fur; typically they do not project beyond the adjacent spines (Fig. 1.9). The spines are usually about 22–25 mm long but may be up to 27 mm (Ognev 1928). Coloration is variable, but generally the base of the spine is brownish, then roughly the lower two-thirds of the spine is pale, followed by a wide brown band ending just short of the pale, sharp tip (Fig. 1.12).

The two European species are much the same size and weight. The total head and body length of adults is 200–300 mm and there is a short, tapering tail about 20–30 mm long. The condylobasal length of the skull is 55–60 mm (Saint Girons 1969, Ruprecht 1972, Corbet 1988, Morris 1991). Females tend to weigh very slightly less than males, but the individual and seasonal variation is such that the difference is not significant. In Britain, adults generally weigh in the order of 600–700 g early in the active season but increase to around 900–1000 g by the autumn; some males may reach 1100–1200 g. This is fairly typical, but it is notable that continental specimens are generally heavier, more commonly exceeding 1 kg and typically around 800–1500 g (Versluys 1975). In Sweden average pre-hibernation weights for males are around 1500–1600 g (Kristiansson 1984). In Israel *E. concolor* averages 720 g but can weigh up to 1000 g (Schoenfeld & Yom-Tov 1985). In Britain, Morris (1983) reported having seen one huge pet hedgehog which weighed 2200 g; one wonders if it could roll-up!

Of the four 'ice-ages' during the Pleistocene, the most recent and coldest covered much of Europe in ice, lasted about 100 000 years and ended about 20 000 years ago (Harrison Matthews 1952). Herter (1965b) suggested that during these ice ages the basic European hedgehog stock became isolated into two main areas: (1) Iberia, southern France and Italy, and (2) south-eastern Europe. Divergence of these two stocks over about 700 000 years of isolation has resulted in the two modern European species, which themselves show a

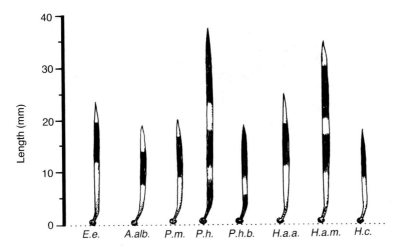

FIG. 1.12 *Diagram showing the characteristics of the spines of various hedgehogs. Note that size and depth of coloration may vary, even on the same individual. E.e. = Erinaceus europaeus, A.alb. = Atelerix albiventris, P.m. = Paraechinus micropus, P.h. = Paraechinus hypomelas, P.h.b. = Paraechinus hypomelas blandfordi, H.a.a. = Hemiechinus auritus auritus, H.a.m. = Hemiechinus auritus megalotis, H.c. = Hemiechinus collaris. Sources: various, principally Roberts (1977). Illustration by the author.*

show a certain amount of racial diversity but are genetically distinct and can also be clearly distinguished by analyses of skull measurements (Geisler & Gropp 1967, Ruprecht 1972, Holz 1978).

As the climate warmed at the end of the glacial period the flora and fauna of Europe very gradually established itself along modern lines. Britain remained connected to mainland Europe until a rise in sea-level around 9500 years ago, by which time hedgehogs had established themselves there. Introductions to various islands have taken place since then (Morris 1991).

There is only limited interfertility between the two European species although Poduschka & Poduschka (1983b) repeated, after several years of trying, Herter's original success in producing an F_1 hybrid litter. Herter (1965b) reported several examples where first generation hybridization had occurred. The Poduschkas were the first to breed an F_2 generation by mating littermates and a hybrid back-crossed to a pure *E. concolor*, but attempts to back-cross hybrids to *E. europaeus* were unsuccessful. Hybrids showed highly variable intermediate characteristics. The readiness with which hybridization occurs in the wild is unknown. Holz (1978) used multivariate analysis to compare the skull measurements of captive bred hybrids with animals found in the sympatric zone (area of species overlap), and concluded that hybridization did not occur naturally, but the observed variability in this zone does indicate some limited crossbreeding (Corbet 1988).

It seems likely that the coexistence of the two species is relatively recent, following habitat changes from agricultural land use (Kratochvíl 1975). Poduschka & Poduschka (1983b) noted a tendency for the eastern species to advance to the west and suggested that the apparent inability of hybrids to breed with pure *E. europaeus* may have contributed to this one-sided advance. In the Czech Republic, Kratochvíl argued that there may be a degree of reproductive isolation between the species because of slight differences in seasonal activity; *E. concolor* apparently awakes from hibernation earlier than does *Erinaceus europaeus*. Little is known about the relationship between these two species at their northern boundary which runs roughly east from Lithuania to the Ural mountains.

The two European species, although very alike, are distinguishable by the colour of the ventral pelage, although this can vary. *Erinaceus europaeus* shows a more well-defined dark 'mask' around the eyes and snout than *E. concolor* (Poduschka & Poduschka 1983b), and the latter species seldom has unpigmented spines. Albino *E. concolor* are extremely rare and Poduschka (1988) described the first known albino of this species, a female which bore a litter of normally coloured young. A more precise distinction between the species can be made by measures of the maxilla which is proportionately longer in *E. concolor*, giving a slightly longer face than *E. europaeus* (Herter 1965b, Ruprecht 1972). The posterior border of the maxilla extends behind the opening of the lachrymal duct in *E. concolor* but not in *E. europaeus* (Corbet 1988). Such differences are hardly visible in live animals, although in parts of Europe where both species occur, some farmers and gypsies distinguish between the so-called 'dog' hedgehog, with a blunt snout and high forehead, and 'pig' hedgehogs, with a pointed snout and flattened forehead (Herter 1965b, 1968, Poduschka & Poduschka 1972). However, Herter commented that the distinction was made even in areas where only one species occurred and he pointed out the variable appearance of hedgehogs as they drew down the skin of the forehead whilst erecting their spines in defence. Probably the distinction is artificial and instead has its origins in gypsy folklore (Chapter 10).

The geographical variation in the European species (*E. europaeus*) has led some to propose various subspecific divisions (Ognev 1928, Herter 1965b). For example, in southern France, Spain, Italy and Corsica, the hedgehogs tend to have a lighter coloured pelage than is normal for more northern *E. europaeus* (Herter 1965b, Saint Girons 1969). But a high degree of individual variability confounds reliable taxonomic separation of these forms. Bretagnolle & Attié (1989) found so much variation in the external and skull characteristics of the hedgehog population around Niort (western central France) that they even found it hard to reliably separate individuals of *E. europaeus* from *Atelerix* ('*Erinaceus*') *algirus*—a north African species introduced to the Mediterranean coasts of France and Spain (see below). They proposed that the population was intermediate between the two species!

In Ireland the hedgehogs have rather dark ventral fur and the premaxilla and frontal bones of the skulls of British hedgehogs meet more often than in their relatives from continental western Europe (Morris 1991). Ruprecht (1972) noted that hedgehogs from Britain had significantly narrower muzzles than those on mainland Europe, and in Poland the muzzles were particularly broad. Searle & Erskine (1985) confirmed earlier reports of a distinct karyotype in British hedgehogs, thus supporting the notion that British hedgehogs have diverged somewhat from those in western Europe. Nevertheless, these and other differences do not necessarily form the basis for a reliable definition of discrete subspecies (Ruprecht 1972, Corbet 1988).

In my field studies of *E. europaeus* in southern England, I have seen a wide variation in pelage colour. It is not unusual for a few unpigmented 'white' spines to be interspersed among the normal brown-banded ones, but in some individuals there are many such spines. The rather coarse fur is usually an even light-brown colour, but individuals may vary from a greyish to a yellowish brown. Some animals are 'blonde' with pink nose and paws (Plate 3), the latter a feature sometimes shown by otherwise normally coloured animals. On Alderney (Channel Islands) such blonde hedgehogs are unusually common (P. Morris pers. comm.). Occasionally true albinos, with a pure white pelage and pink eyes have been reported (Morris 1988a). I have never seen, nor heard of, any melanic (very dark brown or black) animals of this species.

Both European species occur in a similar range of habitat types but usually hedgehogs need a supply of dry broad leaves to make their winter hibernation nests, although burrows and other forms of shelter may be used. Thus they are more scarce in such habitats as coniferous forests, treeless moors, uplands and marshlands. They survive well in urban areas where there are suitably wooded parks, gardens and golf courses and in farmland. However, intensive arable farmland, where copses have been removed, hedgerows replaced by fences and the use of pesticides has reduced the numbers of ground invertebrates, is less likely to support good hedgehog populations. In seasonally dry areas, such as those in southern Europe, hedgehogs may shift their ranges on to irrigated land at certain times of the year (Boitani & Reggiani 1984). Presumably hedgehogs would find it hard to cope in these areas without the benefit of such human influence.

The northern limit of *E. europaeus* (roughly 60°N) coincides with the northern limit of deciduous woodland (Morris 1983). At these latitudes, the long harsh winters and a reduced supply of macro-invertebrates impose severe ecological limits on hedgehogs (Kristiansson 1981a,b). Poduschka & Poduschka (1983a) noted that the most northerly hedgehogs in Finland were 'starvelings' and in poor condition. This century there has been a northward spread of hedgehogs in Finland and Sweden, which seems to be largely a result of introductions by people and their environmental influences (Kristoffersson et al. 1977, Kristiansson 1981b). Today hedgehogs are found even north of the Gulf of Bothnia. Although human introductions have contributed to the population in Finland (Kristiansson 1981b) the presence of *E. europaeus* in a band stretching from Finland to the Urals is unlikely to be purely a result of introductions (Poduschka & Poduschka, 1983a).

A series of introductions from 1870 onwards established European hedge-hogs (*E. europaeus*) in New Zealand and, finding themselves in a niche without much competition, they have since become very common. High densities occur in lowland areas, irrigated pasture, suburban areas and other human-made habitats but they are scarce or absent in arid or permanently damp places such as wet native forest (Wodzicki 1950, Brockie 1975, Morris & Morris, 1988).

The eastern European species (*E. concolor*) has similar ecological require-ments to *E. europaeus*, and appears to have a very similar biology. It too is a species with a wide range (Fig. 1.10), covering a variety of habitat types and a penchant for human-made environments. In the more arid south-eastern part of its range, it thrives in irrigated gardens and agricultural land. Around the coastal plains of Israel it supplements its mainly insectivorous diet by scavenging from human refuse (Schoenfeld & Yom-Tov 1985, Corbet 1988). The fur of this species is somewhat variable in colour but it is typically dark grey–brown, interspersed with light hairs. There is a distinctive area of white hair covering the underside of the chest and neck, which often extends to the flanks around the shoulders (Fig. 1.11b). There is quite a lot of regional variation and several subspecific divisions would seem to be justified. An insular subspecies (*E. c. nesiotes*) with a very extensive white patch, occurs on Crete although this would appear to be karyotypically identical to the mainland form. However the hedgehogs from Rhodes and certain other Aegean islands (*E. c. rhodius*) have statistically discernible karyotypic differ-ences from the mainland form (Giagia & Ondrias 1980). There is a melanic form around the eastern shore of the Black Sea, *E. concolor concolor* (or *E. c. ponticus*) and a pale form (*E. c. pallidus*) with buff-coloured ventral fur from Tobol'sk province in western Siberia (Ognev 1928, Corbet 1988). Holz (1978) described a Romanian/Bulgarian form, characterized by an elongated cra-nium of reduced capacity, but its subspecific status was not established. Poduschka & Poduschka (1972) wrote of the very large 'Thracian' form of this species (from Macedonia) and likened it to ancient descriptions of a large semi-mythical hedgehog-like animal called the Cirogrillus.

Little is published about the natural history of the Chinese hedgehog (*E. amurensis*), which is ecologically similar to both European species in its diet (Liu 1937) and range of habitat types. It may be found in farmland areas, broadleaf forests and various other habitats but does not penetrate into the drier meadow-steppes or coniferous forest zones. Such habitats appear to define the northern and western limits of the range of this species (Corbet 1988). It strongly resembles *E. europaeus* in appearance and can best be distinguished by its skull anatomy, in particular a V-shaped basis-phenoid 'pit'—which is roughly hemispherical in all other hedgehogs (Table 1.1 and Fig. 1.6). There is considerable colour variation ranging from pale to dark, and unpigmented spines are usually present among the normal brown-banded ones. A particularly dark-brown form from Korea has been proposed as a subspecies *E. amurensis koreensis* (Ognev 1928, Corbet 1988).

Genus Atelerix

Apart from some introductions to various islands, mainly the Balearics and the Canaries, and to the Mediterranean coasts of France and Spain (Kahmann & Vesmanis 1977, Corbet 1988), this genus is exclusively African (Fig. 1.13). However, the relationship of this genus with *Erinaceus* from Europe is the subject of continued speculation (e.g. Hübner *et al.* 1991). Butler (1978) described how the early-Pleistocene *Atelerix (Erinaceus) broomi* (from Oldu-

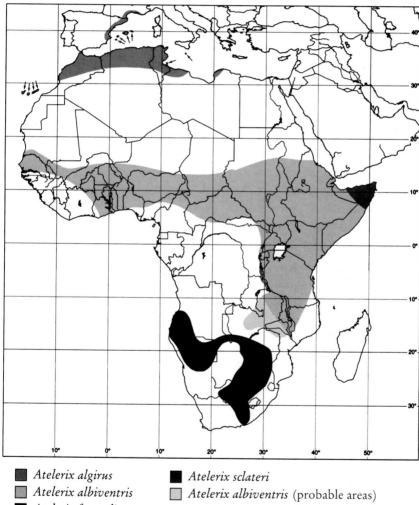

■ *Atelerix algirus*   ■ *Atelerix sclateri*

▦ *Atelerix albiventris*   □ *Atelerix albiventris* (probable areas)

■ *Atelerix frontalis*

FIG. 1.13 *Distribution map of the genus* Atelerix. *Sources: Kahmann & Vesmanis (1977), Happold (1987), Corbet (1988).*

vai, Africa; now extinct) shared many primitive features with *Erinaceus* spp. and *A. algirus*, as well as showing some of the more specialized characters of the other living *Atelerix* species. Possibly an early Pleistocene invasion of a basic *Erinaceus*-type stock into Africa from the north founded the African hedgehog stock, of which *A. algirus* (from north Africa) is the least modified survivor. Subsequent incursions into northern Africa, by the Asiatic genera *Paraechinus* and *Hemiechinus*, seem to have been comparatively recent.

Atelerix are like *Erinaceus* in that there is a 'parting' of the forehead spines (though wider in *Atelerix*). The spines, although generally shorter, are smooth and look much like those of *Erinaceus*, but the pale band at the tip of each spine may be relatively longer (Fig. 1.12). A variable proportion of spines is unpigmented (Herter 1971, Lienhardt 1982). The fur is generally coarse and sparse. The ears are short—around 25–33 mm (Hufnagl 1972)—and although slightly longer than in *Erinaceus*, they still do not project noticeably beyond the adjacent spines (Corbet, 1988). *Atelerix* is characterized by a reduced or absent hallux and a broad shelf at the rear of the palate. The latter feature was found to be one of the most reliable criteria for the separation of *Atelerix algirus* from *Erinaceus europaeus* (with a narrow posterior palatal shelf) in France (Saint Girons 1969, Bretagnolle & Attié 1989). In all *Atelerix* species (also *Paraechinus*) there is a band of whitish fur running across the forehead. In the more southern species this contrasts strongly with the darker fur of the rest of the face, but is poorly defined in the paler-faced Algerian hedgehog. The glans penis has a very distinctive form (Fig. 1.9) with laterally expanded processes, but no spiny or papillate areas on the dorsal surface (no data for *A. sclateri*). *Atelerix* are lighter-bodied and more agile than European hedgehogs, the feet are smaller and their claws less well developed, making them comparatively poor climbers (Herter 1968).

The Algerian hedgehog (*A. algirus*) (Fig. 1.14) is quite large, between 200 and 250 mm or more, with a hind foot length of up to 40 mm and a condylobasal skull length of 50–60 mm (Saint Girons 1969, Corbet 1971, 1988). Although of similar size, it has a more slender build than the European

FIG. 1.14 *The Algerian hedgehog (*Atelerix algirus*). Note the generally pale coloration and indistinct face mask.*

hedgehog. It has a small hallux and a generally pale pelage with varying amounts of brown in the ventral fur (Kahmann & Vesmanis 1977, Corbet 1988). It is the only species of this genus found outside Africa (Fig. 1.13). The Algerian hedgehog is found (probably introduced) in various coastal locations in Southern France (around the Var and eastern Pyrenees) and Spain but may not be as well established as is often assumed (Saint Girons 1969, Corbet 1988). It also occurs on the Canary islands (Fuerteventura, Tenerife, Lanzarote and Gran Canaria), the four main Balearic islands, Malta and Djerba (Tunisia). Various insular forms have been proposed as subspecies—on Fuerteventura (*A. a. caniculus*), the Balearic and Pityusic islands (*A. a. vagans*) and Djerba (*A. a. girbaensis*), but these differ from the mainland population only in minor details (Kahmann & Vesmanis 1977, Alcover 1984). Some workers have also differentiated the Moroccan and Tunisian populations (Corbet 1988). In North Africa, the range of the Algerian hedgehog is limited to the coastal Mediterranean scrub zone of northern Morocco and Algeria, Tunisia and northern Libya as far east as Benghazi. As seems true for most hedgehogs, it seems to do well in areas of human habitation (Hufnagl 1972). It does not penetrate south into the desert, where the 'desert hedgehog' (*Paraechinus aethiopicus*) is found, although the distribution of these two species does overlap in places, notably in Tunisia (Vesmanis 1979, Kock 1980).

The central African, or white-bellied hedgehog (*A. albiventris*) (Plate 4) is very widely distributed across the savanna and steppes of central Africa and down the eastern side from Ethiopia to the Zambezi river (Fig. 1.13), although its occurrence is patchy (Easton 1979). Its range does not extend north into the arid steppe zone of the Sahel region. East of Khartoum (Sudan) isolated populations are found in isolated rocky outcrops (jebels) surrounded by savanna plain (Happold 1969). This species is absent from the central tropical forest and woodland–savanna regions of Zaire and countries further west and avoids the rain forest zones of the southern West African countries, but may be quite common (although rarely seen) in the grassland–bush–farmland habitat on the forest–savanna boundary in Nigeria (Happold 1987). It is commonly found around suburban gardens and agricultural areas around Nairobi (Kenya) (Gregory 1976).

Atelerix albiventris is distinguished not only by its pure white underside (with maybe a little darker fur around the genital region), but also by a vestigial hallux, which is either tiny or absent altogether, hence another common name—the 4-toed hedgehog. It is quite a small animal with a head and body 140–210 mm long, tail 11–19 mm, hind foot 30–34 mm, ear 25 mm, a condylobasal skull length of 37–44 mm and spines up to around 18 mm long (Lienhardt 1982, Happold 1987, Corbet 1988). Of the 69 animals measured by Gregory (1976) around Nairobi (Kenya) all weighed less than 500 g and more than half were in the range of 200–300 g. This suggests a much lower weight in the wild than may be achieved in captivity: up to 675–900 g (Herter 1968). There are no definite subspecies but some may be revealed by the analysis of larger sample sizes in the future (Corbet 1988). From her observations of eight individuals from western Africa (Liberia) Lienhardt (1982) considered that animals from western Africa, although of similar dimensions, differed from eastern individuals in body odour, were more aggressive and had a paler pelage with pink skin on the nose and ears.

The Somalian hedgehog, *A. sclateri*, is known only from northern Somalia and is closely related to the central African hedgehog. It is distinguished from *A. albiventris* only by differences in the roots of the lower third premolar, the presence of a hallux (variably developed) and the rear part of the belly where the fur is dark-brown, though this is variable (Corbet 1988). Like the central African hedgehog it is a small animal with a head and body length under 200 mm, a hind foot less than 30 mm long and a skull under 45 mm in condylobasal length (Corbet 1971). Finds of animals of intermediate appearance suggest that *A. albiventris* and *A. sclateri* may grade into one another in some areas, but more data are required (Corbet 1988).

The southern African hedgehog, *A. frontalis* (Fig. 1.15) is similar in size and general appearance to the previous two species, but even the northernmost *A. frontalis* show no tendency to intergrade with *A. albiventris* (Corbet 1988). The white band across their foreheads is well developed, and extends on either side below the ears. The ventral fur is predominantly a dark greyish brown, but varies in some individuals from white with interspersed black hairs, to 'totally black' (Smithers 1983). There is a relatively narrow, inconspicuous centre-parting of the spines on the crown. The dark band, in the middle of each spine, varies greatly in breadth making some individuals look dark and others pale, and unpigmented spines are commonly interspersed among the others. Although the hallux is somewhat reduced—as is typical of this genus—all five toes are present on the hind foot. Their snouts are sharp and relatively pointed. There are generally three pairs of nipples although additional ones are common (Smithers 1983). Reported *average* dimensions vary somewhat: total length 185–220 mm, tail 19–25 mm, hind foot 30–34 mm, ear 25–27 mm and a bodyweight usually in the range of 300–400 g (studies cited by Smithers 1983). Some individuals reared in captivity and released subsequently achieved weights of around 800 g (Kok & Van Ee 1989).

FIG. 1.15 *The southern African hedgehog (*Atelerix frontalis*).*

Atelerix frontalis is found in a wide variety of habitats and commonly visits suburban gardens, but it generally inhabits areas of scrub, steppe and savanna in southern Africa. Its most northerly range extends to parts of Zimbabwe and isolated locations in southernmost Zambia. Smithers (1983) noted that all recorded locations of this species were within the 300–800 mm mean annual rainfall zone, and that it was absent from either arid regions, or areas with wet ground or a high rainfall ($>$1000 mm year^{-1}). The southern African hedgehog has not been found in south-western South Africa or Natal Province, Mozambique, southern Namibia and the Kalahari desert region of Botswana. In south-western Angola, a subspecies (*A. f. angolae*) has been proposed, mainly on the basis of smaller body size, but the distinction is dubious (Smithers 1983, Corbet 1988). Both Smithers (1983) and Corbet (1988) suggested that records of this species from Natal were likely to be erroneous. Although it hardly seems uncommon (Gillies *et al.* 1991), The International Union for Conservation of Nature and Natural Resources (IUCN) has given *A. frontalis* Threatened Species status ('Rare' category) and it is protected under Schedule 2 in Cape Province and Transvaal, and under Schedule 1 in Orange Free State (Nicoll & Rathbun 1990).

Genus Paraechinus

The 'desert hedgehogs', genus *Paraechinus*, are found from Morocco to India (Fig. 1.16). The genus is characterized by a wide, conspicuous centre-parting of the spines on the crown of the head, and a distinct white band across the forehead (except *P. hypomelas*). The large ears protrude beyond the adjacent spines. The skull has distinctively inflated auditory bullae (the bones encasing the inner ear) and a fairly broad posterior palatal shelf. The spines have a rough surface and are strongly grooved along their length (Fig. 1.9). The hallux is somewhat reduced but is consistently well developed. The glans of the penis has no lateral expansions, but on its dorsal surface there are two tracts of spines. Each of the tracts is single or partly double in *P. aethiopicus* but in *P. hypomelas* each tract may consist of four or five rows of spines (Corbet 1988). In *Paraechinus* the fur on the underside is denser and softer than in either *Erinaceus* or *Atelerix*. The relationship with other genera is unclear and no fossil species have been described (Corbet 1988).

The Ethiopian hedgehog *P. aethiopicus* (Fig. 1.17) has a wide distribution and is the only member of the genus to be found in Africa (Fig. 1.16). It is easily distinguished from the other African hedgehogs (*Atelerix* spp.) by its much longer ears. Its dark face and coronal parting of the spines also eliminates any confusion with the long-eared hedgehog (*Hemiechinus auritus*) which lacks both these features and tends to be larger with longer legs and larger, more strongly clawed feet (Herter 1968). The head and body length varies from 140 to 230 mm, tail length is 10–30 mm (Hufnagl 1972), and the condylobasal skull length averages 48 mm (Vesmanis 1979). Herter (1968) suggested a bodyweight range of 400–700 g but this may include some heavy captive animals. The coloration varies but is generally pale with dark legs. The

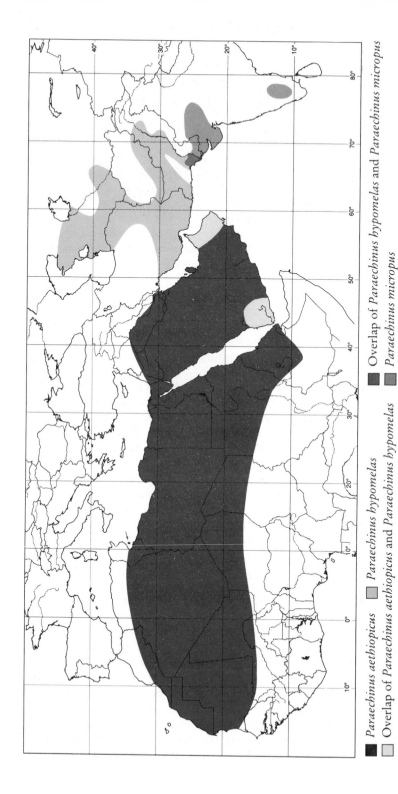

■ *Paraechinus aethiopicus* ■ *Paraechinus hypomelas* ■ Overlap of *Paraechinus hypomelas* and *Paraechinus micropus*

■ Overlap of *Paraechinus aethiopicus* and *Paraechinus hypomelas* ■ *Paraechinus micropus*

FIG. 1.16 *Distribution map of the genus Paraechinus Source: Roberts (1977), Corbet (1988).*

FIG. 1.17   *The Ethiopian hedgehog (*Paraechinus aethiopicus*) from the desert regions of northern Africa.*

ventral fur is a variable mixture of white, brown and black, but some individuals have entirely brown undersides. The grey–black mask is somewhat variable but well defined by a broad white stripe across the forehead (Hufnagl 1972, Corbet 1988). The distribution of this species is hard to map accurately because it occurs in various scattered and rather isolated locations in the Sahara and Arabian desert regions (Corbet 1988). In Libya it is found as far inland as the Fezzan and Kufra Oasis—west of the Rebiana Sand Sea (Hufnagl 1972). Its range extends south, through Egypt and Sudan, to at least central Ethiopia (Awash valley) and possibly further. Populations may be found on the islands of Djerba (Tunisia), Bahrain and Tanb (Persian Gulf). In Arabia the subspecies *P. aethiopicus dorsalis* is characterized by a band of darker spines running down the centre of the back (Corbet 1988). Intriguingly, in Oman and North and South Yemen, *P. aethiopicus* occurs with isolated populations of Brandt's hedgehog (*P. hypomelas*), possibly indicating a more extensive former range for the latter species (Corbet 1988, Delany 1989). Various other subspecific divisions of the Ethiopian hedgehog have been proposed, but sample sizes are, as yet, too small to be reliable (Corbet 1971, 1988). In coastal areas of Egypt and Israel, the Ethiopian hedgehog coexists with the long-eared hedgehog (*Hemiechinus auritus*) and, in Israel, also with the eastern European hedgehog (*Erinaceus concolor*) but little is known about their ecological niche separation other than that *Paraechinus* is the most tolerant of arid conditions and that *Erinaceus* and *Hemiechinus* differ in minor dietary details (Schoenfeld & Yom-Tov 1985) and hibernation pattern (Dmi'el & Schwartz 1984).

Brandt's hedgehog, also called the long-spined hedgehog (*Paraechinus hypomelas*), is found around Oman, the Yemens and on the island of Tanb (Persian Gulf) but otherwise not in the Arabian peninsula. It is found in various locations in Iran, Afghanistan (only Paktia province in the west), to the east of the Caspian sea (Kazakhstan, Turkmenistan), and Pakistan as far east as the Indus valley. Given this fragmented range, it is not surprising that several subspecific forms have been described (Ognev 1928, Niethammer 1973, Roberts 1977, Corbet 1988). In several regions the range of this species overlaps with long-eared hedgehogs (*Hemiechinus* spp.). Brandt's hedgehog has very long spines, up to 36 mm long and, in the dark form (see below), typically three dark bands with the terminal band covering the tip (Ognev 1928, Roberts 1977); Fig. 1.12). Brandt's hedgehog is large and can match the size of a big European hedgehog. Average dimensions are given by Roberts (1977) as head and body length 245 mm (range 205–286 mm), ear 47·2 mm (range 42–55 mm), tail 30·6 mm (range 25–38 mm), hind foot 41·4 mm (range 31–46 mm) and a condylobasal skull length of up to 60 mm (Corbet 1988). The 'Blandford's hedgehog', a subspecies (*P. hypomelas blandfordi*) from the Indus valley (Pakistan) is smaller, with a head and body length averaging 180·4 mm (range 151–205 mm) and shorter spines (Fig. 1.12). The species seems to have two colour forms as some white (not albino) specimens have been collected in Iran, but the species more typically has a striking dark-brown or black pelage with no white band across the forehead (Ognev 1928, Corbet 1988). There is no information about how relatively common the two forms may be. Roberts (1977) described how the dark form tended towards a rufous colour.

Not much is known about the habitat requirements of the Brandt's hedgehog but it is typically found in dry and rather barren rocky areas. However, it may also be found in lowland and agricultural areas, at least in Baluchistan where it is reputed to eat melons (Roberts 1977); see Chapter 3.

The third species of this genus is the pale or Indian hedgehog (*P. micropus*) which is confined to southern Pakistan and India. Corbet (1988) cited a study by Shah & Aravinda (1977) which identified only 74 autosomal arms in the karyotype of this species (88–92 in all other hedgehogs), but Corbet judged that further verification of this finding was required before it could be accepted. It is a pale-coloured hedgehog, with a well-defined dark face and grey–white forehead, a pointed snout and dark legs (Fig. 1.18). The facial

FIG. 1.18   *The pale or Indian hedgehog* (Paraechinus micropus). *Although pale in general coloration, the legs are dark and the facial mask well defined.*

mask, though well defined, is quite variable in shape. It is quite small, weighing up to 435 g, rarely exceeding 160 mm in head and body length, tail 12–13 mm, hind foot 25 mm (range 24–26 mm), and a condylobasal skull length up to 45 mm (Walton & Walton 1973, Roberts 1977, Corbet 1988). According to Roberts the ears are quite short, averaging only 25·5 mm, but the Waltons reported one large individual with 32-mm ears. The spines are medium-sized (19–23 mm) and have white tips (Fig. 1.12) but the colour bands are variable in their intensity and some individuals have a red-golden tint (Walton & Walton 1973, Roberts 1977).

In Pakistan, *P. micropus* is found in dry, sandy areas and tropical thorn forests from Hyderabad southwards. Around Karachi it inhabits semi-arid scrubland and irrigated agricultural land (Walton & Walton 1973). It would seem to be generally rather uncommon and locally distributed in Pakistan (Roberts 1977). It often occurs in the same region as *Hemiechinus collaris*, except for various scattered locations in Rajasthan and the Gujurat regions of India (Krishna & Prakash 1955, Roberts 1977, Corbet 1988). It is absent from the most arid regions of the Rajasthan desert region (India). A map by Krishna & Prakash (1955) suggests that the northern limit of the species range of *P. micropus* is just short of 29°N. The most easterly record is an old one (1870) from Agra (78°E) (Biswas & Ghose 1970). An isolated population of this species, from the Deccan region of central southern India, may have specific status (Biswas & Ghose 1970). Among other features, the hedgehogs from Deccan are reported to lack the posterior callosity of the forefoot, to have shorter ears and a brown collar. However, Corbet (1988), taking some contradictory evidence into account, judged that a subspecific ranking was more appropriate (*P. micropus nudiventris*). Biswas & Ghose (1970) also proposed that the population of the Gujarat region (plus individuals from Jodhpur and Guna) was an intermediate species (also with two subspecific divisions) which apparently overlaps the species range of *P. micropus*.

Genus Hemiechinus

Although its range extends into the Middle East and northern Africa, this genus of 'long-eared' hedgehogs has a mainly Asiatic distribution (Fig. 1.19), and occurs in a variety of habitats including semi-arid regions. The genus *Hemiechinus* seems to be a valid taxonomic grouping but has no close affinity with the other genera of hedgehog (Corbet 1988). The genus can most simply be distinguished by the complete absence of a central-parting of the spines on the crown of the head, although, as in all hedgehogs, a median spineless tract is visible in young babies (Chapter 8). The hallux is well developed, the ventral fur is evenly coloured and there is no face mask. The posterior palatal shelf is narrow (as in *Erinaceus*), and the penis lacks lateral expansions and bears two rows of spines on the dorsal surface of the glans (Fig. 1.9), but these features, like several others, are unconfirmed in the little-known species *H. hughi* from China. The remaining characteristics are rather variable and will be considered separately for each species.

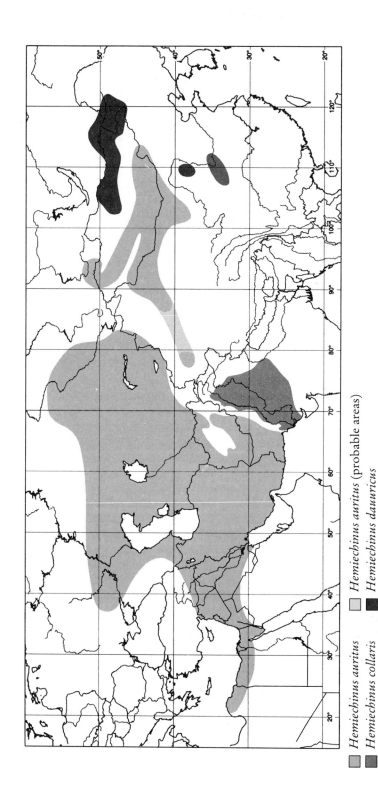

Hemiechinus auritus
Hemiechinus collaris
Hemiechinus hughi

Hemiechinus auritus (probable areas)
Hemiechinus dauuricus

FIG. 1.19 *Distribution map of the genus Hemiechinus. Sources: Krishna & Prakash (1955), Roberts (1977), Mallon (1985), Corbet (1988).*

FIG. 1.20 *The long-eared hedgehog (*Hemiechinus auritus auritus*), a pale form typical of specimens from North Africa and the Middle East.*

The most widely distributed and best-known species is the long-eared hedgehog (*Hemiechinus auritus*) (Fig. 1.20). It inhabits coastal semi-desert, scrub and steppe regions but cannot tolerate very dry desert conditions. It is a common garden animal in Libya, and occurs on agricultural land in Baluchistan (Pakistan) (Hufnagl 1972, Roberts 1977) although in Israel, Schoenfeld & Yom-Tov (1985) noted that this species was more strictly insectivorous than *Erinaceus concolor* and did not eat human refuse (Chapter 3). As its name indicates, it has long, flexible, mobile ears which project well beyond the level of the adjacent spines. If the ears are pressed forward they cover the eyes (Herter 1968). The animal has a long-legged appearance and is fast moving (Hufnagl 1972). The spines are rough and faintly grooved, and the fur is quite soft. The auditory region of the skull is inflated but not to the extent found in *Paraechinus*. The glans penis generally bears two rows of short, broad spines on its dorsal surface. Body dimensions vary but individuals may weigh up to around 500 g, have a head and body length of 170–250 mm, a 15–25-mm tail, and a condylobasal skull length in the range 51–56 mm, depending on the region of origin (Ognev 1928, Herter 1968, Niethammer 1973, Corbet 1988, Al-Khalili 1990). The wide and sometimes discontinuous range of this species—from northern Africa to Mongolia—has led to quite a diversity of forms. Herter (1968) mentioned 16 subspecies, but erroneously described a coronal parting of the spines. Although further taxonomic revision (and further confusion) seems inevitable, Corbet (1988) identified three main subspecific groupings which represent the main trends in the variation of this species.

Hemiechinus a. auritus ranges from western Ukraine to Iran and coastal north Africa as far west as Benghazi (Libya) but also south down the Nile valley as far as El Faiyum (Egypt). Although apparently absent from the Arabian peninsula there is a single record from Bahrain (Al-Khalili 1990). The fur is soft and white with some grey and brown on the head (Corbet 1971, 1988) and the spines are banded in a similar way to those of European hedgehogs (Fig. 1.12). Hufnagl (1972) reported typical measurements for North African animals (hind foot 35 mm, ear 40 mm) and in Israel ear lengths are 31–39 mm (Schoenfeld & Yom-Tov 1985) and average bodyweight is 367 g ($n = 30$, range 230–510 g) (Dmi'el & Schwartz 1984).

Hemiechinus a. albulus occurs in Mongolia, China, eastern Kazakhstan and Kirghizia (Mallon 1985, Corbet 1988). It is similar to *H. a. auritus* but has softer ventral fur. Its measurements and coloration are variable but it is basically white and sandy coloured; Ognev (1928) defined it as a separate species with five subspecific forms. Spines were absent from the glans penis of a single specimen from the west of Xinjiang region, China (Corbet 1988).

Hemiechinus a. megalotis occurs in eastern Afghanistan/western Pakistan (Niethammer 1973, Roberts 1977). It is often considered as a separate species, the Afghan hedgehog, on the grounds of its large size. Roberts (1977) described it as being a rather rufous dark-brown, with long spines (34 mm) bearing three dark bands with only a very small white tip (Fig. 1.12). The average dimensions of 11 animals from Pakistan were: head and body length 251 mm (range 230–270 mm), tail 33 mm (range 22–55 mm), hind foot 41 mm (range 30–55 mm), ear length 47·5 mm (range 38–60 mm). Corbet (1988) reported a head and body length range of 265–300 mm. In Pakistan it is common in steppic upland regions (up to 2500 m) where sub-zero winter temperatures are common (Roberts 1977). Niethammer (1973) demonstrated its subspecific status when he found that the *megalotis* form (average measurements: spines 28·1 mm and condylobasal skull length 56·2 mm) from the south-eastern regions of Afghanistan, graduated into the 'typical' *H. auritus* found in the north (average measurements: spines 25 mm and skull length of 51·9 mm).

The species of long-eared hedgehog found in eastern Pakistan and north-western India, is *Hemiechinus collaris*, sometimes known as Hardwicke's hedgehog or the collared hedgehog and is often referred to as a subspecies *H. auritus collaris*. Bennett (1832) recorded two individuals from 'the Himalayas', which were variable enough for him to describe as two separate species, but both seem to have been *H. collaris* (Corbet 1988). Since there have been no subsequent corroborative finds, these records were regarded as probably erroneous by Corbet (1988). *Hemiechinus collaris* has long ears and soft fur, but is distinguished by its dark-brown fur and spines. The spines, though pale at the base, have a broad dark band covering the upper half of the spines including the tip (Fig. 1.12). The overall effect is a very dark, blackish appearance (Roberts 1977, Corbet 1988). The face is variably paler and there are sometimes lighter patches of fur under the chin. The legs are long and the feet have well-developed claws. Typical dimensions given by Roberts for animals from Pakistan are as follows: head and body length 140–175 mm, tail 23 mm, ear 32–38 mm, spines 17–19 mm. It is found in a variety of habitats from the lowland areas of the Indus river (Pakistan), mainly on the eastern side where it is the commonest species of hedgehog and its range extends eastwards into parts of the Rajasthan desert region, and on across northern India at least as far as Etawah in Uttar Pradesh—roughly 79°E (Krishna & Prakash 1955, Roberts 1977, Pandey & Munshi, 1987).

Very little indeed is known about the natural history of the Daurian hedgehog *H. dauuricus* which inhabits the dry steppe and wooded steppe of eastern Mongolia, the Amur basin region (CIS) and parts of adjacent Manchuria (China) where it is found in the drier regions avoided by the aforementioned Chinese hedgehog (*Erinaceus amurensis*) (Mallon 1985, Corbet 1988). There are also some records of this species from central China (Shaanxi), but there are too few records to reveal the species range between the two areas of its distribution accurately (Fig. 1.19). Ecologically they appear to be very similar to other *Hemiechinus*, feeding on a range of invertebrates and small vertebrates, and using burrows for shelter (studies cited by Corbet 1988). The Daurian hedgehog has a head and body length of around 215 mm long, a 23-mm tail, and moderately long ears which project a little beyond the adjacent spines (Ognev 1928, Corbet 1988); the ventral fur is rather coarse. The spines on the dorsal surface of the glans penis are long and thin and sometimes barbed. The auditory region of the skull is not particularly inflated. The pelage is generally pale, the spines 19–23 mm long and a single dark band (5 mm long) ends about 3–5 mm from the sharp tip (Ognev 1928, Corbet 1988). It is worth noting that Ognev (1928) described this species as a typical *Erinaceus* and considered the inclusion of this species in the genus *Hemiechinus* as a 'complete blunder'! However, he makes no mention of the complete absence of a coronal parting, so typical of *Hemiechinus*.

The last species in this review, *H. hughi*, is perhaps the most obscure and poorly studied hedgehog. It is known only from the central Chinese provinces of Shaanxi and Shanxi and appears to occur alongside *Erinaceus amurensis* in the Qinling mountains a little further south in the subalpine and lower coniferous zone (studies cited by Corbet 1988). It clearly has close affinities with *H. dauuricus*, but there are no data regarding many of the detailed anatomical features required to assess its taxonomic status. Its ears are comparatively short (for the genus) and are no longer than the adjacent spines. The auditory region of the skull is not inflated. The spines are smooth and have a pale band just before the dark tip. The fur is coarser and browner than the Daurian hedgehog; head and body length is 200 mm (Corbet 1988).

CHAPTER 2

Some Features of Hedgehogs

SPINES

HEDGEHOGS are justly famous for their remarkable spines which completely replace the hair of the back and the crown of the head. The spines are modified hairs and therefore made of keratin (a protein). Thin, hair-like spines are found at the border between spines and hair on the forehead and flanks. The number of spines depends upon a hedgehog's age and size, but varies from about 3500 spines on a newly independent youngster, up to 7000 spines or more on a large adult European hedgehog (*Erinaceus europaeus*). Herter's claim (e.g. 1965b, 1968) that European hedgehogs may have as many as 16 000 spines is certainly a mistake (Morris 1983, 1988a). There are no comparable data for most other hedgehog species, although Eisentraut (1952) also counted 7000 spines on an Ethiopian hedgehog (*Paraechinus aethiopicus*). This, and the fact that all the hedgehogs look much alike in terms of their spine density, suggests that there is a roughly similar number in all species, with some variation in relation to body size.

Although many other mammals also have spines (Chapter 1), those of the hedgehog are particularly specialized with an elaborate internal structure that confers properties of lightness, strength and resistance to buckling (see below). Carlier (1893c) gave a detailed description of the histology of the skin and the structure of the spines of *E. europaeus*. The greyish skin of the back and crown has no sweat or sebaceous glands, although these are abundant on the hairy skin and soles of the feet. The epidermis is very thin, but underlying it is a thick, rather corrugated fibrous layer almost devoid of blood vessels, which lie in the deeper layers. With no insulating fur, the absence of blood vessels close to the surface of the dorsal skin is an obvious way of reducing heat loss. Below the level of the spine follicles is a well-developed layer of

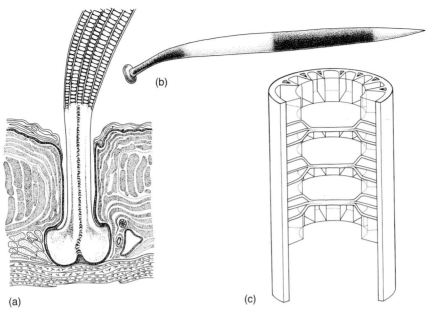

FIG. 2.1 *The features of a spine from a European hedgehog* (Erinaceus *spp.). (a) Vertical section through the skin showing the lower part of a spine and the basal bulb(see text). (b) Side view of a whole spine. (c) 3-dimensional cut-away diagram of a section of spine showing an idealized version of the internal structure; in reality the septa are less evenly spaced and subdivisions at the junction of the spine wall are more variable. Sources: Carlier (1893c), Morris (1983), Vincent & Owers (1986).*

striated muscle, the *panniculus carnosus* (Fig. 2.1a). Under the muscle is a layer of fatty tissue which is especially thick just before hibernation.

Each spine grows from a single large follicle which Štěrba (1976) considered to be fundamentally derived from the fusion of a group of follicles. But Carlier (1893c) considered that each spine was an elaboration of a single hair, a suggestion supported by his detailed description of the intermediate bristly hairs on the flanks. Studying the embryological development of a spine follicle does not resolve the issue, since even at the earliest stages of its development the follicle forms a single unit (Štěrba 1977).

Where the spine emerges from the skin, there is a slender section, angled slightly so that it will flex, should a blow threaten to break the spine or drive it into the hedgehog's own skin (Fig. 2.1). Each spine is erected by means of its own multi-stranded erector muscle (smooth muscle) which originates in the deeper muscle layers (see below). Although the erector muscle is situated on one side of the follicle, some muscle strands pass underneath the follicle and insert on the other side to improve leverage (Carlier 1893c). The erected spines interlock and bristle in all directions, forming an impenetrable array of sharp points (Plate 6).

Each spine is locked into its follicle by a rounded basal bulb (Fig. 2.1a,b) and is so firmly embedded in the skin that if you try to pull one out from a freshly dead animal, considerable force is needed and it will usually snap off at the base first (Carlier 1893c; Harrison Matthews 1952). Carlier described how the weight of the whole dead hedgehog could be supported by one spine alone. Such treatment would be torture for a live hedgehog!

A structural and biomechanical study of hedgehog spines by Vincent & Owers (1986) has confirmed many of the functional properties of hedgehog spines suggested by earlier authors. Porcupines have long spines, designed to break off at the tip and each is filled with a foam-like cortex. The tips of the longer spines have scales to make them more difficult to pull out of the skin of a victim. The spines of hedgehogs, however, are completely different, they are short, smooth-tipped and very resistant to breakage. Inside, the spines are hollow but with a series of transverse septa (which resist lateral compression) complexly attached to the side walls and joined to longitudinal struts ('stringers') which add to the spine's rigidity (Fig. 2.1c). Compared with the spines of the long-eared hedgehog (*Hemiechinus* spp.), those of the European hedgehog (*Erinaceus europaeus*) have deeper longitudinal stringers and more widely spaced septa, each with a more complex insertion into the inside of the spine wall. The spines of tenrecs (Chapter 1) also contain transverse septa, but these are thinner and more narrowly spaced, and there are no longitudinal stringers (Vincent & Owers 1986).

Hedgehog spines do not bend easily, but when they do, they buckle elastically and structural failure occurs only at a force 200 times greater than the force required to buckle the spine. Vincent & Owers (1986) concluded that the short spiny coat of the hedgehog is most suited to absorbing the shock of a blow rather than impaling an assailant in the style of a porcupine. The shock-absorbing qualities of the spiny coat may explain why hedgehogs have apparently little fear of falling from heights; a falling hedgehog rolls-up and erects its spines to cushion the impact. Harrison Matthews (1952) noted that hedgehogs are reputed to drop down small heights deliberately as the easiest way of getting down.

As well as these fancy properties, the spines also have solid, sharp tips and, as anyone who has handled a hedgehog will testify, it is a lot more comfortable to do so when wearing gloves! By the way, I would advise anyone against handling hedgehogs without gloves because the spines can be *very* dirty indeed; sometimes hedgehogs will coat themselves with dog faeces (Chapter 7)! Although the sharp spine tips cause only minor discomfort, they easily penetrate soft skin, injecting dirt and potentially dangerous bacteria.

There are three generations of spines (Poduschka & Poduschka 1986b)—for more details see Chapter 8. About 2 days after birth, the pigmented second generation spines start to grow and mostly obscure the first coat of unpigmented spines (present at birth) by about 2 or 3 weeks. Second generation spines are just smaller versions of the adult spines which gradually replace them from around six weeks (about the age of independence). The adult spines are longer lasting, replaced individually and may not be moulted for up to 18 months (Barrett-Hamilton 1911, Morris 1983).

The longevity of the adult spines is useful to field workers, who can identify animals by clipping short (or otherwise marking) small patches of spines in a coded combination of positions. During 3 years of field research, I reliably identified 108 individual hedgehogs by this method, keeping the clipped patches clear by a trim when required. Sometimes animals which I had not seen for a year could still be identified by their marks.

Continuous spine replacement makes sense for an animal that cannot afford to be without its spiny defences, but some evidence suggests that spine replacement is sometimes particularly intensive. I occasionally found that clipped patches, though still identifiable by the presence of cut stumps, became quite rapidly obscured by a flush of new growth. In further support of this idea, apparently healthy captive animals sometimes moult more spines than usual. Eisentraut (1952) noted that a captive male desert hedgehog (*Paraechinus aethiopicus*) moulted about one-seventh of his spines (up to 260 spines day^{-1}) over 25 days in mid-June which coincided with a flush of newly growing spines. Other animals, though not moulting to the same degree, also appeared to be shedding more spines than usual and he suggested that hedgehogs may undergo periodic partial moults. Similarly, Herter (1971) found that one captive male central African hedgehog (*Atelerix albiventris*) moulted 890 spines during August, almost half the entire number shed over 7·5 months, but this moulting pattern was not shown by other captives. Poduschka & Poduschka (1986b) mentioned that captive female long-eared hedgehogs (*Hemiechinus* spp.) tended to lose a lot of spines at the end of a lactation period, especially if the litter had been large. The Poduschkas were unable to say whether the spine loss was related to endocrine, dietary or other factors.

DEFENSIVE BEHAVIOUR

Hedgehogs are famous for the fact that they defend themselves from attack by 'rolling-up' into a ball, presenting an impenetrable exterior of bristling, sharp spines. However, the widespread idea that hedgehogs roll-up immediately when faced with any danger is quite incorrect!

When danger approaches, the hedgehog's first response is simply to become wary and erect its spines. If the threat is not yet too close, the bristling hedgehog may quickly run away to cover, but otherwise it will freeze and crouch, pulling its spiny dorsal skin down to cover its feet, tail and face. Hedgehogs use a special forehead muscle, the *fronto-dorsalis* (=*fronto-cuticularis* or *preorbitalis dorsalis*) (Fig. 2.2) to draw down the spiny skin of the crown in a 'frown' (Poduschka & Poduschka 1986b). This defends the face while still allowing the hedgehog to keep its eyes and ears open (Plate 7). In hedgehog babies, this forehead muscle becomes functional very early, while they are still blind and cannot yet roll-up (Chapter 8), and shows as a characteristic horizontal crease in the forehead.

Should a hedgehog be subjected to a sudden attack or hear a sharp noise (especially a click, rustle or other high frequency sound—see below), this first

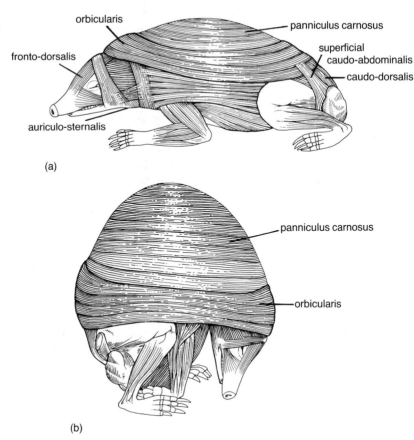

FIG. 2.2　*(a) The dermal muscles of the hedgehog, indicating some of the main muscles involved in rolling-up. (b) A partially rolled-up animal. The muscles overlying the forehead, shoulder and tail-end have contracted, pulling down the* orbicularis *so that it slips over the body. As the* orbicularis *contracts the entire body will become enveloped in the stretched* panniculus carnosus *(see text). Labelling after Grassé (1955); additional diagrammatic sources: Owen (1868), Herter (1965b).*

stage of defence becomes a high-speed flinch. The forehead muscle contracts in an amazingly rapid reflex action, faster than 0.01 s (Poduschka 1969) and the head jerks downwards. At the same time the stretching of the skin musculature (*panniculus carnosus*) stimulates the spine erector muscles and causes a rapid, reflexive bristling of the spines.

　Would-be photographers of hedgehogs are often confounded by blurred pictures caused by the hedgehog's flinch reaction to the sound of the opening camera shutter (Plate 8). Most published pictures of hedgehogs show the spines bristling to some degree, and often the rear end is drawn down, hiding the hind legs and tail. This is why almost all the best pictures of hedgehogs are obtained from animals habituated to the presence of humans. In a totally relaxed hedgehog the spines are completely sleek and the face looks longer as the spines of the forehead lie back from the brow (Plate 1), the body is roughly parallel to the ground and the hind legs are visible. Incidentally, when observing animals in the wild it is relatively easy to tell, by its posture and the lie of its spines, whether or not you are making the hedgehog nervous.

Only if the threat to the hedgehog escalates to physical contact, will it actually 'roll-up'—a remarkable process in which a complex of muscles draws down the spiny dorsal skin to envelop the whole body. This feat is possible only because the dorsal skin and its associated muscles are very flexible and only loosely attached to the body. The *panniculus carnosus* muscle (Fig. 2.2) is thickened at the rim to form a special circular muscle (the *orbicularis*) which, as the roll-up starts, is drawn down—like a hood—over the head and shoulders by various muscles. The flexible ears fold forward, and in the long-eared hedgehogs cover the eyes (Herter 1956,1965b). The rump and tail are tucked inside the 'rim' by the *caudo-dorsalis* and *caudo-abdominalis* muscles (Fig. 2.2). Now the process is completed by the contraction of the *orbicularis* muscle, which acts like the string of a draw-string bag to seal the opening on the underside (Fig. 2.3). Within this bristling, spiny bag of its own skin, the hedgehog's body is tucked tightly head to tail.

If necessary, hedgehogs can remain rolled-up for hours and, apart from the need to keep the *orbicularis* muscle tight, they are quite relaxed. The spine

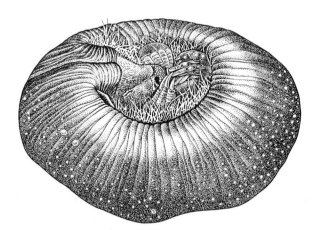

FIG. 2.3 *The appearance of a rolled-up hedgehog without its spines. This unusual European hedgehog, which has lost its spines, shows how the circular* orbicularis *muscle, as it constricts, forms the rim of a 'bag' of skin and muscle which is pulled round to enclose the animal tightly. In a fully rolled-up animal the head and feet are also fully enclosed. Drawing from photographs by P. Morris.*

erector muscles, embedded in the *panniculus carnosus*, are automatically stretched, keeping the spines erect. If the rolled-up animal is prodded, the *panniculus* bunches up locally to increase the density of spines at the point of attack, and the animal may hiss and 'huff'. When the disturbance has ceased, the hedgehog cautiously begins to unroll (Plate 10). Hedgehogs may quickly habituate to human disturbance and tame hedgehogs may be quite hard to get to roll up tightly, although Lindemann (1951) actually trained a tame hedgehog named 'Eri' to roll-up and unroll on command!

As a final illustration of the amazing flexibility of the spiny skin, it is quite possible to pick up a relaxed hedgehog by its spiny scruff and for its body almost to 'fall out' of its loose bag of spiny skin (Fig. 2.4); this is especially noticeable when handling anaesthetized animals.

Although hedgehogs usually rely on a passive defence, the spines may also be used offensively. This is especially well shown in nestling hedgehogs which, when disturbed, jump up in a bucking movement to jab any predator in the face with their spiny backs, often emitting small squeaks at the same time (Chapter 8). Fighting adults will butt at the face and flanks of their opponent with erect head spines. Sometimes when threatened by a predator (as during aggressive encounters with other hedgehogs) the animals may hiss, snort and even 'scream' (see later). All such noises may discomfort a potential predator.

FIG. 2.4   *An eastern European hedgehog* (Erinaceus concolor)*, held by the scruff of its loose, spiny skin. Source: based on a photograph in Poduschka & Poduschka (1972).*

BITING

Hedgehogs rarely bite in defence, although some species can be quite aggressive, hissing and biting in defence of their young (Chapter 8), and hedgehogs may bite each other when fighting.

I have handled wild European hedgehogs hundreds of times and have only once been bitten—although it was little more than a pinch and I was wearing gloves, it was so unexpected I nearly dropped the hedgehog! However, some 'tame' hedgehogs are quite another matter. I once kept a hedgehog (a runt too small to be released) called Emily who would bite quite often. She particularly enjoyed biting Pat Morris, who was at that time supervising my doctoral research, and even savaged him while he was being filmed for a BBC television documentary! Although the bite of a hedgehog is not serious and he managed to keep talking unabashed, it clearly left an impression on him (in more ways than one) as he graphically recounted the incident (Morris 1983, page 27).

TELLING THE SEX OF A HEDGEHOG AND HOW TO UNROLL IT!

The sexes are generally similar in appearance and can be told apart only by getting them to unroll and inspecting their genitalia. In all species the male has a conspicuous penis sheath opening well forward on the belly (roughly where one might expect to see the navel), whereas the vulva of the female is very close to the anus (Fig. 2.5).

The male has no scrotum because the testes are abdominal, but they are placed in pouches inside the body wall and sometimes produce a visible bulge or they may be detected by gentle palpation. Details of the internal reproductive organs are discussed in Chapter 8. Up to 10 nipples are visible in both sexes, but in pregnant or lactating females they may be more prominent and two bands of mammary tissue may be felt running from just anterior to the 'armpit' to the groin. New-born babies are harder to sex: the umbilical cord attachment may be mistaken for the penis sheath, whereas the real penis sheath opening is at first placed quite close to the anus, moving forward as the animal grows. Otherwise, telling the sexes apart is fool-proof, provided you can get them to unroll!

Unrolling a hedgehog is simple and requires only a little practice. Different workers use various methods, but I favour the method taught to me by Pat Morris, which is simple and quick.

(For a right-handed person.) Wear gloves, so you can handle the animal confidently. Gently pick up the hedgehog and hold it so that its rear-end is in your right palm and your left hand is under its front end (nose pointing away from you). Gently bounce it up and down in your hands. It will put out its feet and untuck its snout—now you have a crouching hedgehog. Without hurrying, keep bouncing it gently and allow the snout to poke between the thumb

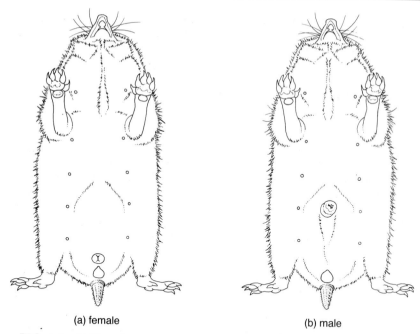

(a) female   (b) male

FIG. 2.5   *Telling the sexes apart is easy. The opening of the penis sheath is placed well forward on the male's belly, whereas the female's vaginal opening is much closer to the anus. In European hedgehogs, both sexes usually have five pairs of nipples.*

and index finger of the left hand and, using gentle but firm pressure, place the thumb on the back of its neck. Now it cannot tuck its head back down. Gently gripping the underside at the rear of the animal with your right fingers, put your right thumb in the small of its back and gently open out the animal by flexing it backwards; if you are not rough or jerky, it will just allow you to open it in this way!

There are other unrolling methods, such as those reviewed by Gregory (1985) but his own preferred method is:

> . . . to hold the rolled up hedgehog head-downwards over a flat surface. It then usually unrolls cautiously and tries to reach the surface. The back legs can then be grasped gently and the animal can be held by them and examined at leisure while it strives to reach the ground.

This is a good method for veterinary use, as intraperitoneal injections and other such drastic procedures can be carried out if necessary (Gregory, 1985), although I would not recommend it to beginners who might drop or hurt the animal. For injections, Saupe & Poduschka (1985), having persuaded the animal to uncurl by heavily stroking its rump, recommended firmly grasping the animal's entire spiny back and holding it down (on its side) on the bench

(Appendix 1). Some authors suggest putting the animal in water, and grasping it as it unrolls to swim (e.g. Kock, 1985), but this may be too much for very weak, hypothermic animals.

THE SENSES IN COMMUNICATION AND NAVIGATION

Hedgehogs have moderately sized eyes, and can probably see well enough in moonlight to distinguish shapes and moving objects. Their vision is principally monochrome: the retina contains only rods and they lack the cones necessary for full colour vision (Bridges & Quilliam 1973). However, Herter (1965b) noted that some of the rods (3·75%) contain cone-type nuclei and found that he could train hedgehogs to discriminate between certain colours, for example, yellow was distinguished from all shades of grey and blue. Thus hedgehogs do seem to have a limited ability for colour discrimination in good light. Similarly, observations by Lindemann (1951) and Herter (1965b) indicate that hedgehogs are not 'short-sighted' (as often stated) and have reasonable visual acuity. Nevertheless, being nocturnal and close to the ground, where low vegetation restricts the view, they are hardly likely to find vision particularly valuable. Humans have very good vision but would not be able to see much if they were crawling about in the middle of a dark wood at night! The other thing that is likely to happen is that one would get a poke in the eye by a stick or thorn, and indeed I have seen many wild hedgehogs with serious eye injuries. Clearly it would be inappropriate for a hedgehog to rely on its eyesight, and the big eyes necessary for improved nocturnal vision would be a liability in the undergrowth! Morris (1985a) radio-tracked one virtually blind male hedgehog which although it blundered about and often ran into things, otherwise led a normal life.

Vision and tactile signals from their long, sensitive whiskers—probably also the long hairs which project from fur on the flanks in some species—are undoubtedly important to hedgehogs, but clearly it is olfaction and hearing, both very acute, that are the dominant senses.

Olfaction

Even the most cursory observation of hedgehog behaviour leaves one in no doubt that their sense of smell is highly developed. The long snout has a large moist tip (rhinarium) and hedgehogs sniff constantly, and often noisily, as they explore their environment. When foraging, hedgehogs detect (presumably by smell) and dig out prey such as leatherjackets (tipulid larvae) concealed in the soil (Chapter 3). The olfactory lobes of the brain are well developed (Chapter 1); their neuro-anatomy is described in numerous papers (e.g. Lopez-Mascaraque *et al.* 1986, Meyer *et al.* 1989, Valverde *et al.* 1989). There is no doubt that, as in most other mammals, odour cues are important in many hedgehog activities, including finding food, detecting potential predators, orientation and place recognition, sexual behaviour, maternal behaviour and other interactions. Unfortunately we still know little about this aspect of hedgehog life.

Although there have been some studies, none has yielded reliable estimations of olfactory performance in hedgehogs. Burton (1969) cited earlier experiments by Adrian (1942) who, using electrodes implanted into the olfactory lobes, established that the sense of smell is indeed acute. Subsequent experiments have added little. Lindemann (1951) carried out numerous rather *ad hoc* observations of captive hedgehogs, using various unlikely odour sources (including vanilla pudding!). He found that hedgehogs could detect crushed beetles (cockchafers and carabids) at a range of up to 1 m (41% success), a dog at up to 11 m (42% success) and mice were reliably detected at 5 m. Sources of food were rapidly located with a performance similar to that of a dog. Bretting (1972) tried to train hedgehogs to associate a food reward with an odour coming from an entrance in a choice chamber. His attempts to determine the olfactory thresholds to various organic substances (valerian, acetic, butyric and proprionic acids) were confounded by his inability to entrain the animals. Three hedgehogs took 1500–2000 trials before they became entrained, and even then behaved unreliably; a fourth never learned what to do, even after 4000 trials! Bretting wisely did not put much weight on his unlikely finding that the olfactory performance of hedgehogs was much poorer than that of dogs and similar to that of humans.

Lindemann (1951) contaminated previously acceptable food items with salt, as well as bitter and sour substances. These were usually all rejected but Lindemann was surprised to find that caustic and strongly smelling substances were not avoided and sometimes even preferred!

Hedgehogs have a well-developed and functional Jacobson's organ (= vomeronasal organ). This olfactory organ is present in the palate of many vertebrates, including snakes who use it to sample scents collected by their tongues. In many mammals (e.g. humans and the higher primates), the organ is found only at certain embryonic stages, but in others it is functionally developed in adults. In the ungulates and many carnivores, the Jacobson's organ comes into play during '*flehmen*', a lip-curling display in which the male 'tastes' the urine of a female to determine her sexual readiness. Nerves from the sensory cells of the Jacobson's organ run separately from those from the nasal olfactory organ, and link to parts of the brain implicated in the control of reproductive physiology and behaviour (the medial hypothalamus and medial pre-optic area) and the ventral medial nucleus which is involved in the regulation of feeding behaviour (Ewer 1973). Wysocki *et al.* (1985) have shown that the Jacobson's organ is capable of taking up high molecular weight, non-volatile molecules in addition to more volatile ones. Presumably its role includes the detection of steroids (including sex hormones) and/or their residues, or other sexually related components of secretions, hence the link with sexual behaviour. In the European hedgehog the Jacobson's organ forms a pair of blind-ending diverticula connected by ducts to the mouth and nasal cavities. The structure of the organ has been described in detail by Poduschka & Firbas (1968), but its functional significance in hedgehogs is not understood. The only observed use of the Jacobson's organ is during the peculiar and unexplained behaviour of 'self-anointing' (Poduschka & Firbas 1968, Poduschka 1977b), which has a very dubious relationship with sexual behaviour (see below and Chapter 7).

Very little is known about how hedgehogs use odours in their interactions with each other and no true 'pheromones' have been properly identified. Although this term has been used by some authors, it should only be used to refer to specific substances which elicit specific responses in the recipient (in a way analogous to hormones). Generally, however, it is reasonable to suppose that odours—and maybe some pheromones too—are important in sexual behaviour (Chapter 8), and may also be significant in other contexts. As an interesting aside, both Herter (1956) and Poduschka (1969) commented that when hedgehogs of different species are placed together, they get very agitated, sniffing, licking and sometimes mounting or even self-anointing. Although there may be initial aggression, they generally calm down and tolerate each other in captivity (Herter 1956).

Although there is little precise information about how odours may be used, there are certain likely sources of odours which include the following:

Sebaceous glands: these glands have been found in the rectal linings of both male and female *Hemiechinus auritus* (Shehata 1981). The secretions, which act as a lubricant during defecation, may also be smelly, especially if combined with bacterial action in or around the glands. Sweat glands around the anus may also add odours to the faeces.

Urine and faeces: these may contain metabolic residues which can be used to convey information about the physiological state of the animal; for example, it is likely that males may be able to detect the sexual readiness of females from odours in the urine.

Lubricating glands in the vagina: secretions of these glands (Deanesly 1934, Shehata 1981) could also be the source of odour signals which may alter in composition during the oestrous cycle, potentially indicating sexual receptivity.

Sexual accessory glands: secretions from these glands may be used as scent marks by males. Such scent-marking behaviour has been clearly observed during pre-copulatory courtship, during which the males marked the ground (and possibly the female) with odorous secretions exuded from the penis tip (Poduschka 1977a, Poduschka & Poduschka 1986b). The exact nature of the secretion is unknown.

A proctodeal gland (a sebaceous gland situated just inside the anal opening): this has been described in the European hedgehog by Grassé (1955). It is a lobulated gland, 6–7 mm long and 4·5 mm wide, and consists of convoluted tubules enlarged in places to form reservoirs. Such a gland probably adds odours to the faeces but no overt scent-marking behaviour using the gland (such as dragging the anus on the substrate) has been observed.

Eccrine sweat glands: in mammals, these are commonly elaborated for scent-marking purposes. Hedgehogs (*Erinaceus* spp. and possibly other genera) have eyelid glands (Meibomian glands) but these are less compact and more sparsely innervated than in rodents and domestic cats. Large multi-lobed sebaceous glands are located in the corners of the mouth (Poduschka 1977a,b, Sokolov *et al.* 1982b). The use of these glands seems to be a component of hedgehog sexual behaviour, at least in the long-eared hedgehogs *Hemiechinus* spp. (Poduschka & Poduschka 1986). Apart from these locations hedgehogs show no specially developed skin glands, although the hairy part of the skin, the circumanal region and the soles of the feet are well supplied by sweat glands, creating the potential for the laying of general body-odour trails. Sokolov *et al.* (1982b) showed the ducts of eccrine sweat glands to be under the control of cholinergic nerves and that the secretory cells are under adrenergic control. Although it has yet to be demonstrated in hedgehogs, there is considerable potential use of such eccrine secretions with the possibility of altering the rate and quality of secretion in response to behavioural cues and physiological state.

'Self-anointing' behaviour: this involves the production of copious quantities of saliva, usually when stimulated by some odour or smelly object. The saliva is frothed up in the mouth and, normally mixed with the stimulus material, is plastered over the animal's back and flanks. This behaviour, which involves the Jacobson's organ, has so far defied convincing explanation but is clearly a process during which the animal goes through a period of intense olfactory stimulation (Chapter 7).

For non-social nocturnal mammals, odours provide an ideal medium for communication with a very high potential for information transfer, both in the face-to-face situations of maternal, sexual and competitive/aggressive behaviour and in the form of longer term 'signpost' odour deposits in the environment. Territorial scent marking is common in mammals, but in hedgehogs it has never been demonstrated and field studies have not shown territoriality in any conventional sense (Chapter 4). Campbell (1973a) observed that single droppings were randomly scattered, with no preferred areas—a finding generally supported by my own field observations, although I once saw a 'latrine'-like pile of about a dozen droppings near a known nest. Nevertheless, some observations of captive *E. europaeus* indicate that faeces are not always randomly placed. Campbell (1975) noted a tendency for animals to defecate near the nest when first emerging and I have observed that captive animals sometimes placed their faeces a few centimetres up the walls of their cage and in their food dishes. Similar observations have been made by Poduschka (1977b) and for captive central African hedgehogs (*Atelerix albiventris*) by Meritt (1981). Meritt also commented on a penetrating odour, 'a combination of motor oil and musk', associated with the faeces which tended to be deposited in a particular corner where the animal also usually urinated.

Secretions from various skin glands, sexual accessory glands and urine mediated odours, though likely to be principally sexual in function, could form marks or trails of territorial significance but, without overt deposition behaviour, would be hard to detect by a human observer. It seems certain that future investigations will reveal many subtle uses of olfactory communication among hedgehogs. Our current ignorance of olfactory communication in general is an almost inevitable result of our own rather pathetic sense of smell and the shortcomings of compensatory technology in this area, although equipment is improving all the time. I refer the reader to Brown & Macdonald (1985) for a good general review of the whole topic.

Sounds and hearing

Humans can only hear sounds up to about 18–20 kHz (this upper limit decreases with age) and sounds above this frequency are commonly referred to as 'ultrasonic'. High frequencies attenuate rapidly in air, thus ultrasound provides a frequency band relatively free of background noise—ideal for short-range reception. If you stand outside with an ultrasound detector, apart from passing bats there is remarkably little sound interference, but the slightest metallic jingle of keys or coins in a pocket comes over as mighty crashes of sound. If you want to see the hedgehog flinch reaction (see earlier), suddenly jingle some keys or click your tongue!

Body sounds, such as blood rushing through the carotid and stapedial arteries, can limit hearing sensitivity at lower frequencies (under 1 kHz) unless adaptations are present to isolate these sounds from the ears. Such adaptations are absent in long-eared hedgehogs (*Hemiechinus auritus*)—the middle ear carotid is not enclosed in a bony canal (Packer 1987). Batzri-Izraeli *et al.* (1990), while mapping the auditory cortex of *H. auritus*, noted a general lack of response to low frequencies (under 2 kHz). Hedgehogs are thus adapted to high-frequency sound reception, a feature common to most insectivores (Lipotyphla) except the moles (Chrysochloridae and Talpidae) which live underground in a low-frequency environment (Packer 1987). Hedgehogs probably use their acute hearing to locate accurately the rustling of invertebrate prey moving in the soil and leaf litter, and to detect the approach of predators (Fig. 2.6). The source of a high-frequency sound is relatively easy to locate because of its short wavelength in relation to ear separation and pinna sizes.

Early studies (Chang 1936, Lindemann 1951, Herter 1956, Poduschka 1968, 1969, and others) did not have access to the high quality ultrasound detection and recording equipment now available, but all commented on the sensitivity of the hedgehog's hearing, especially at higher frequencies. In a simple but convincing experiment (species unstated, probably *Erinaceus amurensis*) Chang (1936) found that the reflex flinch could be induced by pure

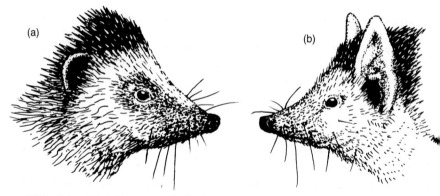

FIG. 2.6 *(a) A European hedgehog (genus* Erinaceus*). (b) A long-eared hedgehog (genus* Hemiechinus*). Partially hidden by fur, the ear pinna of the European hedgehog appears small but it is really quite large at 20–30 mm long. The long-eared hedgehogs have the largest ears, typically up to 40 mm long (longer in some subspecies), more delicate features and shorter fur, both of which add to the impression of very large ears. Also note the moderately sized eyes, whiskers and the wet tip to the nose (rhinarium). Illustration by the author.*

tones (from a calibrated 'Dalton's whistle') in the range 7·6–84 kHz although a maximum response was obtained at about 20 kHz. When such sounds were continued at high volume the hedgehogs even rolled-up! Lower frequencies did not elicit the flinch reflex, no matter how loud they were. In a study of eastern European hedgehogs (*Erinaceus concolor*), Poduschka (1968) noted that sounds that had previously elicited the flinch reflex (clicks, jingles, lip-squeaking noises by people), failed to do so when recorded and played back without the ultrasonic frequencies. Ravizza *et al.* (1969, cited by Poduschka 1977b) showed that long-eared hedgehogs (*Hemiechinus auritus*) can respond to frequencies as high as 45 kHz and, judging by some of the sounds produced by the youngsters studied by Poduschka & Poduschka (1986b), they may hear up to 60 kHz or higher.

It is generally assumed that the expanded auditory bullae and larger ears of the longer eared hedgehog species (genera *Paraechinus* and *Hemiechinus*) endow them with more sensitive hearing, but there have been no audiometric studies. Herter (1956) reported that European hedgehogs could hear the scratching noises of a dung beetle 5 m away. Burton (1969) noted that even hibernating hedgehogs would bristle upon hearing a high-frequency sound.

In certain contexts, sound is an important channel of communication and hedgehogs can produce a wide range of sounds, although some are rarely heard. These range from tongue clicking and tooth grinding sounds to a full-throated scream and include:

Audible high-pitched twittering sounds: these are emitted by neonate babies (Poduschka & Poduschka 1986b).

Shrill piping whistles: these are produced by isolated nestlings and dependent youngsters (all species studied), which stimulate the mother to retrieve a straying youngster. A sonagram for *E. europaeus* showed a fairly pure tone at around 8 kHz (Attié 1990). In *Hemiechinus* such calls, though audible, have ultrasonic components which are strong at 42 kHz, peak at 50 kHz and tail-off at 90 kHz (Poduschka & Poduschka 1986b).

Purely ultrasonic clicks: *Hemiechinus* nestlings produce these at the same time at the isolation calls, but they are not visibly synchronized with the babies' lip movements. They have a maximum amplitude between 40 and 60 kHz and a peak at 64 kHz (Poduschka & Poduschka 1986b). Possibly, a mother alerted by the isolation call would find such high-frequency clicks easier to locate.

Clucking ('le gloussement'): this is a short sound produced by mothers retrieving their youngsters, and by males prior to courtship. It may have a pacifying role, according to Attié (1990), the only worker to describe it in detail.

Snorting, spitting, puffing or huffing: these are all descriptions of what seems to be the same aggressive/warning sound, produced by sharp exhalations through the nostrils (not a vocalization) used by all the species yet studied—for a sonagram see Attié (1990). The sound may be short and sharp, as when rapidly repeated during fights and by females to deter male suitors during courtship rituals (Chapter 8) or drawn out into a snake-like hiss, such as when a hand is inserted into a nest or burrow (Chapter 5).

The 'quack': this unusual vocalization, reported for European hedgehogs (*Erinaceus europaeus*), has been variously described and interpreted (Barrett-Hamilton 1911, Burton 1969, Attié 1990) but seems to be produced when the hedgehog is bothered or in slight pain. I have only recently heard this sound, when one participant in a courtship ritual suddenly uttered a prolonged, rather yowling duck-like sound, repeated loudly, several times (Chapter 8). Two captive hedgehogs were reported to make this sound when confronted with the trail of a strange hedgehog, and once at the first meeting of two animals (Dimelow 1963a). Attié (1990) reported a previously undescribed sound, a rasping growl (*'le grognement'*). The description bears some similarities to a muffled 'quack' and may not have been distinguished by other workers.

The 'scream': this very loud call of distress has been described for European hedgehogs by Barrett-Hamilton (1911) as 'a kind of wail, recalling the cry of a hare when in trouble'. I have never heard a hedgehog 'scream' although there are many accounts (Burton 1969). Barrett-Hamilton cited several early descriptions of these whining cries, including the famous reference in Shakespeare's 'Macbeth' (Chapter 10). He also mentioned an apparently traditional practice among 'country boys' who 'draw a small piece of stick to and fro across their hamstrings' and make the hedgehogs scream! Gregory (1975) described how a central African hedgehog (*Atelerix albiventris*) produced a coarse high-pitched scream repeated regularly at half-second intervals, when it was held by all four feet. On another occasion similar screams were produced by both animals during a fight. Walton & Walton (1973) heard a female Indian pale hedgehog (*Paraechinus micropus*) with young emit a very loud high-frequency scream, clearly audible 10–12 m away, when a kitten climbed into the cage.

During his studies of *Atelerix albiventris*, Gregory (1975) recorded two sounds unknown from other species. The first was a very faint high-frequency twitter, barely audible even at a distance of 20 cm. However, his recording equipment was incapable of registering ultrasonic components. The sound was produced by both sexes (not from animals under 3 months old) and was generally produced when the animal was placed in unfamiliar surroundings, or handled. The second sound was a loud 'serenade', an intriguing bird-like vocalization produced only by mature males as a prelude to courtship (Gregory 1975) (see Chapter 8). Poduschka (1977b) also mentioned the 'schnalz', plus squeaking noises, claimed to be characteristic of Algerian hedgehogs (*Atelerix algirus*). In Pakistan, Walton & Walton (1973) reported that newly captured females with young (*P. micropus* and *H. collaris*) produced a rhythmic high-pitched squeaking for several hours on the first day of captivity although undisturbed.

Senses used for navigation

Precisely how hedgehogs orientate themselves during their extensive nightly wanderings is poorly understood, but Lindemann (1951) and Herter (1965b) both remarked on the excellence of the hedgehog's long-term memory for places, which were remembered even after intervals of several months. They noted that hedgehogs may use well-trodden routes, but it is very clear from radio-tracking studies (Chapter 4) that they more usually navigate freely within their home ranges. The facility with which hedgehogs find their way about gives the impression that they possess a detailed cognitive map of their entire familiar area!

It is likely that hedgehogs navigate using a combination of general olfactory cues (maybe including their own body odour trails) and auditory cues, such as rustling trees or the sounds of running water. Lindemann (1951) considered that visual cues might also be important; from my own field observations I feel that hedgehogs could easily be using the silhouetted shapes of trees, bushes and buildings to help them navigate.

It is hard to know what other environmental cues a hedgehog may use to orientate itself. Maybe hedgehogs use a 'kinaesthetic' sense, in which the turns made and distances travelled are mentally integrated. One newspaper report (Blewett 1979) of a Russian hedgehog 'Topa', presumably *Erinaceus concolor*, recorded a capability for remarkable long-distance homing behaviour. The animal returned to a house (where it had been cared for) over a distance of 48 miles (77 km). Assuming the animal was correctly identified, such a performance tempts speculation about the use of a magnetic sense or orientation using the moon or stars.

Despite tentative reports that hedgehogs may be able to echolocate (Poduschka 1969, 1977b, Poduschka & Poduschka 1986b, Attié 1990) the evidence is very unconvincing. There is a general tendency amongst researchers to interpret any tongue clicks, 'creaks' or similar sounds that crop up on sonagrams as echolocation sounds. Using an ultrasound detector to listen to a tame hedgehog for quite some time, I heard nothing other than the clearly audible whistling and bubbling of air passing through its damp nostrils, plus lip smacking and licking, as it noisily sniffed about. Hedgehogs are notably prone to falling off steps, tables, or into drains and so on. Even though their shock-absorbing spiny coat helps to prevent injury, if they were competent echolocators they would presumably be more able to avoid such incidents.

HOW INTELLIGENT ARE HEDGEHOGS?

The answer to this question depends on a meaningful definition of the word 'intelligent'. All mammals are capable of complex behaviour, and brain development of various kinds may have evolved in response to a combination of ecological, behavioural and physiological selection pressures. Generally, it can be said that low levels of brain development will be found in animals that rely heavily on only one or two senses (olfaction and hearing), occupy a terrestrial (two-dimensional) niche, use passive defence, have limited social interaction, rather stereotyped behaviour, minimum parental association with their young, and a ubiquitous food supply which does not need to be caught (e.g. vegetation). In contrast, greater brain development is related to an increased level of complex social interaction, more highly developed parental care, and behavioural plasticity. Brain development is also associated with the need to process increased sensory input, such as that demanded by living in a niche requiring a high degree of co-ordination (e.g. arboreal) or the need to forage or hunt for elusive, patchily distributed prey. Such generalizations are useful but there are many problems which arise if one attempts, in a more formal way, to correlate brain development with the factors characterizing the ecological niche inhabited by a mammal, although some success has been achieved by Mace *et al.* (1981).

Hedgehogs tend to fit the general ecological model of an animal with a low level of brain development, and their anatomy seems to bear this out (Chapter 1). The olfactory lobes are large and the cerebral hemispheres (= neopallium in Fig. 1.8) are unelaborated and smooth (Herter 1965, Bauchot & Stephan 1966, Mace *et al.* 1981). Nevertheless, hedgehogs forage for a wide variety of patchily distributed prey types, navigate accurately during their extensive movements and also have a high standard of maternal care. Eisenberg (1980) criticized the notion that conservative mammals are limited in their range of social behaviour, including mother–infant relationships. He pointed out that although such interactions are generally brief, they are not necessarily less complex than those of the 'advanced' mammals. Eisenberg also commented that many small mammals tend to have small brains for their body size, irrespective of conservative morphology.

It is fair to say that hedgehogs are not very intelligent, but this does not mean that their behaviour is dull and stereotyped! Rather at odds with their cerebral development, hedgehogs show a great deal of flexibility and individualism in their behaviour. Although Bretting (1972) found training hedgehogs a frustrating experience, both Lindemann (1951) and Herter (e.g. 1965b) have trained hedgehogs to carry out a remarkable number of quite complex tricks. As already mentioned, Lindemann's tame hedgehog 'Eri' learned to roll-up on the command '*Zusammen*' and unrolled upon hearing '*Auf*'; it responded to its name when called and appeared to differentiate between its carer and other people. Poduschka & Poduschka (1972) also found that hedgehogs could become very tame and apparently affectionate towards their carers. Lindemann described how his hedgehogs, by trial and error, learned to pull long rods out of a box in order to obtain an item of food attached to the end of each rod. Herter, for the purposes of his visual discrimination experiments, trained his hedgehogs to open sliding doors. Learned behaviour and an ability to recognize specific locations persisted for weeks or months, and were not forgotten during hibernation.

CHAPTER 3

Diet and Feeding

HEDGEHOGS are indeed insectivorous, but from the bewildering array of accounts I have heard or read, it would appear that they will avidly consume almost any kind of plant or animal food, from pumpkins to live hens and other hedgehogs! Hedgehogs, always idiosyncratic, seem to reserve a good measure of their eccentricity for their diet. However, some stories seem to represent rather exceptional events or are based only on tenuous inferences. For example, I was once told, by a gardener, that his young broad beans had been eaten-off at ground level 'by hedgehogs'. This is not impossible, but it is much more likely that the real culprits were pigeons or slugs.

The British naturalist Maurice Burton, a great popularizer of hedgehogs and collector of hedgehog anecdotes, considered the hedgehog to be as omnivorous as the '...hog' in its name implies. Both he (1969) and Herter (1968) described how, compared with other insectivores, hedgehogs have stronger jaws, blunter teeth and a longer gut. Herter compared the ratio of body to gut length (1:6 or 7) with the stoat (*Mustela erminea*), a strict carnivore (1:4) and the herbivorous rabbit (*Oryctolagus cuniculus*) (1:10). However, the hedgehog has a simple stomach, and a smooth non-complex colon with a poorly defined ileo-colonic junction. There is no caecum and food moves rapidly through the gut, the majority being passed within 12–16 h after ingestion. It is unlikely that much fermentative digestion takes place although lactic acid and volatile fatty acids (indicative of bacterial action) are sometime present in moderate quantities (Clemens 1980). It is now clear from dietary studies of wild hedgehogs (all species so far studied) that they are not really omnivores but predators whose diet consists principally of a wide range of invertebrates, as well as small vertebrates and carrion. Plant material such as windfall fruits, acorns, berries and fungi, although sometimes eaten, has comparatively little importance in the natural diet.

WAYS OF STUDYING DIET

Behavioural observations of naturally foraging hedgehogs usually yield little precise information about what is being eaten. In my experience most small prey are snapped-up so rapidly that reliable identification is impossible.

Most studies of diet have used either rather unnatural 'cafeteria' tests on captive animals (e.g. Lindemann 1951, Krishna 1956, Dimelow 1963b) or relied on the analysis of prey remains found in either the gut contents (obtained post-mortem) or faeces of live animals. These analyses tend to be biased as the more indigestible body parts (e.g. the exoskeletons of inverte-brates) are comparatively easy to find and identify. Insects, notably beetles, may contain a high proportion of indigestible material and thus have less nutritional significance than one might suppose either from their frequency in the diet or from their total energy content as measured by a 'bomb calor-imeter'. About 35% of the energy content of carabid beetles is tied up in indigestible chitin (Wroot 1985b). Soft-bodied prey, although more com-pletely digested, are often identifiable using a wide range of diagnostic clues such as radulae and shell (slugs and snails), mouth-parts (caterpillars and dipteran larvae) and chetae or gizzard-rings (earthworms). In the absence of diagnostic structures it may be possible to separate and identify species-specific proteins by electrophoresis or immunological techniques, but these methods have not yet been used to study hedgehog diet.

A laborious, but useful, approach to dietary analysis is to count the numbers of individuals of each species within each gut or faeces sample directly (e.g. Campbell 1973a, Yalden 1976). If such counts are combined with nutritional analyses of average-sized individuals of each species, it is possible to construct a fairly detailed picture of an animal's nutritional intake (Wroot 1984a). Most studies have combined more than one technique (each with their attendant biases), and also determined either the relative weights of food remains (e.g. Yalden 1976, Maheshwari 1984) or their relative volumes (e.g. Brockie 1959, Obrtel and Holišová 1981, Grosshans 1983). The simplest, most widely used, method of analysis merely records the presence or absence of any particular prey type in each sample, which is then expressed as a percentage occurrence, without regard for relative abundance.

Most studies have probably under-estimated the dietary contributions of soft-bodied prey and carrion, but Wroot (1984a, 1985a) devised an ingenious method to estimate the energy contribution of earthworms. An estimate of the minimum number of segments ingested was based on numbers of chetae (eight per segment), and both the dry weight and energy content of segments were shown to correlate with cheta length. Wroot's method improved realism and removed the need for the assumption that each occurrence of worm remains (e.g. gizzard rings) represented the consumption of a whole worm. Fur, feather or scales in the faeces can reveal that vertebrates (often as carrion) have been eaten but there is seldom any means of estimating the amount consumed.

Only one study, of *Erinaceus europaeus* in Britain (Wroot, 1984a), has seriously attempted to address the difficulties of relating diet to the avail-ability of prey species and their estimated nutritional quality (e.g. total energy content), in combination with field observation of foraging behaviour. This study represents an important first step in the investigation of foraging 'strategy' and the adaptive consequences of food selection (see later).

DROPPINGS

The consistency of hedgehog faeces depends on the diet, but generally, droppings are dark brown–grey or blackish in colour, rather dry and typically show the densely packed remains of invertebrate exoskeletons such as beetle elytra (Plate 11). Droppings are usually found singly, but can be deposited in pairs or, very occasionally, in piles of up to seven or even nine droppings (Obrtel & Hološová 1981). Each dropping is roughly cylindrical, and variably tapered. Average dimensions reported for various species are very similar at around 20–26 mm in length and 7–8 mm in diameter (Obrtel & Hološová 1981, Barquin *et al.* 1986), but there is considerable variation in size; a range of 15–50 mm in length and a diameter of 10 mm has been reported for *Erinaceus europaeus* droppings (Morris 1991).

One of the problems of faecal analysis is that each dropping does not normally represent a stomach-full and the same prey item may get divided amongst several droppings (Obrtel & Hološová 1981). Catching animals after a night of feeding, and keeping them until they have totally emptied their gut, is one way to reduce such errors, and also allows the study of the relationship between observed feeding behaviour and the items later revealed in the faeces (Wroot 1984a).

DIETARY STUDIES OF EUROPEAN HEDGEHOGS

Several dietary studies of both *Erinaceus europaeus* and *E. concolor* have revealed them to be essentially similar in their feeding ecology (Table 3.1). Comparison between these studies is frustrated by the variety of methods used and the various seasonal, habitat and prey species differences in each of the studies. Table 3.2 shows a compilation of the main food types, and their frequency of occurrence in samples, for the eight studies that have presented their data in this form. These data have rather limited value when assessing the relative nutritional importance of food types, but frequency of occurrence data are commonly presented and thus allow some cross-study comparisons, at least when similar food categories are used (regrettably not always the case).

Rather few studies have used the direct-count method which allows more meaningful comparison. Wroot (1984a) adapted such data from three other studies of *E. europaeus* to estimate the amount of dietary energy represented by each prey type (Table 3.3).

When analysed in this way, a remarkable consistency between the studies was highlighted, despite their differing circumstances. Prey such as earwigs

TABLE 3.1 *Summary of details of dietary studies of European hedgehogs in the wild; those incorporating other hedgehog species are excluded.*

Author and date	Species of hedgehog	Study location and habitat(s)	Sampling period	Size and nature of sample
Shilova-Krassova (1952)	*E. concolor*	CIS (Ukraine), mixed woodland & pine forest/plantations.	Spring/summer (1950–1951)	262 droppings
Brockie (1959)	*E. europaeus*	New Zealand, southern North Island & northern South Island, a variety of rural and suburban locations	All year (years not specified)	5 stomachs 90 droppings
Kruuk (1964)	*E. europaeus*	NW England (Cumbria), coastal sand dunes around Ravenglass	March–June (1963)	33 droppings
Campbell (1973a,b)	*E. europaeus*	New Zealand (South Island), pastureland near Canterbury	All year (1970–1971)	230 droppings 60 stomachs
Yalden (1976)	*E. europaeus*	England (East Anglia), various rural locations but mainly game-managed woodland	All year (1966–1969)	137 stomachs (no gut)
Obrtel & Holišová (1981)	*E. concolor*	Czech Republic, general suburbs and parkland around Pisárky (Brno)	April–October (1976–1980)	72 droppings (31 separate samples)
Grosshans (1983)	*E. europaeus*	Northern-West Germany, Schleswig-Holstein, Various rural/suburban locations	April–December (1975–1976)	125 stomachs (with gut)
Wroot (1984a)	*E. europaeus*	SE England (Ashford Middx.), Suburban golf course and surrounding gardens	July–Nov. (1981) April–July (1982)	39 droppings
Dickman (1988)	*E. europaeus*	S England (Oxfordshire), various rural/suburban locations	Nov. (1982)–July (1984)	87 stomachs (with gut)

and isopods, though recorded quite frequently (Table 3.2), provided relatively little potential dietary energy. Adult beetles were less important in total
energy terms than suggested by their incidence in the diet (even less if one
allows for their indigestibility), but retained an important position along with
caterpillars and earthworms, although the latter showed a variability partly
due to methodology. Over the four studies, these three main prey types
together accounted for between 79·5 and 87·2% of dietary energy; other prey
categories, when taken overall, accounted for under 5% each. Despite this
consistency, one clear difference is that the generally low proportion (<5%)
of energy from earwigs is higher (10·5%) in Grosshans' study which was also
one of only two studies to quantify beetle larvae.

It is therefore clear that European hedgehogs feed almost entirely on a
variety of invertebrates; but usually only a few main prey types dominate the
diet. Beetles and caterpillars usually head the list of prey but most studies,
being from different regions (Table 3.1), have their own particular spectrum
of prey items.

Beetles

Generally, beetles are the most numerous and commonly found prey items
but because of their indigestibility (see above) may not be preferred when
there are alternative prey (Wroot 1984a). Carabids (ground beetles) are very
commonly eaten (e.g. Yalden (1976) found them in 60% of stomachs), and
sometimes in large numbers; 144 individuals have been found in one dropping
(Wroot 1984a). Most are medium-sized to small species of the genera
Pterostichus, Harpalus, Nebria, Amara, Bembidion and others. Wroot found
Pterostichus madidus to be the main carabid prey; the much larger *Carabus
violaceus* was found in about 25% of the droppings but only one or two at a
time. Most beetle larvae identified by Grosshans (1983) were carabids. Beetle
larvae, usually of the smaller species, were comparatively unusual in Wroot's
study.

Scarabaeid beetles (which include the dung beetles and chafers) are also
commonly eaten. Many scarabaeids are substantial: Yalden found that they
accounted for almost two-thirds of the 27% (wet weight) of the diet
represented by beetles. Cockchafers (e.g. *Melolontha* sp.) may be eaten in
significant numbers at times when adults emerge *en masse* (Shilova-Krassova
1952). Yalden also recorded cockchafers in May and June and noted that
Serica brunnea were abundant in three stomachs taken in July. Twelve
stomachs (August to October) each contained up to 12 dor beetles (*Geotrupes*
sp.), a genus also recorded by Grosshans.

A wide variety of other beetles are also eaten. Tenebrionids (e.g. genus
Blaps) crop up sometimes and 'mealworms' (the larvae of *Tenebrio molitor*)
are readily eaten in captivity. Kalabuchov (1928, cited by Yalden) found *Blaps
mortisaga* to be quite commonly eaten by hedgehogs (*E. concolor* and *H.
auritus*). Obrtel & Holišová (1981) frequently recorded weevils (46·7%
occurrence) and, more surprisingly, ladybirds (23·3%) which are usually

TABLE 3.2 A summary of dietary studies of European hedgehogs which give '% occurrence' values of food types.

Hedgehog species:		E.c.	E.e.	E.e.	E.e.	E.e.	E.c.	E.e.	E.e.
Study:		Shilova-Krassova (1952)	Brockie (1959)	Kruuk (1964)	Campbell (1973a,b)	Yalden (1976)	Obrtel & Holišová (1981)	Grosshans (1983)	Wroot (1984a)
Insects									
Beetles:	Total	—	37	21	32[f]	74	93	97	100
	Carabidae	3	—	—	3[f]	60	63	78	—
	Scarabaeidae	93	—	—	16[f]	21	10	18	—
	Weevils	<1	—	—	—	—	47	—	—
	Other beetles	—	15	—	23	35	23	27	—
	Beetle larvae	8	5	—	—	—	—	15	10
Orthoptera		—	—	—	—	—	<1[e]	19	—
Earwigs		—	24	—	55	58	70	82	80
Hemiptera:	Homoptera	—	10[i]	—	—	—	<1[e]	2	—
	Heteroptera	2	—	—	—	—	23	2	—
Hymenoptera		—	12[f]	—	4	15	70	42	—
Lepidoptera:	Adult	—	13	—	3	—	—	18	—
	Larvae/pupae	<1	31	—	46	49	17	67	72
Diptera:	Adult	—	13	—	32	12	—	11	—
	Tipulid larvae	—	—	—	—	4	—	—	49
	Other larvae	—	2	94	3[f]	7	—	6	—
Other Insects[a]		2	25[c]	—	2[f]	10	—	—	—
Other invertebrates									
Arachnida:	Spiders	—	21	—	17	18	20	18	—
	Harvestmen	—	—	—	33	18	<1[e]	22	—
Crustaceans:	Woodlice	—	11	18	17	2	—	18	49
	Sandhoppers	—	j	—	—	—	—	—	—
Myriapods:	Centipedes	—	37	—	—	1	—	2	—
	Millipedes	—	35	—	—	40	63	69	—
Earthworms		—	40	—	22	35	—	53	51
Molluscs:	Slugs	—	36	21	30	23	—	26	95
	Snails	—						23	51

Vertebrates								
Amphibians	—	15	—	—	—	—	—	—
Reptiles	6	—	9	—	16	—	<1	8
Birds: Adults/hatchlings	<1	—	21	—	11	<1[e]	—	—
Eggs[d]	—	—	—	—	—	—	—	—
Mammals	2	15	—	—	12	—	3	—
Plant material	2	49[g]	58	95	40	30[h]	82	100
No. guts/droppings in sample	262	90	33	230	137	72	125	39

The use of differing food-type groupings in each study makes direct comparison difficult as % occurrence values in different categories cannot be accurately split or combined without access to original raw data. Inevitably therefore some approximations have been necessary to compile this table.

— Category not used or none reported in this category.

[a] Includes unidentified insects.

[b] My calculation.

[c] Addition of unidentified insect remains and unidentified pupae categories (thus an over-estimate).

[d] Including unhatched chicks.

[e] Estimated from 'importance index' values.

[f] Additional values cited by Yalden (1976).

[g] Maximum of more than one value given.

[h] Grass leaves alone (most commonly found plant remains).

[i] Addition of nymph and adult cicada values (thus an over-estimate).

[j] Reported as rejected.

N.B. Wroot (1984a): undigested 'accidental' inclusions (mites, aphid eggs, thrips, nematodes) omitted from the table.

TABLE 3.3   *A comparison between four studies of diet in European hedgehogs which have used direct counts.*

	% dietary energy			
	Campbell (1973a)	Yalden (1976)	Grosshans (1983)	Wroot (1984a)
Beetles	56·3	41·2	30·0	27·9
Caterpillars	30·9	31·4	43·1	17·7
Earthworms	?	12·3	7·7	33·9
Earwigs	4·8	1·7	10·5	1·5
Slugs/snails	5·3	3·1	1·3	5·6
Diptera larvae	—	2·9	5·2	7·0
Beetle larvae	—	—	10·5	0·4
Millipedes	—	2·2	—	0·3
Woodlice	1·1	0·1	—	0·9
Sample size	230	137	57[a]	39

The counts have been converted to energy equivalents (using conversion factors derived from calorimetric determinations of sample species or near equivalents) and then expressed as a percentage of the total energy these prey represent. Comparability of the data for earthworms is marred by the fact that Campbell did not quantify them at all, Yalden used wet weights, Grosshans apparently combined an unspecified direct-count system with relative volume estimates and Wroot used counts of chaetae to estimate number of worm segments (the most bias-free method).

[a]Grosshans analysed just 57 samples (of the 125 total) in detail.
?Recorded but not quantified.
—Food category not used or none recorded in this category.
Source: based on Wroot (1984a).

avoided. Grosshans also reported silphids (burying beetles), presumably encountered alongside carrion, to be especially important in late summer.

In New Zealand, beetles seem less dominant in the hedgehog diet. Brockie (1959) frequently found them in faecal samples (37% occurrence overall) but never in such abundance that they formed the bulk of any dropping. Neither was it usual to find beetle larvae (15% occurrence) in large numbers, although another study cited found a dropping consisting largely of a common 'grass grub' *Costelytra zealandica*. Campbell (1973b) considered that hedgehogs could be useful in reducing adult populations of this pest. She found up to 424 grass grub beetles per stomach and cited an estimated potential daily consumption of 850 grass grubs per hedgehog.

Some types of beetle are usually poorly represented or absent from the diet, e.g. ladybirds (*Adalia* spp.) were always rejected in food preference tests (Dimelow 1963b). Staphylinids (rove beetles), especially the larger ones, also seem to be avoided altogether (Yalden 1976), or only occasionally eaten (Wroot 1984a).

Caterpillars

Hedgehogs do eat adult lepidoptera, but caterpillars are far more important in the diet, and are clearly a preferred item. Yalden (1976) recorded caterpillars in 49% of samples (26% of the diet by wet weight) and up to 63 individuals in a single stomach; Wroot (1984a) found 56 in one dropping. Species identification of caterpillar remains is often difficult as the heads may be bitten off before eating, but most commonly consumed are the grass-eating larvae (and the pupae) of noctuid moths, such as the large yellow underwing (*Noctua pronuba*). Sometimes called 'cutworms', these caterpillars are also common pests of garden vegetables. Leaf-eating caterpillars (e.g. Notodontidae), although readily eaten, are less frequently encountered down on the ground (Grosshans 1983).

In New Zealand, moth caterpillars are important prey, especially in pastureland. Brockie (1959) recorded a moderate 31% occurrence in faecal samples, but considerable numbers were eaten. Two droppings contained only 'army worms'(*Pseudoletia separata*) which had been in plague proportions in the collection area at that time. Another dropping was composed entirely of the wings of adult army worm moths, presumably newly emerged. Campbell (1973b) reported many larvae, and some gravid adult females of the porina moth (*Wiseana cervinta*)—yet another grass-eating pest in pastureland.

Earthworms

The status of earthworms in the diet is less certain, largely because of variations in methodology between the studies. Species identification of remains is also very difficult; although the common species *Lumbricus terrestris* may be the usual prey, many other species are also acceptable (Dimelow 1963b).

When recorded, earthworms seem to have a significant, but variable, place in the diet (Tables 3.2 and 3.3). Yalden (1976), whilst accepting that much of the semi-digested material was unidentifiable, considered earthworms to be the most important prey, estimated at 13% of the diet (wet weight). Wroot (1984a) found that earthworms contributed about 34% of the total energy intake, and chetae were found in 95% of the droppings in numbers up to an estimated 45 000 per dropping! Although Grosshans (1983) found earthworm remains in 53% of droppings, they contributed only 5% of the total prey volume. Dickman (1988) also found them to be a relatively unimportant dietary item.

In New Zealand, Brockie (1959) found earthworm chetae in 35% of droppings. Campbell (1973b) found earthworm remains in 22% of droppings but also recorded dirt and grit in 50% of stomachs and droppings, a feature strongly linked to earthworm consumption (Wroot 1984a).

Earwigs

Earwigs (Order Dermaptera) are another common prey item (Table 3.2). In Britain and Europe the very common *Forficula auricularia* is the main species eaten. Obrtel & Holišová (1981), Dickman (1988) and Kalabuchov (1928, cited by Yalden 1976) reported that they made up 8·2% of the total number of prey items identified. Yalden found earwigs in 58% of samples and up to 22 in one stomach. Nevertheless, earwigs seem to contribute only modestly to hedgehog nutrition. Yalden noted that they represented only 3.3% of the total wet weight of food, and Wroot's analysis (1984a) found that they only contributed between 1·5 and 10·5 per cent of dietary energy (Table 3.3). In New Zealand, Brockie (1959) and Campbell (1973b) found that hedgehogs frequently ate large numbers of earwigs: both the native *Anisolabis littorea* (especially in sand dunes) and the introduced *Forficula auricularia* in the suburbs.

Molluscs

Hedgehogs cannot break open large, thick-shelled snails such as *Helix pomatia* or *H. aspersa*. Dimelow (1963b) found that captive hedgehogs could only deal with small thin-shelled snails (<18 mm across) such as *Cepaea* or small individuals of larger species. Field studies usually find relatively few snail remains. Wroot (1984a) found snail shell fragments only twice, but Grosshans (1983, in Germany) and Brockie (1959, in New Zealand), found more: 36% occurrence in samples. Brockie found snails (virtually all *Helix aspersa* – presumably small) in 57% of droppings collected from sand dunes. Snails were eaten less in the suburbs and were virtually absent in samples from pasture, orchard and native forest.

Slugs are more consistently important across the studies, and a common small species, the grey field slug (*Agriolimax* sp.) has been generally reported as the main species taken. Dimelow found that most slugs were readily accepted, even large and very slimy ones (e.g. *Arion hortensis, Milax budapestensis* and even one *Limax maximus* 15 cm in length!), but there was a tendency to reject the tougher-skinned species of the genus *Arion*.

Yalden (1976) found that slugs made up 4·1% of the diet (wet weight) overall but noted regional variations in the frequency with which they were eaten (17–59% occurrence).

In New Zealand, Brockie (1959) found slugs in 40% of droppings overall (56% in summer). A wide variety were taken, but the main type was *Agriolimax*, especially in samples from pasture and suburban garden areas.

Wroot's energy analysis (Table 3.3) suggested that, though sometimes eaten in more significant amounts, molluscs contributed between 1·3 and 5·6% of total dietary energy. Slugs are more digestible than arthropod prey and therefore could have a greater relative importance than the figures indicate.

Diptera

Adult flies (Diptera) although eaten, are not important prey. Yalden (1976) recorded 28 (1.6% of identified items), but about half were tiny and probably taken in accidentally; flies contributed only 0·1% of the diet (wet weight). Campbell (1973b) found adult flesh-flies (*Sarcophaga milleri*) in 32% of droppings, presumably eaten in association with carrion.

More important are dipteran larvae or pupae. Maggots, probably eaten in conjunction with carrion, crop up occasionally in stomach samples but are easy to miss in droppings. Crane-fly larvae (Tipulidae) and pupae, commonly known as leatherjackets, are taken from grassland and lawns—hence their importance in Wroot's (1984a) golf-course study site. Yalden reported a figure of 1·2% of the diet (wet weight) in mainly rural locations. Dickman (1988), without quoting figures, noted that leatherjackets were more commonly consumed in suburban areas.

Myriapods

Centipedes (Chilopoda), normally *Lithobius* sp., are infrequent dietary items (Yalden, 1976, Obrtel & Hološová 1981, Grosshans 1983). Dimelow (1963b) remarked that they might have been eaten more often had they not been so fast and adept at escape, and cited speeds of up to 28 cm s^{-1}!

Millipedes (Diplopoda), on the other hand, are common prey items and in some studies assume importance. Dimelow (1963b) reported them to be a firm favourite, seldom rejected. But despite her finding that polydesmid millipedes were acceptable prey items, almost every millipede identified in the hedgehog diet has been a member of the Iulidae, such as *Cylindroiulus* spp. and *Julus* spp. Most studies have recorded fairly high percentage occurrences for millipedes (37–69%) but evidently most are small. Yalden (1976) found that they accounted for only 3·4% of the diet (wet weight). Grosshans (1983) reported a figure of 5·6% of total prey volume; all very different from the 40% given by Obrtel and Hološová (1981)! Wroot (1984a) found them unimportant in terms of dietary energy.

Crustacea

Woodlice (Isopoda), despite being abundantly available, are never consumed in significant numbers. Brockie (1959) reported that woodlice were unpalatable and always refused by captive animals. Dimelow (1963b) found that only *Armadillidium* sp. (with relatively poorly developed odour-producing lateral plate glands) were readily accepted. Of the few woodlice eaten, the genera *Oniscus* and *Armadillidium* have been positively identified as prey in

Britain and Europe. In New Zealand, *Porcellio scaber* was eaten quite frequently (11–17% occurrence in samples), but only in small numbers (Brockie 1959, Campbell 1973b).

Hedgehogs feeding around a gull colony in coastal dunes (north-west Britain), ate modest numbers of sandhoppers (Amphipoda) of the genera *Talitrus* and *Talorchestia*. Kruuk (1964) recorded them in 18% of faeces (8% of total diet by estimated weight). In contrast, Brockie (1959) reported that *Talorchestia*, although abundant, was never eaten in New Zealand; not even when crushed and offered to hungry hedgehogs.

Hymenoptera

Several studies have reported single bees and wasps as occasional prey items, but nests of bumble bees (*Bombus* spp.) may sometimes be raided (Yalden 1976, Grosshans 1983). The opportunistic consumption of dead and moribund honeybees (*Apis* sp.) from under a hive was observed by Obrtel & Holišová (1981), and Yalden (1976) found eight honeybees in one stomach. All these studies concluded that most bees are consumed when dead or comatose but there are reports of hedgehogs attacking active bees, seemingly indifferent to their stings (see later)!

Obrtel & Holišová found that most of the Hymenoptera in their hedgehog's diets were ants (60% occurrence), usually *Lasius* spp. or *Myrmica* spp. Grosshans (1983) recorded ants as quite frequent, but in very small numbers, indicating that they may have been taken accidentally, a conclusion shared by both Yalden and Brockie who recorded only occasional ants.

Arachnida

Various arachnids are quite commonly found in hedgehog diets (Table 3.2), but are usually few in number and the species are small. The most usual spiders identified are wolf-spiders (Lycosidae), nocturnal hunters which were particularly common food items in Campbell's study on New Zealand pastureland. Even so they accounted for only 3–6% of the diet (also Brockie 1959). Harvestmen (Opiliones) are also very common prey in some studies (e.g. Campbell 1973b), although in others they may be only occasional items (e.g. Obrtel & Holišová 1981).

Arachnids, although frequently eaten, contribute only a small proportion of the diet according to most studies: for example 0·2% of the diet (wet weight) in Yalden's (1976) study.

Hemiptera (Bugs)

Bugs, such as aphids (Homoptera), are unusual in the diet and are generally rejected in preference tests (Dimelow 1963b). Wroot (1984a) reported intriguing finds of up to 9000 undigested aphid eggs in a few droppings collected in the autumn. Despite the abundance of cicadas (*Melampsalta* spp.) in the

Wellington suburbs (New Zealand), only a few were eaten (Brockie 1959). In the Czech Republic, Obrtel & Holišová (1981) also reported only occasional homopterans (spittle-bugs; *Philaenus* spp.) but found heteropterans to be fairly frequent items (23·3% occurrence), particularly the firebug (*Pyrrho-coris apterus*) which was found in 13.3% of samples.

Orthoptera

Only Grosshans (1983) found grasshoppers (Acrididae) in moderate numbers (15% occurrence) in the summer months. Otherwise they are reported only occasionally, although Brockie (1959) found large wetas (cricket-like orthop-tera of the family Stenopelmatidae) in 5% of droppings in New Zealand.

Other foods

Apart from the prey reviewed above, a wide and variable range of other items may be ingested (possibly accidentally) such as thrips (tiny insects, Order Thysanoptera), mites and nematode worms. More substantial occasional items are sometimes reported. One hedgehog in Wales was seen to be crunching up a swan mussel (*Anodonta cygnea*), still in its shell (Venables & Venables 1972)! A highly variable catalogue of human food wastes may also be scavenged; in Israel *E. concolor* included minced meat and vegetable matter in its diet (Schoenfeld & Yom-Tov 1985).

Food of vertebrate origin is also on the hedgehog's menu. For now, I shall confine the review to the findings of dietary studies, but see later for some accounts of audacious acts of predation on birds and their eggs, mice and snakes, and other feeding feats.

Brockie (1959) reported the active predation of frogs (*Hyla aurea*) in New Zealand and Kruuk (1964) witnessed attacks on black-headed gull eggs and chicks (*Larus ridibundus*), but most other studies lack reliable distinction between predation and carrion feeding. Yalden (1976) found 19 occurrences of mammal remains (in 12% of stomachs) including an almost complete mouse (*Apodemus* sp.), remains of a shrew (*Sorex* or *Neomys*) and a mole (*Talpa* sp.). Some rodent fur was probably from nestling mice or voles, but lagomorph fur was probably from the hare or rabbit commonly used as bait in the gamekeepers' traps from which many of the samples were obtained. Yalden found the remains of what appeared to be bird eggs in up to 15 stomachs. Only one unidentified feather and four occurrences of vole remains (*Microtus*) were found by Grosshans (1983). Campbell (1973b) found hedge-hog hair in 30% of stomachs and 50% of droppings, and presumed it to originate from grooming rather than cannibalism. In a study of *Erinaceus concolor*, Shilova-Krassova (1952) found vertebrate items in almost 9% of droppings. These included mice (five occurrences), lacertid lizards (16 occur-rences) and a bird and a snake (single occurrences). Other reports include single finds of a feather (Obrtel & Holišová 1981) and some lizard scales (Schoenfeld & Yom-Tov 1985).

Plant material

Reports of plant material in the diet of the two European hedgehog species have included the remains of the leaves and seeds of grass and other plants, moss, conifer needles, bark scraps, fibrous roots, straw, apples and a wide variety of other fruit (e.g. Shilova-Krassova 1952, Brockie 1959, Campbell 1973a, Yalden 1976, Obrtel & Hološová 1981, Grosshans 1983). Hedgehogs in grassland and suburban areas tend to ingest the most plant material. For example, Wroot (1984a) found plant material in every dropping examined, but this was mostly grass clippings from the frequently mown lawns of the golf course, plus a fine mush of plant material, also reported by Yalden (1976), thought to be from the guts of caterpillars and other herbivorous prey.

No study has found any evidence of the plant remains being digested and Yalden noted how items had not even been chewed! The consensus view is that virtually all plant material eaten by hedgehogs is accidentally ingested, either in the guts of herbivorous prey, stuck to their bodies, or simply grabbed in the same mouthful as the prey item. Hedgehogs may also eat, presumably by accident, other non-food items, such as scraps of plastic and paper, and there is a report (Grosshans 1983) of a hedgehog with a large amount of cotton wool in its gut—I shudder to think what may have attracted a hedgehog to such an item!

Nevertheless, there are a few examples where European hedgehogs may have deliberately eaten plants. In New Zealand, Brockie (1959) found that 19% of droppings from pastureland contained young leaves and buds of clover (apparently eaten intentionally) and cited an account of hedgehogs eating clover from plots at Massey Agricultural College. In a Czech suburb, Obrtel & Hološová (1981) noted that plant material in droppings increased in October, when other food sources were declining. This could have been the result of active selection of plants as food, although they thought it unlikely.

DIETARY STUDIES OF NON-EUROPEAN HEDGEHOGS

There have been very few rigorous dietary studies of non-European species, but the food types seem much the same as their European counterparts. Nevertheless, non-European species appear to be somewhat more voracious predators of vertebrates, especially the long-eared hedgehogs (*Hemiechinus*) and desert hedgehogs (*Paraechinus*). Of course the prey species themselves, and the balance of prey within the diet will vary with circumstance and habitat, but it is a fair bet that the food of unstudied species will be scarcely different from those already studied.

Unfortunately some studies of *Hemiechinus* species have also included other sympatric hedgehog species such as *Erinaceus concolor* and *Paraechinus micropus* and the results have been presented without distinguishing between them. Probably the dietary differences between these species are not great, but one study in Israel (Schoenfeld & Yom-Tov 1985) briefly commented that *H. auritus* seemed to be more strictly insectivorous/predatory than *E. concolor* which scavenged vegetable material and human food remains from refuse, particularly in the spring. No such remains were found in the stomachs or faeces of *H. auritus* (also Roberts (1977) below).

Kalabuchov (1928, cited by Yalden 1976) examined the faeces or stomach contents of 24 *E. concolor* and 11 *H. auritus* from the Ukraine and Northern Caucasus (CIS) but the species were not distinguished in the results. Beetles dominated the prey items (85% of the 582 individual prey identified) but earwigs (8·2%) and caterpillars (4·2%) also featured. Other invertebrates totalled less than 1% of prey items, but plant material was commonly found. Vertebrate prey (about 2% of items) included four occurrences of small lizards (sand lizard, *Lacerta agilis*; Eremias lizard, *Eremias arguta*), three small passerine birds and four mammals, including mice (*Mus musculus*) and voles (*Microtus* sp.).

Reviews by Brockie (1959) and Corbet (1988) have cited various studies of the food of *H. auritus* in the former USSR. (e.g. Bibikov 1956, Gromov & Yanushevich 1972). All show strong similarities to a more recent study by Zherebtzova (1982), which revealed an almost total reliance on invertebrates (98·8%), primarily insects (86·7%). The most important insect groups were beetles (mainly Tenebrionidae), termites, lepidoptera (adults and caterpillars), but a very wide range of other insects and invertebrates were included. Vertebrates were not numerically important prey, but included an interesting array of small rodents such as jirds (*Meriones meridianus*), snakes (including a saw-scaled viper, *Echis carinatus*) and some lizards. In contrast to other studies, no amphibia were listed.

Roberts (1977) treated *H. collaris* as a subspecies of *H. auritus* and therefore commented on them together. He noted that, unlike other hedgehogs in Pakistan, this species showed no interest in vegetables or ripe fruit. Roberts augmented reports by Krishna & Prakash (1956) and Prakash (1959) with his own observations and recorded a wide range of food species including termites, scorpions, various crickets and grasshoppers, beetles (especially dung beetles e.g. *Helicopris bucephalus*), spiny-tailed lizards (*Uromastix* spp.), sand boas (*Eryx johni*) and toads (*Bufo andersoni*). He thought it likely that the eggs of any ground-nesting birds, such as the crested lark (*Galerida cristatus*) would also be eaten. Intriguingly, captive specimens showed no interest at all in worms or snails!

Roberts distinguished *H. auritus megalotis* as a separate species (*H. megalotis*) and, although its diet appeared to conform to the general pattern for *Hemiechinus* species, anecdotal reports of it eating melons and mulberries suggested it to be particularly omnivorous (see *Paraechinus hypomelas* later).

A comprehensive study of the food of *H. collaris* was carried out by Maheshwari (1984) in ravines near Agra (India). The stomach contents of 165 hedgehogs living in this area of steep slopes, with a wide variety of trees and mixed vegetation, were collected over three seasons: winter, summer and monsoon (see later). Overall, insects were the largest food category and

TABLE 3.4 *Percentage occurrence and percentage dry weight of various food items in the stomachs of 165 hedgehogs* (Hemiechinus collaris) *collected from the wild over 2 years.*

Food items	No. of stomachs in which occurred	% Occurrence	% Dry weight
Earthworms	67	8·85	10·22
Arthropods:			
Coleoptera	114	28·24	30·83
Diptera	70	7·63	3·28
Lepidoptera	47	3·79	2·37
Dermaptera	18	1·79	1·17
Hymenoptera	49	6·00	2·09
Arachnida	39	4·42	2·30
Chilopoda	36	5·26	10·40
Diplopoda	16	2·31	1·52
Isopoda	10	1·73	0·20
Vertebrates:			
Amphibians	66	8·42	13·41
Reptiles	78	8·16	7·29
Birds	27	2·79	0·52
Mammals	45	7·42	10·34

19 stomachs were found to be empty.
Source: Maheshwari (1984).

contributed 40% of the diet (dry weight). Beetles turned up in 114 stomachs and accounted for over 77% of the total insect weight (Table 3.4). The status of other invertebrates in the diet was rather seasonally variable but overall, centipedes (10·4%) and earthworms (10·2%), were most important with arachnids, millipedes and woodlice together accounting for only just over 4%.

Maheshwari found vertebrate items to be rather important, not just by dry weight assessments (31·56% of the diet, including a few feathers and birds' egg fragments) but also by number. Amphibians, reptiles and mammals together accounted for 24% of prey items (Table 3.4).

Unfortunately, studies by Krishna and/or Prakash (1955–1960) of *H. collaris* and *Paraechinus micropus* from the desert regions of Rajasthan (India) did not always clearly distinguish between them. The stomach contents of these species revealed, once again, a diet principally of insects and other arthropods. Overall, 53% of the items identified were insects of various kinds, including orthoptera and termites, but nearly half were beetles. Some stomachs were stuffed full of dung beetles (*Helicopris bucephalus*). Other arthropods (e.g. Solifugid spiders) and a considerable number of vertebrate items, including toads, lizards, bird eggs and a few mammals, made up the rest of their diet. Intriguingly, as also observed for *Hemiechinus* by Roberts (1977), captive animals of both species refused earthworms (living and chloroformed), although earthworms are part of the natural diet (Maheshwari 1984).

Little is known of the diet of *H. dauuricus* (from the Gobi desert), although it seems to conform to the general pattern of the genus. Sokolov & Orlov (1980, cited by Corbet 1988) reported that it feeds on insects, especially orthopterans and beetles, as well as small rodents, snakes and frogs. Nothing at all is known of the feeding ecology of the closely related species *H. hughi* from China.

In Pakistan *P. hypomelas* will apparently tackle almost any prey from venomous snakes to beetles (Roberts 1977). In years when the desert locust (*Schistocerca gregaria*) is plentiful, this forms the bulk of their diet. Roberts reported that this species was particularly frugivorous, eating the Russian olive (*Eleagnus hortensis*), planted along the roadsides in cultivated areas, and (like *H. auritus megalotis*) is reputed to feed on ripe water melons in Baluchistan, and to eat fallen mulberries (*Morus alba*).

In dry steppic vegetation around Ain El Hadjel (Algeria), *P. aethiopicus* is reputed to eat mainly insects and reptiles, such as agamid lizards and snakes (Sellami *et al.* 1989). In Oman its diet includes hymenoptera and grasshoppers (Delany & Farook 1989).

Liu (1937) investigated the stomach contents of 47 hedgehogs, probably *E. amurensis*, from Peiping (North China). Almost 95% of the dietary items were fly larvae, notably the maggots of *Chrysomyia* (about 64% of food items), *Musca* (28%) and *Eristalis* (3%). Other invertebrates identified were mole-crickets, earwigs and beetles. A few unidentified hairs were found in three stomachs and five feathers in another. Liu concluded that the hedgehogs had been foraging around manure heaps and old-style latrines, and performed a useful role in controlling pests. Occasional plant remains (about 1% of items) included vegetable leaves and melon seeds but were thought to be accidental inclusions from the middens and he discounted reports of melon-eating. However, Liu did note one stomach entirely full of fruit—jujubes (*Zizyphus jujuba*), which must have been actively selected!

The diet of the African genus *Atelerix* has not been well studied, but the information available suggests that these hedgehogs conform to the typical hedgehog pattern. Studies cited by Corbet (1988) indicated that the diet of the Algerian hedgehog (*A. algirus*) on the Balearic Islands consisted of snails, centipedes, insects, some small vertebrates (snakes, lizards, frogs) and a truffle-like fungus (*Melanogaster variegatus*). Foods readily accepted by captive animals have included earthworms, locusts, mealworms, and a range of fish and meats; fruit was almost always rejected (Herter 1964). However, a study of plant seed dispersal in the Canary Islands (Barquin *et al.* 1986) found *Plocama pendula* berries (Family Rubiaceae) in 30 faecal samples from Algerian hedgehogs. The hedgehogs apparently travelled some distance to eat the berries, possibly for their water content. Barquin *et al.* (1986) also noted anecdotal evidence that, in Tenerife, hedgehogs commonly eat corn on the cob (*Zea mays*) and pumpkins (*Cucurbita pepo*).

In southern Africa, *A. frontalis* is reported to eat beetles, ants, termites, grasshoppers, moths, centipedes, earthworms, slugs, frogs, small rodents, eggs and chicks of ground-nesting birds, vegetables, fruits and fungi. Millipedes may be sought soon after they emerge with the onset of the rains (Smithers 1983, Corbet 1988).

Studies of the central African hedgehog, *A. albiventris*, have listed ants and other insects, lizards, snakes, bird eggs and chicks, as well as small rodents (Meritt 1981). Kingdon (1974) added earthworms, snails, slugs, crabs, fruit, fungi, roots and groundnuts to the menu. Herter (1971) reported that captive individuals would eat small slugs (*Agriolimax*), relished locusts and a wide range of insects including the larvae (mealworms) and pupae of tenebrionid beetles, dead houseflies and dead bees or wasps. Fruit and vegetables were generally refused, as were wax-moths (*Galleria mellonella*) and lime hawk moths (*Mimas tiliae*). Such captive experiments, however, merely show a process of discrimination and do little to reveal natural predilections. One tame *Erinaceus europaeus*, which I kept for 3 years in Britain, was also very keen on locusts!

Plants as a source of water

There may be some truth in the suggestion that some hedgehogs in arid climates may eat fruit or other plant material as a source of water. However, it is notable that Maheshwari's (1984) study of *Hemiechinus collaris* near Agra (India) found no vegetable material at all. Also, Krishna (1956) reported an absence of plant material in the diets of both *H. collaris* and *Paraechinus micropus* from the Rajasthan desert region (India), and captive animals rejected all vegetable foods: a finding that contradicts claims by locals that hedgehogs destroy vegetation by eating stems and roots. Furthermore, Chandra (1985), in a rather nasty experiment, reported that captive *H. collaris* when offered only green vegetation would not feed and died within 18 days!

In fact, dehydration may be less of a problem than one might at first imagine. It is cooler at night, when hedgehogs are active, and insects, along with many other invertebrates, have a relatively high water content (60%; Versluys 1975). Droplets of water from dew, rain, or exuded by low plants are probably lapped up when foraging, and puddles or other sources of water will be used where possible.

OPPORTUNISM, SEASONALITY AND FOOD SELECTION

Changes in prey availability throughout the year, or from year to year are inevitably reflected in the hedgehog's catholic and flexible diet. Most authors use this fact to argue that it is an unselective, opportunistic feeder (e.g. Maheshwari 1984). Care should be taken here! Hedgehogs may indeed be opportunistic, exploiting high quality prey items that suddenly present themselves, but modern models of optimal foraging 'strategies' (based on the principles of evolution by natural selection) can be used to predict that, given a certain variation in the nutritional quality of prey items, hedgehogs ought to have evolved into selective foragers. Hedgehogs certainly exhibit an ample array of dietary preferences and aversions! For a careful explanation of such models, I refer the reader to the books by Krebs & Davies (1984, 1987) in which the evolutionary theories, the models and their attendant concepts, such as 'switching', are well discussed and illustrated with examples.

A clear prediction of foraging theory is that foragers can sometimes increase their net nutritional intake by 'switching' to specialize on easily accessible prey items which are then taken disproportionately in relation to overall prey availability. This can reduce 'costs' such as the time (or energy) spent in the search for prey and quality discrimination, and can also result in improved prey handling efficiency—effectively raising the net profitability of the prey.

A possible example of 'switching' by hedgehogs is the exploitation of the brief superabundance of adult cockchafers (*Melolontha hippocastani*) in May (Shilova-Krassova 1952). Of 262 hedgehog (*E. concolor*) droppings collected, 222 were from pine and oak plantations (Izyumski forest, Khar'kov region, Ukraine), and 40 from a pine forest (Buzuluk forest, Chkalovsk, south-eastern Russia). Apparently, around early May, hedgehogs temporarily moved into these woodlands specifically to exploit the glut; cockchafers occurred in all droppings and accounted for 76% of all prey items. Captive hedgehogs from the Buzuluk forest, fed an exclusive diet of *Melolontha*, ate from 87 to 103 per 24-h period!

In the Izyumski pine plantations, the hedgehogs also dug up large numbers of the larvae of June cockchafers (*Amphimallon solstitialis*). In one small area, hedgehogs reduced the density of June beetle grubs in the soil from 15·2 to 6·4 m^{-2}. Hedgehogs may have some economic value as predators of these species, which are serious pests both as adults and larvae. Obrtel & Holišová (1981), working in suburban parkland near Brno (Czech Republic), also noted that adult June cockchafers were exploited as they emerged *en masse* at dusk.

In New Zealand, hedgehogs (*E. europaeus*) apparently 'switched' to feed almost exclusively on grass grub beetles (*Costelytra zealandica*) and porina moths (*Wiseana cervinta*) during their flying seasons. Up to 424 grass grub beetles were found in a single hedgehog stomach (Campbell 1973b). Hedgehogs were also observed to exploit an autumn 'plague' of army worms (a caterpillar, *Pseudoletia separata*) on pastureland, and a midsummer glut of gravid female huhu beetles (*Prionoplus reticularis*) in pine woodland (Brockie 1959).

Seasonal variation in diet

Seasonal variation in the diet of non-European hedgehog species has been little studied, except for one investigation of *H. collaris* over three seasons in

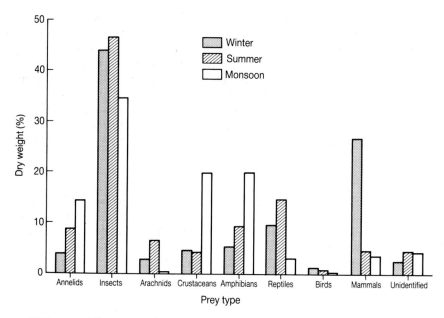

FIG. 3.1   *The seasonal occurrence (expressed as % dry weight) of the various prey types found in 165 hedgehog stomachs (*Hemiechinus collaris) *from ravines near Agra (India). Source: Maheshwari (1984).*

India (Maheshwari 1984). Although Maheswari did not consider the seasonal variation to be significant, it is apparent from his published data (Fig. 3.1) that in the wetter climate of the monsoon, creatures that need humid conditions to be active, like earthworms and amphibia, became more important in the diet. 'Crustaceans' were also more represented in the monsoon but, apart from woodlice, this category also included millipedes and centipedes, making generalizations difficult.

In the two European hedgehog species, all relevant studies have revealed a dynamic, constantly changing balance of prey in the diet. However, most have made only rather general attempts to relate diet to prey availability, and only Wroot (1984a) has seriously considered the issue of prey selection.

In the study of *Erinaceus concolor* by Obrtel & Holišová (1981), several prey species, although consumed throughout the active year, showed seasonal variation in the diet. Millipedes peaked in importance in spring and again in autumn. Ground beetles were important mainly in spring and earwigs in summer. Ant workers (plus soil from raided ant heaps) were common items from June to September.

As already mentioned, two studies of *E. europaeus* in New Zealand have shown the exploitation of brief seasonal superabundances. Apart from these events, food species were taken more or less in relation to their availability, although many could be found all year round. Setting aside details of habitat differences, Brockie's (1959) results revealed peaks (in percentage occurrence) of slugs and beetles in summer, snails and millipedes in spring, worms in spring and autumn, and moth caterpillars (including the plague of army worms already mentioned) in late summer/autumn.

Three of the European studies looked more closely at seasonal variation in the diet of *E. europaeus* (Yalden 1976, Grosshans 1983, Wroot 1984a). These studies share quite a few similarities, but also differ in many details, hardly surprising in view of the habitat differences!

The study on a suburban golf course by Wroot (1984a), despite its small sample size, is the most comprehensively analysed of all the dietary studies so far. Using a form of multiple regression analysis Wroot investigated relationships between the proportions of 10 prey types in the diet, in relation to time of year and weather variables. Three of the four main prey species (caterpillars, beetles, earthworms and leatherjackets) showed significant variation in relation to time of year, the exception being earthworms. Wroot also noted a significant seasonal variation in beetle larvae which featured more in warm weather, as did earwigs. Figure 3.2 shows an overview of monthly variation in the dietary energy contributions of the prey categories. A strength of Wroot's study is that he went on to relate observed dietary variations to simultaneous determinations of prey availability in the field.

Comparisons between these three European studies can only be tentative, but all showed a rather similar predominance of beetles during the summer (also shown by Brockie 1959, Campbell 1973b). Grosshans reported that adult carabids, apart from an early peak in May (presumed to be new adults from over-wintering larvae), were eaten fairly consistently throughout the year. However, there was a very noticeable increase in the numbers of beetle larvae (presumably about to over-winter) in the late autumn. In Yalden's study the importance of different beetle types in the diet varied; weevils peaked in May, carabids in June and, as also noted by Grosshans, scarabaeid beetles increased in dietary importance in the late summer.

Also common to the studies was a significant increase in the numbers of caterpillars eaten in the late summer–early autumn (also Brockie 1959); Yalden alone reported another, earlier peak in April to May.

Earthworms were eaten at any time of year, their availability linked to damp conditions (Wroot 1984a). Although earthworm consumption did not relate to season specifically, both Wroot and Grosshans (also Brockie 1959) noted increases in early spring and late autumn.

All the studies found a summer increase in the number of earwigs consumed, although the dietary importance of this group varied greatly. Earwigs were particularly well represented in the German study. A rapid increase in their consumption started in July, apparently when the imago stage is reached, and in August they comprised over 50% of the diet (relative volume).

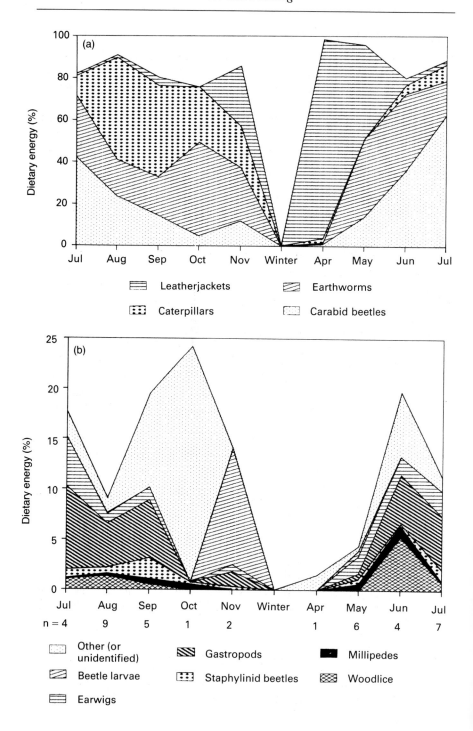

Leatherjackets

Earthworms

Caterpillars

Carabid beetles

n = 4 9 5 1 2 1 6 4 7

Other (or unidentified)

Gastropods

Millipedes

Beetle larvae

Staphylinid beetles

Woodlice

Earwigs

Prey selection and preference

Although the nature of the habitat, prey availability and the sheer chance of encountering particular prey, are fundamental determinants of what can be eaten, hedgehogs clearly select some prey over others if presented with a choice.

Dimelow (1963b) carried out food preference tests on captive hedgehogs, nine of which were offered 73 species of adult invertebrates (plus some larvae) in a series of 167 trials. Although a rather unnatural approach, several interesting agreements and contrasts with field studies have emerged, for example the frequent rejection of woodlice was in accordance with dietary data (e.g. Brockie 1959, Yalden 1976, Wroot 1984a).

In Britain, Yalden (1976) found millipedes to be commonly eaten (recorded in 40% of stomachs), whereas Wroot (1984a) found them to be rather unimportant, and not a preferred item (see below). In New Zealand, Brockie (1959) reported millipedes to be frequent in the hedgehog's diet in sand dunes and pasture, and that they were occasionally eaten in large numbers; but millipedes were not noted by Campbell (1973b). This variable importance of millipedes is somewhat at odds with Dimelow's finding that they were highly preferred items. She suggested, as did Brockie, that foraging hedgehogs seemed to be attracted to their cyanide-like odour.

The assumption that hedgehogs feed opportunistically and unselectively on whatever is available was challenged by Wroot (1984a) whose findings strongly suggested selective feeding to maximize energy intake. Wroot estimated the available energy of prey species using calorimetric analysis of pitfall-trap samples and formalin extractions of earthworms. He then compared the available energy of prey with their representation in the diet, thereby indicating the extent to which the hedgehogs were preying selectively, or simply consuming species in direct proportion to their availability. Using an average of four different selection-index calculations, he sorted prey into three groups: highly selected items (leatherjackets, caterpillars and earwigs); an intermediate group (earthworms, molluscs and carabid beetles); and a least selected group (staphylinid beetles, millipedes, beetle larvae and woodlice). However, the distinction between the first two categories is blurred by the inherent sampling biases of pitfall trapping, which underestimates the true availability of many slow-moving species.

Hedgehogs showed a partiality for soft-bodied prey which, generally speaking, tended to be more available during wetter weather, such as during the spring and autumn. Soft prey, like slugs, caterpillars, leatherjackets and

FIG. 3.2 *Area charts showing the percentage of dietary energy contributed by each prey type to the diet of the European hedgehog* (Erinaceus europaeus) *in suburban/golf course habitat in southern England (1981–1982). Values are monthly averages of figures obtained for individual droppings. n = number of droppings obtained per month. (a) The four main prey types, (b) seven additional prey categories. Source: Wroot (1984a).*

earthworms, containing moderate to large amounts of energy, are slow-moving and relatively digestible.

Earthworms, which on average contain nine times more energy than other major prey items, were taken when conditions were wet enough for them to become surface-active. Wroot did, however, find evidence to suggest that worms, although frequently eaten, were not strongly selected for, but became more important in the absence of other more preferred species. Dimelow's observation that earthworms, though generally eaten, were seldom selected first adds weight to this suggestion, but the reason for this lack of preference for apparently high quality prey remains obscure.

In drier weather, Wroot noted that carabid beetles were eaten roughly in proportion to their availability. However, during their maximum availability in August the hedgehogs reduced their intake of carabids, apparently to exploit the increased numbers of caterpillars. Carabids are indigestible, fast-moving and commonly employ chemical defences, all of which may explain why hedgehogs seem to prefer alternatives when available (also Dimelow, 1963b). Hard exoskeletal parts may also deter hedgehogs—Dimelow noted that large female stag beetles and cockchafers were eaten but the hard elytra and mouthparts were rejected.

At this point, it might be salutary to point out that although the energy content of food is very important, some foods satisfy particular nutrient requirements and may thus be more important than apparent from their energy content or the amount consumed. This, and the problems of more accurately assessing prey availability, digestibility and selection by the foraging hedgehog, may mean that further studies need to use enclosed animals with an artificially limited range of prey types.

Does diet change with age?

For hedgehogs it is unlikely that much more than the general 'rules' underlying selective foraging 'strategies' would be innately determined. Given the seasonal variations in prey availability and variety of habitat types exploited by hedgehogs, there would seem to be benefits in maintaining a flexible approach to prey selection, based on behavioural modification through experience. Young animals, while maturing physically and behaviourally, might well show differences in their diet and foraging skills, when compared with more experienced mature animals.

There is increasing evidence of such dietary change in hedgehogs. Dimelow (1963b) pointed out that youngsters were more likely to try, unproductively, to tackle large thick-shelled snails, and to take unpalatable items such as woodlice. Yalden (1976) noted that there was a tendency for older animals to take significantly more earthworms, carabid beetles and slugs than younger animals, which tended to rely more on vertebrate carrion. He suggested that young animals may learn to deal with the more tricky prey items as they mature.

So far, the best support for the idea that age-related differences in diet may exist has come from a study of *Erinaceus europaeus* by Dickman (1988). However, its intriguing findings must remain tentative, because of the small sample of hedgehogs in some age groups, the considerable limitations of the accuracy of age determination methods (Chapter 9) and the confounding effects of combining animals collected from a variety of rural and suburban habitats.

Dickman found the dominant prey-size category (estimated from measurements of remains) for animals of all ages, to be in the range 0·05–0·49 g with rather few prey over 2 g, although a few much heavier items were consumed. Youngsters included a larger proportion of small prey (<0·05 g) but as they grew older the hedgehogs gradually took more soft-bodied and larger prey, supporting the suggestion that many of these are higher quality, preferred prey (Wroot 1984a). The mean weight of prey items was significantly associated with age class, and in rural animals this increased from 0·50 g for animals aged 2 years to a maximum of 1·27 g at age '5'; for suburban animals a mean of 0·72 g at age 2 increased to a maximum of 1·22 at age '7'.

The above observations by Dimelow and Yalden gain general support from Dickman's findings that hedgehogs ate more molluscs (slugs and snails), larvae and carabid beetles as they aged, but fewer arachnids and earwigs. Older hedgehogs in the suburbs ate fewer woodlice and in rural areas consumed fewer myriapods, but more scarabaeid beetles (Fig 3.3).

Dickman used calculated dietary 'niche' breadths and overlaps to hypothesize that the niche separation between certain age classes might even be sufficient for them to be considered as separate feeding niches. Young animals apparently took a wider selection of prey types than older animals which tended to specialize. Such differences may expand the niche breadth of the hedgehog population as a whole, and have the effect of reducing competition within the species. This kind of dietary niche expansion is theoretically likely in a habitat where biological productivity is fairly constant and there is little feeding competition from other species. Hedgehogs in Britain very roughly fit this scenario, but Dickman suggested that niche expansion would be most pronounced in places such as New Zealand, where a dense hedgehog population exploits the insectivore niche in the virtual absence of competitors. This fascinating idea awaits investigation.

Where do hedgehogs forage?

Hedgehogs spend most of their time foraging (Chapter 7) and appear to exploit a wide variety of natural and man-made habitats. For *Erinaceus europaeus* in Italy, Boitani & Reggiani (1984) showed that 'bush' and *maquis* were important foraging areas but much less so in summer when wet meadows were favoured (36·5% of observations). Refuse tips were used at a low level throughout the year, but slightly more so in November. In Britain, in mixed rural habitat (Rycote, Oxfordshire) hedgehogs tended to prefer

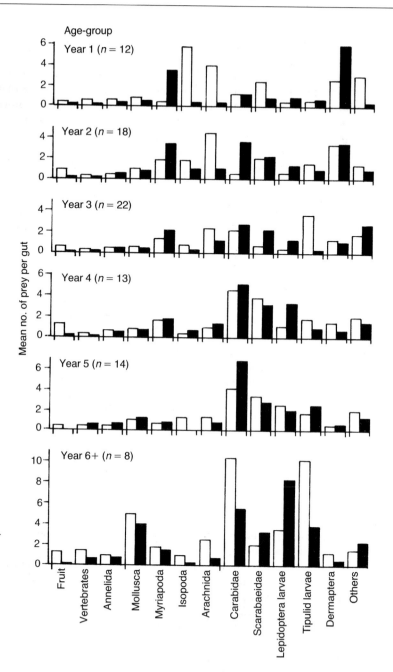

FIG. 3.3 *The prey types eaten by different age-groups of European hedgehog from Oxfordshire (England). Open bars = suburban animals, black bars = rural animals. 'Vertebrates' includes birds and mammals, 'Others' includes Hymenoptera and Diptera. Source Dickman (1984).*

grassland and to avoid arable land (Doncaster 1992). Both *E. amurensis* (Liu 1937) and *E. concolor* (Schoenfeld & Yom-Tov 1985) have also been reported to forage in refuse areas.

My study of *E. europaeus* on a British suburban golf-course (Reeve 1981) revealed nothing definite about habitat preferences, but it seemed to me that hedgehogs favoured 'edge-habitat', the boundaries between open and more densely vegetated areas, a zone which may harbour a maximum choice of invertebrate prey types. Despite his own reservations about methodology, Wroot (1984a), using the same study area, has provided the only data specifically relating habitat and foraging, and the results showed several interesting features.

The golf-course and suburban gardens could be classified into five habitat categories (trees, long-grass/tree interface, long grass, short grass, garden), and hedgehogs generally spent similar amounts of time in each, although males apparently spent more time foraging in gardens than females. Analyses of data for 15 'hedgehog-nights' showed associations between the habitat in which the hedgehogs foraged and their diet, as revealed by the contents of their faeces (produced later in temporary captivity). Carabids in the diet were associated with time spent in long grass and trees, earthworms with short grass and to a lesser extent with the long-grass/tree boundary, slugs with both long and short grass, caterpillars and leatherjackets mainly with gardens, and earwigs with time under trees. These associations appeared to reflect prey availability (estimated by pitfall trap catches) in the various habitats.

Hedgehogs tended to forage in open areas (long and short grass) later on in the night, maybe because moisture-loving prey become increasingly available as the dew forms. It is tempting to speculate that habitat use may not be haphazard but, to an extent, 'strategically' organized to maximize feeding efficiency.

Foraging behaviour and prey handling

Because hedgehogs spend most of their active time searching for food, foraging is not easily separated from general activity (discussed in Chapter 7). Several studies of captive European hedgehogs have found evidence of a bimodal feeding rhythm, i.e. with two peaks of activity, the first around 21:00–24:00 hours and a second smaller peak at around 03:00 hours (Kristoffersson 1964, Campbell 1973b, 1975). Captive studies by Herter (1965b, 1971) of all four hedgehog genera (*Erinaceus, Atelerix, Paraechinus and Hemiechinus*) also found a basically bimodal rhythm but the later peak was less distinct, seemingly split into two. Although I found no evidence to suggest similar rhythmicity in my field study of *E. europaeus* in Britain (Reeve 1981), Wroot (1984a) showed clear evidence of a trend towards a bimodal foraging pattern. Wroot used the same study area as I did, but concentrated on obtaining much more detailed individual behavioural records, especially with respect to duration and location of feeding. He suggested that the bimodality arose in the following way. A hedgehog that was able to fill its stomach early in the night might be less active for a period while its stomach emptied, but would then resume feeding in the early morning. Animals that, for whatever reason, failed to fill their stomachs early, would feed more continuously. This might explain some of the variability between individuals and between studies. Observations by Yalden (1976) can be used to support this notion. He noted that although hedgehogs normally consume around 57–71 g of food daily (Kruuk 1964, Morris 1967), the maximum weight found in any of the tightly filled hedgehog stomachs in his study was only 32 g. He surmised, therefore, that a hedgehog would need to fill its stomach twice each night.

When foraging, a hedgehog generally progresses in a slow meandering walk, frequently punctuated by short bursts of speed and brief pauses to sniff the air or ground. Errant prey items are usually snapped up with a rapid darting movement, while items buried in the litter, grass or soil surface are quickly rooted out. The hedgehog is always very alert, constantly sniffing and listening, and deals with prey very quickly. It seems most likely that prey are detected mainly by their odour; however, sound also seems to be important in detecting the movements of prey among leaf litter. However it is achieved, prey detection is evidently very effective; I have many times seen hedgehogs suddenly dart forwards, or to one side, to pounce on something up to half a metre away. Hedgehogs may also forage in a more rapid and linear style, during which they cover much more ground but still 'keep an eye out' for suitable prey which they will pause to eat. Wroot (1984a) showed that, during foraging, over 70% of hedgehog movements were very short, with relatively few rapid movements; although, exceptionally, speeds of up to 50 m min^{-1} were recorded. Males tended to travel faster than females while foraging and both sexes travelled fastest in short grass and progressively slower as cover density increased.

Hedgehogs will dig food items out of rotten wood and the soil surface but do not seem to dig deeply for their food (Burton 1969). They are well-known to make small holes, a few centimetres across, in lawns when in pursuit of prey such as leatherjackets, especially under plantains. This habit was noted by early naturalists, who assumed that roots were the desired target, and embodied in English literature: 'The Hedgehog underneath the plantain bores' (Tennyson, 1864; line 850 of *Aylmers Field*).

Hedgehogs can be quite athletic in pursuit of prey and one has been seen to pounce on and consume a large moth (Burton 1969), but fast-moving species, such as carabid beetles and centipedes, can be evasive. Dimelow (1963b) noted that, although centipedes were preferred to millipedes, they escaped more easily. She also observed the techniques used by hedgehogs to subdue and eat various prey types. Beetles were seized from the side or hind end and readily crushed although various hard body parts such as elytra and mouthparts were sometimes left (also Brockie 1959). Taking beetles in this way would avoid biting on (or being bitten by) the hard, powerful jaws of some of the larger predatory beetles. Worms were seized by the hind end and chewed forwards towards the head, and occasionally turned round and bitten up and down along their length, before being chewed forwards again. Only small thin-shelled snails were eaten, and these were crushed-up whole. Hedgehogs were seen to wipe slime from large slugs, such as *Limax maximus*, with their front paws before eating them piecemeal. Worms and slugs were sometimes regurgitated and then reingested. Having observed her captive hedgehogs using their tongues to flick small prey items into their mouths, Dimelow suggested that a foraging hedgehog might hold its tongue ready for use, extended between the widely spaced front incisors.

Dimelow found that hedgehogs refused to eat any dead or moribund prey and Herter (1965b) also noted that dead, motionless or very inactive food is sniffed over for a long time whereas mobile prey is quickly seized. Maybe avoiding prey in such poor condition reduces the risk of consuming prey heavily burdened by parasites (Chapter 9). However, hedgehogs do eat vertebrate carrion and, as noted earlier, stinging insects like bees and wasps have been reported on several occasions as being eaten when dead or comatose.

When dealing with vertebrate prey or carrion, hedgehogs, lacking the dentition of a true carnivore, bite persistently at the flesh. They gnaw into live prey, subjecting them to a lingering and grisly death. Barrett-Hamilton (1911) referred to accounts of this kind of behaviour meted out to a variety of small vertebrates, and in some cases even the bones of the prey were eaten.

Although some accounts may suffer from elaboration, there is ample evidence of hedgehog attacks on birds (see later), mice, frogs and lizards in which the prey are usually held down by the hedgehog's body and forepaws and eaten rear-end first. Krishna (1956) described similar attacks, by semi-captive *Hemiechinus collaris* and *Paraechinus micropus*, on a range of living vertebrates including rats, lizards, a small snake, toads and frogs. In the last two cases, the entire prey were eaten, bones and all! Herter (1965b) described how, just like dogs, hedgehogs may shake prey such as lizards and mice. Barrett-Hamilton cited the case of one hedgehog reputed to have seized a hare by the hind leg and Burton noted one account of a hedgehog feeding on the udder of a live sheep while she was caught, and held fast, by her wool in briars!

Burton (1969) claimed that hedgehogs can outrun mice and cited one report in which a live mouse was quickly seized in a 'tug-of-war' by three hedgehogs in a compound, and another in which a hedgehog killed a mouse by rolling on it. It is unlikely, however, that hedgehogs would normally be able to catch very active prey such as mice, although nestlings and moribund animals are likely victims. Furthermore, experiments carried out by Herter (1965b) have demonstrated that hedgehogs are *not* effective mousers, whatever their reputation in Europe.

Hedgehogs are sometimes reported as being cannibalistic. Some reports merely record the eating of new-born babies by mothers, when disturbed by intrusive researchers (Prakash 1955b). Burton (1969) however, recorded four cases of adult cannibalism and quoted one account which claimed that on two separate occasions captive hedgehogs had killed and eaten one of their number, and had even eaten the bones. Krishna (1956) described how captive

Hemiechinus collaris and *Paraechinus micropus* would avidly feed upon hedgehog carcasses placed in their cage. Traces of hedgehog hair have been found in droppings by some workers, but Brockie (1959), who found hair in 15% of stomach and faecal samples, attributed this to grooming. Although it is quite possible that hedgehogs could, under certain captive conditions, kill and eat each other, it seems more likely that many of the cases of so-called 'cannibalism', both in captivity and the wild, are really the result of feeding on the corpses of hedgehogs that have died from other causes. In Brockie's study, one exceptional dropping contained 500 spines! These had been pulled out by the roots, indicating that a rotting hedgehog carcass had been consumed.

HEDGEHOGS AS PREDATORS OF GROUND-NESTING BIRDS

It is clear from the dietary studies already discussed that hedgehogs are capable of killing and eating small vertebrates such as mice, frogs or snakes. Thus it is likely that, given the opportunity, they would be equally able to kill and eat the eggs, nestlings, and possibly the adults of some ground-nesting bird species. Hedgehogs have long been blamed for losses of game birds and poultry and despite the protestations of some hedgehog-lovers, it is clear that hedgehogs are not entirely innocent. Nevertheless, most objective studies reveal that only a very small percentage of losses are attributable to hedgehog predation. Such findings sharply contrast with the anecdotes and opinions of many gamekeepers who claim that hedgehogs take important numbers of eggs (especially in areas where nests are confined to hedgerows), will kill incubating adult birds and even kill penned pheasant poults. Some natural historians of the past consistently claimed them to be significant predators.

In Britain an Act of Parliament in 1564 put a bounty on hedgehogs in some parts of the country. Old churchwardens' records list bounty payments of 2d in 17th century Westmorland and 4d in Oxfordshire and Bedfordshire in the 18th and 19th centuries (Barrett-Hamilton 1911). When these bounties ceased, gamekeepers continued to trap and kill hedgehogs, as they still do in Britain today. Since the Wildlife and Countryside Act (1981) hedgehogs enjoy a degree of protection, but still fall victim to traps set for other species. Many estates have ceased to report the number of hedgehogs killed in this way (Tapper 1992).

Barrett-Hamilton (1911), Cott (1951) and Burton (1969) between them refer to a veritable feast of ancient accounts of the hedgehog's depredations of poultry and game birds. These are too numerous and long-winded to present here, but include references to authors such as Duncan (1882), Atkinson (1844), Bell (1837), Alston (1866), Buckland (1883–1885), Lydekker (1893–1894) and Brehm (1912). These, and many others, contain testimonies, apparently eager to add to the bad reputation of hedgehogs as ruffians.

Two quotes, taken from Cott (1951), exemplify the genre:

He [the hedgehog] prowls at night, like an owl, looking after the nests of pheasants, partridges, corncrakes and larks: he kills the old ones if he can, and sucks their eggs if he can't.

('Rusticus' 1849)

A captive animal was observed to eat the contents and shell of a hen's egg:

He hit it sideways with his sharp canine teeth, and made a hole in it just big enough to thrust in his little black nose, and then with his tongue licked out the contents, and mightily he seemed to enjoy it, little thinking what evidence he was giving against the rest of his species.

(Buckland 1900)

Hedgehogs are thus cast by tradition into a split character, in which they are viewed not only as charming and useful consumers of invertebrate pests, but also as having a malicious side to their nature.

Such ambivalent views are widespread. Around 1870, the European hedgehog was deliberately introduced (as an asset) to New Zealand. However, Wodzicki (1950) reported a belief, widespread among New Zealanders, that hedgehogs damaged domestic and wild birds; they were deemed responsible for a recent decline in the numbers of ground-nesting game birds, such as pheasant (*Phasianus colchicus*), quail (*Coturnix coturnix*), chukar (*Alectoris chukar*), wild duck, as well as pipits (*Anthus* spp.) and skylarks (*Alauda arvensis*) (all introduced!). Wodzicki cited stories of hedgehogs eating eggs from a skylark's nest, molesting or attacking chicks or hens, and 'sucking' eggs. Hedgehog control was thus favoured by Acclimatization Societies and Sporting organizations throughout the country. From 1939 a bounty of 3d per snout, increased to 6d in 1940, was paid by the Vermin Control Board. In 1939–1948, a total of 53 647 snouts were submitted for the bounty in the North Island alone. Wodzicki considered that there were too few data to assess the impact of such controls, but did nevertheless note the apparent continuing expansion of the hedgehog's range in New Zealand.

Cott (1951) used four hedgehogs as tasters in a survey of the palatability of the contents of fresh eggs from 25 bird species. The aim was not to investigate natural food choices of hedgehogs; most species included would not normally be available to hedgehogs and no eggs from partridge (*Perdix perdix*), pheasant, quail, larks or pipits were used. In order of preference, kittiwake (*Rissa tridactyla*), eider (*Somateria mollissima*), razorbill (*Alca torda*), gannet (*Sula bassana*), domestic chicken (*Gallus gallus*), lapwing (*Vanellus vanellus*), common tern (*Sterna hirundo*) and coot (*Fulica atra*) were the most palatable species. Cott noted that, despite some exceptions, hedgehogs showed fairly good agreement with human tastes. Generally, larger eggs were more palatable, as were eggs from colonial or cliff-nesting species. Cryptic eggs were usually more palatable than immaculate or distinctively marked eggs.

Cott's study, in which game species were not tested and eggs were offered without shells (with no alternative foods), cannot form a basis for assumptions about the behaviour of wild hedgehogs. However, hedgehogs have been reported to be predators of colonial ground-nesting birds such as terns and gulls (see later). Cott gave evidence that hedgehogs will eat partridge eggs (apparently preferred to pheasant eggs) but only anecdotes were used to support the idea that they take significant numbers.

Burton (1969) found that hedgehogs were normally disinterested in, or unable to open, whole domestic hens' eggs, but readily ate cracked and opened eggs. Lindemann (1951) stated that hedgehogs were only a danger to eggs smaller than 39 × 28 mm, e.g. partridge and quail. Similar experiments by Krishna (1956) in India showed that hedgehogs (*Hemiechinus collaris* and *Paraechinus micropus*), similarly could not cope with an intact hen's egg but could break pigeons' eggs between their jaws. Burton suggested that some hedgehogs may learn to break open hens' eggs and become 'addicts'. Kruuk (1964) observed a technique (similar to that described by Buckland earlier) in which a large hole was opened in the blunt end and the shell was sometimes crushed up entirely by the end of the meal.

Field studies and observations clearly show that hedgehogs can cause some damage to the eggs and nestlings of ground-nesting birds. In 1964 Kruuk studied hedgehog predation in a large black-headed gull (*Larus ridibundus*) colony (about 8000 pairs) at Ravenglass (Cumbria, UK). A combination of captive studies and field evidence indicated that a single hedgehog, if it ate nothing else, might eat or damage an average of 4·5 eggs in one night. Captive hedgehogs, fed *ad libitum* on freshly killed gull chicks, consumed an average of 71 g each night; best estimates for the wild were an average of 2·5 hatching eggs or chicks. Wild hedgehogs ate only part of their victims and would thus kill more chicks than required. Although gulls apparently provided the hedgehogs with roughly 30% of their food, other food types were more important (Table 3.5).

Possibly some hedgehogs specialized in raiding nests for a few nights at a time, as a number of droppings consisted entirely of young gull and/or egg remains. The hedgehogs feeding on eggs appeared to have diarrhoea.

Kruuk's study shows the best evidence of significant hedgehog predation although such losses were estimated at no more than 2–3% of the 800 broods each year. Foxes did considerably more damage, which was most severe in 1962, when they killed 825 (5%) of the 16 000 adult birds, 1100 young birds (about 4% of the 8000 broods) and a large number of eggs.

Most other studies also show either similarly low levels of damage or somewhat questionable predator identification. Middleton (1935) indicated that out of 1232 partridge (*Perdix perdix*) nest losses recorded from various parts of Britain, only 16 (1·3%) could be attributed to hedgehogs. On the same estate, however, 33·8% of nest losses were attributed to foxes and 27% caused by accidents during farm work. Cott (1951) suggested that this was an artificially low figure for hedgehog predation, resulting from effective population control by gamekeepers. A study by Jenkins (1961, cited by Yalden 1976) found the hedgehog to be the main predator, taking 3·4% of all eggs laid. However, most losses had other causes; mowing operations broke 3·1%

TABLE 3.5   *Analysis of faeces of hedgehogs, collected near gulleries.*

Prey species	% Total estimated weight organic matter	% Occurrence
Insects	41	94
Snails (*Cepaea*)	3	21
Beachhoppers (*Talitrus, Talorchestia*)	8	18
Vegetation	17	58
Gull-chick down	29	30
Adult gulls	2	9
Eggshell	—	21
	100%	

Total weight = 111·3 g. Total number of faeces = 33: 46% of the total organic weight of the faeces consisted of sand. Gull-chick down was probably obtained mainly from chicks still in the egg. 'Adult gulls' probably refers to carrion; two of the three droppings containing gull feathers came from hedgehogs caught in the act of eating a gull killed by a fox.
Source: Kruuk (1964).

dogs and cats accounted for 6·6%. Yalden (1976) considered that, from the descriptions of damage and circumstances, foxes were more likely to have been the true predators in a report by Axel (1956), who blamed hedgehogs for severe damage to the nests of common terns (*Sterna hirundo*) in the Dungeness Bird Reserve (Kent, UK).

Because there can be no direct witness to every attack, accurate predator identification remains the main problem in the assessment of the impact of hedgehogs upon bird populations. In Kruuk's (1964) study the tracks in the sand, combined with the faecal analyses, assured accurate identification of the hedgehog as the marauder in many, if not all, cases.

Green *et al.* (1987) devised useful criteria for the identification of the predators of eggs, based on the type of shell damage. Mammal predation, in general, was associated with crushing of the fractured edges of shell fragments, and the spacing and diameter of tooth puncture marks were used to indicate the mammal species. Incisor marks, attributed to hedgehogs by their close spacing (less than 5 mm apart) and large tooth diameter (51% of the spacing), were identified on two clutches of wader eggs on a coastal grazing marsh at Elmley (Kent, UK). Because hedgehogs are not normally associated with the bog or marshland areas often used by waders for nesting, it was not surprising that hedgehog damage was light. Elmley was the only site of the five studied where hedgehogs were known to occur.

In an analysis of hedgehog stomach contents, mostly from game managed areas, Yalden (1976) found bird remains in 16% of stomachs and pieces of egg in 11%. This could be taken as lending support to the gamekeeper's traditional view that hedgehog predation is significant. These data, however, reflect the common use of addled eggs as bait for the traps used to catch many of the hedgehogs, and it is uncertain to what extent these items were actively predated.

Accounts of attacks on adult birds are widespread but, although not especially rare, seem to represent rather isolated incidents. The hedgehog's method of dealing with large prey is exemplified by Kruuk's (1964) description of how hedgehogs attacked large and full-grown black-headed gull chicks. The hedgehog would grab its victim anywhere on the body, often a leg (which was sometimes broken in the process), and then sit on top of it to hold it down, while removing feathers and gnawing into the flesh of the rear end. The victims usually took some time to die.

Two species of hedgehog in India (*Hemiechinus collaris* and *Paraechinus micropus*) have been observed to use a similar style of attack when, in a rather cruel experiment, they were presented with a helpless pigeon in captivity (Krishna 1956). Burton (1969) cited an account of a hedgehog's attack on a live chicken where it had seized the breast and removed a number of feathers which lay scattered about. He reviewed 19th century copies of the *Field* which contained many claims of hedgehog attacks on young chickens, ducks and turkeys, of a hedgehog trying to nose a partridge off her nest of eggs (while she beat it with her wings), and of another caught trying to carry off a pair of two-thirds grown partridges. Stocker (1987) has witnessed a hedgehog eating a full-grown pigeon, attacking ducks and even a Canada goose (*Branta canadensis*). Observations such as these indicate that hedgehogs, under some circumstances, are certainly able to attack and kill quite large animals.

There is a clear need for further rigorous studies, in which the predators are properly identified, to determine the true extent of hedgehog predation of bird eggs and/or nestlings, and its impact upon their populations. Species with altricial young remaining in the nest, such as pipits and larks, are clearly vulnerable to predation for longer than those with precocial young, which flee the nest soon after hatching, such as partridge and pheasant. It therefore remains doubtful whether predation pressure by hedgehogs, though real enough, has any significant impact on game populations or wild ground-nesting birds generally. However, under some circumstances hedgehogs may well present a problem. The poor breeding success of ground-nesting birds, notably arctic terns (*Sterna paradisaea*) and ringed plovers (*Charadius hiaticula*), on North Ronaldsay (Orkney Islands, UK), was attributed by some to predation by hedgehogs. The flourishing hedgehog population, possibly over 1000 in 1984, was supposed to have descended from a single pair introduced to the island in 1972. A programme to translocate hedgehogs to the mainland commenced in 1985–1986 and about 200 hedgehogs were moved, an action heavily criticized by Stocker (1987). However, the hedgehog population of this 984-ha island seems to have been in dramatic decline anyway. A study (currently in preparation) revealed a population of roughly 514 in 1987 which has subsequently fallen to around 105 (H. Warwick pers. comm.). Warwick concluded that the continued poor status of the island's ground-nesting birds suggests that other known factors (e.g. shortages of fish, predation and damage by other birds and mammals—including humans and livestock, disease, etc.) may have been responsible for the decline in the first place, although the effect of the hedgehogs may not have been negligible.

Currently, similar concerns exist about the potential effects of introduced hedgehogs on breeding waders, in nature reserves on North and South Uist and Benbecula (Outer Hebrides, UK).

SNAKES IN THE DIET

Snakes, an unlikely sounding dietary item, deserve a special mention. In Britain and Europe, hedgehogs have long been famed for their ability to overcome venomous snakes such as the adder or viper (*Vipera berus*). Viper-killing has become embedded in the general folklore surrounding hedgehogs and old accounts sometimes colourfully portray the two species as dire enemies! Barrett-Hamilton (1911) quoted an excellent example by Topsel in *The Historie of Foure-Footed Beastes and Serpents* (1658):

> There is mortal hatred betwixt the Serpent and the Hedge-hog, the Serpent seeketh out the Hedge-hog's den, and falleth upon her to kill her, the Hedge-hog draweth it self up together round like a foot-ball, so that nothing appeareth on her but her thorny prickles; whereat the Serpent biteth in vain, for the more she laboureth to annoy the Hedge-hog, the more she is wounded and harmeth herself, yet notwithstanding the height of her minde, and hate of her heart, doth not suffer her to let go her hold, till one or both parties be destroyed.
>
> The Hedge-hog rowleth upon the Serpent, piercing his skin and flesh, (yea many times tearing flesh from the bones) whereby he scapeth alive and killeth his adversary, carrying the flesh upon his spears, like an honourable banner won from his adversary in the field.

Satunin in 1895 (cited by Ognev 1928) claimed snakes to be the preferred food of hedgehogs, but it is clear from all formal studies of diet that snakes are not commonly eaten, possibly because they are normally hiding away at night. Modern accounts of hedgehogs predating adders are widespread in the popular literature of European countries, and descriptions of the technique used by hedgehogs to subdue the snakes bear a strong general resemblance to Topsel's account. Herter (1965b) showed a photograph of such a fight. The following summary is an amalgamation of the main features of several of these accounts.

Upon meeting an adder the hedgehog immediately bristles and shields its snout and legs by pulling down its spiny skin. The hedgehog then approaches and tries to bite the snake along its body (Fig. 3.4). The snake retaliates by striking at the hedgehog; however, the hedgehog's spines are longer than the snake's venomous fangs and the snake cannot bite through to the skin. After many such futile strikes the snake may injure itself and become exhausted; additionally the snake's store of venom is likely to have been expelled

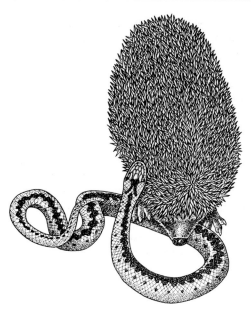

FIG. 3.4   *A hedgehog fighting a viper.*

uselessly. The hedgehog, when possible, uses its prickly body to pin down the snake, and gnaws at the snake in any convenient place until it bites through its backbone. The hedgehog then chews along the body towards the head until the snake is completely dead and can be eaten. Herter (1965b) mentioned that the entire snake, including the head and poison sacs, may sometimes be eaten.

Poduschka & Poduschka (1972) described how a young captive-reared hedgehog used its spiny coat as a shield to fend off a small stick which was gently poked at it and suggested that the strikes of snakes would be parried in the same way. From this observation one may infer that this kind of response, although probably not specific to encounters with snakes, is present in inexperienced youngsters and therefore seems to be innate.

The legendary immunity of hedgehogs to adder venom, also referred to by many early sources, seems to be partly true. Ognev (1928) cited experiments which indicated that hedgehogs were 35–40 times more resistant to comparable doses of adder venom which were also injected into white mice, and guinea pigs of the same size as the hedgehogs. Ognev also cited experiments by Satunin who subjected hedgehogs (*Paraechinus*) to being stung by scorpions (order Scorpiones) and bitten by horned vipers (*Cerastes cerastes*). Apparently the hedgehogs were not affected by such treatment and eventually ate both the snakes and the scorpions.

More recent confirmation of the hedgehog's resistance to adder venom has been provided by de Wit & Westrom (1987a,b) in Sweden, who found that plasma from *Erinaceus europaeus* contained three macroglobulin proteinase inhibitors which, when purified, neutralized the haemorrhagic activity of the venom. It is clear from several accounts, however, that venom immunity is either incomplete or is individually variable, because although some hedgehogs show no symptoms at all (Räf 1988) or no more than some local swelling when bitten by adders, for others the bite is fatal. Herter (1965b) described symptoms of extreme thirst and fasting, followed by death between 3 h and 8 days later. Possibly a hedgehog might survive if the venom dose is small and then acquire increased immunity, or if the first snake-bite injects a large dose of venom, it may die despite a degree of innate immunity. Although adders and various other species of snake are eaten, Knight (1962) indicated that, in Britain, hedgehogs are less ready to eat the grass snake (*Natrix natrix*, Family Colubridae) which, although not venomous, exudes a foul defensive odour from glands at the base of its tail. It seems, however, that very similar odours from another Colubrid, the Asian rat snake (*Ptyas mucosus*), did not deter a captive hedgehog (*Hemiechinus collaris*) which caught and ate a 33-cm specimen (Krishna 1956). It is interesting that the description of the attack on this non-venomous species was essentially identical to the way a European hedgehog deals with a viper.

HEDGEHOG RESISTANCE TO TOXINS AND POISONS

This is yet another controversial topic where most evidence is drawn from disparate observations and piecemeal experiments. It seems that hedgehogs, as well as having a degree of immunity to adder venom, also exhibit some tolerance of the chemical defences of many prey species. For example, *E. europaeus* will commonly eat millipedes and carabid beetles which use distasteful and/or noxious substances in defence, although some other distasteful species such as woodlice, staphylinid beetles and some ladybirds, seem to be avoided. Roberts (1977) claimed that hedgehogs (*Hemiechinus auritus megalotis*) are immune to the stings of scorpions and to poisonous solifugid spiders. Herter (1965b) reported that hedgehogs seemed to be immune to insect toxins generally. He drew attention to the fact that hedgehogs will eat Meloid beetles such as the oil beetle (*Meloë* sp.) and the blister beetle (*Lytta* sp.). These beetles, generally avoided by other predators, contain cantharidin, claimed to be 3000 times more toxic to humans than to hedgehogs (Burton 1969). Ognev (1928) reported that one hedgehog (*Hemiechinus auritus*) had eaten 50 such beetles without ill effect. Bees, wasps and ants are all eaten, sometimes in considerable numbers and without apparent harm. Herter (1965b) wrote how one hedgehog with 52 bee stings showed no obvious discomfort!

Hedgehogs are sometimes reputed to possess unusual resistance to a variety of poisons, anaesthetics, agricultural biocides and diseases. However, although there have been some substantiated examples, this Rasputin-like reputation is based largely on supposition (Chapter 9).

FEEDING FOLKLORE

No natural history of hedgehogs could fail to mention the extensive folklore surrounding their feeding habits. Some stories, as we have seen, have a fair basis in fact, and even the following should not be discounted out-of-hand, though I have relegated two of the most dubious tales to a brief treatment here. Most authors have concluded that these stories, although they may contain grains of truth, are, at the very least, somewhat fanciful and rather embroidered. Burton (1969) was less dismissive and recounted many testimonies of people who claimed to have seen such hedgehog behaviour.

Suckling cows

In European folklore, hedgehogs have long been accused of suckling dairy cows, supposedly reducing milk yields and helping to spread foot and mouth disease (Chapter 9). Herter (1965b) and Morris (1983) both pointed out that hedgehogs do like milk and might lick drops of milk leaking from the full udders of recumbent cows. Herter completely dismissed the idea that a hedgehog could fit a cow's teat into its mouth and suckle effectively, and Morris noted that a cow would be unlikely to tolerate impassively the attentions of a hedgehog. In contrast, however, Burton (1969) cited several testimonies to support the traditional view, that hedgehogs do deliberately take milk from cows, and in quantities sufficient to affect morning milk yields! Certainly these testimonies and Burton's personal observations present a fairly substantial support for the idea that hedgehogs will attack cow udders!

To my knowledge, there is only one published veterinary report of genuine hedgehog damage to a cow's teat (Smythe 1967) where a farmer saw a hedgehog hanging on to one. The hedgehog was then kicked off by the cow, and killed by the farmer. The teat had shallow longitudinal incisions on either side, apparently caused by the hedgehog's incisors being dragged down the teat. Smythe found no milk in the hedgehog's gut, but noted that a number of other cows on the same farm had also suffered torn teats. Another report where, on two occasions, the tip of a teat had been 'neatly shaved off' with almost surgical precision, was attributed to hedgehogs, using no clear criteria (Corcoran 1967). In neither of these reports had the cow been suckled! Stocker (1987) suggested that such damage could result from a hedgehog's attempts to eat the udder itself, rather than suckle from it. This is not an unreasonable idea because, as already revealed, hedgehogs will try to eat any animal flesh that presents itself; a report of one eating the udder of a helpless sheep has already been mentioned. To my mind it is most unlikely that a hedgehog could take significant amounts of milk from a cow, but I have little doubt that a hedgehog *could* take hold of a teat and chew at it. Even if there was no obvious injury to the teat, the distress caused to a cow attacked in this way could well reduce milking performance.

Fruit gathering

The traditional story of hedgehogs gathering fruit, by rolling on it, impaling it on their spines and carrying it away, was apparently originally written down by Pliny more than 2000 years ago and has since been repeated throughout Europe, illustrated in medieval bestiaries (Fig. 3.5), and even crops up in China. The fruit mentioned varies, and reviews of this topic tell of apples, figs, grapes, pears and strawberries being used (Burton 1969, Herter 1965b). Most stories also refer to hedgehogs carrying the fruit to a cache of some sort and some versions even claim that hedgehogs will climb trees, to dislodge fruit, and throw themselves down on the apples! The story is constantly reinforced by modern accounts; for example Lane Fox (1989) in a newspaper article claimed that a hedgehog was taking apples from his garden '...*plainly guilty because one apple was sticking to his backside*'.

FIG. 3.5 *Part of an illustration from a 12th century medieval manuscript depicting hedgehogs rolling on apples and carrying them away on their spines. Redrawn.*

This old story, if taken at face-value, is the most unlikely of all the food-folklore 'myths'. Hedgehogs, as we have seen, may eat fruit, but it is rare for them to consume a significant quantity. No field study of hedgehogs has revealed any tendency to cache food, neither do they take food to their young, or use the spines to carry any other item. Even nesting material is always carried in the mouth. Hedgehogs could conceivably climb a very rough or sloping tree trunk, but I have never witnessed it, nor has anyone else I have questioned. Herter (1965b) was astonished that people should believe such stories and claimed that it was impossible for hedgehogs to impale fruit on their spines by rolling upon their backs, because the skin musculature, needed to hold the spines erect, immediately slackens in this position.

Pat Morris has demonstrated, on a BBC television wildlife programme (*The Great Hedgehog Mystery*), that one can stick a slightly mushy apple forcefully onto the back of a bristling hedgehog and it will stay put while it walks away (also Herter 1965b). But to duplicate such an event in nature would require some rather unusual circumstances. Maybe a slightly soft apple might fall on to a hedgehog that just happened to be bristling at the time!

Burton (1969), once again, was reluctant to discount completely the many, apparently genuine, testimonies to fruit gathering he had collected. Instead, he offered an intriguing, if slightly contrived, explanation, which he also tested on several occasions with a half-grown captive hedgehog in an area of fallen crab apples. This hedgehog was known to self-anoint when stimulated by the odour/taste of dead leaves (Chapter 7). During the throes of self-anointing it did, on several occasions, temporarily pick up apples on its spines and punctured many more. Such accidental transport of fruit would not require any rationalization of the behaviour in terms of diet or food storage, and if observed would seem to reinforce the popular fable of fruit gathering.

FEEDING HEDGEHOGS

Feeding hedgehogs in the wild

Wild hedgehogs are fed by huge numbers of householders who take consider-able pleasure in their garden visitors. Traditionally they are fed bread and cow's milk, which many hedgehogs seem to relish and is often favoured by enthusiasts (e.g. Coles, 1983). Bread and cow's milk, as long as it is a *very* minor component in an otherwise natural diet, probably does little harm but hedgehogs fed mainly on bread and milk soon develop a greenish diarrhoea and may suffer serious enteritis. A good quality tinned cat or dog food (meat) is a better alternative both for captive and garden animals. It is a common mistake to assume that animals will instinctively reject unsuitable foods. Captive hedgehogs will gorge on a wide variety of unnatural and unsuitable foods (including bread and milk), and a wild hedgehog in Orpington (UK) was reported to have licked sulphuric acid from a car battery (Morris 1966)!

Studies of *E. europaeus* in Britain show that, although hedgehogs may regularly travel some distance to food bowls in gardens, they do not seem to become over-dependent (Morris 1985a). They often skip visits to the feeding bowl and will continue to forage normally both before and after their feast which may be punctuated by periods of foraging and trips out of the garden. Usually several peripatetic hedgehogs will visit food bowls.

Feeding captive hedgehogs

In my view the casual 'rescue' of apparently sick or orphaned wild animals is justified only when one is certain that the animal is truly abandoned or very ill and will suffer greatly without human aid. Proper care will usually involve veterinary treatment (Chapter 9 and Appendix 1), careful feeding and later rehabilitation into the wild. This is not a responsibility to be taken lightly, and one should be prepared for failure when animals are already seriously ill.

Diet is a key aspect of the care of sick, orphaned, injured or seriously underweight hedgehogs. Nowak (1972, 1977) promoted the idea of caring for underweight youngsters from autumn litters during the winter and releasing them in the spring.

Although there are distinct differences in their methods, Poduschka & Saupe (1981) and Stocker (1987, 1988) are both good sources of advice on the care of captive animals, including suitable diets and proven procedures for rearing captive hedgehogs. Both emphasized the importance of avoiding cow's milk in the diet, especially in young unweaned animals. Poduschka's account named a series of appropriate powdered milk substitutes and advocated that the feed be made up incorporating fennel or camomile tea to prevent certain digestive problems characterized by a swollen stomach and soreness around the anus. Calcium and vitamin supplements (B, C and D) were also recommended. Frequent feeding was recommended for youngsters under 100 g, at least every 3–4 h by day and 4–5 h by night.

Stocker advised against powdered milk substitutes and advocated a diet of fresh, or freshly defrosted, unpasteurized goat's milk with added colostrum (ratio 2:1), for rearing unweaned babies. Colostrum is usually kept by goat breeders, but when unavailable, a mixture containing raw egg is better than no colostrum at all. However, Dimelow (1963a) claimed that raw egg white inhibited vitamin B synthesis by gut bacteria and therefore was unsuitable for an adult's diet. The milk mixture, slightly warmed and with added vitamins, should be given until at least 41 days old, about 2 weeks after starting solid food. The mother's natural licking of the urinogenital area to stimulate urination and defecation must be simulated; Stocker suggested the gentle use of a damp tissue. The British Hedgehog Preservation Society (BHPS) (1987) mentioned that 'Lactogen' was a safe milk substitute. They noted that 'Lactade' contains a lactose-digesting enzyme which thus makes cow's milk more acceptable, though still not ideal, for use with hedgehogs.

Care is needed to avoid under- or over-feeding and regular weighing is necessary to monitor growth. Although there are large individual differences

in size and growth, Poduschka & Saupe (1981) suggested that the maximum
desirable weight gain for a growing hedgehog was about 50 g per week. At
first a syringe or pipette is needed to feed the babies but at around 3 weeks
they may be taught to lap from a dish. Stocker advised that at this stage, when
their first incisors erupt and weight gain may start to slow, a high quality
puppy food may be introduced. For more mature babies the goat's milk
mixture should be increasingly supplemented by a more solid diet of good
quality meat, such as dog or cat food (at first liquidized) with added vitamins,
dried-insect food, and mealworms (only in small quantities as they have a high
fat content). Poduschka & Saupe considered that readiness for independent
feeding was indicated by tooth eruption and that the diet could incorporate
foods such as mashed banana, various meats and ants' eggs, with mealworms
and ground mussel shells to add roughage.

At roughly 6 weeks, young hedgehogs should have graduated to the meat-
based diet, with fresh drinking water, suitable for captive adults. I advise
anyone who is faced with the problems of rearing youngsters, or otherwise
caring for hedgehogs, to read Stocker (1987, 1988) or, for readers of German,
Poduschka & Saupe (1981). The BHPS also publish useful advisory booklets.
It is also a good idea to contact an animal rescue centre or wildlife hospital
with the veterinary contacts, facilities and experience required (see Appendix
3). Returning such animals to the wild requires care and a gradual rehabilitation programme of increasing freedom with the opportunity to feed on
natural prey.

Well-grown or adult hedgehogs of all species are relatively easy to feed.
Although it is an attractive idea, captive hedgehogs should not usually be
offered natural prey items like slugs, worms, beetles and so on, gathered from
the wild because they may carry the infective stages of serious parasite
infections which may be fatal if untreated (Chapter 9). If you have taken on an
underweight or sick animal, it is obviously easier, and maybe better for the
animals, to have a carefully formulated artificial diet. The faeces of a well-fed
and healthy captive hedgehog should be firm, dryish and well formed with no
green slime or blood flecks.

A meaty pet food, plus mineral/vitamin supplements, makes a suitable basic
food for all species. Herter (1956) successfully maintained five hedgehog
species on a staple diet of chopped raw ox hearts. In longer term captivity and
for fast-growing young animals, care must be taken to balance the diet and to
include variety and roughage. Specialist foods, such as those used in zoos
containing ants' eggs and insects are also suitable. Meritt (1981) fed captive
Atelerix albiventris on fruit and baby food vegetables, cooked minced beef,
milk, hard-boiled egg yolk and 'Zu/Preem' (a canned specialist animal food).

Poduschka & Saupe (1981) suggested feeding only about one to two heaped
tablespoons of food daily. The valuable ability of the hedgehog to 'tank-up'
upon encountering a large source of food in the wild can lead to obesity
problems in captivity. Adult weights of both species of European hedgehogs
vary enormously and commonsense should be used in judging how obese an
animal is for its body size. Generally, for British hedgehogs, a weight of up to

around 1000 g is reasonable for an adult, although a few may weigh up to half as much again. In areas with colder winters such as Scandinavia and Continental Europe, and at higher altitudes, normal adults tend to be rather heavier at up to 1400 g. An *E. concolor* reared in captivity by Poduschka reached 1730 g.

In captivity hedgehogs will eat an amazing variety of foods, too many to list here (Lindemann 1951, Dimelow 1963a, Herter 1968 Poduschka & Poduschka 1972). It is certain that many of these foods were unsuitable and most recent publications strongly discourage 'treats' of chocolate, confectionary or seasoned foods. This is important because hedgehogs may gluttonously gorge themselves on particular foods and sometimes develop a passion for them that restricts their intake of proper food. Nougat chocolate became a major preoccupation of hedgehogs kept by Nowak (1972). In general, food should not be provided *ad libitum*. Herter (1968) noted one lactating female *E. concolor* (from Rumania) that ate 120 g of chicken meat, as well as a sparrow weighing 24 g and 85 g of milk, in a single night, a total of more than one-third of her 650 g bodyweight! Another hedgehog provided with *ad libitum* mealworms (high in fat) ate 1880 g in 19 days with a weight increase of almost 68% (689–1155 g). Captive *Hemiechinus collaris*, from Rajasthan, ate an average of 297 grasshoppers (*Chrotogonus*) daily, about 119 g (Chandra 1985).

CHAPTER 4

Home Range and Territoriality

HOME range is a commonly used term to describe the area over which an animal normally travels in pursuit of its routine activities (Jewell 1966). This is a useful general concept, but differences in what is regarded as 'normal' or 'routine' can lead to confusion when comparing studies. An animal may explore and become familiar with areas surrounding its normal home range, it may also shift its range in response to changing conditions or even be migratory. Therefore, it is essential to note the time-scale over which the range has been measured.

It is also very important to distinguish the concept of home range from that of 'territory' which refers to an area, part or all of the home range, that is defended to exclude or restrict access by conspecifics (Burt 1943, Jewell 1966).

Before the availability of radio-tracking, workers usually relied on traps, arranged in a grid across the study site, to recapture marked individuals repeatedly and so gradually build up a picture of their range. Although it remains a useful approach for many species and in certain study situations, trapping has obvious drawbacks when studying animal movements. Traps confine animals and disrupt their behaviour; furthermore the use of baited traps alters food availability in the study area. Radio-tracking has its own methodological problems (see below), but it does allow animals to move freely and researchers can locate individuals according to a planned schedule. Evaluations of home-range area can be derived from recorded locations (or 'fixes') in a variety of ways, some almost identical to those used for grid-trapping data (Macdonald *et al.* 1980, Trevor-Deutsch & Hackett 1980, Voigt & Tinline 1980).

One exciting new aspect of radio-tracking is that it permits continuous monitoring to provide detailed route maps of a hedgehog's movements, revealing exactly where it has been and how far it has travelled. The distance travelled during an activity period is of great biological significance, especially for foraging animals, such as hedgehogs, who must travel a certain distance in order to find enough food items. If data on distance travelled, speed and use of habitat are augmented by behavioural observations detailing the time spent in various activities (e.g. feeding, locomotion, etc.), the resulting activity budget can form a realistic basis for studies of individual foraging and energetics. Simple representations of home range as an area cannot match such versatility, but nevertheless do provide a valuable indication of the area of habitat(s) used by an animal to fulfil its needs—bearing in mind factors such as population density, habitat type and so on. Maps showing the spatial organization of individual home-range areas can also provide useful insights into territoriality and 'social' relationships within the study population.

Most studies of hedgehog range have used simple determinations of home-range area, drawing concave or convex polygons around plots of all the known locations of an animal during specified periods. More detailed statistical analyses of location data are possible, and may be pretty, but often add little biological meaning and may make unrealistic mathematical assumptions (Macdonald *et al.* 1980). While statistical methods do provide valuable aids to the identification of activity clusters or the enhancement of sparse data (Voigt & Tinline 1980), it can often be just as revealing simply to look at maps showing habitat features with presentations of the animal's movements (e.g. Reeve 1981, 1982, Boitani & Reggiani, 1984). Two simple techniques which may be used to show areas of concentrated activity, or 'core areas', within an overall range are shown in Figs 4.1 (a combination of continuous and discontinuous location data) and 4.2 (superimposed route maps from continuous observations).

Although radio-tracking data may be described as continuous, in practice each period of activity is recorded as a series of consecutive fixes. It is obvious that longer intervals between fixes reduce the accuracy of the revealed route, but the significance of the error also depends on the level of the animal's activity. Correctly mapping the precise location of the animal at each fix can also be a problem, especially when following animals through dense woodland or across featureless open grassland. I was fortunate to work on a golf course with numerous clear landmarks—many of which were numbered! Animals may also disappear into private gardens or other inaccessible areas where direct observation is impossible and triangulated fixes, also subject to a variety of errors, are the only choice.

The attachment of a transmitter package to a hedgehog poses several problems. Collars or bands are generally impractical because hedgehogs have a poorly defined neck, lack a 'waist' and have a small tapering tail. The pioneering study of European hedgehogs in England by Morris (1969) used a home-made 27 MHz system with a flexible external loop aerial incorporated into an elastic harness which, passing either side of the forelimbs, held the transmitter dorsally over the animal's shoulders. Moors (1979) in New Zealand used a harness of silicone rubber tubing placed around the hedgehog's neck. Such elastic harnesses allowed the hedgehogs to roll-up adequately for defence, but they must have constrained natural movements to

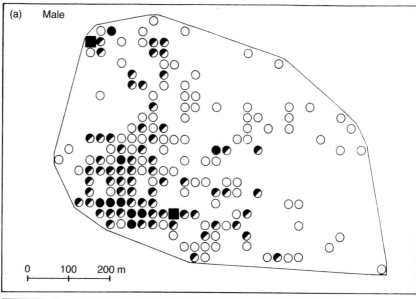

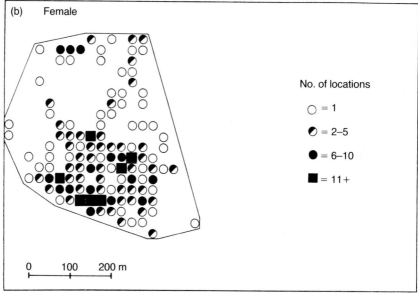

FIG. 4.1   *The differential use of home range of (a) a male and (b) a female European hedgehog on a suburban golf course in southern England. Data were collected during 12(a) and 13(b) whole nights of radio-tracking active animals during 1979. The study area (delimited by the rectangular border) was divided into 25-m² grid cells and the frequency of locations in each is plotted. Note that much of the range is infrequently visited and the male's range is much larger than that of the female. See also Fig. 4.2. Scale in metres. Source: Reeve (1981).*

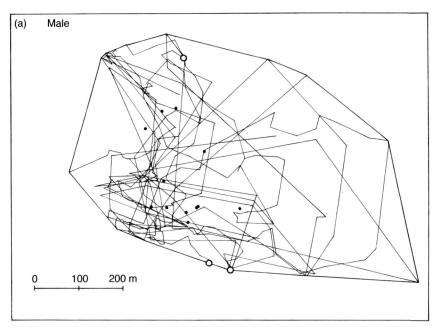

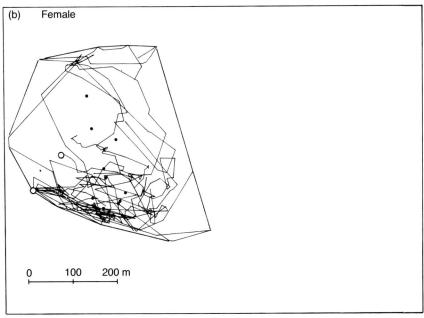

FIG. 4.2   *Routes taken by the animals shown in Fig. 4.1 (minimum straight line distances between fixes shown). Study details as for Fig 4.1. Nests are marked with an open circle, the black dots show the geometric centre of activity for each night's movements. Scale in metres. Source: Reeve (1981).*

some extent. The spiny skin is very muscular and mobile and in Morris' study hedgehogs frequently escaped from their harnesses.

In contrast, gluing transmitters to the dorsal spines has been very successful and used by almost all of the more recent studies, e.g. Kristiansson & Erlinge (1977), Berthoud (1978), Reeve (1980), Boitani & Reggiani (1984), Kristiansson (1984), Morris (1985a), Schoenfeld & Yom-Tov (1985), Dowie (1987). Philchagov (1988) stitched the transmitters to the hedgehogs' spines!

Attaching transmitters (or other tags) to the spines has shown itself to be reliable and does not seem to inhibit free movement. Minimizing the weight of transmitter packages is important, but the miniaturization of electronic components is only part of the problem. The transmitter must be robustly encased in waterproof resin and the battery weight required for a good power delivery and long life can often be high. In the studies reviewed in this chapter transmitter weights varied from 12 to 28 g but one study used 30–40-g packages (Boitani & Reggiani 1984). The design and weight of the transmitter aerial also provides a trade-off between transmission range and possible adverse effects on the animal. Whip antennae or trailing wires can give a good range—up to around 1500 m in one study (Boitani & Reggiani 1984) but may snag on objects or interfere with nest building (Moors 1979). Integral aerials, such as the iron-dust rod used in my own transmitters (Reeve 1980), avoid such problems and have no external connections to break or let in water, but may weigh more and perform less well than whips.

Advances in component design should mean that current and future studies can benefit from smaller lighter transmitters with reduced power consumption and improved performance, as well as the additional telemetry of physiological variables such as body temperature and heart rate. However, even if small, well-designed transmitter packages weighing only a few grams are used, one should not discount the possibility that carrying a transmitter may modify natural behaviour or adversely affect performance; the effects could be subtle and hard to quantify. Nevertheless, few problems have been reported in hedgehog studies. Schoenfeld & Yom-Tov (1985) found that transmitter packages had no effect on measures of body condition during the study period, but one animal died as a direct result of the package becoming entangled in grass. In my own study, animals also appeared unaffected by their transmitters but, by sad coincidence, one of my hedgehogs also died after its transmitter became caught in long grass, trapping it outside during a day of heavy rain.

It is notable that during radio-tracking studies the frequency and level of observer disturbance can be high. Several studies, including mine, have involved stealthily following animals, typically at distances of 20 m or more, but some workers (e.g. Boitani & Reggiani 1984) frequently spot-lighted animals! I temporarily taped small luminous tags to the transmitter (out of the animal's sight) and used deep-red torch-light in an attempt to minimize disturbance of the animal during tracking, but I still needed to contact an animal to attach the light. Permanently attached lights could have attracted unwelcome attention from the public or predators. Image-intensifying equipment might seem an ideal aid to covert night-time observation, but the image-intensifier I tried emitted a high frequency whistle which irritated me and could well have disturbed the hedgehogs.

Although informal observations and mark–recapture studies have yielded valuable information, almost all of our more detailed knowledge of the natural ranging behaviour of hedgehogs comes from a few radio-tracking studies of the European hedgehog (*Erinaceus europaeus*). An exception is one combined study of the eastern European hedgehog (*E. concolor*) and the long-eared hedgehog (*Hemiechinus auritus*) which occur together in Israel (Schoenfeld & Yom-Tov 1985). Despite the major benefits of radio-tracking, one must bear in mind the methodological problems associated with transmitter package design and performance, triangulation and mapping errors, fix frequency, the effects of observer disturbance, and so on. It would be very surprising if the different habitats and climates in each of the studies did not result in differing patterns of activity and ranging behaviour, even for the same species. However, much of the variation in the data reported by the studies below could also be attributed to differences in the methods used to obtain raw data in the field, and in the subsequent analyses and interpretations of 'home range'.

STUDIES OF HOME RANGE IN *ERINACEUS EUROPAEUS*

The public image of the European hedgehog as a rather bumbling, sedentary creature seemed to be confirmed by early capture–recapture studies. Herter (1956) cited a 1928 study by Lüttich on a North Sea Island (Spiekeroog) which indicated a range roughly 200–300 m around the nest. Herter also reported that translocated animals generally settled within 2·5 km of the release point. In contrast, Kruuk (1964) followed the tracks of hedgehogs on sand dunes at Ravenglass (Cumbria, UK) and showed that they made trips of 'several kilometres' and trails up to 4 km were found (Morris 1969, citing Kruuk pers. comm.). Kruuk marked 15 hedgehogs, but none was recovered, possibly indicating a very mobile population.

Radio-tracking studies from several countries (reviewed below) have provided a new perception of hedgehogs as active, bustling animals which may sometimes travel several kilometres during their nightly activities.

Britain

Morris (1969), as part of a multi-faceted study, was the first to experiment with radio-tracking hedgehogs in a West London deer park. Technical constraints and problems of harness design limited the data gathered, but he estimated that an animal could feasibly find enough food for one night during the course of about 300 m of intensive foraging. Later, in collaboration with Morris, my own study involved a capture–recapture and radio-tracking study

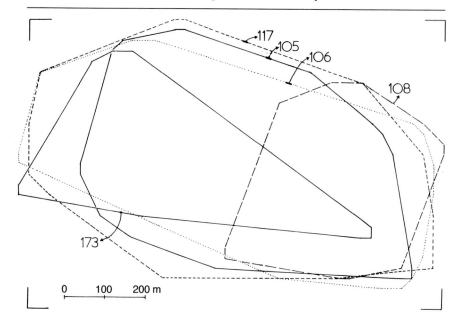

FIG. 4.3   *Overlapping seasonal home-range areas (minimum area convex polygons) for five male European hedgehogs living on a suburban golf course in southern England. The corner markings represent the limits of the study area. Data for animals located more than 10 times in 1979. Number of locations for male 105 = 433, 106 = 532, 108 = 97, 117 = 277, and 173 = 13 locations but this animal's range also extended outside the study area. Scale in metres Source: Reeve (1981).*

of 107 marked hedgehogs over three seasons (1977–1979) (Reeve 1980, 1981, 1982). The site was a West London suburban golf course (about 40 ha) surrounded by houses, gardens and busy roads. The habitat was a mixture of open grass fairways interspersed with rough grass, scrub and wooded areas and the hedgehog population density was about 0.83 ha^{-1}.

The hedgehogs, including the few females known to be lactating, were active continuously throughout the night. Animals showed no evidence of maintaining territorial boundaries and their home ranges overlapped, often completely, irrespective of sex (Figs. 4.3 and 4.4). There was also a marked tendency for animals of both sexes to remain in the same general area year after year (Fig. 4.5).

Recapture records supported the suggestion by Berthoud (1978) that the young have a dispersal phase which occurs in the first few months of life, establishing their future adult range before, or shortly after their first winter.

Using data from six adult males and seven adult females, seasonal range area estimates (convex polygons) were extremely variable but adult males had, on average, significantly greater range areas (32 ha) than adult females (10 ha) (Table 4.1). Results from three subadults suggested range areas similar to

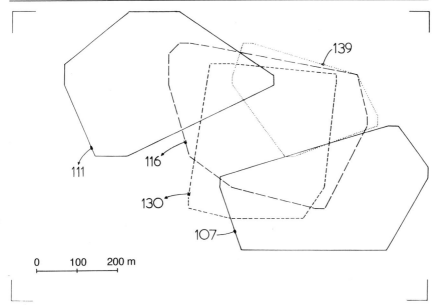

FIG. 4.4   *Overlapping seasonal home-range areas (minimum area convex polygons) for five female European hedgehogs living on a suburban golf course in southern England. Details as for Fig. 4.3. Number of locations for female 107 = 62, 111 = 154, 116 = 106, 130 = 17, 139 = 30. Scale in metres. Source: Reeve (1981).*

those of females, averaging 12 ha. These calculated range areas were based on between 30 and 532 locations (capture locations and radio-fixes).

All-night route maps were obtained over 83 'hedgehog-nights' for 12 radio-tracked animals. Because the number of fixes taken affects the reliability of each calculated route length, only routes derived from over 20 fixes (up to 70) per night were used. Straight line distances between fixes were measured. There were statistically significant sex differences in minimum nightly distance travelled, with averages of 1690 m and 1006 m, based on three males and three females, respectively. Subadults (one of each sex) averaged 1188 m (Table 4.2).

Thus males were revealed as wide-ranging in comparison with females, not only accumulating seasonal ranges about three times larger, but travelling on average 68% further each night. Males moved with a mean speed of 3·73 m min^{-1}, significantly faster than females (2·19 m min^{-1}) and subadults (2·17 m min^{-1}). Hedgehogs can put on surprising bursts of speed. I timed one hedgehog, not in any way disturbed, running easily across an open stretch of grass at 60 m min^{-1} and Wroot (1984a) reported speeds of up to 120 m min^{-1}!

The rapid and wide-ranging movement of males is generally presumed to result from searching for receptive females during the 'rut' (e.g. Campbell 1973a, Berthoud 1978, Kristiansson 1984). I could not determine male ranges

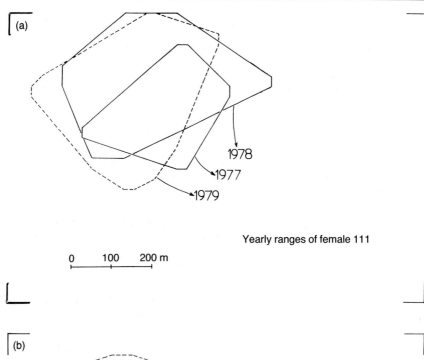

Yearly ranges of female 111

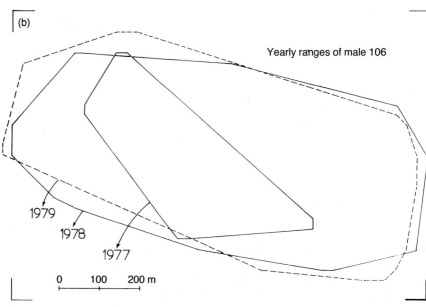

FIG. 4.5 *Yearly ranges of female 111 (a) and male 106 (b), showing that they remain in the same locality in consecutive years. The corner markings represent the limits of the study area. The apparently small size of the 1977 ranges is a result of the limited data obtained that year. Scale in metres. Source: Reeve (1981).*

TABLE 4.1   *Summary of hedgehog cumulative home-range area estimates from studies which include radio-tracking.*

Species Age/sex	Mean range area (ha)	(s.d)	Range of values	n	Study notes
E. europaeus					
♂ Adult	32	8·9	15·5–41·5	6 ⎫	Reeve (1982); sexes
♀ Adult	10	2·2	5·5–12·0	7 ⎬	significantly different
♂♀ Subadult	12	2·5	10·0–15·0	3 ⎭	
♂ Adult	46·5	15·8	25·0–67·7	5 ⎫	Kristiansson (1984); sexes
♀ Adult	19·7	8·4	8·1–29·5	6 ⎬	significantly different
♂ Subadult	9·2 ⎫			⎭	
♀ Subadult	3·4 ⎭	(Not radio-tracked)			
♂ Adult	57·13	36·6	5·5–102·5	9 ⎫	Boitani & Reggiani (1984);
♀ Adult	29·08	20·08	10·0–56·2	5 ⎭	no significant sex difference
♂ Adult	6·4	—		11 ⎫	Morris (1986)
♀ Adult	6·9	—	—	12 ⎬	
♀ Adult[a]	11·0	—	—	10 ⎭	
♂ Adult	27·0	—	—	— ⎫	Dowie (1988) (summary
♀ Adult	6·0	—	—	— ⎭	data only)
E. concolor					
♂ Adult	1·56	0·82	0·8–2·27	4 ⎫	Schoenfeld & Yom-Tov
♀ Adult	1·58	1·25	0·14–2·38	3 ⎟	(1985); no significant sex difference in either species
H. auritus					
♂ Adult	4·98	3·36[d]	1·64–9·97	5 ⎟	
♀ Adult[b]	2·85	1·43[d]	0·86–4·2	4 ⎟	
♀ Adult[c]	2·08	1·65[d]	0·17–4·25	6 ⎭	

s.d. = standard deviation; *n* = number of individuals (for Morris, 1986 = number of hedgehog-nights).
[a]Lactating females.
[b]Non-lactating females.
[c]Non-lactating and lactating females.
[d]Recalculated from published data.

outside the breeding period because sexual activity (from mid-May to September) spanned virtually the entire active season, with no identifiable post-mating period, unlike the Swedish study (see below) in which a clear reduction in male activity was shown late in the season. However, in my study, range data from one male, with 274 locations obtained before late May and 258 subsequent locations, do support the idea that males range less widely when sexually inactive (Table 4.3 and Fig. 4.6).

Morris (1985a), using the same suburban golf course as a study site, described a 4-week (mid-August to mid-September 1982) investigation of the effects of supplementary feeding on hedgehog movements. He calculated

TABLE 4.2 *Average nightly distance travelled: data from six studies of hedgehogs* (Erinaceus europaeus).

Time of year	Age/sex	Mean nightly distance (m)	n	Study notes and method used to estimate distance per night
Seasonal				
	♂ Adult	1690	14	Reeve (1982): (UK); sum of
	♀ Adult	1006	8	minimum distances between
	♂♀ Subadult	1188	9	fixes, seasonal total
June				
	♂ Adult	1761	19	Kristiansson (1984): (Sweden);
	♀ Adult	782	21	calculated values from average
August				speeds and activity
	♂ Adult	1013	29	duration
	♀ Adult	974	30	
August/September				
	♂ Adult	1158	17	Morris (1985a): (UK); sum of
	♀ Adult	660	13	minimum distances between
				fixes.
July/August				
	♂ Adult	868	11	Morris (1986): (UK); sum of
	♀ Adult	570	12	minimum distances between
	♀ Adult[a]	693	10	fixes
July/August				
	♂ Adult (old)	1785	19	Morris (1988b): (UK); sum of
	♂ Adult	933	9	minimum distances between
	♀ Adult	957	17	fixes
Summer (no details)				
	♂ Adult	1417	—	Dowie (1987): (UK); sum of
	♀ Adult	915	—	minimum distances between
				fixes. Mixed farmland & pasture
				(Kent)
October				
	♂ Adult	328	—	Pasture (Gloucestershire)
	♀ Adult	471	—	

n = number of hedgehog-nights.
[a]Lactating females.

minimum distance travelled per night for 30 'hedgehog-nights' during which animals were followed for at least 3 h and the position of the following day's nest was known. For males the mean distance travelled (1158 m; $n = 17$ hedgehog-nights) was about 75% larger than that for females (660 m; $n = 13$) (Table 4.2). This statistically significant sex difference corroborates the findings of my own previous study, and clearly showed that even when food was abundant (in food bowls) males still travelled further than females.

TABLE 4.3   *Changes in nightly distance travelled and average speed for male 106; April to July 1979.*

Date	Distance travelled (m)	Average speed (m min^{-1})	No. fixes per night
30 April	739	1·61	46
8 May	986	2·59	61
14 May	1227	2·77	51
4 June	1535	3·63	28
19 June	1128	2·66	34
17 July	1039	2·49	40

Source: Reeve (1981).

Morris (1986) reported a brief study (July to August 1983) of three hedgehogs in an area dominated by mixed (mainly deciduous) woodland, scrub, grassland and cultivated areas surrounding the buildings of Alice Holt (near Farnham, Surrey, UK). Good data were obtained for two females (one with a litter of five) and one male; a useful total of 33 'hedgehog-nights' of activity were monitored. Each animal was located a minimum of six times per night over 10–12 nights.

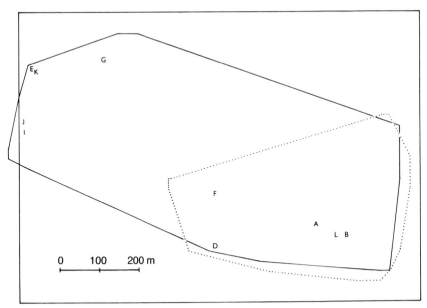

FIG. 4.6   *The home range (minimum area convex polygon) of a male (106) before (....) and after (——) 20 May 1979, when courtship activity had begun. Before this date he used only nests A and B but afterwards he used seven others and once a resting site without a nest (L). Scale in metres. Source Reeve (1981).*

Again males travelled, on average, further each night than did females, in this case about 38% further (868 and 625 m, respectively). The female with the litter had remained active during parturition and lactation and did not appear to return to the nest to feed the babies at night. It is interesting to note that her average distance travelled per night and range area is slightly higher than for the other female (Tables 4.1 and 4.2).

In Morris' study the number of fixes used to calculate routes was sometimes rather small, but even so there was a fairly clear tendency for these 'forest' animals, more especially the males, to range rather less widely than those in more open habitats both in Britain and elsewhere. This could be due to single or combined factors such as higher quality or more frequently available food items, habitat effects on ease of movement, population density or possibly even a relative preponderance of females.

Only two British radio-tracking studies have been carried out in rural farmland; these showed fundamentally similar results to those from other open habitats. Morris (1988b) tracked five adults on about 55 ha of pasture and hayfields at Newtown (Isle of Wight, UK) in the summer of 1984. The hedgehog population density was low, estimated at about one per 3 ha. Data suitable for detailed analysis were obtained for only three animals (two males and a female), but these were tracked for 45 hedgehog-nights, including two nights of continuous observation (Table 4.2). As in Morris' previous study, a minimum of six locations per hedgehog-night was generally aimed for, but his conclusion, that around 20 or more fixes per night were preferable for the more active hedgehogs, corroborated my own findings (Reeve 1981). In the Newtown study the mean interval between locations of individuals was 39 min, although a few lapses of more than 2 h did occur.

As usual in these studies, even allowing for methodological problems, the variation in measured nightly minimum distance travelled and range area was high even for the same individuals. This variation was not linked to weather conditions, which were fairly stable throughout the study. One older male was especially active, with a cumulative range area of about 37 ha, and he covered at least 1 km almost every night and over 2 km on a third of all nights tracked. One night he walked a measured minimum distance of 3·14 km, a British record for a radio-tracked hedgehog! Possibly because they were less reproductively active than the older male, the ranges of the younger adult males—cumulative range areas around 10–12 ha and mean minimum distances travelled of 547–957 m per night—were more like that of the female.

The second rural study was carried out by Dowie (1987,1988) using two study sites. At Divers Farm (Kent, UK), a mixed farm with cereals, orchard and pasturelands, movement data collected during the summer appeared similar to that from earlier work, but no detailed comparisons are possible because only summary data were presented. Males travelled on average about 55% further than females each night, and generally ranged over much greater areas (see Tables 4.1 and 4.2). The second site, Folly Farm (Gloucestershire, UK), was mainly pastureland surrounding an area of wildfowl pens. It is notable that this October study showed males to be less wide-ranging than females (Table 4.2). It was suggested that at this time males were not searching for mates and late-breeding females were more active in search of food in order to build body condition before hibernation.

Sweden

Kristiansson & Erlinge (1977) tracked an adult female for 5 days in June and an adult male for 3 days in July, in open fields, gardens and small copses

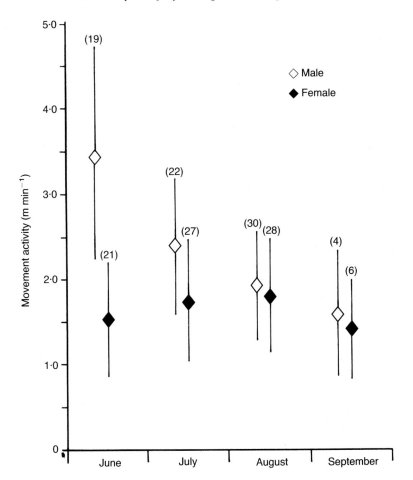

FIG. 4.7 *Average speeds (m min⁻¹) are shown for male and female European hedgehogs in southern Sweden over the June–September period. Numbers in parentheses show the number of tracking nights and vertical lines show the standard deviation for each mean. Total duration of activity was not significantly different between the sexes but both increased their active period from an average of 8·2 to 9·2 h in the post-mating period. Source: Kristiansson (1984).*

around the village of Revingeby (near Lund, Sweden). The female moved
between 700 and 1000 m each night and the male around 800 m during 8 h of
activity, using three nests in 3 days. The home-range estimates, 2·3 ha (female)
and 3·7 ha (male), appear comparatively small because *concave* polygons were
used to define range area. Capture–recapture data indicated that individuals
used the same areas during the summer and autumn. Further studies using
capture–recapture and radio-tracking were carried out in the same area
(Kristiansson 1984). Estimates of home-range area (convex polygon) and
distance travelled are presented in Tables 4.1 and 4.2. As in almost all other
studies, adult males, on average, ranged much more widely than females and
subadults. The estimates of home range fall between those from my study in
Britain (Reeve 1982) and the Italian study (Boitani & Reggiani 1984).

Kristiansson's study revealed that in Sweden the hedgehogs showed a
distinct post-mating period phase (after July 16) during which the previously
extensive movements of the males, on average 1761 m per night, declined to an
average of 1013 metres per night. Females, in contrast, increased their distance
travelled from an average of 782 m to 972 m. These changes in distance
travelled and a lengthening of the duration of activity in the post-mating
period are reflected in the changes in the average speeds of males and females
shown in Fig. 4.7.

Switzerland

Berthoud (1978) tracked seven males and five females during two years of
study near Yverdon (Switzerland) in an area of mixed habitats, ranging from
meadows and natural lakeside vegetation, to forestry plantations, arable
fields, market gardens and areas of human habitation.

The hedgehogs were radio-tagged for between 4 and 12 weeks and were
followed on fine nights, mainly from 21:00 to 02:00 hours, which Berthoud
claimed to be their principal activity period. Feeding range (*'terrain de chasse'*)
seemed to alter during the year in response to food availability. Observations
suggested that when food was abundant, animals foraged systematically for
several hours, but when food was scarce they covered many hundreds of
metres, without stopping. The day nesting site was often some way from the
feeding range. In the seven cases studied, this distance varied from 0 to 400 m
(mean 254 m) and the hedgehogs regularly used convenient routes such as
forest or agricultural tracks. Berthoud's study, in contrast to all others, clearly
suggested that the hedgehogs were territorial, especially in early May when
they apparently maintained a strict perimeter. Territory sizes were between
1·8 and 2·5 ha. Females never left their own territories which were contiguous
but non-overlapping. However, this study contained some rather equivocal
information. Although it was asserted that boundaries were maintained, no
marking behaviour was observed. Despite the strictly delimited territories
reported, frequent movements into the territories of others did not elicit
aggressive responses. Observations did suggest, however, that animals tra-
versing the ranges of others moved in a rapid trot, whereas in their own
territories their movements were less direct. If anything, this suggests a

mutual avoidance system of spatial organization (as found in my own studies, see later), rather than a system of territorial boundaries.

As in other studies, individuals reoccupied their previous year's range after the winter, and males wandered extensively during the breeding season; one male walked a route of 3·2 km on at least five occasions.

Italy

Boitani & Reggiani (1984) radio-tracked European hedgehogs in a 160-ha study area around Lake Burano in the Mediterranean coastal *maquis* region along the coastlines of Tuscany and Lazio (Italy). The area contained a brackish water lake and reed marsh, cultivated fields and meadows separated from the sea by sandy dunes. Juveniles were not tagged, but 14 animals weighing from 520 to 1020 g were tracked between March 1980 and July 1981.

Observations were obtained either by spot locations (at least twice per night) or by extended following at a distance of around 20 m, with recorded fixes every 10–15 min. Visual contact was prolonged wherever possible by a torch shone on the animals. Home range was very variable, with calculated areas (convex polygons) of between 5·5 ha in the period before hibernation and 102·5 ha during periods of maximum activity. In contrast to other studies, areas that were obviously unused, such as the lake, were excluded from the area calculations. Data on total range area from the Burano site seem to confirm the findings of other studies in that male ranges tended to be larger than those of females. Although five of the nine males tracked had range areas larger than any of the five females, the huge variability in range size (males 5·5–102·5 ha, females 10·0–56·2 ha) means that the difference was not statistically significant (Table 4.1). In this habitat nightly distances covered were reported at around 3–4 km for both sexes, but detailed data were not presented. Ranges consistently overlapped widely and each covered a variety of habitats.

When in the cultivated areas and around the three small refuse sites, animals tended to concentrate their activities, re-visiting the same sites several times, but when in the *maquis*, recorded locations were more dispersed. It would seem that the *maquis* is a poor habitat, with hedgehogs travelling considerable distances to meet their food and reproductive needs. In June and July when the weather was dry the hedgehogs tended to move from the rather arid *maquis* into the pasture and agricultural land, concentrating in the damper areas. The most frequented habitat was wet meadow, especially in the summer and autumn, dry meadow being more popular in spring. Food abundance, in turn affected by available moisture, seemed to be an important determinant of habitat use.

Russia

Philchagov (1988) radio-tracked hedgehogs during spring and summer around Kalinin (north-west of Moscow), in 3·5 km^2 of mixed habitat consisting of arable land, pasture, scrubland, copse and woodland. Oddly,

Philchagov added to the resident population by translocating hedgehogs into the study area. She used luminous tags and followed animals at a distance of 15–20 m. Hedgehogs were usually active for between 7–12 h each night although there was little activity on nights with sub-zero temperatures, even during the rut. Altogether four adult males, four adult females (two lactating) and two subadult females were observed for between 28 and 67 h each. The hedgehogs' movements closely resembled those already described in previous studies, although the activity of the Kalinin hedgehogs seems particularly erratic.

Overall, the hedgehogs travelled from 0·7 to 2·5 km per night, but the two lactating females tended to move further (average of four nights: 1397 m per night, range of values 1015–2001 m) than other females. Sexually active males ranged more widely and travelled further (up to 2500 m) than females or non-rutting males. As in Kristiansson's (1984) study there was a distinct post-rut period, prior to hibernation, during which the males were less mobile. Philchagov detailed the activity periods of the movements of individuals, but presented only selected home-range data.

Nearby, in the Yaroslavl region, a previous study by Karaseva *et al.* (1979) reported range sizes from 0·5 to 11·2 ha (males) and 0·8 to 3·5 ha (females). Both sexes usually moved between 100 and 600 m per night but whereas females very rarely exceeded this range, males often did and one travelled around 3 km. Intriguingly, Karaseva *et al.* noted that although the ranges of males overlapped, those of females did not, a feature observed in no other study except Berthoud (1978).

New Zealand

The only published radio-tracking study of hedghogs in New Zealand (*E. europaeus*) was a study of nesting by Moors (1979) on sand dunes at Pukepuke (see Chapter 5). The only relevant data collected were distances separating an individual's nests, which for males were up to 650 m, and for females up to 130 m.

Capture–recapture studies, all in open habitats, have yielded more useful data, although two of them (Campbell, 1973a,b, Parkes 1975) concentrated on feeding range rather than total home range. An 18-month study by Parkes (1975) involved 150 individuals with 356 recapture locations. The study area in the Manawatu (North Island, New Zealand) contained a mix of vegetation types on very sandy soil: mainly pasture but including pine plantations. The estimated population density varied from 1·1 ha^{-1} (winter) to 2·5 ha^{-1} (summer). Using convex polygons Parkes estimated mean 'feeding ranges' for adult males, females and juveniles (Table 4.4.). Parkes (1972, cited by Campbell 1973a) also used a probability ellipse method to estimate total home range to be 7·0 ha (males) and 12·9 ha (females).

Campbell's (1973a,b) study area was irrigated pastureland near Canterbury (New Zealand). Over 2·5 years, 100 individuals were marked, with 20 recaptured between 10 and 46 times. Although she was unable to estimate

TABLE 4.4 *A summary of published feeding range estimates from two New Zealand studies.*

	Mean feeding range (ha)	No. individuals	Mean no. sightings per individual
Campbell (1973a)			
Females	2·8	7	—
Males	2·4	7	—
Juvenile females	2·0	3	—
Juvenile males	1·9	3	—
Parkes (1975)			
Females	3·6	10	12·9
Males	2·5	4	6·7
Juveniles	2·5	6	8·5

Source: Campbell (1973a) and Parkes (1975).

density and total home range reliably because of her small (8-ha) study site and low capture rates, she did estimate an 'average minimum feeding range' of 1·9–2·8 ha (mean 2·4 ha), see Table 4.4. Also in New Zealand, Brockie (1974a, cited by Kristiansson 1984) gave average home range (both sexes) as 18 ha (range of values 5·1–25·9 ha).

New Zealand has a mild climate, no natural predators (although hedgehogs have few anyway) and in suitable habitats the hedgehog population density seems to be higher than in Europe (Morris & Morris 1988). It is noteworthy that even with a high population density and presumably significant intra-specific competition, there is no evidence of territoriality. All the New Zealand studies have shown greatly overlapping individual ranges, and Campbell (1973a) noted no overt aggression.

STUDIES OF HOME RANGE IN OTHER HEDGEHOG SPECIES

In Israel, Schoenfeld & Yom-Tov (1985) radio-tracked 20 *Erinaceus concolor* (reported as *E. europaeus*) and 15 *Hemiechinus auritus*. Transmitters were normally attached for up to 4 months, but one male was tracked for 12 months. The study area, in the town of Givatayim near Tel Aviv, was an open space of about 0·5 km^2 of mixed habitats including waste ground with refuse (both organic and inorganic), a deserted citrus orchard, a wooded area and areas of sandstone with shrub cover. The ranges of both species overlapped with individuals of their own and the other species.

The range areas of four male and three female *E. concolor* were about 1·6 ha (both sexes; see Table 4.1) and they travelled around 300 m nightly at maximum walking speeds of about 17 m min^{-1} (measured over 5 min). These range sizes fall within the range observed in New Zealand for the ecologically similar *E. europaeus* (Parkes 1975, 0·5–5·7 ha; see Table 4.4) but are much smaller than in all other studies. Such apparent species differences are just as likely to be circumstantial, explained by the more localized sources of food and the rather omnivorous diet (with a proportion from domestic refuse) in the *E. concolor* study.

Hemiechinus auritus, although smaller, tended to walk further (around 1 km nightly) and faster, with a maximum walking speed of 200 m min^{-1} (measured over 5 min). It is noteworthy that Zherebtzova (1982) reported an average speed equivalent to 17–20 m min^{-1} for *H. auritus* and considered it capable of covering a remarkable 7–9 km during one 7–8·5-h activity period! Schoenfeld & Yom-Tov (1985) found *H. auritus* to be more strictly insectivorous than *E. concolor*, a possible factor in the apparent species difference in ranging behaviour. As in other hedgehog studies, males had larger average range areas (4·98 ha) than females (2·85 ha for non-lactating females; see Table 4.1) Interestingly, in contrast to the observations of *E. europaeus* by Morris (1986) and Philchagov (1988), two lactating females had comparatively small ranges (0·17 and 0·88 ha).

There is a frustrating lack of further studies of ranging behaviour in non-European hedgehogs, but at least we know that some *Hemiechinus* and *Paraechinus* are no less speedy than their European cousins! Hufnagl (1972) reported a speed of 10 km h^{-1} (167 m min^{-1}) for *P. aethiopicus* (followed by car over 10 min); Nowak & Paradiso (1983) cited speeds equivalent to 38·1 metres min^{-1} (when frightened or chasing a toad) and 18·3 m min^{-1} (normal 'trot') for hedgehogs in the Rajasthan desert (India), but it is unclear whether these data related to *P. micropus* or *H. collaris*, both of which are found in this area. Information about Brandt's hedgehog (*P. hypomelas*) is limited to a comment by Roberts (1977) that it might be somewhat more nomadic than other species. There is a clear need for much more fundamental work on all these and other, as yet unstudied, hedgehog species.

TERRITORIALITY AND 'SOCIAL' BEHAVIOUR

Hedgehogs generally fit Eisenberg's (1981) pattern of a 'type one' basic mammalian social system with a fundamentally solitary life-style. Males take no part in parental care and the young disperse soon after being weaned. Whether or not such an animal would be territorial is expected to depend on factors such as the distribution and abundance of resources like food, nest sites and sexual partners, as well as the relative costs of defending them against conspecifics. Kristiansson (1984) suggested that a simple analysis of daily range length in relation to home-range area could be used to indicate that, at least in theory, both male and female *E. europaeus* could economically defend a territory. He concluded, however, that territoriality was not favoured because of a complex of other factors, including patchy food dispersion and the unpredictable location of potential mates.

Field observations suggesting territorial behaviour in hedgehogs are rare and largely circumstantial. Nowak & Paradiso (1983) indicated that the desert hedgehog *P. aethiopicus* may be rather sedentary, occupying a single burrow and the same range all year and this could be construed as evidence for possible territoriality. The rather contradictory evidence used by Berthoud (1978) to suggest territorial behaviour by *E. europaeus* (see earlier) lacks support from all other studies which clearly show that hedgehogs do not defend any kind of exclusive area. Their home ranges often overlap, sometimes completely, with other individuals of either sex: e.g. for *E. europaeus* by Parkes (1975), Campbell (1973a), Reeve (1982), Boitani & Reggiani (1984), Kristiansson (1984) and for *H. auritus* and *E. concolor* by Schoenfeld & Yom-Tov (1985). All these studies also noted an apparent lack of territorial defence reactions from active animals, even when near each other. Despite the hedgehog's excellent sense of smell, there have been no reported observations of wild hedgehogs overtly using faeces, urine or specialized scent glands to mark boundaries or other locations (see Chapter 2).

Morris (1969) was the first to suggest that, rather than maintaining a defended area, European hedgehogs might use mutual avoidance to allow non-simultaneous use of the same area and thus avoid direct competition. Indeed, field studies have shown that hedgehogs rarely meet directly, and adults are usually found together only during courtship or when attracted to a localized food source—when fights sometimes ensue. Otherwise, fights are extremely rare, Wroot (1984a) saw only one during more than 102 h of close observation (6154 observations). In my study (Reeve 1981) involving 3460 behavioural records (2568 of which were clearly visible), I recorded only 17 non-sexual encounters. Only four of these encounters were fights in which the animals attempted to butt or bite one another, and another four involved no more than some snorting and flank to flank manoeuvring. All such aggressive encounters were brief, only involved males and there were no injuries. The remaining encounters occurred when animals (of either sex) approached to within a few metres of each other, then paused, sniffed the air and changed direction. The animals were silent, showing no overt aggression and I could only be sure that an encounter was taking place when both participants were clearly visible; thus such encounters were probably under-recorded. Similar descriptions by other workers (Campbell 1973a, Boitani & Reggiani 1984) provide evidence for the suggestion that hedgehogs use body odour cues to maintain a 'personal space'. Boitani & Reggiani (1984) noted that hedgehogs of the same sex were never separated by less than 20 m. If hedgehogs do use body odours in this way, there may be some association with the intriguing behaviour of 'self-anointing' (Chapter 7).

The idea that hedgehogs may use a system of mutual avoidance has thus gained general support from field observations. Similar 'social' systems have been reported for domestic cats (*Felis catus*) (Leyhausen 1963), and several other carnivore species including racoons (*Procyon lotor*), kinkajous (*Potos flavus*) brown and black bears (*Ursus arctos* and *Ursus americanus*) (studies cited by Ewer 1973).

Although normally shunning each other's company, hedgehogs can sometimes be very tolerant of the presence of others. Schoenfeld & Yom-Tov (1985) recorded 10 adult *Erinaceus concolor* under a dense hedgerow 11 m long and 2 m wide. Similarly, when food is put out in gardens, it is not uncommon to find several hedgehogs close together or even feeding from the same bowl. Lindemann (1951) showed that captive hedgehogs would sometimes try to attack each other on sight (when separated by glass) but at other times they would be more tolerant. Studies of captives have shown that hedgehogs can form hierarchical relationships when confined together (Lindemann 1951, Dimelow 1963a, Herter 1965b) but the hierarchies bore little relation to apparent physical size or prowess and the relationships were not constant (Lindemann 1951). The so-called 'dominance hierarchy', in which individuals hold a 'rank' relative to others, is very much a human conceptual construct which has often been applied anthropomorphically to animals forced to compete for resources by the conditions of captivity, whereas in nature they would avoid doing so by other behavioural means. Although the concept is not without value if applied cautiously in the analysis of complex competitive interactions which occur naturally in highly social animals, such as the primates (Deag 1980), its application to wild hedgehogs seems inappropriate.

HEDGEHOG RANGING BEHAVIOUR: A SUMMARY OVERVIEW

Only the European hedgehog (*E. europaeus*) has been the subject of more than one radio-tracking study and generalizations are risky given our sketchy or non-existent knowledge of home range in other hedgehog species. Hedgehogs can sometimes travel up to 3 or 4 km per night, but a few hundred metres (up to around 1 km) is more typical, especially for females and non-breeding males. European hedgehogs seem to remain in roughly the same area for several years, possibly for their entire adult life. There is good evidence that none of the species studied are territorial and European hedgehogs appear to minimize potentially competitive interactions by mutual avoidance.

Theoretical predictions of minimum feeding range can be obtained from models such that devised by McNab (1963) which uses observed interrelationships between body size, basal metabolic rate, range size and food type; hedgehogs (insectivores) fall into the 'hunter' category. Predicted minimum feeding range area (based on adult bodyweights) is roughly 3–6 ha, a figure in line with the minimum ranges recorded for hedgehogs (Table 4.1). Thus the results obtained from field studies broadly match theoretical expectations. Naturally, such a minimum range might often be exceeded under certain circumstances, e.g. food availability may be low or variable, or intake may exceed normal maintenance levels to build body condition before and after hibernation. Home range may also be large for reasons other than food supply; sexually active males search extensively for receptive females, and the range must encompass suitable day-time nesting sites as well as feeding areas.

CHAPTER 5

Nest Construction and Use

THE vital importance of nests and refuges in the lives of small mammals is not always fully appreciated. As in other mammals, studies of hedgehogs have usually concentrated on other aspects of their biology and the behaviour of active animals. But refuges are of very great significance in hedgehog ecology and provide both concealment and protection from weather:

(i) as a day-time retreat during active seasons ('summer nests' or 'day nests').
(ii) for breeding females and their litters of altricial young ('breeding nests').
(iii) for periods of up to several months, during which the hedgehogs may hibernate or aestivate (undergo a summer period of torpor) when there is harsh weather and/or food shortage ('hibernacula' or 'winter nests'; there is no distinct term for aestivation nests).

I prefer the descriptive terms above for the refuges used by hedgehogs, even though they sometimes hide in rock crevices or burrows in soil (a normal practice for some species). Although the term 'nest' carries mental associations with the provision of bedding materials (not always used) and breeding, it is a simple term in common use. 'Den' is sometimes used but because of its connotation with caves or hollows is inappropriate for above-ground nests. Knight (1962) suggested the alternative 'home' but this implies a degree of exclusivity and permanence which is also rather misleading.

The nests of hedgehogs both in the wild and in captivity are fairly well described for several species, but there are few studies of the way in which free-living hedgehogs use their nests. Nests are usually well-concealed and very difficult to find (Plate 13). To determine which individual (if any) is inside, one would have to disturb both the nest and the occupant; animals in rock crevices and burrows would have to be dug out! For these reasons serious long-term behavioural studies are virtually impossible without radio-tracking and most useful information has been obtained during the home-

117

range studies already discussed in Chapter 4. However, although the hedgehog in western Europe (*Erinaceus europaeus*) is again the most comprehensively studied species, we can build up reasonable comparative information about several of the other species from the many descriptive accounts of nests found in the wild and the reported activities of captive animals.

NEST CONSTRUCTION

The two species of European hedgehogs (*Erinaceus europaeus* and *E. concolor*) appear to use a similar range of nest types and sites, depending more on circumstance than on species differences. Many previous studies (e.g. Chard 1936, Knight 1962, Dimelow 1963a, Morris 1969) have suggested that summer nests, in comparison with winter nests, are relatively insubstantial, used casually and often dispensed with altogether. Although this is often true, there is in fact no clear distinction between the construction of summer and winter nests despite the obvious requirement for hibernacula to be especially well sited, robust and carefully constructed, if they are to provide effective protection for torpid animals over long periods. Of course, a poor quality or badly sited summer nest is less likely to cause serious problems for its occupant, but it must be remembered that hedgehogs are active from roughly March to November, during which the weather may be anything but clement!

In my own study in Britain, I found that most of the 58 summer nests examined conformed closely to the detailed description of winter nests by Morris (1973) although the need to avoid undue disturbance meant that I could not measure wall thickness. They were built and used all through the summer, a fact also noted by Berthoud (1978) in Switzerland and in other radio-tracking studies. It would seem that where suitable nesting materials are to be found summer nests are normally fairly robust. Indeed my own observations show that sometimes summer nests, possibly somewhat refurbished, may be adopted as hibernacula as winter approaches. Although hedgehogs usually use a nest of some kind during summer days, sometimes they lie outside a nearby nest or simply rest under the cover of vegetation. During 3 years of field observations, I have found hedgehogs lying outside in this way on only three separate occasions; when approached, they remained still, but bristled and crouched defensively. Ognev (1928) recounted similar incidents for hedgehogs in the CIS and Boitani & Reggiani (1984) reported five such instances in Italy during warm weather. In Israel, Schoenfeld & Yom-Tov (1985) reported 13 cases where animals simply hid in the foliage, in one exceptional case with its head under foliage and its back exposed! The suggestion that nests are not built in summer could originate from field work carried out only in fine weather, when the hedgehogs may not depend on a nest for weather protection, although they could still benefit from the concealment provided by a day nest. Dimelow (1963a) reported that captive animals did not build a nest when the ambient temperature exceeded 16°C.

In my study, in Britain, the summer nightly minima were rarely as high as 16°C. On the three occasions when a radio-tracked animal used no nest the nights were cool (down to 11–14°C) but the following days were warm (21–28°C). Oddly, on other similarly warm days the same animals used nests.

Even in the summer in Britain the nights and early mornings can be chilly and dewy at ground level, and as the hedgehog generally retires at around dawn it is hardly likely to be feeling overheated! Nest sites are usually heavily shaded by vegetation or other objects and are thus unlikely to become very hot by day. Both summer and winter nests in natural habitats are most commonly found above ground, under brambles or other ground vegetation, and are normally constructed of dry broad leaves, although other construction materials may be used depending on the local vegetation, and a burrow may be used (see later).

In mild climates such as in New Zealand (Parkes 1975, Moors 1979) the nests may be relatively flimsy, constructed merely of grass or pine needles, but in colder temperate areas, hedgehogs typically build fairly substantial nests to rest in during the day and a very robust hibernaculum. Morris (1973), in his study of 185 hibernacula in Britain, pointed out how well-made nests using broad leaves have very good qualities of weather-resistance and insulation upon which hedgehogs depend for protection when hibernating. He found that a good nest will keep an internal temperature of between 1 and 5°C even with an outside temperature range of −8 to +10°C. In Denmark, Walhovd (1979) found that although ambient temperatures ranged from −11 to +13°C, the temperature inside four occupied nests remained above freezing for 78–99% of the time and most commonly ranged from 0 to 4°C. Of course, the temperature inside inhabited nests is also affected by the temperature regulation of their occupants, who actively maintain a body temperature above freezing. Between 1 and 4°C seems to be an appropriate body temperature for a hibernating *E. europaeus*, low enough to conserve energy while avoiding the freezing of tissues which would result in frost-bite (Chapter 6).

The availability of suitable nest sites and materials, as well as the animal's ability to make a good nest, are likely to be some of the most critical factors determining winter survival in colder climates. This is probably why hedgehogs are not normally found above the tree-line in mountain areas, although they may persist in areas with a good scrub cover, and the northern limit of their distribution in Scandinavia and the CIS coincides strikingly with the northern limit of deciduous (broadleafed) trees.

Good descriptive accounts of materials and methods used in nest construction are to be found in virtually all popular works about hedgehogs. Descriptions generally agree, with only minor differences, but few contain much hard data. Morris' studies (e.g. 1973) have provided the best data on winter nest construction and the following account derives largely from his observations. Several further studies, including my own (Reeve & Morris 1985), have corroborated and extended this work to the construction and use of summer nests.

Nests above ground

These are not merely heaps of leaves with 'no definite arrangement' as supposed by Barrett-Hamilton (1911), but carefully made structures forming a compact dome 30–60 cm in diameter. The nest may be based in a shallow depression or scrape in the soil and thus often does not protrude greatly from a surrounding depth of leaf litter. The nest walls are typically of closely packed dry broad leaves forming a laminated structure up to 20 cm thick. The best and most durable nests are those supported externally by springy low-lying vegetation such as brambles, or lodged under tree stumps, fallen logs and so on (Tables 5.1 and 5.2). Morris' study of winter nest sites showed that nest orientation was not significantly predisposed to any particular direction nor were nests sited with respect to shelter from the sun. Thus sun-warming of some winter nests did occur and most animals aroused and moved to new nests at some time during the winter months.

The hedgehog builds its nest by gathering up dry leaves in its mouth (not on its spines!) until it has created a substantial pile, well packed under the supporting vegetation. Knight (1962) reported sufficient material being gathered over 1 night, but Berthoud (1982) wrote that unless there is a convenient mass of suitable material, the hedgehog may need 2 or 3 days and many trips to amass sufficient material. Using a burrowing and rolling action, the hedgehog forms the nest chamber within the leaf pile by combing actions of its paws and spines, effectively aligning the leaves and compacting them to form the typical laminated structure of the walls. More leaves may be added from the inside as necessary, until the walls are tightly packed and firmly braced against the supporting vegetation outside. The finished nest has a roughly spherical inner chamber which may be lined with softer vegetation such as moss, leaves or hay (Herter 1968). The chamber is a fairly tight fit for the hedgehog which just has room to curl up inside. The entrance may be

TABLE 5.1   *Choices of winter nest site for the European hedgehog* (Erinaceus europaeus) *in Britain.*

Location	No. of nests in each site	% of total in each site
Under low brambles	54	29·2
Under brushwood (woodpile)	38	20·5
Against log	24	13·0
Under grass tussock	23	12·4
Among nettle stalks	15	8·1
Under loose leaves	14	7·6
Other sites	17	9·2
Total:	185	100·0%

Source: Morris (1973).

TABLE 5.2   *Details of 58 summer nest sites and construction.*

Nest site	n
1. Nests supported from above and the side (67·2%)	
Under brambles	21
Under sticks and dead wood	4
Under loose pile of leaves	4
Under piles of logs	3
Miscellaneous (under or inside—paint tin, iron sheet, garden shed, concrete slab, compost heap)	7
2. Nests supported on one side only, or unsupported (24·1%)	
Against base of tree or bush	10
Against earth hummock, metal water tank, or wall	3
Free standing in leaf litter	1
3. In burrows (8·6%)	
Short tunnel resembling rabbit burrow	4
Horizontal passage into tree stump	1

Of 67 daytime resting sites located only 58 were accessible enough for close inspection. Of those 58·5% were in thorny or stinging undergrowth (brambles (*Rubus*), holly (*Ilex*), hawthorn (*Crataegus*) or nettles (*Urtica*)).
Source: Reeve and Morris (1985).

concealed or may sometimes form a short tunnel of leaves; Fig. 5.1 illustrates the presumed construction process.

Morris has emphasized the importance of external support for the winter nest. A well-made nest, despite being occupied for 4–6 months at the most, may last for a year or more, occasionally even up to 18 months. Its tightly packed structure limits the action of detritivores and decomposer organisms hence outlasting the surrounding leaf litter which has mostly broken down and vanished in about 6 months (see later). Many nests are used only briefly before being abandoned and only a few of these may be re-occupied later, though Morris (1988a) made it clear that winter nests are never used again the next winter.

Moors (1979) examined 30 nests in sand dunes around Pukepuke lagoon in the Manawatu (New Zealand). Most of the nests (87%) were in tussocks on the sand dune slopes or crests; the slacks and hollows, which become waterlogged in wet weather, were avoided. Nests were sited amongst dense vegetation and built mainly of dead marram grass stems with the incorporation of rushes, pine needles and other available on-site materials. The nests were spherical (20–30 cm diameter with walls 0·5–5 cm thick) and usually well constructed but four of the 26 in dune tussocks were flimsy, hardly covering the hedgehog inside. There was no evidence of permanent nest entrances and the hedgehogs merely closed the hole in the wall after entering and did not seal exit holes upon leaving. Moors, finding only one torpid animal during his

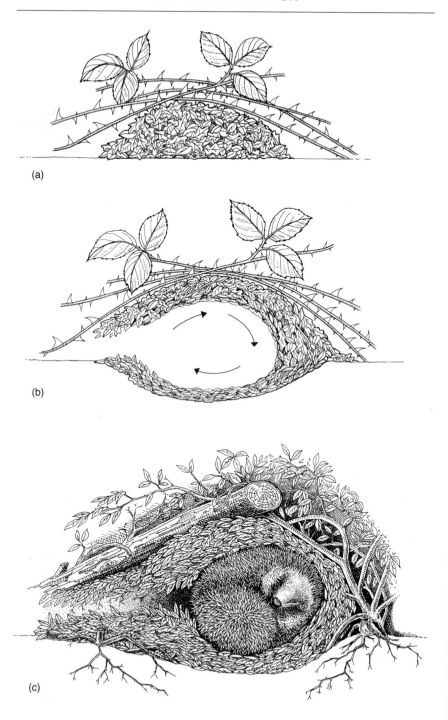

(a)

(b)

(c)

study, concluded that in the relatively clement climate of the Manawatu, in which hibernation is not obligatory, nest construction was less critical than for British hedgehogs.

In Tuscany (Italy) Boitani & Reggiani (1984) detailed 120 *E. europaeus* summer nest sites, of which there were: 34 (28·3%) among bushes of the sand dunes; 30 (25%) under brambles; 24 (21·7%) in tall grass, usually on ditch embankments; seven (5.8%) in dry leaves under downy oak thickets; seven (5·8%) at the base of rush clumps; five (4·2%) under pine needles; four (3·3%) under ferns; four (3·3%) under cane. The use of grass nests was more common in summer while of seven hibernation nests found, all but one were in dry leaves among brambles.

Schoenfeld & Yom-Tov (1985) also gave details of 52 *E. concolor* summer nests in Israel. Out of 52 nests 26 (50%) were under foliage, dry grass and man-made objects such as polyethylene sheet or paper. Thirteen (25%) were under hard cover (e.g. rocks) and lined with a few leaves or grasses. In the remaining 13 cases the animals used no nest but simply rested, usually in a concealed place.

Hedgehog nests have been reported in an amazing variety of natural and anthropogenic places: hidden spots in hedgerows; amongst almost any kind of dense ground vegetation; rock crevices; hollow tree trunks; piles of leaves, logs or brushwood; areas under the raised floors of garden and agricultural out-buildings; a disused coal cellar and even barn attics and a thatched roof!

Breeding nests are by nature temporary constructions having a similar basic structure to the ones already described and they vary considerably in their constituents. Of course they are much larger so as to accommodate the mother and her litter of around four or five youngsters which will each weigh over 200 g before finally leaving the nest. Lüttich (1928, cited by Herter 1956) related that a female may build a makeshift nest extension for herself in order to get some peace from the youngsters! However, Herter commented that he had never seen this himself despite many years of observing captive animals. In the wild the mother may build and use more than one nest while rearing the litter and, unless she abandons or eats the young, will almost certainly move the youngsters promptly to a new nest if disturbed (Chapter 8).

When asleep by day hedgehogs do not roll up tightly as is often supposed but usually sleep on their side, muscles and spines relaxed, only partially curled and with head and legs protruding. In warm weather or in the warmth

FIG. 5.1 *Presumed method used by a European hedgehog to build a nest using broad leaves. (a) A leaf pile is collected under some ground vegetation (or other supporting structure), in this case, brambles and twigs. (b) The hedgehog forms a nest chamber by rotating its body within the leaf pile to compact the leaves which are restrained by the brambles. (c) The finished nest has firm walls of layered leaves and a tightly fitting nest chamber which may be lined with moss. There may be a short entrance tunnel. Main source: Morris (1973).*

of captivity they may stretch out, belly flat to the ground, and they may lie partly out of the nest entrance. At the slightest disturbance the hedgehog is instantly ready to bristle and roll up tightly in the nest. Even hibernating hedgehogs will do this and anyone finding a hedgehog in its nest may well suppose that they spend the whole winter tensed and bristling. Such disturbed hedgehogs may make a snake-like hissing or a coarse 'huffing' noise to deter intruders.

Nests in burrows

The use of burrows by European hedgehogs is reported widely and it would seem to be quite a common practice for both summer and winter nests. In Britain several workers have reported the use of simple, blind burrows up to a metre or more in length with a small chamber at the bottom (e.g. Chard 1936, Lancum 1951, Knight 1962, Reeve & Morris 1985). Such burrows may have been dug by the hedgehog or taken over from rabbits. During my own study (Reeve & Morris 1985) four summer nests were of this type (roughly 7% of the 58 nests in the sample).

In southern Russia, Ognev (1928) described hedgehogs (*E. concolor*) making large above-ground nests of leaves and grass, and in the steppes beneath boxthorn bushes or under 'feathergrass'. However, although above-ground nests are still used, hedgehogs of both European species in continental Europe and the CIS seem more ready to excavate elaborate burrows than in Britain. This may be a response to the harsh continental winters, although the use of burrows is by no means confined to the winter since they also make elaborate summer nest burrows.

Herter (1956, 1968) reported that European hedgehogs occasionally dig their own burrow in the ground. His description of a 30-cm tunnel, frequently with two openings (one being plugged depending on the wind direction) seems more complex than the rather simple burrows described in Britain.

Ognev (1928) related several good examples of nesting burrows which I have paraphrased and summarized here as they contain some unique features.

The southernmost records are from the wormwood and 'feathergrass' steppes of the Askaniya-Nova region (east of Odessa on the northern side of the Black Sea; roughly 42.5°N 54°E). An *E. concolor* burrow was found in a soft earth mound next to an old fox earth. The 2-m passage slanted downwards to about 1 m in depth. The hedgehog was seen asleep at the burrow entrance in the shade, and retreated when approached.

Two very elaborate burrows, apparently breeding nests, were also found in this region. The first was abandoned and consisted of a lower chamber in the form of a rounded unlined 'hall' 14 cm deep and 30.5 cm long, plus an upper chamber with a strong roundly arched ceiling (26 × 22 cm) so that a wide entrance to the lower chamber was formed in the front. Wormwood twigs made up the ceiling sides the central part being packed with concentric arches of grass. The second burrow was of exactly the same form and locality but still in use with one young still inside, another resting outside the nest.

Around Orenburg (just south-west of the southernmost tip of the Ural range near the Kazakhstan border, roughly 52°N 55°E) *E. concolor* used simple burrows on hillsides and gradual slopes. Winter nests are in gently sloping burrows, often sited between the roots of bushes and trees, up to about 152 cm long and reaching a depth of no more than about 76 cm.

In the centre of the Ryazan region (55°N 39°E, just south-east of Moscow) where there is little forest, an occupied *E. concolor* breeding nest burrow, lined with leaves, was found amongst the dense grass of an orchard.

The most northerly record of a winter nest burrow is from the Olonets region which, at around 61°N 33°E, is close to the northernmost range of *E. europaeus*). The burrow was large with many exits and filled with aspen leaves. Although I shall discuss nest sharing later, it notable that Ognev stated that 'Almost always several hedgehogs are located in a single nest for winter hibernation'.

Frustratingly there are few ecological data available for the Chinese hedgehog *E. amurensis* (Corbet 1988). Its habitat ranges from treeless cultivated areas to forest and forest-steppes. This species appears to shun truly arid areas and its northern distribution is, like *E. europaeus* and *E. concolor*, largely confined to the northernmost limit of deciduous forest. It would thus seem reasonable to suppose that this species is broadly similar to the other two, making use of either above-ground nests in a variety of forms or burrows, depending upon circumstance.

The Genus Hemiechinus

This genus of long-eared hedgehogs may tolerate fairly arid regions of grass and scrubland but tend not to be found in severe desert conditions. There is considerable subspecific variation within the widespread species *H. auritus* (Chapter 2) which is likely to have resulted in a variety of nesting strategies, but the literature available often lacks detail and suffers from the taxonomic confusion surrounding this genus. An example of this problem is a report by Nowak & Paradiso (1983) that *H. auritus* hibernated in colder parts of its range (such as the mountains of Pakistan and the Punjab of northern India), but they did not state whether above-ground nests or burrows were used. Furthermore, according to Corbet (1988), it is likely that they were writing about what is now termed *H. collaris* for the northern Indian records (called *H. auritus collaris* by many earlier authors). When active, typical hedgehogs of this genus seem to use simple burrows as day nests. Herter (1956) mentioned that captive *H. auritus* chose not to line their nests under piles of stones. This, plus the fact that a captive female gave birth on the smooth sandy floor of their nest box which she had cleared of any debris, licking the young clean (Poduschka & Poduschka 1986b), suggests that no nest lining is used, even in breeding nests. Nowak & Paradiso (1983) surmised that, in Egypt, this species uses existing shelter and seldom digs its own burrow, but acknowledged that elsewhere it is reputed to build burrows of up to 150 cm long.

Ognev (1928) quoted an account of *H. auritus* nesting in steppe and semi-desert areas of the CIS, pointing out a preference for soft ground (such as the sandy slopes of dunes) in which it can dig relatively deep burrows which descend at a slight angle. It may also make use of rock fissures. In Libya, Hufnagl (1972) reported that they hid under stones or in 'small caves' and also used short single-entranced burrows.

A radio-tracking study of *H. auritus* by Schoenfeld & Yom-Tov (1985) confirmed that this species' preference for burrowing was also true in Israel. Out of 37 resting places 26 (70%) were burrows, 10 (27%) were depressions under stones and one was in a pile of foliage at the base of a tree. The burrows were mostly L-shaped 10–50 cm long and 10–17 cm in diameter and usually opened out onto a slope. Burrow air temperature, mainly determined by soil temperature, was more constantly around 25°C (range 20–28°C) while the ambient temperature ranged between 15 and 36°C. The presence of a hedgehog in the burrow had little effect on burrow temperature. Contrastingly in above-ground nests, nest air temperature was 1–2°C higher than ambient when a hedgehog was present.

In soft soil *H. auritus* was able to dig a 10-cm hole in 5 min and could dig several burrows during one night, changing its resting place almost nightly. Although adult hedgehogs only ever nested singly, they used the burrows of other hedgehogs in their absence.

Interestingly Schoenfeld & Yom-Tov clearly reported finding three Y-shaped breeding nest burrows, each with young in one branch and a female in the other. This Y-shape is not mentioned by other reports of nests in this genus. Ognev (1928) related an account of an *H. auritus* breeding burrow with five blind young in a sandy region (with brome grass and *Euphorbia* spp.); took the form of a 'flat chamber' dug in a small mound. A short passage (roughly 10 cm long) led from the unlined nest to the exterior.

Krishna & Prakash (1955) reported that wild *H. collaris* and *Paraechinus micropus* from the deserts of Rajasthan (India) both used very similar individual burrows, invariably under hedge or dense bush and never in open ground. If disturbed by a stick inserted into their burrow they made a snake-like hissing noise, presumably similar to the noise previously mentioned for European hedgehogs.

Krishna & Prakash noted that in firm soil the burrows were simple, with a straight passage 30·5–61 cm long and 20–35·5 cm deep. The single entrance was 6·5–10 cm in diameter and the inner blind ends were dilated slightly to form a chamber typically 9–13 cm in diameter but of rather larger diameter in breeding nests (11·5–18 cm); no lining material was mentioned. In areas with looser soil, burrows 122–152 cm long have been observed. The animal lies in the burrow either half rolled-up or fully stretched. Roberts (1977) reported that *H. auritus* occupy the same burrow all year, but this does not match the impression gained from the prolific burrowing observed by Krishna &

Prakash. One animal, kept by Roberts in an open enclosure in the Punjab, dug a burrow and hibernated in it from 8 November to 2 March.

Krishna & Prakash's study included careful observation of digging technique which involved powerful lateral strokes of the broad-clawed forelimbs to loosen and forcefully throw earth out behind. Once the burrow reached around 30 cm in length the hedgehog periodically reversed up the burrow and kicked out the accumulated earth, with rapid alternating movements of the hind feet. Hedgehogs were never seen to use their snouts in digging. In firm soil they usually completed their 30–38-cm burrows in 3 or 4 h. As their spines make reversing in burrows rather awkward the hedgehogs entered and left their burrows head-first, somehow turning round in the remarkably small space inside. Interestingly, Krishna & Prakash observed that the hedgehogs protected their faces when pushing into a burrow, by pulling down the anterior portion of the *orbicularis* muscle over the snout. This requires no special adaptation because all hedgehogs use this ability in anti-predator defence. It may well be used by all hedgehog species when burrowing.

Roberts (1977) gave a brief account of nesting in the very large subspecies *H. auritus megalotis* in Pakistan where it is found in steppic mountain regions up to 2500 m and is quite common at altitudes of roughly 900 m. It is similar to ordinary *H. auritus* in that it is solitary and digs its own burrow (sited under a large stone or rocks) and, with well-developed claws on its fore-feet, is capable of digging in quite hard soil. Observations of captive animals indicated that, by day, they usually sought out dark corners, presumably a response to being unable to burrow. In summer months they will aestivate during periods of food scarcity. In regions where the winters may be very cold, with temperatures down to −6·5°C, they hibernate.

The Genus Paraechinus

Few details are known of the nesting habits of these three species of desert-adapted hedgehogs, but one can sketch out a general picture using several accounts.

In two of the species the use of burrows very similar to those found in *Hemiechinus* seems usual. But *P. hypomelas* seems to be a more wide-ranging, nomadic form, hiding out by day in rock crevices and less inclined to burrow. Roberts (1977) observed that compared with other hedgehogs, they seemed ill-adapted to burrowing, with noticeably longer-looking legs and shorter, blunter claws. Captives tended to seek higher ground before their daytime rest. However, Ognev (1928) recorded that, at least in some conditions, they will burrow. According to local reports east of Ashkhabad (an arid area close to the Iran border, east of the Caspian sea) *P. hypomelas* hides in burrows 1 m deep during the day, often in the sandy embankments of railway tracks. Nothing is known about its nesting behaviour when breeding.

As already mentioned, Krishna & Prakash (1955) found that *P. micropus* and *Hemiechinus collaris* shared rather similar habits, but *P. micropus*, though always found in burrows in the wild, avoided digging its own burrows when in semi-captivity, preferring instead to remain under logs or under dense bushes, or to use burrows vacated by *H. collaris*. Roberts (1977) suggested that *P. micropus* is rather a sedentary species often keeping to the same burrow and range throughout a 12-month period. Generally observations support the impression that this species, rather like *P. hypomelas*, is a reluctant burrower but is certainly a capable excavator since Krishna & Prakash (1955) described a remarkable three-chambered burrow in which three captive individuals rested by day!

Where *P. micropus* is found there is generally plentiful insect life even in winter. However, it is likely to aestivate during periods of drought or food scarcity and captive animals have been known to undergo prolonged fasts (3–4 weeks) without apparent harm (Roberts 1977).

Very little detail is known about the nesting habits of *P. aethiopicus*. Hufnagl (1972) merely stated this fact and reported that in Egypt and the Fezzan (Libya) it has been found resting by day 'in cliffs', presumably in rock crevices. In northern Algeria it may nest in clumps of vegetation (Sellami *et al.* 1989), and in Egypt it may use burrows under shrubs or amongst rocks (Osborn & Helmy 1980 cited by Corbet 1988). On the evidence from captive animals kept by Herter (1956, 1968) it would seem that this species can dig well, excavating burrows with many entrances and exits, but does not line its nest. A female *P. aethiopicus* kept by Eisentraut (1952) gave birth to a single baby in a sand and peat hollow making no use of the hay, woodshavings and leaves available.

The Genus Atelerix

From the few reports of wild and captive animals it appears that these hedgehogs behave much like the others found in semi-arid regions. They can use a wide variety of refuges but most reported nest sites are above-ground. Kingdon (1974) reported that *Atelerix albiventris* was not found in water-logged areas and most common on well-drained soils in areas where they can sleep in termitaries, rock crevices, buildings or under tangles of brushwood or dry leaf litter. As in other species they may sleep curled up or lie full-length.

Summary

Overall it is quite noticeable that hedgehogs of all species have broadly similar nesting habits. Various habitat types provide different refuge possibilities and so it is not particularly surprising that those hedgehog species from hotter and more arid climates tend to rely more on burrows than those in Europe. In arid areas there may be a dearth of nesting cover and suitable leaf litter for use as nest lining and in any case the need for thermal insulation may be less. Furthermore, in an underground burrow or deep in a rock crevice, the environment would be cooler, with a higher humidity and more effectively buffered against environmental fluctuations than in a nest at the surface. Thus the hedgehog using a burrow in such an environment can maintain homeostasis more easily. Conversely in cold climates the buffering effect of a burrow would moderate a harsh climate in exactly the same way.

NEST USE

Summer nests

As with many other aspects of hedgehog behaviour there are very large individual differences in nesting habits that often belie generalizations. However, the few detailed studies of European species do share some consistent features with my study in Britain (Reeve 1981, Reeve & Morris 1985). Although some nests are flimsy and used a few times at most, the majority are well constructed and are strong enough to be used periodically throughout the active season. Such nests may be abandoned for days or even months before being re-used, and may even be used later as a winter nest. Both sexes may use several nests during one season, change their nests quite frequently and are rarely faithful to the same one for any period, although 'old favourites' may be revisited often. One extremely restless male used 15 nests, and changed nest 41 times in only 68 days! Males, probably because of their larger ranges, tended to use more nests and changed site significantly more frequently (about every 3 days) than non-breeding females (about every 10 days). Details of these results are shown in Fig. 5.2 and Table 5.3. For successfully breeding females, which normally remain with their offspring in one place, one would naturally expect even fewer nest changes.

When following radio-tracked animals, especially males, I found it very hard to guess in which of the many known nest sites my hedgehogs would end up. Existing nest sites seemed well known to the animals. Sometimes after a long night of following an individual, just when I was thinking that I would be out all day as well as all night, it would apparently decide abruptly to retire and make a rapid and very accurate bee-line for its choice of day nest. Sometimes the distances travelled in the last 'dash' were considerable (several tens of metres) and sometimes the nest would be, as far as I knew, a site previously unused by the animal.

Morris (1986) in a brief radio-tracking study of three hedgehogs in forest habitat in Britain noted similar patterns of nest use. One female used three nests in 21 days with four nest changes, another with young used three nests in 20 days and changed twice, and a male over 19 days made six changes among four nests. Another study in farmland by Morris (1988b) yielded similar data. One particularly active adult male used at least eight different nests in 20 days, whereas a female used only three or four nests in 16 days.

The study by Boitani & Reggiani (1984) who located 120 nests while radio-tracking *E. europaeus* in Tuscany (Italy) also confirmed this general pattern of nest use (Table 5.4). All non-hibernating hedgehogs used more than one nest, the majority (62%) being occupied more than once. Of the nests that were re-used, some were permanently abandoned after a few days while others (64%)

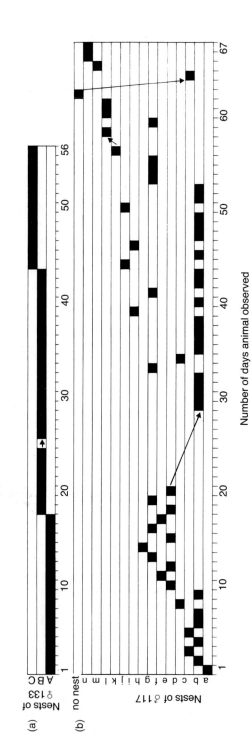

FIG. 5.2 *The different nest use patterns of a selected female* (a) *without young, and a male* (b) *European hedgehog in Britain. The black bars indicate periods of nest occupancy, the arrows indicate days when no observations were made. In the study there was a clear tendency for females to use fewer nests and change nests less frequently than males, although not all showed such a clear difference as these two animals. Source: Reeve and Morris (1985).*

TABLE 5.3 *Nest use in radio-tracked European hedgehogs in Britain showing the number of days each animal was tracked, the number of nests used in that time and the number of nest changes made.*

Year	Animal no.	Tracking period (days)	No. of nest sites[b]	No. of change	Days/nest	Days/change
Males						
1978	106	39	10	26	3·9	1·5
	117	49	7	15	7·0	3·3
1979	105	72	4	15	18·0	2·1
	106	118	11	42	10·7	2·8
	108	32	4	25	8·0	2·9
	117	68	15	41	4·5	1·7
	136	7	2	1	3·5	7·0
	173	9	2	4	4·5	2·5
	176[a]	42	3	13	14·0	3·2
Females						
1978	107	29	2	4	14·5	7·2
	111	42	6	10	7·0	4·2
	139	14	9	8	1·5	1·7
	150[a]	33	6	7	5·5	4·7
1979	107	88	6	27	14·7	3·3
	133	56	3	2	18·7	28·0
	139	40	4	3	10·0	13·3
	180[a]	73	3	6	24·3	12·2

[a]Juveniles.
[b]Includes resting sites where no nest was used.
Source: Reeve and Morris (1985).

were returned to after periods of between 1 and 169 days. In the spring, when there is a general increase in activity, nests are more frequently changed, with longer lapses in occupancy. Statistically significant sex differences, along the lines already described, are apparent from these Italian data. Females used the same nest continuously for longer periods, thus both the total number of nests used and the number of changes of nest in any given time were less than for the males. This is likely to be, but (as evidenced by my own study) not necessarily, due to litter rearing by females. The mean distances separating the consecutively used nests of males are, as might be predicted from their larger home ranges, significantly greater than those for females. Using Boitani & Reggiani's data I have calculated an overall mean separation of consecutively used nests for eight males of roughly 593 m (range 50–4300 m!) and for five females about 244 m (range 50–386 m).

The tendency in the Italian study for females' nests to be more tightly clustered in their smaller home-range areas was also evident in other radio-tracking studies, including my own. Five male and four female *E. europaeus*

TABLE 5.4 Nest use data of active hedgehogs using published data (and values calculated using these data) from a study of Erinaceus europaeus in Italy.

Hedgehog no.	No. of days observed	No. of nests	Days/nest	Maximum no. of days of use of same nest	Maximum no. of days of continuous use of same nest	Mean distance between consecutive nests (m) (range)
Females						
203	88	12	7·3	12	12	140 (50–375)
204	64	9	7·1	20	20	133 (75–225)
205	98	11	8·9	13	13	270 (50–950)
218	31	5	6·2	7	7	386 (250–590)
219	23	4	5·75	6	3	292 (100–600)
Mean		8·2	7·06	11·6	11·0	244·2 (Mean of means)
s.d.		3·33	1·22	5·6	2·55	107·59

Males				{16}	{16}	
206[a]	76	10	7·6	7	3	535 (50–950)
213	53	10	5·3	7	3	1351 (150–4300)
214	32	9	3·56	4	2	923 (100–2360)
215	45	16	2·8	6	3	675 (50–1750)
216	30	11	2·73	2	—	437 (125–750)
217	53	10	5·3	10	8	341 (50–700)
220	17	4	4·25	3	2	233 (125–350)
221	24	8	3·0	5	4	251 (100–550)
Mean		9·75	4·32	5·29	3·67	593·25 (Mean of means)
s.d.		3·56	1·68	2·69	6·44	383·21
Statistically significant sex difference?		No	Yes **	Yes *	Yes *	No

s.d. = standard deviation of mean. Two-tailed independent sample t-test results: * $p < 0.05$; ** $p < 0.01$.
[a]206 excluded from some calculations as activity interrupted by hibernation periods.
Source: Boitani & Reggiani (1984).

were tracked by Moors (1979) in a area of sand dunes in the Manawatu, around Pukepuke lagoon (New Zealand). Nest separation was very variable, but averaged around 300 m for males (range 50–650 m) and 60 m for females (range 15–45 m). On farmland in Britain, Morris (1988b) found the nests of an adult male to be widely spread within its large home range and consecutively used nests were separated by 150–930 m or more (values estimated from the map published). In contrast, Morris found three of the female's nests to be separated by only 50 m or less; two were so close that they might have been the same nest. A fourth nest, used only once, was 250 m from the rest.

The nest use patterns revealed by these studies are generally corroborated by other workers such as Kristiansson's studies in Sweden, but can show subtle variations as in the study by Berthoud (1978) who radio-tracked seven *E. europaeus* in the region of Yverdon (Vaud, Switzerland). He reported that they made a principal summer nest in the forest which was occupied regularly and one or several secondary refuges, used only occasionally, scattered around their feeding range. Outside the study area, many principal nests were observed in parks or gardens. This description implies a rather less haphazard pattern of use than has been found in other studies.

There is always a strong possibility that hedgehogs, which are very sensitive to any disturbance (such as researchers poking around their nest sites), may change their nests more frequently when under investigation than would occur naturally. In my own study, although my presence during their active period could have had an unsettling effect, I am confident that nest disturbance did not normally occur. In some other studies, however, nest disturbance may have influenced the results, as the researchers themselves have acknowledged. For example in Moors' study the longest period of consecutive use of a nest was 3 days, and in the study in Israel by Schoenfeld & Yom-Tov (where the nest sites were inspected daily), the *E. concolor* all changed nesting places nightly, with the sole exception of a female with a litter who remained at the same nest for 18 days. They also reported that the other species in the study (*Hemiechinus auritus*) changed nest burrows frequently; even breeding females moved their litter to a new nest nightly. Such extraordinary mobility was quite likely to be a result of disturbance.

Winter nests

There has been only one major study of winter nest use: Morris (1969, 1973) documented 185 winter nests in a West London park (UK). The park was dominated by open grassland, but broadleafed plantation areas were favoured for winter nesting by the hedgehog population. Because of the relatively small size of these areas and despite the problems of finding the well-concealed nests, a thorough nest survey was possible. Low temperature seemed to trigger nest building and nest occupancy was highest when temperatures were at their lowest (Fig. 5.3).

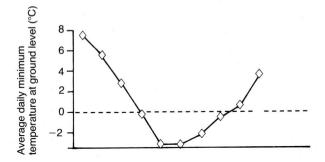

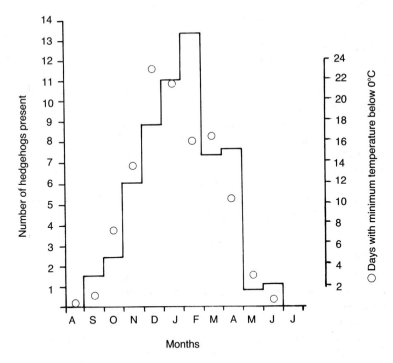

FIG. 5.3 *Relationship between average monthly temperature and mean number of European hedgehogs present in their hibernacula (southern England). Source: Morris (1973).*

Hibernation was rarely continuous and most animals became active and moved nests at some time during the winter. This is not surprising as a study of captive hibernating hedgehogs by Kristoffersson & Soivio (1964a) indicated that spontaneous arousal was quite normal at any time during the winter. Only four animals in Morris' study did not move during a sunny spell in February and all were nesting in heavily shaded sites. New nests were built throughout the winter and more nests were built than were lost, resulting in peak nest numbers in February and March. In April hedgehogs normally left their hibernacula and few new nests appeared until the following winter.

Morris kept a monthly log of the complete life-histories of 167 nests. Nests were generally durable with an average life-span of 6·4 months; well-supported nests lasted an average of over 7 months but poorly-supported nests only about 3·5 months (Fig. 5.4). To serve a hedgehog throughout the winter, a nest would have to last about 5 months or more, but fewer than half the nests lasted this long. Since nest building is likely to be a skill that improves with experience, some of the poorer quality nests may well have been built by first-time hibernators.

Occupancy periods varied greatly but averaged only just over 2 months, although one animal stayed in the same nest for 6 months. Some nests were repaired and re-used while others were permanently abandoned. Interestingly, 10 nests were occupied, then abandoned for up to 4 months and later re-occupied. Some others were empty at first then occupied later, suggesting they were 'spare nests'.

At the end of the winter, in Britain usually from April onwards, a hedgehog may leave its hibernaculum completely or continue to use it intermittently for a further few weeks (Knight 1962, English & Morris 1969). Hibernation in the milder climate of New Zealand is not obligatory and Brockie (1974a) found hibernating hedgehogs in winter between late April and early September with the greatest numbers from July to September. As in Morris' study, the numbers found hibernating fluctuated in any particular month apparently in response to varying severity of climate.

As previously mentioned, despite the many descriptions of hedgehog winter nests and hibernation in the literature, there are no behavioural data regarding the other genera (all of which are known to hibernate or aestivate) nor are there other comparably detailed studies of natural winter nest use in other *Erinaceus* species. Hibernation itself will be discussed in Chapter 6.

Nest sharing

At several points in this chapter I have mentioned the fact that hedgehogs may occasionally share nests. Albeit very unusual, it is intriguing that they occasionally abandon their normally solitary habits.

Although sole occupancy was the general rule, winter nest sharing by *E. europaeus* was reported by Morris (1973). He described three double-chambered winter nests which had presumably contained two occupants and two other similar nests which were briefly in dual occupation. Morris

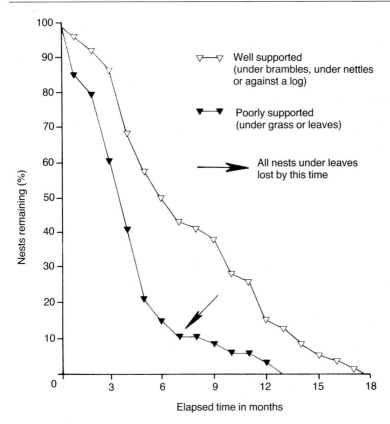

FIG. 5.4 *The difference in longevity between well-supported and poorly-supported nests of European hedgehogs in southern England. Data from 167 nests. Source: Morris (1973).*

speculated that nest sharing may have involved the newly weaned young of an incompletely dispersed litter; however, the animals were not disturbed hence their age and sex are unknown. Ognev (1928), who described winter nests in burrows around Olonets, claimed that it was usual for several hedgehogs to share a single nest for winter hibernation.

One can only guess why hedgehogs should cease to be unsociable and nest together. The suggestion that the nest-mates may be siblings is plausible and so is the idea that a female may remain with one or more of her young from a late litter. In the cold of winter there may be energy conservation benefits for group-nesting. Under extremely cold conditions, in locations where there may also be a shortage of high-quality nesting sites, benefits of group-nesting, such as energy conservation and shared use of nesting materials, may outweigh possible competition losses. Such losses could include being displaced from the optimum location in the burrow, disturbance, injury and possibly even predation by another hedgehog, disease and parasite transmission.

I have found only one published report of adult wild hedgehogs sharing a summer nest. Schoenfeld & Yom-Tov (1985) mentioned that a male and a female *E. concolor* were found sharing a day nest in Israel only 20 cm apart from each other. However, nest sharing is not uncommon in captivity even when there are surplus nesting sites available (Morris 1973). Krishna & Prakash (1955) reported that three captive *Paraechinus micropus* simultaneously shared a burrow (see earlier).

All other reports of wild hedgehog nesting suggest that just one animal per nest is the rule. However, radio-tracking studies have brought to light the remarkable fact that one hedgehog may use the summer nest of another in its absence. This phenomenon of non-simultaneous nest sharing has been shown in *Hemiechinus auritus* in Israel by Schoenfeld & Yom-Tov (1985) and in my own study of *Erinaceus europaeus* in Britain (Reeve & Morris 1985).

During 2 years of my study there were seven such instances but because routine searching of all known nest sites would have caused excessive disturbance, such 'nest sharing' was only detected when a radio-tagged animal used the known nest of another. It may be of no importance but it is worth mentioning that in my study all the second-users of nests were females and all but one of the previous occupants were males.

The true prevalence of such behaviour is unknown but it seems likely to be quite common and therefore could have important implications for the transfer of certain diseases and ectoparasites. Nests certainly have a potential role in the transmission of ticks, mites and fleas (Thompson 1936) and, as discussed by English & Morris (1969), may provide a protected environment which allows hedgehog ringworm fungus to persist and thus serve as a route for the infection of hedgehogs who make use of the nest.

The non-simultaneous use of summer nests by others is likely to be simply a pragmatic use of existing resources in the hedgehogs' environment. Why build a nest, or travel significant distances to an alternative site if there is a vacant nest nearby? Naturally one does not know if, or under what circumstances, there may be competition for the use of a nest. Judging by their general lack of belligerence, any dispute over occupancy would be quickly over and under normal circumstances the loser would simply make do with another site or hide-out nearby.

CHAPTER 6

Hibernation and Energetics

HIBERNATION

MAMMALS and birds are 'endothermic', i.e. able to warm their bodies above the temperature of their surroundings using internal, heat-producing (thermogenic) metabolic processes. Their body temperature is under homeostatic control, and is usually regulated within fairly tight limits (homeothermy). Reptiles, amphibians and fish are 'ectothermic' and generally depend on external heat sources to warm their bodies; consequently they undergo a greater range of body temperature fluctuations (poikilothermy). However, endothermy is an energy-expensive strategy, so mammals generally conserve energy by insulating their bodies with fat and fur, and by using nests, burrows and so on. Furthermore, many mammals (and some birds) strategically conserve energy by 'turning down the thermostat' on a daily and/or seasonal basis. Hibernation and aestivation (its summer equivalent) are seasonal strategies to conserve energy during adverse conditions. Deep hibernation is characterized by a drastic reduction in overall metabolic rate resulting in a greatly reduced body temperature (commonly as low as 1–5°C in hedgehogs), lowered oxygen consumption, low heart and ventilation rates with periods of apnoea (cessation of breathing) and a torpor more profound than sleep. It is helpful to distinguish between hibernation torpor and normal sleep; nevertheless, certain features of temperature and breathing regulation during hibernation do resemble an exaggerated 'slow wave sleep' (Lyman 1982, Malan 1982).

Hibernation in mammals is a widespread and much-studied phenomenon, but there is considerable variation in the habits and physiological mechanisms of hibernators, and many questions remain about even the most intensively studied species. Among the insectivores, periodic shallow torpor is known to occur in shrews (particularly the Crocidurinae, or white-toothed shrews), some golden moles (Chrysochloridae), and the tenrecs (Tenrecidae) which may also enter a more prolonged seasonal torpor. All species of spiny hedgehog seem able to enter a deep hibernation or aestivation during adverse conditions, but only *Erinaceus europaeus* is well studied. The unqualified use of the word 'hedgehog' in this chapter relates only to this species, and since hibernation physiology is so complex, patchily understood, and variable among species, generalizations should be tentative.

How hot is a hedgehog?

In captive non-hibernating European hedgehogs (*Erinaceus europaeus*), average body temperature is 35·4°C (±0.5) and there is a clear circadian (24 h) rhythm with a peak at midnight (GMT) and a minimum at noon (in Scotland; Fowler & Racey 1990b). In Germany, Herter (1934) reported a cycle from 03:00 to 15:00 hours. The wide range of 'normal' body temperatures reported reflects this circadian variation but also results from the various measuring methods used, e.g. thermometers or thermocouples held against the skin, inserted rectally or down the oesophagus, inserted by needle or surgically implanted. Nevertheless, typical body temperatures reported by most studies (e.g. Shkolnik 1980, Liu *et al.* 1990) fall within the 33·5–36·75°C range reported by Herter (1934, 1965b). Herter found that at extreme ambient temperatures (over 35°C or under −3°C) body temperature rose as high as 38°C, and the hedgehogs showed discomfort.

Reported temperature ranges for *Atelerix albiventris* and *A. algirus* are 32·9–35·4°C and 34–35·6°C, respectively (Herter 1964, 1971). Both *Erinaceus concolor* and *Hemiechinus auritus* averaged around 33°C when active at an ambient temperature of 11°C (Dmi'el & Schwartz 1984). Eisentraut (1952) reported an average of 35·4°C (range 31·2–36·2°C) for *Paraechinus aethiopicus*.

To summarize, 'normal' body temperature for hedgehogs seems to be around 35 ± 2°C, with only small differences between species. The adaptive aspects of body temperature and energetics are briefly considered later (p. 157).

The hibernation season

The two European species of *Erinaceus* are together naturally spread across more than 30° of latitude: from the seasonally arid zones of the Mediterranean and Middle East to the northern limit in Sweden and Finland where winters are severe. The hibernation period varies according to climate, individual condition and sex. At the northern limit of its range *E. europaeus* hibernates for 200 days or more, from October to April (Kristiansson 1984). In northern Europe and Britain, the hibernation period starts in October but animals may remain active well into November; most resume normal activity by the end of April (Walhovd 1975, 1990, Morris 1991). In Britain, females dominated my September catches and no males were found in October. Final arousal was as early as March in males, but females were infrequently caught before early May (Reeve 1981). Other studies have revealed a similar sex difference (e.g. Morris 1969, Göransson *et al.* 1976, Berthoud 1978, Vasilenko 1988).

Further south through central France to Italy and Spain, the hibernation period becomes progressively shortened and more variable, and some individuals may not hibernate at all (Herter 1968, Saboureau 1986). In the mild climate of New Zealand, a study by Brockie (cited by Kristiansson 1984) showed that only about 21% of the autumn population hibernated in mild winters, compared with 63% in more severe winters.

In Israel, Schoenfeld & Yom-Tov (1985) found that *Erinaceus concolor* seldom hibernated and were most readily trapped in the winter and spring (February to May). *Hemiechinus auritus*, however, were found hibernating from November to March and none was caught from December to February. So these two species, living in the same region, apparently occupied different climatic niches, although both were found active throughout the range of ambient temperatures (6–27°C) and relative humidities (40–100%) recorded in the study area. Dmi'el & Schwartz (1984) could maintain both these species in hibernation at a constant ambient temperature of 11°C.

Southern African hedgehogs (*Atelerix frontalis*) may hibernate throughout June and August in the eastern Orange Free State where winter minimum temperatures may reach −9°C (Kok and Van Ee 1989). But in Pietermaritzburg (Natal), where it is generally 5–7°C warmer, captives penned outside hibernated for only 1–3 days at a time during June to July (Rowe-Rowe 1974). In Pretoria wild hedgehogs are scarce from May to August and Gillies *et al.* (1991) found that captives could be maintained in hibernation at ambient temperatures of 15°C and below.

So what governs the hedgehog's 'decision' to hibernate? If kept warm and fed during the winter, a hedgehog may not hibernate at all, although it may show a lack of appetite and enter torpor rather readily (Dimelow 1963b). A fairly reliable way to induce hibernation is simply to lower the ambient temperature. In Germany, Herter (1934, 1965b) found that captive *E. europaeus*, when in a ready state, hibernated at ambient temperatures under 15–17°C; possibly the upper temperature limit compatible with hibernation (Krumbiegel 1955, cited by Kayser 1961). Although hibernation was not guaranteed, body temperature started to cool to around 15–30°C (usually about 10°C above the ambient), accompanied by variable levels of torpor. At ambient temperatures below 5·5°C the animal either hibernated, or resisted and remained active (also Dimelow 1963b; Kristoffersson & Suomalainen 1964). In Finland, Kristoffersson & Soivio (1964b) found that hedgehogs from Germany tended to hibernate at slightly higher ambient temperatures than local animals kept under the same conditions. This may reflect possible genetic differences between the populations (Kristoffersson & Soivio 1967, Saure 1969).

Experiments to compare the temperatures favouring hibernation in various hedgehog species by Herter (1964, 1965b, 1968), found that *E. concolor* (from eastern Europe) hibernated at higher temperatures than the more northerly distributed *E. europaeus*. Oddly, captives from hot countries became torpid at 19–24·5°C (*E. concolor nesiotes* from Crete, *Atelerix algirus* and *Paraechinus aethiopicus* from northern Africa, *Hemiechinus auritus* from Palestine). One explanation might be that these animals may be adapted to aestivate (enter summer torpor) as protection against heat and drought, but evidence from other studies in Israel and South Africa (see above) indicate that the critical season for hedgehogs is the brief cool winter and not the hot dry summer (Dmi'el & Schwartz 1984, Schoenfeld & Yom-Tov 1985, Kok & Van Ee 1989, Gillies *et al.* 1991).

So it seems that persistent cold is a primary governing factor in hibernation. When kept at 4°C, *E. europaeus* hibernated until June or July (Kramm *et al.* 1975), and a constant temperature of 11°C would induce hibernation in *E. concolor* and *Hemiechinus auritus* at any time of year (Dmi'el & Schwartz, 1984). However, hedgehogs may not readily hibernate unless in an appropriate physiological condition, and in nature the timing and duration of hibernation seems to be governed by a complex of environmental and hormonal factors. Secretion of melatonin (a hormone secreted mainly by the pineal gland) is increased by darkness, thus levels vary in response to circadian and seasonal photoperiod (light–dark cycles). In males, melatonin levels are naturally elevated in the autumn to midwinter period (testosterone levels are low). From January onwards melatonin declines as photoperiod increases, testosterone levels rise and gonadal activity recommences so that animals are fully sexually active upon final arousal (Saboureau 1986, Fowler 1988, Fowler & Racey 1990a; see Chapter 8). Male hedgehogs treated with melatonin implants had lowered levels of plasma testosterone and thyroxin, especially in the autumn (Fowler & Racey 1990a)—a confirmation of melatonin's known antigonadotrophic effects (Willis 1982). Furthermore, in males testosterone inhibits hibernation and its absence prolongs it (Saboureau 1986). Since the administration of melatonin in September advances the onset of testicular reactivation in the spring it may be that some internal 'timer' (responsive to photoperiod in the autumn) strongly influences the timing of spring arousal in males (Saboureau 1986, Fowler 1988, Fowler & Racey 1990a). In females, hormone-implant experiments on intact and ovariectomized animals have indicated that the timing and length of hibernation is linked more to changes in ambient temperature and food availability, than to levels of gonadal hormones (Saboureau 1986).

Photoperiod, melatonin and sex hormones are clearly just some of the endogenous factors regulating seasonal rhythms. The idea of an internal 'timer' sounds feasible, especially as hedgehogs hibernate in the virtual darkness of a thick-walled nest or burrow. However, hedgehogs just might be able to sample the photoperiod during their brief periodic arousals (see later). The effects of temperature have already been considered but food availability (e.g. Saboureau 1986) and body condition may also be significant. Gillies *et al.* (1991) found that *Atelerix frontalis*, induced to hibernate in conditions of reduced photoperiod and lowered temperature, entered significantly longer periods of torpor if food was restricted. This suggests a facultative control over torpor according to energy availability.

The observed sex differences in the timing of hibernation are intriguing. Males might gain net fitness benefits by risking early arousal to obtain access to females as early as possible in the season; early litters have the best chance of surviving the following winter. Males may have less time for feeding when competing for newly aroused females, and therefore benefit from improved body condition before the mating season starts. Although there may be less food available earlier in the year, while the females remain inactive there would be less competition for food and males keep energy costs down by ranging less widely than during the rut (Chapter 4). Females, however, who seldom conceive at the first oestrus in any case (Chapter 8), have a month of gestation to increase body condition at a time when food is presumably more abundant. Mature females may start hibernation later than males in the autumn because of the extra time taken to regain condition after the rigours of late litter rearing.

White fat, brown fat and thermogenesis

Before it can hibernate, a hedgehog must build up its body condition with large 'fuel' reserves of fat. Fat is the main energy storage tissue in animals because it has a high yield of energy for its weight (39.33 kJ g^{-1}) and is compact to store (Willis 1982, Gillies *et al.* 1991). Ordinary 'white fat' (adipose tissue) is mainly deposited subcutaneously and among the mesenteries of the abdominal cavity. In hibernators this fat provides a long-term energy supply to keep the animal's metabolism ticking over, but a second kind of fat store, 'brown fat' (brown adipose tissue), has a more specialized function. Brown fat was first recognized in hibernators, in which it may form substantial deposits—called the 'hibernating gland' by some early workers.

All tissues, as they respire, contribute to thermogenesis in mammals, but some may also be used to boost body temperature when needed. This is usually achieved by contraction of the skeletal muscles (as in shivering or voluntary exercise) or by 'non-shivering thermogenesis' which is principally, although not exclusively, achieved by brown fat tissue (Himms-Hagen 1983, Lyman & O'Brien 1986; see Table 6.1). Although brown fat is a key feature of hibernators, it may also be well developed in other mammals (especially rodents). Its presence in young humans (it may be 2–5% of the weight of a new-born baby) has aroused great interest in its role in thermoregulation and the possible pharmacological manipulation of its function in the treatment of obesity (Trayhurn & James 1983).

Brown fat tissue can generate impressive amounts of heat; up to around 400 W kg^{-1} (Girardier 1983). The cells are packed with large brownish mitochondria (organelles controlling cellular respiration) with a unique thermogenic physiological pathway (Olsson 1972b, Nicholls & Locke 1983). A rich blood supply delivers the oxygen necessary for rapid respiration,

TABLE 6.1 *Categories of thermogenesis that may be influenced by hormones.*

	Category of thermogenesis	Major site(s)	Major hormones		
			Direct	Permissive	
Obligatory (or essential)	(1) Essential thermogenesis	All organs	None		
	(2) Endothermic thermogenesis	Most organs	Thyroid		
	(3) Post-prandial thermogenesis	Intestine, liver, white adipose tissue		Insulin	
Facultative (or optional)	(4) Diet-induced thermogenesis	Brown adipose tissue	Noradrenalin	Thyroid Glucocorticoids(?) Insulin Sex hormones(?)	
	(5) Cold-induced non-shivering thermogenesis	Brown adipose tissue	Noradrenalin Glucagon(?)	Thyroid Glucocorticoids Insulin Melatonin(?)	
	(6) Cold-induced shivering thermogenesis	Skeletal muscle	Acetylcholine	Glucocorticoids Catecholamines	
	(7) Exercise-induced thermogenesis	Skeletal muscle	Acetylcholine	Glucocorticoids Catecholamines	

Source: Himms-Hagen (1983).

distributes the heat generated, and transports the breakdown products of fat to 'fuel' vital tissues. The numerous small fat droplets in brown fat cells are more rapidly accessible than the large droplets in white fat cells; they may also differ in their fatty acid composition (Laukola & Suomalainen 1971, Åkesson 1972, Girardier 1983).

In hedgehogs there are several, symmetrically distributed, lobes of brown fat (Carlier 1893d). The largest mass lies around the axillary region ('armpit') forming a rough triangle, the tip of which passes forwards to the junction of the clavicle and sternum to form a lobe in the neck which associates closely with the external jugular vein, the thyroid and thymus glands, and the neck musculature. The forward extension of the axillary lobe also continues over the shoulder to the back, where it spreads behind the scapula to the spinal column. It then branches both anteriorly and posteriorly to form small lobes between nearly all the muscles of the back and neck, adjacent to the spinal column. The main superficial deposits of brown fat around the thorax, neck and along the spinal column are typical of small mammals and together form a vest-like arrangement, strategically placed to dispense heat to the thorax and central nervous system (Girardier 1983). However, areas of brown fat around the aorta, though common in other hibernators, are small or absent in hedgehogs (Carlier 1893d). In small mammals generally, and maybe also in hedgehogs, minor deposits of brown fat may be associated with various abdominal organs such as the adrenals, autonomic ganglia and kidneys, the suprailiac region and many other minor locations (Girardier 1983).

In a hedgehog ready for hibernation, the lobes of brown fat are a strong orange–brown and may represent up to 3% of the total body weight; the colour gradually darkens as the fat is used (Carlier & Lovatt Evans 1903, Suomalainen 1935). As brown fat is used, the proportion of water in the tissue increases, presumably derived from the metabolism of fats, as no water is drunk. Should any brown fat remain after final arousal it will continue to regress, but where hibernation is prolonged it may be reduced to a few fibrous cords by the time of final arousal (Carlier & Lovatt Evans 1903).

Brown fat provides a vital source of rapidly metabolizable energy, controlled principally by the sympathetic nerve endings which densely permeate the tissue, and by circulating adrenal hormones (the sympatho-adrenal system). Thermostatic control is achieved by sensors in the hypothalamus, in the cervical region of the spinal cord, and the skin (Werner & Vens-Cappell 1982, Girardier 1983, Landsberg & Young 1983, Horwitz *et al.* 1986, Werner & Riecke 1987, Fowler 1988). Brown fat can operate at low temperatures (Girardier 1983) and during arousal is promptly mobilized to raise the hedgehog's temperature, from around 1–5°C to its normal level within 3 h or so. Thus brown fat effectively 'jump-starts' the hedgehog's metabolism, but although it may be the principal thermogenic tissue, there are contributions (as yet unquantified) from other thermogenic processes, such as shivering (skeletal muscle contractions) and the vigorous pumping of the heart. An overview of the body changes during arousal from hibernation is given later.

Entry into hibernation

When considering the complexities of hedgehog physiology, the importance of something as simple as the winter hibernation nest (hibernaculum) should not be forgotten. A hedgehog relies on a well-sited winter nest for concealment, and would soon die of exposure but for its weatherproof properties (Chapter 5). The insulating nest buffers external temperature changes and helps to maximize energy efficiency during hibernation.

Entering hibernation is a controlled process, and not simply an abandonment of thermoregulation (Lyman 1982) but the factors favouring the onset of hibernation are complex and incompletely understood. Early claims of a single hibernation 'trigger' substance were ill-founded (Kayser 1961) and continuing studies are progressively revealing the complexity of physiological variables involved. Some influential factors have already been mentioned (photoperiod, temperature and food availability) but injections of insulin (causing an artificial hypoglycaemia) can also induce 'hibernation' even in the summer. Although insulin is important in the management of body stores of glycogen (a starch-like carbohydrate) prior to hibernation (Herter 1968), such induced hypoglycaemia may simply mimic an effect of fasting, which presumably also lowers blood glucose levels. Hibernation is characterized by very low levels of insulin in the blood and an insensitivity to its action (see later). Low levels of thyroxin, observed in fasting hedgehogs in the autumn, may also be a factor (Saboureau 1986), although Herter (1965b) stated that hedgehogs from whom thyroids had been removed, and hedgehogs with thyroid hormones added to their diets, all hibernated normally.

The state of hibernation

Hibernation is not a static state, but one which changes in response to external stimuli, and is naturally punctuated by spontaneous arousals and periods of activity (see later). One of the many problems of studying hedgehog hibernation is that the animals are very sensitive to being touched or moved, or having blood samples and measurements taken. The consequent changes in internal state are so rapid that many studies, while aiming to measure variables from live animals in deep hibernation, have in fact monitored the first stages of an artificially induced arousal! This, along with numerous other methodological problems, is one of the main reasons why so many questions remain about the state of hibernation in hedgehogs (and other animals), and why physiological measurements are so variable.

The hibernation state is controlled by the integrated action of neural and endocrine control mechanisms, and there are many differences between hibernation and the active state. In hibernation the slowing down of metabolic rate, to 1 or 2% of the levels in active animals (Kayser 1961, Tähti 1978), results in a remarkable number of physiological changes. Whereas some have a functional or adaptive significance, others are simply side-effects of low body temperatures, neural and endocrine suppression or fasting. For example, the depletion of ascorbic acid (vitamin C) in various organs of hibernating hedgehogs (Kayser 1961) would occur during any prolonged fasting.

The energy conservation benefits of low body temperature and depressed overall metabolic rate are plain, but severe cold requires a boost in metabolic heat production to prevent freezing of the tissues. At an ambient temperature of $-5°C$ hedgehogs consumed 22 times as much oxygen as they did at $4°C$ (Soivio *et al.* 1968). A significantly raised ambient temperature also increases metabolic demand, caused by a passive rise in body temperature. Therefore, either very cold, or unusually warm, winter weather will increase the use of body reserves, shortening the period over which hibernation can be sustained, and may stimulate arousal (Kayser 1961). The optimum body temperature during hibernation seems to be around $4°C$, although the exact figure depends on bodyweight (Kayser 1961, Kristoffersson & Soivio 1964b, Tähti 1978). The effect of surface area on body heat loss (or gain), normally so important in warm animals, would be negligible during hibernation, as the body and ambient temperatures are similar. This again highlights the significance of the temperature-buffered environment of the hibernation nest.

Heart rate and respiration

The low metabolic demand of a cool hedgehog is matched by a reduced breathing rate and lowered heart rate. When active at normal body temperatures, the heart rate is usually around 200–280 beats min^{-1}, but this falls to around 147 beats min^{-1} when asleep (Eklund *et al.* 1972, Kramm *et al.* 1975, Gunderson 1976). Heart rate is naturally very variable and it changes rapidly in response to disturbance. Despite the range of values reported in the literature (from 2 to 48 beats min^{-1}), Kayser (1961) concluded that the heart rate of deeply hibernating hedgehogs fluctuated around 5 beats min^{-1}, a value typical of many other hibernators. He found that the slightest touch raised the heart rate to 10 or more beats min^{-1}, and merely connecting up pre-implanted electrodes raised the rate to 20–25 beats min^{-1}. The normal heart rates of hedgehogs hibernating at around $4°C$, measured by ECG (electrocardiograph), were found to be between 2 and 12 beats min^{-1} by Kristoffersson & Soivio (1964b) and an average of $13·7$ beats min^{-1} by Eklund *et al.* (1972), but Kramm *et al.* (1975), who obtained measurements by palpation, reported 25 beats min^{-1}!

The hearts of hedgehogs show many physiological features which may be related to a resistance to ventricular fibrillation and maintained function at low temperatures. The ECG shows a prolongation of all components and the S–T segment is short or absent (Sarajas 1954, Eklund *et al.* 1972, Duker *et al.* 1986). The heart muscles of hedgehogs (and other hibernators) have a reduced adrenergic innervation and low noradrenaline content (Owman & von Studnitz 1972, Duker *et al.* 1986). Glycogen accumulations in the heart muscle provide a local fuel store and the heart has a high activity of alpha-GPDH (glycerophosphate dehydrogenase), an enzyme in the pathway that converts fats to energy (Thorell *et al.* 1972, Sokolov *et al.* 1982a). The fatty acids in the membranes of the heart muscle cells may become more un-saturated to preserve membrane permeability (Liu *et al.* 1991) and the flow of sodium, potassium and calcium ions across the membranes is maintained better than in non-hibernators. Calcium availability may be particularly important in the maintenance of membrane permeability and muscle contrac-tability at low temperatures (Wang 1982, Willis 1982, Duker *et al.* 1986). General aspects of calcium physiology and parathyroid gland activity during hibernation are considered in Kayser (1961) and Senturia *et al.* (1972).

Breathing rates are also very variable, averaging 25 min^{-1} in resting non-hibernating animals, but about double that figure in active animals (Kristof-fersson & Soivio 1964b). During hibernation at around 4°C, the average breathing rate drops to 13 min^{-1} or less (Kramm *et al.* 1975). However, as in other hibernators, there are periods during which breathing ceases altogether (apnoea). In China, Chao & Yeh (1950, 1951, cited by Lyman 1982) timed an apnoeic period of 65 min in *Erinaceus amurensis*. Apnoea lasting 150 min was recorded for *E. europaeus* by Kristoffersson & Soivio (1964b) although the average duration was around 56 min. Each apnoeic period started with an expiration and ended with a burst of 40–50 breaths over about 3–5 min before the next apnoea (Fig. 6.1). Periodic apnoea is usually exhibited only in deeply torpid, undisturbed animals at body temperatures around 4°C, and at normal atmospheric levels of oxygen and carbon dioxide (Kristoffersson & Soivio 1964b, Tähti 1975).

Hibernators generally have a very efficient anaerobic metabolism—torpid hedgehogs can tolerate up to 2 h or more in a pure nitrogen atmosphere (no oxygen) 'without permanent damage' (Biörck *et al.* 1956a). However, although there may be some shift towards anaerobic conditions (Olsson 1972a), oxygen deficiency in the body is unusual in hibernation despite low breathing rates. The reasons for this are complex but, in simple terms, temperature- and acidity-related changes in blood chemistry result in a raised oxygen affinity of haemoglobin and a reduced metabolic demand (Johansson & Senturia 1972a, Kramm *et al.* 1975, Tähti & Soivio 1975, Malan 1982). Metabolic suppression results from a low body temperature and low levels of several hormones in the blood, but infrequent breathing also causes carbon dioxide to accumulate in the blood (raising its acidity) which further inhibits glycolysis (the metabolism of glucose). Periodic apnoea is therefore an effective energy saving strategy that also reduces evaporative water losses from the lungs. For a more detailed review see Malan (1982).

Hibernation-related changes in red blood cell count, haematocrit (percent-age volume of red cells in whole blood) and blood haemoglobin content have also been observed, however, no clear picture has emerged from the studies so far (e.g. Biörck *et al.* 1956b, Kramm *et al.* 1975). A detailed study by Suomalainen & Rosokivi (1973) found a slow increase in red blood cell counts during hibernation from 10·18–14·52 million mm^{-3}, and in haematocrit from 38·8–50·5% (October and March values, respectively). However, they noted that several factors such as sex, age, stage and depth of hibernation, and the use

(Above) *The European hedgehog (Erinaceus europaeus). Note the alert stance of an undisturbed, active animal.*

(Right) *Hedgehogs are able swimmers but may be unable to escape from steep-sided garden ponds.* PHOTO: PAT MORRIS.

3. (Left) *A 'blond' European hedgehog from Britain. Unlike an albino, it has normally coloured eyes but pink skin on the nose and paws. The pale coloration makes it easy to see how dirty some hedgehogs can get!*

4. *A female central African hedgehog (Atelerix albiventris) from Kenya, with her litter of four (aged around 12 days). PHOTO: MARTIN GREGORY.*

5. *Long-eared hedgehog (Hemiechinus spp.). PHOTO: PAT MORRIS.*

6. *The bristling spines of a European hedgehog (Erinaceus europaeus). Note how they interlock and point in all directions.*

The first line of defence is to crouch and draw down the spines to cover the face and limbs. This European hedgehog is normally coloured except for its pink nose and paws.

8. *Sharp sounds, such as the click of a camera shutter, trigger a very fast reflexive flinch which has blurred this photograph of a central African hedgehog (Atelerix albiventris). PHOTO: MARTIN GREGORY.*

9. *A loosely rolled-up European hedgehog turned on its back. The spiny skin of the forehead and rump is tightly clamped together to encase the animal completely if it is threatened.*

10. *If left undisturbed the hedgehog soon unrolls. This partially unrolled European hedgehog is lying in a 'bowl' of spiny skin, the rim formed by the orbicularis muscle.*

11. *A fresh hedgehog dropping.*

12. (Right) *The author locates a young European hedgehog tagged with a radio transmitter. PHOTO: PAT MORRIS.*

13. European hedgehog nests are typically made of broad leaves tucked under brambles or other ground vegetation. This one was concealed under a disused trailer overgrown with grass.

14. My tame hedgehog 'Emily' self-anointed whenever she smelled this old woollen carpet.

15. Self-anointing by a nestling central African hedgehog. PHOTO: MARTIN GREGORY.

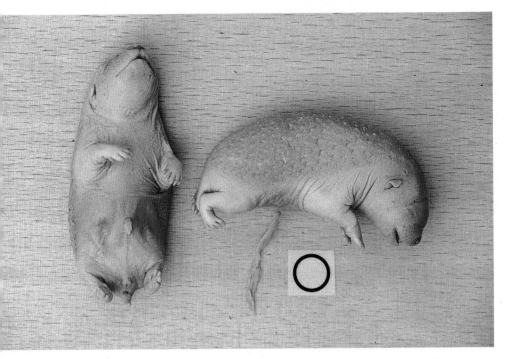

6. *Stillborn full-term European hedgehogs (scale 10 mm).*

7. *Exploring outside the nest, a young European hedgehog about 4 or 5 weeks old.*
    PHOTO: IAN CONDON.

18. (Top) *Courting European hedgehogs.*

19. (Above) *Hundreds of tiny parasitic mites (Caparinia erinacei) are visible on the skin of this central African hedgehog (Atelerix albiventris). PHOTO: MARTIN GREGORY.*

20. (Right) *Crossing the road is risky.*

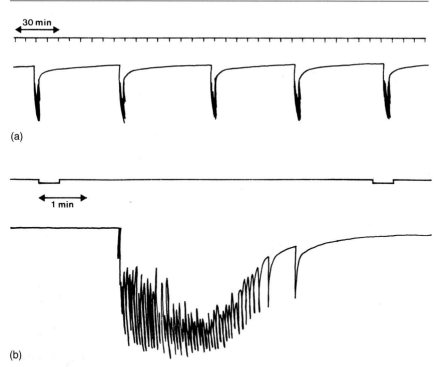

(a)

(b)

FIG. 6.1 *Kymograph of the respiratory movements of a deeply hibernating European hedgehog at a constant ambient temperature of 4·2 ± 0·5°C. (a) A trace showing periods of apnoea lasting about 56 min and periods of breathing lasting about 4 min. Inspiration is downward; the time marker interval is 7·5 min. (b) Expansion of one period of breathing consisting of about 50 inspirations (time marker interval is 7·5 min). At the end of an apnoeic period the arterial partial pressure of oxygen may be down to 10·5 ± 3·7 mm Hg, but after a series of breaths it can rise to 120 ± 27 mm Hg (Tähti & Soivio 1975). Source: Kristoffersson & Soivio (1964b).*

of anaesthetics, strongly affected the variables measured—all of which helps to explain the often contradictory information from other studies. Changes in red blood cell counts and haematocrit may also be linked with lowered blood volume during hibernation (Eliassen 1961, Kayser 1961), but the suggestion that the spleen (which breaks down old red cells) may amass red cells removed from circulation was doubted by Carlier (1893b) and effectively refuted by Biörck *et al.* (1956b). Weight changes (both losses and gains) of the spleen during hibernation have been reported, as well as rapid weight changes when hedgehogs were suddenly removed from the cold (Senturia & Johansson 1972). However, such changes may be more related to the spleen's immunological role as an accessory organ of the lymphatic system (Kayser 1961).

The neuro-endocrine system in hibernation

Despite a massive reduction in metabolic rate, the important homeostatic control centres in the hypothalamus remain responsive and functional, even in deep hibernation. Sanchez-Toscano *et al.* (1989) found that in hibernating hedgehogs the neurons of the supraoptic nucleus of the hypothalamus had more highly branched dendrites which bore roughly double the density of dendritic spines (receptive structures). These neuronal changes were interpreted by Haynes (1989) as a mechanism by which hedgehogs 'amplify their brains' weak signals' during hibernation. Nervous tissue from hibernators remains functional at lower temperatures than in other mammals (Willis 1982), but some areas of the brain (the cerebellum and cerebral cortex) apparently become virtually inactive (Giacometti *et al.* 1989).

The maintenance of the hypothermic state is controlled principally by two neurotransmitters, 5-HT (5-hydroxytryptamine, also known as serotonin), and noradrenaline (= norepinephrine). On current evidence, it seems that when 5-HT concentration is raised and noradrenaline reduced (associated with a decline in sympathetic nervous activity) the result is cooling and the maintenance of hibernation, whereas the converse situation stimulates thermogenesis and arousal from hibernation (Uuspää 1963a,b, Owman & von Studnitz 1972, Saarikoski & Suomalainen 1975, Sokolov *et al.* 1982a, Willis 1982).

In seasonal hibernators endocrine function is typically depressed at the onset of hibernation (Willis 1982) and during torpor the very low body temperatures must limit endocrine activity. The thyroid gland is regressed during the autumn and early hibernation period and there are low plasma levels of thyroxin—an important regulator of metabolic rate. However, there may be significant endocrine activity during the periodic arousals. This is exemplified by the progressive increase in gonadal activity in males, during the latter half of the hibernation period, in which the arousal periods are used to build-up to a full sexual readiness at the time of final arousal from hibernation (Chapter 8). The adrenal glands reach their minimum weight during hibernation (Senturia & Johansson 1972, Saarikoski & Suomalainen 1975), but later in the hibernation period the relative weight and cortex thickness of the adrenal glands increase and the thyroid also resumes activity (Pinatel *et al.* 1970). This pattern of resumption of endocrine activity later in the hibernation period is also found in other seasonal hibernators (Willis 1982).

Energy metabolism

During hibernation, hedgehogs rely on their fat reserves and carbohydrate metabolism virtually ceases—hence there are very low levels of the pancreatic hormones glucagon and insulin (Hoo-Paris *et al.* 1982). Insulin promotes glucose uptake by cells (lowers plasma glucose levels) while glucagon has the opposite effect by promoting the breakdown of stored glycogen to glucose. Evidently, both glycolysis and gluconeogenesis (the synthesis of glucose from glycerides (fats), amino acids and so on) are greatly reduced during hibernation torpor (Forssberg & and Sarajas 1955, Kayser 1961, Hoo-Paris *et al.* 1982, 1984a,b, Castex & Hoo-Paris 1987). Measures of glycogen storage and mobilization in active hedgehogs show enormous variability depending on their activity and feeding (Saarikoski & Suomalainen 1971). This makes comparisons with hibernating animals difficult and may explain some of the inconsistencies between studies but Sokolov *et al.* (1982a,b) noted a general agreement on the accumulation of glycogen in heart muscle during hibernation (see earlier).

Although very variable, normal blood sugar concentration in active animals is around 125 mg 100 ml^{-1} (Kayser 1961), but as hibernation begins, it may plunge to around 54 mg 100 ml^{-1} (Suomalainen 1935). Similar results have been observed in other studies (Sarajas 1967, Thorell *et al.* 1972). Blood glucose concentration remains low throughout hibernation, but slowly increases during early arousal to achieve normal levels in newly aroused hedgehogs (Suomalainen 1935, Sarajas 1967).

With carbohydrate metabolism at such a low level, it is clear that hibernating hedgehogs get their energy almost entirely from the metabolism of their fat reserves—as suggested by the RQ (Respiratory Quotient) values of around 0·7 reported by most studies (Kayser 1961, Dmi'el & Schwartz 1984). 'Lipid' is a general term for any hydrophobic substance (sterols, prostaglandins, etc.), but in this context the term 'lipolysis' usually refers to the hydrolysis of glycerides (fats). Glycerides are transported in the blood as lipoproteins (i.e. in association with protein molecules). Glycerides are broken down and converted to acetyl-coenzyme A, then oxidized in the Krebs cycle to release energy. Overall, rather little is known about the management of fat metabolism during hibernation, despite a number of studies. Laplaud *et al.* (1989) found that plasma concentrations of certain lipids (cholesterol, glycerol and phospholipids) and lipoproteins peaked when testosterone and thyroxin were at minimal levels, i.e. at a time when lipid supply exceeds metabolic demand. Johansson & Johansson (1972) found a similar pattern of change in total serum fat, triglycerides and cholesterol.

During deep hibernation, when energy is principally obtained from lipolysis, it is likely that the brain (and other vital tissues) would also make direct use of the energy metabolism of ketone bodies (themselves produced by lipolysis). Ketone bodies are converted into acetyl-coenzyme A and fed into the Krebs cycle. This has not been investigated in hibernators (Willis 1982), but is a well-known phenomenon in fasting humans.

During hibernation there seems to be no significant use of proteins for metabolic energy (via gluconeogenesis) and there is no particular accumulation of blood urea (produced from the oxidation products of amino acids) during hibernation in hedgehogs, or other hibernators (Kristoffersson 1965, Willis 1982). In line with the general depression in metabolic rate and cellular activity, there is a reduction in overall protein metabolism during hibernation (Sokolov *et al.* 1982a, Hoo-Paris *et al.* 1984b, Giacometti *et al.* 1989).

Adenosine triphosphate (ATP) is the substance at the heart of energy delivery in cells. Although the ATP content of various tissues may change greatly during hibernation (Kristoffersson 1961), Lyman (1982) concluded that levels of ATP (often in superabundance anyway) are far less important than the capacity to synthesize and mobilize it rapidly.

Osmoregulation

During hibernation, infrequent breathing and low body temperatures minimize evaporative water loss from the respiratory tract, but what about urine production? The slow metabolic rate during torpor means that there are few metabolic wastes to eliminate, requiring little in the way of kidney function. This is just as well, because active kidneys have a high metabolic demand and constantly nipping out of the nest to urinate would be less than convenient! Blood flow is reduced through the kidney by vasomotor control (Harrison Matthews 1952), and the increased viscosity of blood at low temperatures is also likely to ensure a slower rate of filtration. Although urine may not be produced in important amounts during torpor (Clausen & Storesund 1971), water is produced by fat metabolism (Kayser 1961) and any surplus may be cleared by urination during brief periods of arousal (Dmi'el & Schwartz 1984).

Studies of changes in the levels of various ions (potassium, magnesium, sodium and chloride) in the blood plasma and various tissues have shown major inconsistencies (Suomalainen *et al.* 1969, Clausen & Storesund 1971, Senturia *et al.* 1972, Tähti & Soivio 1977). It is unclear if the changes observed are passive effects of low body temperature or a result of active physiological management; neither is it known whether such changes have adaptive significance, represent physiological constraints or are effectively neutral.

Other changes during hibernation

Changes in the gut are largely confined to an involution (shut-down) of the secretory glands in the gut lining. However, bile release into the gut continues during hibernation as does the activity of the exocrine pancreas (Carlier 1896, Kayser 1961, Clausen & Storesund 1971), although Thorell *et al.* (1972) reported average pancreas weights in November and January to be, respectively, only 35% and 46% of the July average of 5.18 ± 1.22 g.

During hibernation, huge numbers of white blood cells (leucocytes) migrate from the blood to form aggregations in the lymph glands, the lungs, the connective tissue around the gut, and around the pancreatic and bile ducts (Carlier 1893a, Inkovaara & Suomalainen 1973). In some locations, such as around larger blood vessels, the leucocytes form dense gland-like masses. The blood count of leucocytes falls from 18 to 20 thousand mm^{-3} to anything from 1 to 3 thousand mm^{-3} (Carlier 1893a). After arousal, the distribution of leucocytes quickly returns to normal, although the rate of change varies with leucocyte type and the tissue (Inkovaara & Suomalainen 1973, Suomalainen & Rosokivi 1973). No one is sure why these changes take place, the leucocytes may just be stored (or disposed of) in these sites but both the lungs and intestine are in particular need of immunological protection during torpor. Suomalainen (1960, and later studies) advanced a theory that many observed physiological changes, including the reduced blood leucocyte count are all symptomatic of an adaptation response (Selye's syndrome) to the chronic stress of cold and fasting.

Overall blood protein levels show no significant seasonal variation (Johansson & Senturia 1972b). Nevertheless, Biörck *et al.* (1956b) noted lowered concentrations of globulins during hibernation, especially gamma-globulins which fell from 0·90 g 100 ml^{-1} (June) to 0·52 g 100 ml^{-1} (January), possibly reducing the capacity for immune response. The same study also recorded a doubling of the normal blood platelet count to 875 thousand mm^{-3} during hibernation. Although this, and reduced levels of an anti-clotting enzyme (tissue plasminogen activator) in the heart, lung and kidney (Pandolfi *et al.* 1972), indicates a need to compensate for slow blood clotting at low temperatures, it seems to me that clot formation in the sluggish, viscous blood flow is a more serious potential problem.

Hibernating — or dead?
Hibernating hedgehogs are not 'dead to the world' but very sensitive and may be roused by disturbance or any deterioration in their nest environment. Although responsiveness varies individually and at different times during hibernation, merely touching the hedgehog will normally trigger bursts of muscle action potentials, a bristling of the spines, raise the heart rate and elicit other physiological changes which may lead to arousal (Kayser 1961, Kristoffersson & Soivio 1964d).

The bristling response is a useful way of checking whether any accidentally uncovered hedgehog is alive and hibernating, or dead! If it bristles (even slightly) when touched, re-cover it. Most likely it will become active after a few hours and move to a new nest, but if it stays, leave it strictly alone! Too many disturbances will prematurely use up the animal's fat reserves reducing its chances of survival.

Arousal from hibernation

The popular idea that hibernators enter a deep and untroubled 'sleep' at the onset of winter, and only 'awaken' when spring returns, is simply a myth! Hedgehogs, like all deep hibernators, arouse spontaneously several times during the hibernation period. Undisturbed *Erinaceus europaeus* wake from hibernation every 7–11 days on average (Kristoffersson & Soivio 1964a, Walhovd 1979, Wroot 1984a). During periodic arousals hedgehogs often remain in their nests before hibernating again a few hours later, but they can remain active for some days and may change nest (Chapter 5). Under constant conditions (ambient temperature of 4·2 ± 0·5°C) they wake, on average, 15–22 times, and spend only 80% of the hibernation period in hypothermia; even less at temperatures of +10°C or −5°C (Kristoffersson & Soivio 1964c, Soivio *et al.* 1968, Walhovd 1979). In Israel, Dmi'el & Schwartz (1984) found that, at a constant ambient temperature of 11°C, hibernation bouts of *E. concolor* lasted 5–27 days (average 9·3 days), but those of *Hemiechinus auritus* were more regular and short (average 4·8 days). The arousal periods were 20–25 h in both species but the number of arousals in *Hemiechinus* was higher (average 5·3 month^{-1}) than in *Erinaceus* (average 2·9 month^{-1}).

Although European hedgehogs are less commonly found active outside the nest in freezing conditions, winter activity has been recorded even at $-7°C$ (Walhovd 1978). It is thus a mistake to assume that hedgehogs found active in the winter are in need of 'adoption'. Only clearly underweight or obviously distressed hedgehogs should be taken into care.

Reports conflict as to whether or not hedgehogs (all genera) feed during arousal periods and in some studies some individuals will feed whereas others ignore any food or water provided (Ranson 1941, Walhovd 1978, Herter 1965b, Dmi'el & Schwartz 1984, Kok & Van Ee 1989, Gillies *et al.* 1991). Hedgehogs do not store food and, because prey may be scarce, they probably do not feed under natural conditions. Captive *E. europaeus* can hibernate successfully without any food or water (Kristoffersson & Soivio 1964a). Nevertheless, anyone finding a hedgehog active during the hibernation period could offer it a meal of some suitably meaty pet food which, if accepted, would probably benefit the hedgehog.

Although even brief periods of torpor effectively conserve energy, it is still unknown why periodic arousals from deep hibernation are seemingly unavoidable. One arousal, maybe lasting only 3–4 h, consumes the energy equivalent of several days in hibernation (Tähti & Soivio 1977). Periodic arousals occur even in conditions of constant darkness (Kristoffersson & Soivio 1964a), but they could be cued by a latent endogenous rhythmicity which persists even in hibernation (Willis 1982). Maybe a progressive depletion of some vital substance, or metabolic waste accumulation occurs, although neither urea nor lactate accumulate. However, arousal must 'reset' many metabolic functions to normal, for example the rapid resumption of carbohydrate metabolism, and a restoration of the ionic balance of cell membranes (Willis 1982). Although hedgehogs, and other hibernators, may urinate during the arousal periods (Dmi'el & Schwartz 1984) experiments have shown that arousal occurs irrespective of bladder fullness (Willis 1982).

Whatever factors are involved, there does seem to be a progressive 'irritability', a readiness for arousal, towards the end of each hibernation bout (Kristoffersson & Soivio 1964a).

The arousal process

Arousal involves neural and hormonal regulation of heart rate, respiration rate, blood pressure, oxygen consumption and body temperature and takes about 2–5 h in the laboratory. However, the arousal of hedgehogs penned outdoors averaged almost 12 h (Fowler & Racey 1990b) indicating that it may take longer in the wild. A hedgehog remains inactive, with closed eyes while its body temperature remains under 20°C, but as it warms further, its eyes open and it may move the front end of its body. The animal may then stand unsteadily and shiver. When the body temperature reaches 28–30°C it may begin to totter about (Suomalainen & Suvanto 1953, Herter 1965b).

The problem with studying natural arousal in more detail is that the investigative technique itself will probably induce rapid arousal. Moving the animal, say into an experimental chamber for monitoring purposes, and to take blood samples or use any invasive or acute methods, will almost certainly distort the results obtained. In an attempt to determine the difference between induced and truly spontaneous arousals, Tähti & Soivio (1977) monitored hibernating hedgehogs (at a constant ambient temperature of 4·2°C) using permanently implanted monitoring equipment. Measurements of oxygen consumption, breathing rate, temperature and other physiological changes were monitored during several spontaneous and induced arousals, the latter initiated by a 'mechanical stimulus' to the neck spines. They found that induced arousal evoked a more vigorous thermogenesis, an abrupt disappearance of apnoea, an acceleration of heart rate and raised blood pressure, all occurring together shortly after the stimulus. Peak oxygen consumption occurred 30 min earlier and was 36% higher than in spontaneous arousals. In spontaneous arousals, heart rate increased *before* the initiation of continuous respiration or any other sign of arousal. Figures 6.2 and 6.3 show the pattern of change in some key physiological variables during arousal.

In the early stages of arousal the body is warmed by brown fat thermogenesis and the vigorous pumping of the heart, which must work hard to move the cool and viscous blood through constricted peripheral blood vessels. In a study of induced arousals, Edwards & Munday (1969) found that

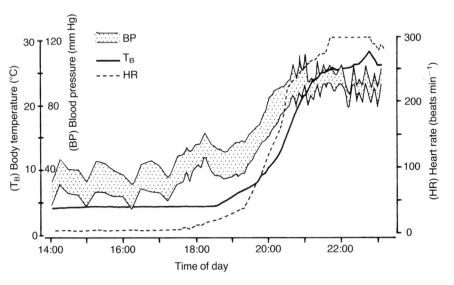

FIG. 6.2 *Changes in blood pressure, body temperature and heart rate during a typical spontaneous arousal from hibernation in the European hedgehog. Before the onset of the arousal the spontaneous rhythm of blood pressure change (caused by periodic apnoea) is clearly visible. Source: Tähti & Soivio (1977).*

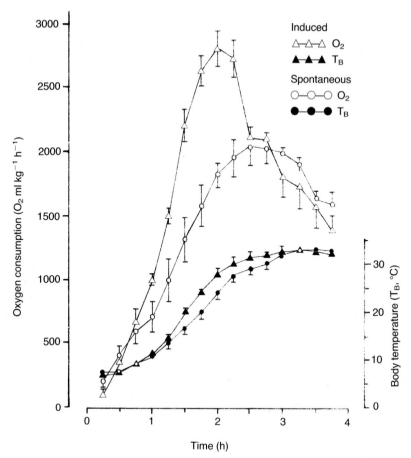

FIG. 6.3   *Changes in oxygen (O_2) consumption and body temperature (T_B) during induced and spontaneous arousals. Data are mean values (n = 4), bars denote standard error. Source: Tähti & Soivio (1977).*

three of their six subjects aroused much more rapidly than the others. Brown fat tissue led the rise in body temperature, raising its temperature by an average of $6°C\ h^{-1}$ (slow arousers) and $20·6°C\ h^{-1}$ (fast arousers). The heart, although lagging 2°C behind the brown fat, showed similar rates of warming. Physiological studies confirm that lipids are mobilized and intensively used to provide energy during arousal (Suomalainen & Saarikoski 1967, 1971, Willis 1982). Once the body temperature rises above 15°C, glucose turnover increases as carbohydrate metabolism re-establishes. Glucagon secretion rises particularly rapidly in the late stages of arousal with body temperatures over 20°C. Though clearly temperature dependent, the secretion and action of insulin and glucagon are also complicated by other factors (Hoo-Paris & Sutter 1980, Hoo-Paris et al. 1982, Willis 1982).

Studies of cardiovascular changes by Kirkebö (1968) have shown that during the early stages of arousal, heart strokes are slow and heart output initially rises faster than heart rate. The strokes then progressively shorten to 0·1 s at 35°C (heart rate 250 beats min^{-1}). As is typical in other hibernators, the anterior of the body warms first, then an increased circulation in the abdomen and posterior half of the body causes a sudden rise in rectal temperature (see also Edwards & Munday 1969). An observed decline in the resistance of peripheral blood vessels may be more to do with the lowering of blood viscosity as the body warms than the vasodilation of peripheral vessels.

HEDGEHOG ENERGETICS

Evolutionary aspects of energetics

Hedgehogs are conservative, both morphologically and in the niche they inhabit (Chapter 1), and are commonly categorized as primitive thermoregulators. This conclusion is based mainly on their somewhat low body temperature, 3–4°C lower than the typical 38°C of an 'advanced' eutherian mammal, and the fact that they may undergo considerable body temperature fluctuations. But is such a conclusion justified?

While accepting that certain conservative mammal groups (e.g. monotremes and marsupials) have a relatively low resting metabolic rate and low body temperature, Dawson & Grant (1980) revealed them to be sophisticated homeotherms and refuted the long-supposed direct association between increased metabolic rate, body temperature and homeothermic competence. A low 'thermostat-setting' incurs lower energetic costs than a high 'setting' and could alternatively be viewed as energetically superior! Long-standing assumptions about the primitive thermoregulatory capacities of hedgehogs are similarly refuted by Shkolnik (1980), who showed them to be competent homeotherms. On a slightly different tack, Crompton *et al.* (1978) and Taylor (1980) suggested that homeothermic capacity in mammals may have evolved in two stages. The first involved the invasion of a nocturnal niche, using fur as insulation and an ability to increase heat production in the cold. The second stage was a move to a diurnal niche which involved a 3–5-fold increase in resting metabolic rate, and an increased body temperature.

Crompton *et al.* reported evaluations of the metabolic rates of hedgehogs (*Erinaceus europaeus*), tenrecs (*Tenrec* sp. and *Setifer* sp.), echidnas (*Tachyglossus* sp.) and opossums (*Didelphis* sp.), when active in a treadmill. They argued that more typical 'mammalian-type' energetics are found in monotremes and marsupials, who are supposed to have a diurnal ancestry, although some modern representatives, e.g. the echidna, are secondarily nocturnal. On the other hand, the hedgehogs and tenrecs, having remained in the nocturnal niche, have retained 'reptilian-type' energetics. Such arguments, however, rest not only on the details of the analysis of results (Dawson & Grant 1980) but also upon assumptions about biological trends in evolution and their adaptive consequences.

Although hedgehogs are in many ways conservative they are capable of well-regulated hibernation, which may be regarded as a specialized rather than a primitive characteristic (Poczopko 1980). Furthermore, Shkolnik (1980) reviewed the evidence of studies of *Erinaceus europaeus*, *Hemiechinus auritus* and *Paraechinus aethiopicus* and concluded that hedgehogs, despite having a somewhat lower body temperature, are no less effective at thermoregulation than other mammals. The tendency to become hot (hyperthermic) at environmental temperatures close to body temperature is shared by most other nocturnal mammals and may, in some circumstances, be viewed as an economical adaptation to cope with a hot environment (Shkolnik 1980). Kayser (1961) showed that active hedgehogs increased heat output as temperature drops, just as in other non-hibernating mammals. The data presented showed a linear increase in metabolic rate of over two and a half times as the ambient temperature was reduced from 30 to −4°C. Kayser nevertheless found that hedgehogs regulated imperfectly outside this temperature range.

Adaptive specialization

Although from a wide range of climates, all hedgehogs have a similar body temperature (see above), but they do have different thermoregulatory adaptations. The Standard Metabolic Rate (SMR) of *Erinaceus*, when normalized to 38°C (assuming a Q_{10} of 2·5) is what one might expect for a typical eutherian, but the normalized SMR values of the desert species are lower: about 26% and 49% lower for *Hemiechinus* and *Paraechinus* respectively (Table 6.2). A lowered metabolic rate is a common adaptation to hot and arid

TABLE 6.2 *Standard resting metabolic rates of three species of hedgehogs.*

Species	No. of animals	Body mass (g)[a]	Body temperature (°C)[a]	Metabolic rate ($\dot{V}O_2$) Measured (ml h^{-1})	% of predicted[b]
Erinaceus europaeus	5	749 ±183	34·00 ±0·74	337·05	98
Hemiechinus auritus	8	397 ±60	33·75 ±0·61	150·86	74
Paraechinus aethiopicus	5	453 ±59	34·19 ±0·64	108·75	51

[a]Mean ± standard deviation.
[b] $\dot{V}O_2$ (ml h^{-1}) = 2·3 M(g)$^{0.75}$ (Dawson & Hulbert 1970).
Source: Shkolnik (1980).

TABLE 6.3 *Evaporative water loss (E) in relation to metabolic rate (M) in hedgehogs at various ambient temperatures (T_a).*

$T_a(°C)$	20	T1.c.[a]	35	40
Erinaceus				
T_B (°C)	34	34	37·5	38–39
E (mg H_2O g^{-1} h^{-1})	0·8	1·0	2·6	6·7–10
E/M (%)	9·0	22·5	55·0	101–120
Hemiechinus				
T_B (°C)	33·8	33·8	36	37·5–39
E (mg H_2O g^{-1} h^{-1})	1·0	1·0	2·2	4·0–8·2
E/M (%)	9·3	30	48	106–160
Paraechinus				
T_B (°C)	34·2	34·2	35·5	36·2–38·5
E (mg H_2O g^{-1} h^{-1})	0·45	0·55	0·65	3·3–4·5
E/M (%)	7·6	30	57	108–137

[a]Lower critical temperature: for *Erinaceus*, 29°C; for *Hemiechinus*, 30°C; for *Paraechinus*, 31°C. T_B = body temperature.
Source: Shkolnik (1980).

conditions among mammals because it conserves energy in a harsh environment where food may be scarce and it greatly reduces evaporative water loss (Table 6.3). A low overall thermal conductance (rate of heat exchange of the body core with the environment) may also help maintain body temperature (Shkolnik 1980). Intriguingly, unlike *Erinaceus* and *Hemiechinus* and many 'advanced' mammals, *Paraechinus* does not respond to increases in ambient temperatures by raising its overall thermal conductance, which is usually achieved by vasomotor control of peripheral blood vessels. Although this lack of response to environmental temperature changes could be construed as 'primitive', Shkolnik (1980) considered such a mechanism to be dispensable in a nocturnal mammal.

Kayser (1961) reviewed the findings of studies by Issaakian & Felberbaum (1949) and Issaakian (1955) which showed that active *Hemiechinus auritus* regulated its temperature better than *Erinaceus europaeus* in response to environmental fluctuations during the summer. Intriguingly, their studies also revealed that wild hibernators regulated their temperature better than captive ones. Whatever the value of laboratory studies of thermoregulatory capacities, it must be emphasized that such conditions bear little relationship to the situation in the wild. Wroot (1984a) pointed out that in the field, the rate of heat loss by thermal conductance (body heat loss), outside the thermoneutral zone, is affected by factors such as air speed, evaporative cooling and heat absorption from outside sources (usually the sun for diurnal animals).

Energy requirements

Weight loss and energy use during hibernation

As fat reserves are depleted during hibernation, hedgehogs usually lose a great deal of weight. For European hedgehogs estimates of weight loss vary: around 25% in England (Carlier & Lovatt Evans 1903, Morris 1984), 20–40% in Sweden (Kristiansson 1984) and an average 40% (maximum 50%) loss for captives after 160–170 days of hibernation in Finland (Kristoffersson & Suomalainen 1964). Kok & Van Ee (1989) noted weight losses in the order of 15% for semi-captive southern African hedgehogs (*Atelerix frontalis*) which did not feed during 3 months of hibernation.

Assuming a weight loss range of 25–40%, Morris (1984) estimated that, in Britain, a youngster in its first season must achieve a minimum pre-hibernation weight of roughly 450–550 g. In continental Europe, where hedgehogs are somewhat larger, Poduschka & Saupe (1981) suggested a minimum pre-hibernation weight of around 700 g, but according to evidence from Denmark Morris' estimate may be more realistic (Walhovd 1975, 1990).

Measures of daily weight loss of captive hibernating European hedgehogs are fairly consistent at around 0·2–0·3% of bodyweight, or 1–2 g (Camus & Gley 1901, Kristoffersson & Suomalainen 1964, Kramm *et al.* 1975, Wroot 1984a). These data are also consistent with a study of *Erinaceus concolor* and *Hemiechinus auritus* in which both species lost an average of around 1·2 g day^{-1} during a 4-month hibernation at 11°C (Dmi'el & Schwartz, 1984). Wroot's (1984a) estimate that a hibernating 600-g European hedgehog would consume an average of 1 g of bodyweight per day provides a useful 'rule of thumb' to gauge the minimum weight gain to survive a hibernation period.

To determine energy use during hibernation, oxygen (O_2) consumption may be used to calculate energy use (4·74 cal ml^{-1} O_2). However, the effects of body temperature on metabolic rate must be corrected for, before studies can be meaningfully compared. *Erinaceus europaeus* hibernating at around 4°C used 0·0106–0·0148 ml O_2 g^{-1} h^{-1} (Tähti 1978), equivalent to about 0·7–1·0 kcal day^{-1}, in line with the 0·0109 ml O_2 g^{-1} h^{-1} given by Kayser (1961: figure corrected to 4°C assuming $Q_{10} = 2·3$) and the 0·0148 ml O_2 g^{-1} h^{-1} (corrected figure) given by Dmi'el & Schwartz (1984) for *E. concolor*. Oddly, Dmi'el & Schwartz found O_2 consumption to be twice as high in *Hemiechinus auritus*, for no clear reason but possibly because of its smaller size and slightly poorer insulation.

Although such figures provide metabolic guidelines, total energy use during the hibernation period will vary with ambient conditions, bodyweight, the degree of disturbance and the number of arousals. Dmi'el & Schwartz (1984) calculated that the cost of keeping a normal body temperature for 1 day is roughly equivalent to 7 days of torpor, and that 85% of energy consumed during the whole hibernation period was used during the short periods of awakening (very close to Kayser's estimate of 90%).

TABLE 6.4　*Comparisions between estimates of resting metabolic rate for European hedgehogs at 25°C reported in the literature.*

Authors	Ambient temperature (°C)	Resting metabolic rate at 25°C (ml g^{-1} h^{-1})[a]
Hildwein & Malan (1970)	25	0·490
Shkolnik & Schmidt-Nielsen (1976)	30	0·630[b]
Tähti (1978)	25–26	
June		0·557
August		0·433
October		0·357
Wroot (1984)	13–25	0·514[b]

[a] Volume O_2 or CO_2 depending on study.
[b] Calculated from regression equation.
Source: Wroot (1984a).

Energetics and food requirement in active hedgehogs

In an investigation of energetics and feeding in hedgehogs, Wroot (1984a) used respirometry (based on CO_2 production), to obtain measures of the metabolic rate of newly captured wild hedgehogs during various activities, including locomotion in an unpowered treadmill. There were no significant differences between males and females, either in the time spent in the treadmill, or in their average speed (about 20–23 m min^{-1}). The metabolic rate of active hedgehogs varied from about 2·65 ml CO_2 g^{-1} h^{-1} (adjusted to 25°C) at a speed of 8 m min^{-1} to about 3·2 ml CO_2 g^{-1} h^{-1} at 33 m min^{-1}. Measures of resting metabolic rate from several studies are presented in Table 6.4.

The large volume of air in the respirometry chamber in Wroot's study meant that Daily Metabolic Requirement (DMR) could be determined more accurately than instantaneous metabolic rate. Interestingly, he found that the DMR of a hedgehog that was not rapidly changing weight could be quite accurately estimated from only its weight the average air temperature and the duration of its activity (when hedgehogs spend most of their time foraging average speed is rather constant; see Chapters 3, 4 and 7).

Wroot estimated a daily requirement for a hedgehog (500–700 g) to be about 90–140 kcal (377–586 kJ), equivalent to around 18–28 g dry weight (60–90 g wet weight) of food per day—equivalent to something like 230–400 caterpillars or leatherjackets! Such estimates of daily intake are close to the 71 g suggested by Kruuk (1964) and the 57 g suggested by Morris (1967). The filled stomach of a hedgehog contains about 32 g of food (Yalden 1976) thus it must be filled two or three times per night, resulting in bimodal or trimodal feeding rhythms (see Chapters 3 and 7).

CHAPTER 7

Behaviour: the Ordinary and the Extraordinary

MANY aspects of hedgehog behaviour are considered in context elsewhere in this volume, for example: communication (Chapter 2), aggression and defence (Chapters 2, 4 and 8), feeding and habitat choice (Chapters 3 and 4), movement patterns (Chapter 4), nesting (Chapter 5), sexual and maternal behaviour (Chapter 8). In this chapter I shall first examine the way hedgehogs usually spend their active hours, and then focus on two of the more extraordinary and unexplained aspects of hedgehog behaviour.

NOCTURNAL ACTIVITY RHYTHMS AND GENERAL BEHAVIOUR

Hedgehogs are not normally active during broad daylight and animals that are seen active during the middle of the day are often found to be ill. Nevertheless, healthy animals are sometimes active during the day—maybe because they have been disturbed, or perhaps they are still hungry. Certainly the pressures of litter rearing may drive lactating mothers to increase their level of activity (Chapter 4). One lactating female European hedgehog, radio-tracked around Kalinin (Russia), was active almost as much during the day as at night (Philchagov 1988). It seems that although hedgehogs 'prefer' to be nocturnal, it is clearly not obligatory. I observed that during the short mid-summer nights in Britain, hedgehogs tended to emerge before sunset and some retired to their nests well after dawn (Fig. 7.1). Later in the season, the hedgehogs remained active later in the darker mornings—maybe they took advantage of the extra foraging time to improve body condition before hibernating, or prey abundance might have been declining, or changes in prey type could have required a re-scheduling of foraging behaviour.

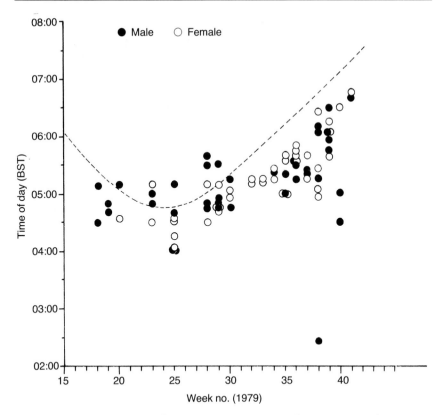

FIG. 7.1   *Known time of retirement to a nest in relation to time of sunrise for radio-tracked European hedgehogs in Britain. Dashed line shows the time of sunrise (British Summer Time). Source: Reeve (1981).*

As briefly mentioned in Chapters 3 and 6, studies of caged hedgehogs have tended to reveal a bimodal activity rhythm with a main peak in the evening (21:00–24:00 hours) and a second smaller one at around 03:00 hours (e.g. Kristoffersson 1964, Campbell 1975). Similar results were obtained by Herter (1934, 1971) in studies of a range of captive species (*Erinaceus europaeus*, *Paraechinus aethiopicus*, *Atelerix algirus*, *A. albiventris* and *Hemiechinus auritus*) although the resumption of feeding in the early morning was quite variable and the data from *E. europaeus* seemed to suggest three activity peaks (Herter 1934, 1965b). However, in captivity, feeding rhythms may dominate the overall activity pattern. Nevertheless, field studies of European hedgehogs have also tended to reveal a similar, but less well-defined, bimodal feeding rhythmn (Campbell 1975, Wroot 1984a). However, with regard to *general* activity, I found that the animals were active throughout the night and their speed of movement varied erratically with no apparent rhythmicity. Animals only occasionally took short rests (not in a nest) at various times during their nocturnal excursions. This pattern of activity has also been shown in other radio-tracking studies of European hedgehogs in Sweden (Kristiansson & Erlinge 1977) and Russia (Philchagov 1988), although Philchagov reported a surprising amount of day-time activity.

How does a hedgehog spend its time?

The only reliable way to answer this question is to observe as many individuals as possible, in the wild, for prolonged periods; usually only possible in a radio-tracking study. Here, I shall briefly present the findings of two such studies, my own (Reeve 1981) and Wroot (1984a), both of which used the same study area—a golf course in the West London suburbs (UK). Both studies used behavioural 'spot-checks' at 1-min intervals during periods of observation, a method based on the assumption that the relative frequency with which any particular behaviour is recorded reflects the proportion of time a hedgehog devotes to that behaviour. Of course, we could only properly observe animals out in the open, so the recorded repertoire is artificially limited to overt behaviour and excludes hidden activities such as nest building, and maternal behaviour in the nest.

Whereas Andy Wroot was trying to obtain a detailed activity budget for a study of foraging and ecological energetics, my priority was to obtain as many location fixes as possible for up to four different animals each night. This means that his data are more regularly timed and continuous than mine, because my observation periods were interrupted by frequent tours around the study area. There are many practical difficulties with behavioural field studies—especially at night—and subjective judgements may vary; for example, when does a fast walk become running? Simultaneous behaviour such as locomotion and foraging can also cause recording problems for the observer and very brief activities (e.g. scratching) are likely to be somewhat under-represented in 'spot checks'. We both had problems with animals that spent long periods out of sight, mainly in nearby private gardens, during which we could only distinguish active from inactive animals by the modulation of the radio-signal caused by their movements. Despite a few procedural differences both sets of data are fairly comparable. I have re-categorized the raw data from both studies to produce an equivalent classification of activities, the relative frequencies of which are presented in Fig. 7.2.

As can be seen, Wroot found that his male subjects spent more time out of sight in the gardens around the study site than the females, a feature related more to the larger home ranges of the males than to any sex difference in habitat choice. My results showed no sex difference of any significance except perhaps a tendency for males to be found on the move more often. The disparity in the level of locomotion probably reflects observer differences in differentiation between the combined activities of walking and foraging. As in my study (Chapter 4), Wroot found non-sexual meetings to be rare among the hedgehogs and recorded only one, a fight.

Both studies showed that around half or more of the hedgehog's time is

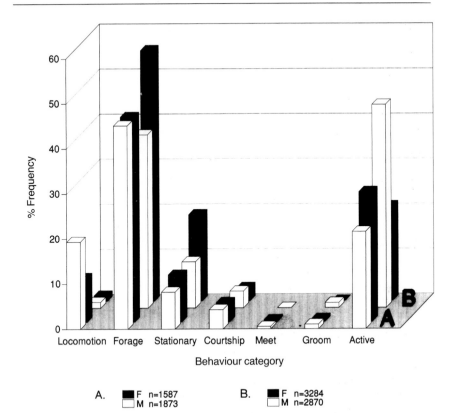

FIG. 7.2 *Bar graphs showing the percentage frequencies of activities recorded for* Erinaceus europaeus *(males and females) on a suburban golf course (southern England).* n = *the number of behavioural records for each sex (M/F). Behaviour categories: Locomotion = walking or running, Forage = foraging for food or feeding, Stationary = paused/stationary outside the nest, Courtship = courtship/copulation, Meet = any non-sexual encounter with another hedgehog, Groom = scratching/biting at fur or spines, Active = active but unspecified behaviour (usually hidden from view). Source:* **A.** *N. Reeve unpublished data, from 1978–1979;* **B.** *Wroot (1984a), data from 1981–1982.*

spent foraging, during which the animal keeps up a fairly steady meandering walk, punctuated with pauses and short bursts of rapid movement. When foraging, a hedgehog will constantly sniff the air and ground, occasionally pausing to listen intently (Plate 1). Most of the rest of the time was taken up with simply walking and occasional pauses. Bouts of courtship only accounted for around 4% of observations overall; other encounters were very infrequent. Assuming that hedgehogs hidden from view behave in the same way as when they are visible, Wroot's data indicate that hedgehogs spend around 58% (males) or 65% (females) of the time foraging (respectively, 41%

and 64% in my study). However, Wroot (1984a) pointed out that active animals concealed in the gardens, where food is abundant, were likely to be foraging virtually all the time. This led him to suggest that hedgehogs really spend about 68–84% of their time foraging, a value which fits well with Berthoud's (1982) estimate of 72% .

Extraordinary Behaviour

With our inability to participate in its sensory world, the life of a hedgehog may often seem a trifle mundane to us. Yet our knowledge of hedgehog behaviour is far from complete, and some bizarre activities still await convincing explanation.

Self-anointing

This strange and unique behaviour has been observed by almost everyone who has kept or studied hedgehogs (e.g. Lindemann 1951, Eisentraut 1952, Herter 1956, Burton 1957, 1969, Poduschka & Firbas 1968, Walton & Walton 1973, Brockie 1976, Brodie 1977, Gustato *et al.* 1984, and others). Each researcher has his or her own ideas about the signficance of the behaviour, but it still defies full explanation.

Self-anointing is usually elicited when the hedgehog detects certain substances, commonly with a strong smell or taste—although there are exceptions. The hedgehog sniffs, licks and chews at the substance and produces mouthfuls of frothy saliva. It then 'spits' the saliva on to its back and flanks (mainly the spiny areas but sometimes also the fur) by turning its head back over its shoulders and using flicking motions of its tongue (Fig. 7.3). The result is that the hedgehog spatters itself with saliva which is either mixed with the triggering substance or (presumably) contaminated with its odour. The activity may be brief, with only one or two spitting actions, or may last an hour or more but during this period the hedgehog is highly absorbed and difficult to distract from its actions. It chews, salivates and spits with almost

FIG. 7.3 *Detail of a self-anointing hedgehog showing the flicking action of the tongue, as described by Poduschka & Firbas (1968).*

frenzied movements, contorting its body to reach the more inaccessible areas on both sides.

Although the triggering substance is usually taken into the mouth, hedgehogs sometimes self-anoint as a response to odours alone (Herter 1956), but Gustato *et al.* (1984) noted that the more licking and chewing that took place, the more prolonged was the anointing. The hedgehogs may appear rather tired and dazed after their behaviour but they tend to have an increased appetite (Lindemann 1951). Lindemann also observed that only healthy animals would anoint themselves.

The behaviour was originally called *Selbstbespucken* or *Selbstbespeicheln* ('self-spitting') by early German researchers, and Burton (1957) coined the now commonly used English name of self-anointing. This bizarre behaviour seems to be common to all spiny hedgehogs and has been observed in several species representing all four genera. The diversity of natural and unnatural substances known to elicit the behaviour is such that it is hard to identify common characteristics, although they generally have an acrid or pungent odour. However, the substance is sometimes totally innocuous; apparently hedgehogs have self-anointed when presented with only distilled water (Burton 1969)! The list of substances reported to trigger self-anointing is truly mind-boggling; it includes other hedgehogs, dog urine and faeces, tortoises and toads, fox fur, human sweat, leather and polish, various glues and varnish, insulating tape, enamelled or glazed surfaces, fish, egg, coffee, cream, tar, soot, creosote, tobacco and its smoke or ash, soil, many kinds of plants or their parts, wool, nylon stockings, cotton, newsprint, valerian, perfumes and cosmetics (Lindemann 1951, Herter 1956, Burton 1969).

Lindemann (1951) and Herter (1956) both considered that none of the substances that triggered self-anointing was acceptable as food, but Burton's list also included tinned cat-food, boiled fish, slugs and worms, all of which are eaten readily. One animal, Rufus, self-anointed for three hours after taking food of any kind (Burton 1969). Oddly several other strong-smelling substances, petrol, paraffin, turpentine, vinegar, olive oil, whisky and cognac, do not elict self-anointing (Lindemann 1951, Gustato *et al.* 1984). The substance does not have to be novel (as claimed by Lindemann) because hedgehogs may be repeatedly stimulated by the same trigger substance; for example my pet hedgehog, Emily, habitually chewed an old woollen carpet and anointed herself (Plate 14). However, a stimulus that induces self-anointing on one occasion may fail to elicit any response from the same individual on another occasion (Burton 1957). Self-anointing has been reported for animals of both sexes, solitary individuals, when animals meet (both sexual and non-sexual encounters) and in animals of all ages—including nestlings when still blind (Plate 15).

Because natural behaviour may become distorted in captivity and is often incomprehensible outside its natural context, looking for the behaviour in the wild is an obvious strategy but one that has been rarely pursued. Herter (1956) did mention that he had seen wild hedgehogs with spittle on their backs, but the first detailed observations were provided by Brockie (1976) who examined

929 wild hedgehogs in New Zealand and observed foamy saliva on the backs of 19 (eight females, 11 males). He found no connection between self-anointing and moon phase, wind direction or strength, time of night or ectoparasite burden (although there are no hedgehog fleas in New Zealand, mite infestations are common).

Brockie concluded that self-anointing might be a means of presenting a sexual odour, possibly of a type similar to the androgen-related odour secreted into the saliva of the male pig (*Sus scrofa*) which prompts the female to stand ready for copulation. The data he cited in support of this idea were interesting but not at all conclusive. He did not observe wild animals actually anointing in a sexual context, but found spittle-covered animals only during those months in which courtships were observed. In 19 observations of courtships he found animals that had evidently recently anointed themselves on five occasions.

During my 3-year field study in Britain (1977–1979), I found only nine animals that showed clear evidence of recent self-anointing, three of which were subadults. Usually I could not tell what the trigger substance had been, but on two occasions the animals had apparently plastered themselves with dog faeces! Luckily, I also witnessed three instances of wild hedgehogs (two adults and a subadult) self-anointing in the field: to my knowledge the first such observations. The animals were alone and the trigger substances were dog faeces, a white painted post (not freshly painted), and a rag used to wipe golf clubs. Unlike Brockie, I found animals that had self-anointed outside the breeding season and not in the context of courtship or any other meeting of hedgehogs. A laboratory study of five female European hedgehogs in Italy (Gustato *et al*. 1984) also recorded self-anointing during July–December, though much less in December. My pet hedgehog Emily self-anointed at all times of the year and alone. I therefore find it hard to accept Brockie's suggestion that self-anointing has a principally sexual function; if it were so then why was this behaviour apparently absent from three-quarters of the courtships he observed? Why do both sexes do it? Why should the subadults in my study do it? Why do nestlings do it? Brockie accounted for the latter by suggesting that the nestlings' enhanced odour would aid retrieval by the mother in the event of them straying—a suggestion of a more general odour function (see below).

A possible link with sexual behaviour is raised again by the findings of an investigation by Poduschka & Firbas (1968). They observed that during the licking and chewing movements of self-anointing, the foamy saliva was brought into contact with the oral openings of the nasopalatine ducts which lead to the Jacobson's organ—a specialized olfactory organ in the palate that is known to be important in the sexual behaviour of some mammals, notably the ungulates and many carnivores, but is also implicated in feeding behaviour (Chapter 2). A characteristic feature of self-anointing is a peculiar flicking with the underside of the tongue against the roof of the mouth, an action that may help (in conjunction with serous gland secretions which flush the organ) to clear the froth from the nasopalatine duct, apparently making way for another sample of saliva mixture (Poduschka & Firbas 1968).

Whether or not the function of self-anointing is sexually related is uncertain, but what does seem definite is that the process effectively transfers the odours of the trigger substance and the hedgehog's saliva on to its spines and that the hedgehog uses all its chemoreception options (smell, taste and Jacobson's organ) in what must be an intense sensory experience. The newly anointed hedgehog seems to have a characteristically sharp smell which is not simply the smell of the trigger substance (Brockie 1976, Reeve 1981). The spines will not mat together like fur and have an enormous surface area, making a perfect odour dispersal system. Bearing all this in mind, it seems almost inconceivable that such behaviour is anything other than some form of personal scent marking. The functional explanation may simply be that self-anointing forms a strong personal body odour, which combines elements of the trigger substance and salivary secretions. The role of the Jacobson's organ could be to monitor the composition of the mixture.

Personal odours have the potential for use in a variety of situations such as the formation of odour trails around the home range, the detection and/or mutual avoidance of other hedgehogs (Chapter 4), and a general broadcast of body odours which may convey information in aggressive and sexual encounters, as well as in interactions between a mother and her young. This 'social' use of body odour might also help to explain why hedgehogs will sometimes anoint when presented with another strange hedgehog.

Although the idea of a general purpose personal odour is attractive, it is largely speculative and some aspects of self-anointing remain hard to explain. What is the significance of the peculiar range of trigger substances? If the behaviour provides the animal with a fundamentally important 'social' odour, why is the behaviour so rarely observed in the wild? One of the strangest aspects is that the hedgehogs become so engrossed in their anointing that they become a potentially easy target for a predator.

Despite a lack of hard evidence, the 'general body odour' explanation seems to me to be more tenable than most of the many alternatives that have been proposed, the most likely of which I describe below.

The odours may camouflage the hedgehog's own smell, or make it repellant to predators: at first this idea seems sound—hedgehogs will anoint themselves with dog faeces, grass and other substances in their environment which might act as olfactory camouflage. However, to the human nose, the hedgehog's odour is strongly *enhanced* by the behaviour (Brockie 1976, Reeve 1981). Furthermore, Lindemann (1951) conducted 60 trials using a dog that was keen on hedgehogs, and found that hedgehogs were always detected at an average of 12·5 m, whether or not they had self-anointed. It is thus unlikely that the camouflage would be effective and the smell of most of the trigger substances would probably not repel a predator, although some of the more noxious alternatives could have such an effect.

FIG. 7.4   *Hedgehogs are more supple than is often supposed and may use the long claws of the hind feet to scratch and groom the more inaccessible parts of their bodies. Source: based on a photograph in Poduschka & Poduschka (1972).*

Self-anointing may groom and condition the spines, and/or kill ectoparasites: this is unlikely since the spines do not need to be kept supple, and need no conditioning, in fact they become relatively soggy when soaked. The spines and skin are not cleaned by self-anointing, they are always made dirtier (Lindemann 1951, Herter 1956). Hedgehogs, contrary to common belief, can groom their spines by scratching with their long hind claws (Fig. 7.4) and can reach much of the body with their mouths, although it is true that they pay little attention to personal hygiene! If the saliva mixture is effective in killing ectoparasites (which are found all over the body) it would be senseless to apply it mainly to the spines, although Dimelow (1963a) also observed thorough licking of the fur of the groin region. Neither is self-anointing a response to particularly heavy infestations because captive hedgehogs without any ectoparasites also anoint themselves. As a final dismissal of this idea, most trigger substances are clearly not effective pesticides—if they worked one might expect hedgehogs to have lighter ectoparasite burdens—and rolling in mud would probably give better results! Long-eared hedgehogs (*Hemiechinus auritus*) often sand-bathe, which may help to explain why they have comparatively few ticks (Schoenfeld & Yom-Tov 1985, see Chapter 9).

The trigger substance may add an irritant factor to the spines, increasing antipredator effectiveness: Brodie (1977) conducted experiments to show that the spines of hedgehogs who had self-anointed using toad skins (*Bufo* spp.) became coated with the toxic secretions from the toad's skin glands. It is not at all surprising that spines coated in this way (or artificially) with toxic toad skin secretions caused severe local reactions when jabbed into the arms of volunteers. But Brodie's oft-repeated suggestion that self-anointing is an adaptation to apply irritant substances to the spines, enhancing their effectiveness against predators, is baseless. If he had conducted the experiment with any of the innocuous substances with which hedgehogs also commonly anoint themselves, the results would have been totally different! Much more interesting is the fact that spines coated only with saliva caused no reaction, demonstrating that the saliva itself is not toxic (although he did not state how, or under what circumstances, the saliva was collected).

The behaviour may have no adaptive function: the anointing may be a non-functional response to a smell or taste stimulus—like the catnip response of cats (Burton 1969). Although self-anointing and the catnip response seem similar in many respects, such as the frenzied actions and its occurrence irrespective of sex or age, the catnip response in many (but not all) of the cat family, evokes recognizably sexual behavioural elements (Ewer 1973). In hedgehogs the behaviour is triggered by a much wider range of substances and self-anointing does not resemble any other type of behaviour. Burton (1969) suggested that self-anointing could be a relic of some ancestral cooling behaviour, triggered out of its original context; the saliva is an inconvenience and simply cleared from the mouth, using the spines, as quickly as possible. However, if the spitting was just a way of clearing the mouth why would the hedgehogs bother to spread it over the more inaccessible parts of its spiny coat? Anyway, it seems to me that the poorly vascularized spiny back would be a poor choice of site for the application of saliva in any cooling behaviour and more cooling would result from using the thin, vascular skin of the limbs and belly. Even in the tropics, hedgehogs have not been reported to cool themselves in this way, and being nocturnal probably do not need to. It seems unlikely to me that self-anointing is really non-functional. If there were no benefits to the behaviour, its expression would certainly be a selective disadvantage, as it leaves the hedgehog very vulnerable to predation.

Therefore, despite the lack of a clear functional explanation of self-anointing, it seems most likely that this intriguing behaviour is indeed some kind of scent-marking behaviour, involving the sensory use of the Jacobson's organ. Further detailed observation and experiment are needed to understand its role, but until such data are available, it is clear that this popular debate will continue!

As a postscript, it is pertinent to point out (as have many previous authors) that the spiny 'hedgehog' tenrecs (Chapter 1) use a scent-marking behaviour with some similarities to hedgehog self-anointing. As in hedgehogs, the behaviour can be released by a variety of chemical stimuli, but in tenrecs the urine from another individual frequently serves as a releaser. While sniffing and licking at the urine the tenrec salivates on to it, and the resulting puddle is then wiped onto the animal's flanks by repeated alternate strokes of the forepaws; the muzzle may also be wiped in a 'washing' action (Gould & Eisenberg 1966). Thus the tenrecs also make use of the large evaporative surface of the spines for odour disperal, although the technique used is somewhat different. Although it is virtually certain that it is a form of scent marking, no further functional details are known.

Running in circles

This strange behaviour is something I have never seen, but is well documented in the European hedgehog (*Erinaceus europaeus*). A particularly good description is given by Boys Smith (1967) who, over a period of a month (May–June), observed a hedgehog (sex unknown) which almost every night would run in a large circle for long periods in the same part of the garden. The circle varied a little but typically was 15 yards (nearly 14 m) in diameter, and the hedgehog ran anticlockwise at a steady speed of about 4·5 miles h^{-1} (7·2 km h^{-1}) for up to 2 h or even longer, easily visible in the light of nearby street lamps. About one-third of the circular route was on a gravel drive, the remainder on a grass lawn, and the hedgehog easily mounted and dismounted the stone border between the two areas. This hedgehog always appeared and ran as night fell, but also at various times during the night. Apart from the circle-running the animal seemed to behave normally, was aware of the approach of an observer, foraged normally between running bouts and would feed on bread and milk if provided. One night the hedgehog disappeared and was never seen again.

Similar behaviour has been observed by Dimelow (1963a) in captive animals when placed on a laboratory floor—some would run in either direction but others would always turn clockwise or anticlockwise. Other circle-running incidents have several times been reported in letters to newspapers, some of which were reviewed by Burton (1969). While Burton felt unable to offer any explanation, except to say that it may have some relationship to courtship circling, Morris (1983) suggested that such circle-running might be an abnormal behaviour resulting from some kind of infection, or pesticide poisoning. Tentative support for the latter idea is that circle-running seems to be a relatively recently reported behaviour, being confined to the period since the 1960s, when relatively large amounts of garden pesticides began to be used (Morris 1983). Blind animals can behave fairly normally (Morris 1985a), so this is unlikely to be a factor in circle-running; however, maggot- or mite-infested ears, viral or bacterial infections of the ears or nervous tissue, or parasite infestations (Chapter 9) could all cause such behaviour.

CHAPTER 8

Reproduction

A S the hibernation period varies in different climatic regions (Chapter 6), the timing and duration of the breeding season also varies in different populations and between species. European hedgehogs (*Erinaceus europaeus*), kept outside or in a laboratory, may become sexually active more than 2 months earlier than in the wild (Allanson & Deanesly 1935).

Hedgehogs usually breed seasonally and sexual behaviour begins soon after the end of hibernation, but the seasonal pattern may vary and some species may breed throughout the year. The sexual cycle of male *E. europaeus* varies regionally. In Fennoscandia, testis activity usually starts in January (during the hibernation period) and maximum testosterone secretion and spermatogenesis occurs in May (shortly after final arousal from hibernation). The rut ends around mid-July when testis activity rapidly declines and remains low until the following January (Saure 1969). Similarly, in Sweden, the rut peaks in late May and early June but then rapidly declines; Kristiansson (1984) observed no courtships in August. In these countries late litters are exceptional.

In the rest of Europe, although testis activity starts at around the same time, full spermatogenesis and endocrine activity are found as early as March or April, and there is an earlier emergence from hibernation. Testis activity may persist until August but declines to a minimum from the end of September onwards. Consequently late litters are quite common. Walhovd (1981) presented numerous records of young born in August–October in Denmark. In central France the rut is divided into two phases, in spring and in late summer, with gonadal regression in September–November (Saboureau & Dutourné 1981).

In England, the breeding season starts in earnest around mid-May, shortly after the females have emerged from hibernation (Reeve 1981). Exceptionally, nestlings have been found as early as April, courting animals have been found up to the end of September and there are records of some litters in October (Barrett-Hamilton 1911, Morris 1966). In England and Wales, Morris (1961) found a pregnancy rate of 52% ($n = 25$ adult females) in September,

173

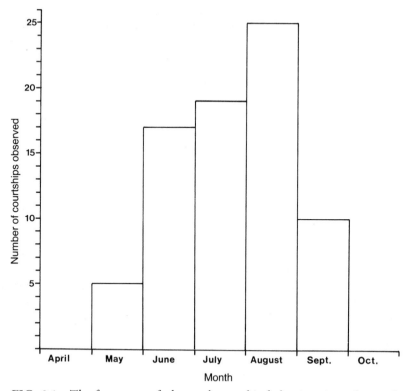

FIG. 8.1 *The frequency of observed courtship behaviour in each month (1977–1979 data combined) for European hedgehogs inhabiting a suburban golf course in southern England. Source: Reeve (1981).*

comparable to the average 44% ($n = 63$) rate during the May–July period. Therefore, even though the majority of sexual activity occurs from May to mid-August, courtship or pregnancies may be found during most of the active year—roughly March–October (Deanesly 1934, Herter 1965b, Reeve 1981; see Fig. 8.1).

Introduced *E. europaeus* in New Zealand have a breeding season centred around November–March (equivalent to the April–August breeding season in Europe) but the mild climate permits breeding well outside this core period (Parkes 1975).

In the northern Caucasus (Chechenko-Ingushetiya region, CIS) *E. concolor* ruts mainly during the first 20 days of April. Vasilenko (1988) found a 40% pregnancy rate in the first 20 days of May; at the same time males showed maximum testis size. Lower pregnancy rates (15·4% were found in late May and the first 10 days of July (no data for June). Later, only lactating females were found and males showed reduced testis size. In the humid, subtropical Black Sea coast, the rut is about 2 weeks earlier. Samples from locations extending as far south as Kobuleti (Georgia) revealed pregnancy rates of about 32–41% (late April–early May). Vasilenko suggested that youngsters may breed later in the year. Further south, in Israel the rut is also relatively advanced, with courtships observed from March to late May (Schoenfeld & Yom-Tov 1985). In central Europe, Poduschka (1969) noted that females may produce two litters, one at the end of May and a second at the end of August.

The breeding season of the Indian species of long-eared hedgehog (*Hemiechinus collaris*) generally resembles that of *E. europaeus*. Around Jaipur and in Uttar Pradesh (Agra and Etawah), reproductively active females are found from March to August, with most Graafian follicles in the ovaries in May and June. Pregnancies occur from April to the end of August, but females may undergo a period of anoestrus at any time of year. In these regions, and also in the Punjab and in the Indus valley around Karachi (Pakistan), males reach peak sexual condition in April–May (active spermatogenesis from March to August) and become sexually regressed by October (Walton & Walton 1973, Goyal & Mathur 1974, Kanwar *et al.* 1980, Asawa & Mathur 1981, 1986, Pandey & Munshi 1987).

However, in some very arid habitats breeding may be delayed. In ravines and scrubland around Agra, wild *H. collaris* breed from June to September (Maheshwari 1982) and in Rajasthan (north-western India) litters are generally born in August and September (sometimes in July), (i.e. mating from June to August). Breeding thus falls between a period of extreme heat in May–June and cooler weather in December and January, and the young can benefit from an increased food availability resulting from the monsoon rains of July–August (Prakash 1960, Maheshwari 1982, 1984). Similarly, in Pakistan, most litters are born during August and September, at the height of the monsoon when insect prey are most abundant (Roberts 1977).

In the regions of Pakistan inhabited by the subspecies *Hemiechinus auritus megalotis* (sometimes called the Afghan hedgehog) there is no monsoon, and mating probably takes place straight after emergence from hibernation. Litters are therefore produced in the late spring (but sometimes as early as mid-April) and early summer (Roberts 1977). *Hemiechinus auritus* in Afghanistan may start breeding in April; lactating females have been caught in July (Niethammer 1973).

In Pakistan, *Paraechinus micropus* breeds in the monsoon period and litters are born when prey are most abundant, July to September (Roberts 1977) or July in the deserts of Rajasthan (Prakash 1960). In Rajasthan, Bidwai & Bawa (1981) found high levels of spermatogenesis in captive males from April to August, but a period of regression and sexual inactivity from September to March. Spermatogenesis resumed in late March–April. Thus it seems that just as in *Hemiechinus* and *Erinaceus* the males are sexually functional well in advance of the period in which breeding occurs.

Little is known about Brandt's hedgehog (*Paraechinus hypomelas*). In Baluchistan (Pakistan), births may occur from late spring (one captive gave birth on 28 May) to early summer, but there is no evidence of a second litter.

The subspecies (*P. hypomelas blandfordi*), whose range extends to the Indus Basin, possibly breeds throughout the year in non-mountain areas where there is some monsoon influence (Roberts 1977).

In Libya, *Atelerix algirus* breeds from April to early June but sometimes produces a second litter in July (Hufnagl 1972), a similar pattern of seasonal breeding to that already described for the other genera. However, central African hedgehogs (*A. albiventris*) from Nairobi (Kenya) are sexually active throughout the year (Gregory 1976) and captives (from Togo, West Africa), kept in a 12:12 h light–dark régime, produced litters in every month (Brodie *et al.* 1982). But further south, in Zambia and Zimbabwe, *A. albiventris* breeds seasonally; the young are born in November, about 2 months after emerging from aestivation (Kingdon 1974).

Around Bloemfontein and north-eastern South Africa, hedgehogs (*A. frontalis*) hibernate from June to August and the young are born during the warm wet summers, usually between October and March but sometimes as late as April (Smithers 1983, Yates 1984, Kok & van Ee 1989). Nothing is known about the breeding season of this species in the more arid regions to the south and west.

REPRODUCTIVE ANATOMY AND PHYSIOLOGY

Predictably, it is the reproductive biology of the European genus *Erinaceus* that has been most frequently studied, but we also know a little about *Hemiechinus*. Sadly, there is a lack of even basic information about most hedgehog species, but it does seem that all hedgehogs share a fundamentally similar breeding biology that is modified, mainly with respect to seasonality, under widely differing ecological circumstances. The external appearance of the genitalia of both sexes is described in Chapter 2.

The male reproductive system

Apart from the enormous seasonal variation in size (see later), and the unusually large relative size of the seminal vesicles in mature animals, the basic sexual anatomy is unremarkable (Fig. 8.2). However, past studies have not always agreed on the homology and naming of the various sexual accessory glands (Marshall 1911, Allanson 1934, Kanwar *et al.* 1980). I have adhered to the terms used by Allanson (1934).

Studies of *Hemiechinus collaris* (Goyal & Mathur 1974, Kanwar *et al.* 1980, Maheshwari 1982) have indicated no functional or anatomical differences in the reproductive organs between the males of this species and *Erinaceus europaeus* as described by Allanson (1934).

Among the most noticeable features are two very large multi-lobed seminal vesicles, supported by connective tissue and lying dorsal to the bladder. They do not store sperm but produce copious amounts of a secretion heavily loaded

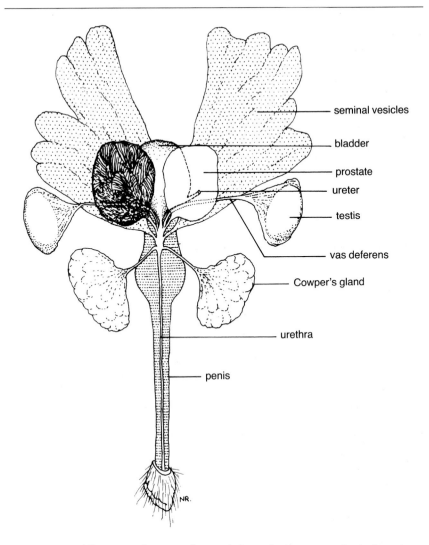

FIG. 8.2 *The genital tract of an adult male European hedgehog in breeding condition. The penis (shown in section) has been shown stretched backwards. Source: based on Allanson (1934). Illustration by the author.*

with a suspension of transparent protein crystalloid masses (Marshall 1911, Allanson 1934, Stieve 1948). On each side, the ducts from these lobes unite in a common sheath which runs into the muscular wall of the urethra. A pair of prostate glands, supported by peritoneal folds, form a flattened mass ventral to the bladder. Additionally, two well-developed glands lie outside the pelvis tucked behind the ischia in the thigh/buttock region, and a long duct runs from each to the urethra. Although considered to be Cowper's glands by certain authors (Owen 1868, Allanson 1934) not all workers have agreed on their homology (Marshall 1911).

The vas deferentia and the ducts of the seminal vesicles and prostate run within the urethral muscle and open into the urethral bulb just before the point of entry of the ducts from the Cowper's glands. The bulb itself contains two glandular masses (only visible in sections) with multiple ducts entering the urethra (Allanson 1934).

The copious secretions of the large accessory glands may be important in the formation of a vaginal plug which retains a quantity of sperm and mucus in the uterus. The plug is a milky gelatinous mass, apparently of clotted ejaculate, which forms within a couple of hours of copulation but disappears by the time fertilized ova are found in the uterus (Stieve 1948, Herter 1956). However, in a major study of female hedgehogs by Deanesly (1934) (see below), no vaginal plugs as such were found. Instead, citing earlier work by Courrier, she noted that, during the breeding season, the whole of the upper vagina was often found to be filled with a thick fluid containing sloughed epithelial cells mingled with the secretions of the cervical and vaginal glands. Thus the gelatinous contents of the upper vagina may be partly or entirely produced by the female. The formation of a post-copulatory vaginal plug in other animals is usually a male 'strategy' to avoid sperm competition from possible later matings by other males. This may be so in hedgehogs but, from the above evidence, such a functional interpretation of the 'vaginal plug' remains in doubt. It is notable that the sperm persist in the uterus for a remarkably long time after copulation, and may be found well into the first stages of pregnancy, although it is not known for how long they remain potent (Deanesly 1934).

Hedgehogs are ascrotal, that is to say the testes remain attached to the inside of the body wall and do not descend into a scrotum. In rut, however, the testes occupy a perineal pouch in the body wall, and are detectable from the outside (Marshall 1911). Most eutherian mammals use a countercurrent heat exchange in the blood supply of the spermatic cord and the pampiniform plexus to cool the testes. This is also likely (although unconfirmed) in European hedgehogs whose testes are also insulated from the body cavity by poorly vascularized pads of fat. The testes are maintained at an average of $1\cdot4 \pm 0\cdot2°C$ below body temperature in active animals from January to October (the period of gonadal activity). This temperature differential is not maintained during hibernation and is more variable ($\pm2°C$) in active animals from October to December when there is virtually no spermatogenesis (Fowler & Racey 1987). Lohiya & Dixit (1975) considered that countercurrent cooling of the testes did not occur in *Hemiechinus collaris*, but noted the testicular temperature to be $1\cdot0°C$ lower than rectal temperature ($34°C$) in anaesthetized animals.

The 'bulbo-cavernosus' type penis is long and flexed when at rest. Erection is achieved by engorgement of the *corpus cavernosum* and also by muscles which run down the length of the penis and insert on its dorsal surface (Owen 1868). The erect penis protrudes from its sheath by several centimetres, but I have not found exact measurements in the literature—hardly surprising in view of the problems presented in obtaining such data! The penis of European hedgehogs shows no significant seasonal size changes, but increases with age and body size. In adults it may weigh from 2·5 g up to around 6 g, whereas in immature animals it may weigh from 1 to 2·5 g (Allanson 1934). Allanson suggested that penis weight may be used to distinguish immature animals from adults in the spring.

The urethra opens on to a special projecting process of the glans penis (Owen 1868) but the form of the glans penis is somewhat different in each of the four genera (see Chapter 1). It is surprising however, that more people have not remarked upon the observation by Poduschka (1969), that in young *E. europaeus* (about 2 months old), the penis tip is a dark olive-green, which changes to a more conventional pinkish-red in adulthood.

Seasonal changes in the male reproductive system

Male European hedgehogs show marked seasonal changes in the size and activity of sexual organs (Allanson 1934). Early in the season, full sperm production precedes the development of the accessory glands (seminal vesicles, prostate and Cowper's glands) but these then develop remarkably, possibly becoming larger in proportion to body size than in any other mammal (Marshall 1911, Allanson & Deanesly 1935). In Germany, Stieve (1948) reported the total weight of accessory glands to be as much as 92 g (8·4% of bodyweight). The reproductive tract of a male European hedgehog at the height of the rut may account for up to 10% of his weight and the seminal vesicles alone may have increased 10-fold in weight, often reaching 20–30 g (Allanson 1934). Allanson found that accessory gland weights peaked in late-April and May but changes in the volume of secretions of these glands were a potential source of error. Well-developed accessory glands were found until August. At the end of the breeding season these organs regress rapidly to a small fraction of their maximum size and become quiescent.

Allanson (1934) found testis weight, even when indexed with body size, to be a poor indicator of sexual activity. The total weight of both testes increased from roughly 1 to 2 g (December–May), but there was great individual variation with some testes weighing up to 5 g per pair. The diameter of the seminiferous tubules increases dramatically from 130–150 μm during quiescence to 190–210 μm when fully active and their epithelial lining thickens from 47 μm during hibernation to 72 μm in breeding animals (Allanson & Deanesly 1935, Machin & Arnanz 1989). In both *E. europaeus* and *H. collaris*, even when hibernating and sexually regressed, some residual spermatogenic activity persists in the tubules but this proceeds only as far as the primary spermatocyte stage (Allanson 1934, Goyal & Mathur 1974, Machin & Arnanz 1989). The seasonal size change of the epididymides parallels that of the testes. Together the epididymides weigh 0·3–0·5 g when regressed, but 0·75 g or more at the onset of the rut. The tubule walls become thinner, the epithelial lining thickens from about 30–35 μm to 45–50 μm and the lumen dilates as the tubule diameter increases at the onset of sexual activity (Allanson 1934).

European hedgehogs in Finland show an identical pattern of seasonal sexual change, which differs only in details of its timing (Saure 1969). Two Indian studies of *H. collaris* from the Punjab (Kanwar *et al.* 1980) and Uttar Pradesh (Maheshwari 1982) also showed virtually the same pattern of change, apart from some differences in absolute values and seasonal timing. Kanwar *et al.* found that monthly average bodyweight varied from 161 to 289 g (average of six or seven animals per month). The total weight of testes peaked at 1·1–1·6 g (April–May) but fell to less than half that value (range 0·38–0·58g) from July–November. Minimum and maximum monthly average weights of other organs (total weight) in these animals were as follows: prostate (0·15–1·316 g), seminal vesicles (0·22–1·81 g), epididymis (0·11–0·40 g). Seminiferous tubule diameter was about 98–151 μm when regressed, but about 190 μm during peak sexual activity. The diameter of the epididymis tubules similarly increased from 81 μm to 175 μm.

Seasonal hormonal changes

The hormonal changes underlying these cyclic changes have aroused considerable interest, but some studies which measure simultaneous changes in several hormones are too complex to present in any detail here. Even so, it is unusual for studies to measure metabolic clearance rates or rate of utilization by target tissues, and discussion is further limited by our incomplete understanding of the regulation and action of many of the hormones.

Stated simply, testosterone is secreted by the Leydig cells (interstitial cells) of the testis in response to the gonadotrophic hormone LH (luteinizing hormone) from the pituitary. Spermatogenesis results from a combination of these changes and an increase in FSH (follicle stimulating hormone) which stimulates the Sertoli cells (de Kretser 1984). In European hedgehogs, Teräväinen & Saure (1976) showed changes in steroid metabolism in the hedgehog testis in line with the stages of testis activity defined histologically by Saure (1969) and numerous other studies of *E. europaeus* have added further detail (e.g. Saboureau & Dutourné 1981, Dutourné & Saboureau 1983, Machin & Arnanz 1989). In the second half of the hibernation period, increases in Leydig cell activity and increased plasma testosterone levels precede the development of the seminiferous tubules and spermatogenesis by about a month. Such processes probably occur only during the arousal periods that punctuate hibernation, rather than at body temperatures close to 0°C (see Chapter 6). As the breeding season ends, Leydig cell regression and a decline in plasma testosterone levels happen about 1 month prior to the involution of the seminiferous tubules (Saboureau *et al.* 1982). Plasma levels of LH and testosterone are closely related in a clear seasonal rhythm: peak values in February–April and a rapid decrease at the end of the summer, with minimum levels in October–November (El Omari *et al.* 1989).

However, such a simple view belies the complexity of hormonal systems. The action of hormones may be mitigated by yet other substances. In France, Saboureau *et al.* (1982) measured seasonal changes in the plasma concentrations of both testosterone and a protein which binds to testosterone in the

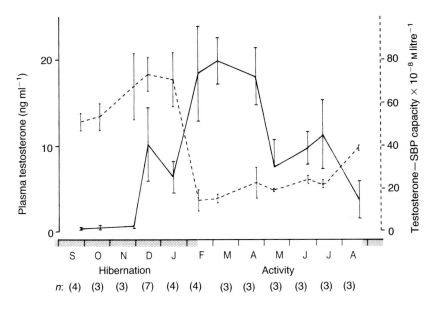

FIG. 8.3 *Average monthly levels of plasma testosterone (———) and plasma testosterone binding protein capacity (- - - -) in adult male European hedgehogs (from France). Values are monthly means (vertical bars denote standard errors); the numbers of animals (n) per month is shown in parentheses at the bottom. The shaded months represent the hibernation period. Source: Saboureau et al. (1982).*

plasma and makes it unavailable to target organs. The protein shows a roughly inverse pattern to the testosterone concentration and is at a minimum level in February (close to the time of final arousal) when testosterone has started to peak (Fig. 8.3).

In humans, thyroid hormones are thought to increase the production of the testosterone binding protein, but in hedgehogs the converse is true and our understanding of the regulatory mechanisms involved is far from complete. Intriguingly, during hibernation when protein metabolism generally is depressed (Chapter 6), the binding protein is maintained at high levels in the blood.

The complexity of this topic is further illustrated by Fowler's (1988) study (in Scotland, 57°N) of daily and seasonal changes in plasma testosterone, melatonin, β-endorphin, prolactin, thyroxin and cortisol in the plasma and urine. All but cortisol showed annual cycles (Fig. 8.4). Seasonal changes in testosterone were as described above, but the spring/summer period of raised testosterone was 2 months shorter than in studies in France (46°N) by Saboureau—matching field observations of breeding activity. In line with field observations (Chapter 6) that have suggested an earlier spring arousal and autumn onset of hibernation in males, thyroxin levels rose and fell

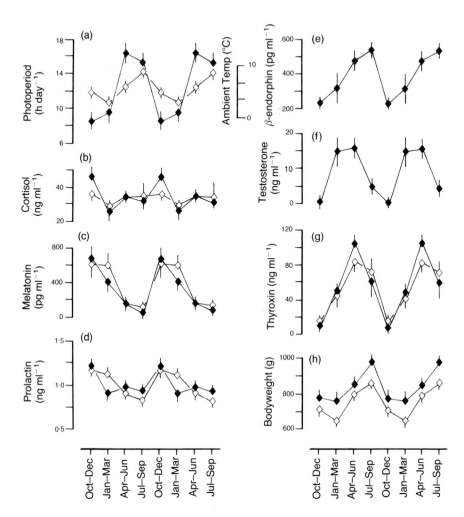

FIG. 8.4 *Mean quarterly values for body weight, hormonal and environmental data for European hedgehogs (northern Britain). Each cycle is shown twice. (a) Photoperiod (◆) and ambient temperature (◇), (b) urinary (◆) and plasma (◇) cortisol, (c) melatonin in male (◆) and females (◇), (d) prolactin in males (◆) and females (◇), (e) β-endorphin, (f) testosterone, (g) thyroxin in males (◆) and females (◇), (h) body weight of males (◆) and females (◇). Values are means ± standard error for 4–6 animals per month. Source: Fowler (1988).*

1 month earlier in males than in females. β-endorphin was also at significantly higher levels during the active season but peaked in July–September. Prolactin was significantly elevated during the hibernation period for both sexes—it has wide ranging functions but is antigonadotrophic in males. The pineal hormone melatonin (also antigonadotrophic) was present in significantly higher concentrations when the nights lasted 14 h or longer, equivalent to the November–February period (see Chapter 6).

The female reproductive system

Most descriptions of female reproductive anatomy (all hedgehog species) closely conform to the detailed account of *E. europaeus* by Deanesly (1934) which also forms the basis for the following summary (see Fig. 8.5).

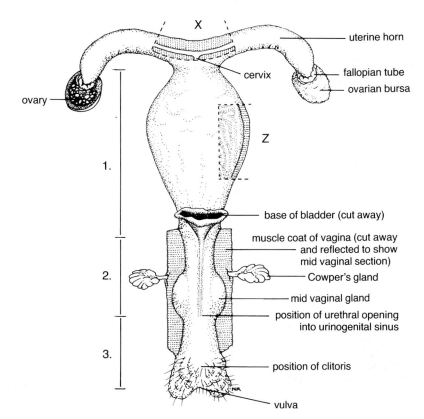

FIG. 8.5 *The reproductive tract of a female European hedgehog in breeding condition. 1. Upper vagina, 2. mid vagina, 3. urinogenital sinus (lower vagina). X = cut away of uterus to show continuity of lumen between uterine horns, Z = cut away of upper vagina to show relatively thin, wrinkled wall. Source: based on Deanesly (1934). Illustration by the author.*

The highly vascular, rather lumpy looking ovaries are roughly U-shaped, bent round a thick muscular hilus and totally enclosed by a tough peritoneal capsule (bursa). The ovary tissue is fibrous with some fat-containing cells but no true interstitial cells. Within and attached to each ovarian capsule is a well-developed ciliated parovarium which conveys released ova into the fallopian tube. Wrapped around the tip of the uterine horn, and supported by the bursa, is the fallopian tube (50–80 mm long), which narrows as it passes through the thick muscular uterine wall to open into the uterus. Each uterine horn is about 5 mm in diameter and 15–20 mm long and the lumen is continuous across the top of the cervix, allowing unimplanted blastocysts to pass from one horn to the other. The single narrow cervical canal opens into the thin-walled upper vagina which extends from the cervix to the level where it unites with the urethra. From here, in the mid-vagina, the lumen is smaller, and the urethra runs within its thick muscular wall for about 20 mm (breeding adult), before opening into the lower vagina or urinogenital sinus, which is itself up to about 20 mm long. Several large lymph nodes lie under the epithelium in this area. The clitoris projects into the urinogenital sinus and sometimes contains a small cartilage. The overall size and weight of the reproductive tract, especially the upper vagina, varies with maturity and the reproductive cycle (see later), but the vagina is always open ('patent').

The cervix and vagina are well supplied with mucous secretions from epithelial glands. Level with the base of the bladder, within the upper vaginal epithelium, lie a small pair of branched tubular mucous glands. A pair of larger glands is situated on either side of the urethra, just behind the urethral opening and a similar but smaller pair lie either side of the clitoris. Lying outside the vaginal wall are a pair of distinctive fan-shaped glands consisting of numerous irregular tubules set in dense fibrous tissue. These seem to be homologous to the Cowper's glands of the male, and each gland unites to form a single duct which empties its secretions into the mid-vagina.

The reproductive tract of *Hemiechinus collaris* is virtually identical in size and anatomy to that of the European hedgehog, except for the lack of a pair of 'greater vestibular glands' (Cowper's glands) (Asawa & Mathur 1986, Pandey & Munshi 1987). Secretions from vaginal glands—more widely distributed throughout the lining of the upper and lower vagina than in the European species—may compensate for the lack of Cowper's glands. Oddly, Maheshwari (1984) featured Cowper's glands in a sketch of the female reproductive tract of *Hemiechinus collaris*, but judging from the position in which they have been drawn this is probably an error. Shehata (1981) described paired glands ('the female prostate') with ducts opening into the vagina, in *Hemiechinus auritus* from Egypt. These seem to be equivalent to Cowper's glands, but no diagram was given.

Seasonal and oestrous cycles of the female

Although sometimes stated otherwise (e.g. Stieve 1948, Herter 1956, Asdell 1964), it is clear that European hedgehogs are spontaneous ovulators (Deansely 1934) and, like most other mammals, do not require the stimulus of copulation to induce follicular rupture (ovulation). However, because hedge-hogs may become pseudopregnant, some authors have assumed that hedge-hogs are 'induced ovulators' like the rabbit (*Oryctolagus cuniculus*), ferret (*Mustela furo*), domestic cat (*Felis catus*) and others. In fact pseudopregnancy can also be found in species such as laboratory mice (*Mus musculus*), rats (*Rattus norvegicus*) and golden hamsters (*Mesocricetus auratus*), which ovu-late spontaneously but require the stimulus of copulation to stimulate the release of prolactin from the anterior pituitary—a hormone necessary for full corpus luteum function (Short 1984). If copulation does not take place, a short period of 'dioestrus' occurs, during which the corpus luteum does not proliferate and only secretes progesterone for a few days before regressing. Hedgehogs seem to fit this category, and are 'seasonally polyoestrous', i.e. they show a succession of oestrous cycles at a particular time of year. Cycles not accompanied by mating result in a brief dioestrous period, during which the corpora lutea are small, fibrous and hardly luteinized. After infertile matings however, the corpora lutea are large, developing and well vascular-ized (identical to the corpora lutea of true pregnancy), resulting in a 7–10 day period of pseudopregnancy before oestrus recurs (Deansely 1934; Fig. 8.6). Unfortunately Deansely was unable to estimate reliably the durations of the other components of the oestrous cycle. Occasionally, females that have just copulated are found to have not yet ovulated (Stieve 1948), but in two such cases reported by Deanesly (1934) the follicles, although large, were not yet mature. It would seem that such cases represent a mis-timing of copulation rather than evidence for induced ovulation.

The reproductive organs generally regress during the winter anoestrous period. In the ovaries, follicles cease development and degenerate markedly, as do luteal bodies. Several small follicles may collapse together to produce glandular-looking cell masses (Deansely 1934). The ovaries also become smaller and relatively poorly vascularized during hibernation (Arnanz & Machin 1987). Uterine regression probably results from lowered sex hormone secretion (Lescoat *et al.* 1985). A month or two before the hibernation period ends, there is some development of the uterine lining and follicles in the ovaries (Walin *et al.* 1968). Thus, as in the males, there is some sexual activation during the hibernation period, although it occurs relatively late-on.

Deanesly (1934) revealed that, as the breeding season re-commences, the ovaries gain weight, become active, and after several ovulation and dioestrous/pseudopregnancy cycles become rather like small mulberries in appearance. Large follicles show well-developed granulosa cells and are around 1 mm in diameter (range 0·7–1·25 mm) just prior to ovulation. The ovum itself is 70 μm in diameter (84 μm in *Hemiechinus collaris*; Kumar & Pandey 1990). In unmated females the follicles vascularize, but the granulosa cells hardly luteinize and they regress to about 0·5 mm by the time of the next ovulation—remaining thus for some time. The more well-developed corpora lutea of pregnancy and pseudopregnancy grow to a diameter of 1·1–1·4 mm and often merge. These are maintained during subsequent cycles and they remain very well vascularized.

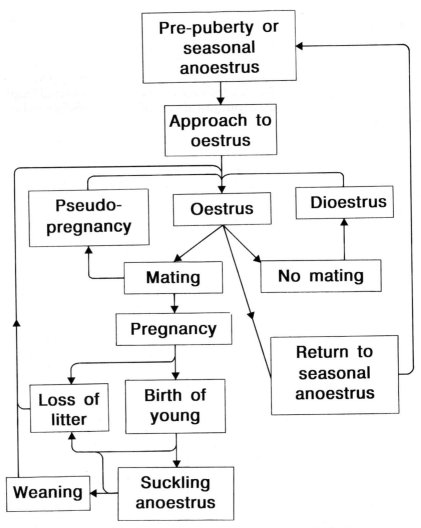

FIG. 8.6 *The reproductive cycle of the female European hedgehog. Source: based on Deanesly (1934).*

In Britain, Deanesly (1934) found that the first oestrus of the breeding season usually passes without copulation taking place. Females may also have two, three or more pseudopregnancies before a true pregnancy is established. The corpora lutea of pseudopregnancy may persist and, after several such cycles, a proliferation of the uterine lining occurs in readiness for pregnancy. Thus the sterile cycles contribute to a maturation of the reproductive system. However, as already mentioned, there are occasional reports of pregnancies as early as April in Britain. Deanesly found that pseudopregnancy was not associated with age, reproductive history, low bodyweight or low uterus weight. The possible adaptive significance (if any) of this rather unusually high level of infertility remains obscure.

During hibernation the uterus weighs an average of only 0·07 g in prepubertal hedgehogs and 0·53 g in parous females (ones that have previously bred), but in May it weighs, respectively, 0·52 g and 1·00 g (Deanesly 1934). According to Stieve (1948), the vagina is 40–45 mm in overall length and 8–12 mm across during oestrus. Just after mating it was 45–55 mm long and oval in section with a diameter of 16–18 mm (dorso-ventral) and 20–25 mm (transverse). Uterus size in parous females during anoestrus varies according to the degree of involution since the last pregnancy (Allanson & Deanesly 1935). In Britain, glandular development of the uterus lining precedes the onset of oestrus and may be found as early as the end of March. Similar changes are also found in the secretory accessory glands: the Cowper's glands, mid-vaginal and clitoral glands. Nielsen & Owman (1972) showed significant spring and summer proliferation of adrenergic nerve endings of the uterus (reaching a density unknown in any mammal apart from the domestic cat) and suggested that this was somehow linked to increased sex hormone activity.

Immediately after birth the uterus weighs an average of 2·41 g (range 1·4–3·4 g) but during lactation anoestrus it regresses once more to 0·66 g (range 0·049–0·76 g) (Deanesly 1934). The vagina enlarges at the onset of the breeding season and becomes dilated during oestrus. As oestrus approaches, the vaginal epithelium proliferates and stratifies. Prior to ovulation the epithelial cells form a cornified layer, which persists during dioestrus but sloughs away following copulation and during early pregnancy. During pregnancy and lactation the vaginal epithelium remains thin. This general type of epithelial growth cycle is typical of many mammals (e.g. laboratory rodents) and investigators can determine the stage of the oestrous cycle of live animals by simple examination of the cells obtained by vaginal smears.

Evidently, the ovarian cycles and periodic changes in the reproductive organs of female long-eared hedgehogs (*Hemiechinus collaris*) from Rajasthan and Uttar Pradesh are comparable to those of the European hedgehog (Asawa & Mathur 1986; Munshi & Pandey 1987). Vaginal smears from captive animals yielded the data seen in Table 8.1, a total cycle length of about 8–10

TABLE 8.1   *The average duration of the oestrous cycle and its phases (in days) in captive* Hemiechus collaris.

Study	n	Prooestrus	Oestrus	Metoestrus	Dioestrus	Total cycle length
Asawa & Mathur (1984)	25	1·9 (1–3)	1·2 (0·5–2·2)	1·8 (1–2·5)	2·5 (1·5–4·5)	7·9 (5–9·4)
Munshi & Pandey (1987)	10	2·5 (1–5)	3·9 (1–7)	2·2 (1–5)	1·8 (1–2)	9·9 (6–14)

Range of values given in parentheses; *n* = sample size.

days on average. The female probably ovulates in the middle of the oestrous phase (Asawa & Mathur 1986). Poduschka's (1969) estimate of the duration of oestrus in *Hemiechinus* species at up to 6 days seems to be an over-estimate, but is within the range reported by Pandey & Munshi (1987). Zherebtzova (1982) reported that if a litter is lost, there may be a repeat mating within 6 days of birth.

Apparently a post-partum oestrus is not usual in European hedgehogs (Deanesly 1934, Herter 1956), although Morris (1961) noted that one female rapidly returned to breeding condition when her litter was removed immediately after birth, and produced another litter 38 days later. But Deanesly (1934) showed a rapid regression of the vagina after birth and a prolonged anoestrus lasting for at least the first part of the lactation period. Females who have reared a litter return to the same cycle of dioestrous/pseudopregnancy as earlier in the season and do not appear to be any more fertile than first-time mothers. Deanesly noted several females who had mated after lactation without becoming pregnant.

Does *Erinaceus europaeus* rear more than one litter per season?

Hedgehogs are polyoestrous and under favourable conditions could potentially raise two litters in a season (Deanesly 1934). However, in Britain and Europe many authors have simply assumed late litters to be second litters–usually said to be born any time from August onwards (e.g. Barrett-Hamilton 1911, Harrison Matthews 1952, Herter 1968).

In Fennoscandia there are no late litters and no opportunity for the rearing of a second litter in the short breeding season. Females may not reach maturity until their third summer (aged 2 years; Kristiansson 1981a, 1984).

In Britain and northern Europe, late litters are common, but it is uncertain how many of them can be successfully raised second litters. Deanesly (1934) noted that six of 16 animals caught in July had ovulated since pregnancy and one female was found with an early pregnancy in July who had mammary gland development typical of that found in late lactation. Such evidence does support the idea that some individuals may breed twice, but significant mammary development may occur during pseudopregnancy and some of the previously pregnant females found ovulating in July could have suffered abortions or the early death of their young. These would be hard to distinguish from those who have reared a litter to independence. Signs of recent pregnancy in females caught in winter (Deanesly 1934) could represent the late first pregnancies of young females born the previous summer.

It is undeniable that some females could rear two litters to maturity, but I know of no field study confirming this for an identified female. Conception as early as the first of May would bear a litter in early June that would reach independence in early July. If the female conceived again *immediately*, birth would follow in mid-August and independence in mid-September—leaving no more than 1 or 2 months for the young to prepare for hibernation at a time of diminishing food supply. Thus the survival of second litters would only be likely under the best possible conditions, and from females that have had the minimum number of dioestrous or pseudopregnant periods.

It seems to me that an adult female (with a potential life-span of two or more seasons) would gain fitness benefits by building up body condition in the autumn to maximize her chance of surviving the winter. She could rear her next brood in the spring, rather than sacrificing her resources for a potentially doomed late litter. I therefore suggest that in Britain and northern Europe, most late litters will be from females that have not successfully reared young that season.

In the mild climate of New Zealand, hedgehogs are sexually active from late August–September to March–April and may not hibernate. Under these circumstances, as in central and southern Europe, many late litters might indeed be second broods (Wodzicki 1950, Brockie 1958, Parkes 1975).

COURTSHIP AND MATING

Hedgehog courtship (pre-mating behaviour) is very conspicuous and many people have been roused by the sounds of this noisy nocturnal ritual. But despite numerous accounts, remarkably little is known about what actually goes on during courtship and the biological significance of the behaviour observed. Neither is it known why so many matings do not result in pregnancy (see above) nor why so many courtships are unconsummated.

Courtship behaviour is basically similar in all hedgehog species for which we have information (Herter 1965a), but with many minor species differences. Poduschka & Poduschka (1986b), contrary to Herter's observations, found that captive *Hemiechinus* did not circle and snort in the way typical of the European hedgehog, although the male did still try to herd the female about. Gregory (1975) described the courtship behaviour of *Atelerix albiventris* as very similar to that of the European hedgehog, except for the male's courtship 'serenade' (see later). The following account is based mainly on published accounts of courtship in wild European hedgehogs plus my own field observations. Captive studies do add substantial detail to our knowledge, but many behaviour patterns may be distorted in captivity, especially when animals are disturbed or closely confined. Suppression of oestrous, homosexual behaviour and an enhanced libido when presented with another species of hedgehog, have all been observed in studies of captives by Poduschka (1969, 1981b). Furthermore, for normal sexual behaviour to occur, an area of 40 m² or even 100 m² should be made available, although courtship may take place in a much smaller area (Poduschka 1977a,b).

Courtship behaviour

Courtship appears rather unfriendly and may be mistaken for a fight. As the male approaches, the female reacts aggressively with a lowered forehead, bristling spines and a loud, rapid snorting. This characteristic sound has been variously described (Chapter 2) but can be well imitated by a sharp exhalation through the mouth, while forming the letter 'F'. The female may continue snorting, at a rate of about 3 s^{-1} (my own data), with only a few short pauses, for a couple of hours or more! Her flanks pump vigorously, and each snort is accompanied by a small jerk of the body which may initiate an aggressive forward lunge at the male. Some accounts wrongly suggest that it is either the male, or both animals, making this noise, but although the male may make an identical noise during purely aggressive encounters, he usually remains virtually silent during courtship (Degerbøl 1943, Rook 1959, Herter 1965a, Reeve 1981).

The male approaches the female and then attempts to herd or circle her. She may run away at first, but eventually stands her ground and, keeping up a rapid snorting, turns to face the flank of the male, butting him with erect head spines—sometimes hard enough to bowl the male on to his back! The couple may take up a face-to-face position with the female retreating before an advancing male (Rook 1959). As the male circles, he changes direction occasionally and periodically attempts to mount from behind but is often dislodged by the female who turns quickly to box him away. This ritual may last for anything from a few minutes to several hours, but is often inconclusive and copulation is infrequently witnessed. I have seen only five definite copulations (under 7% of courtship observations in the field). The position of the female during copulation is somewhat variable but typically she presses her belly to the ground while raising her tail-end to expose her genitalia. The male mounts from behind, scrabbles for purchase on the spines of her back with his forepaws, and commonly grips the spines around her shoulders with his teeth. The female may also raise her head and forequarters, thus arching her back into the classic 'U' shape of lordosis. Degerbøl (1943) recorded that a male remained mounted for 3–4 min during which three copulations occurred. Stieve (1948) described each copulation as consisting of 10–11 rapid thrusts. Campbell (1973a) mentioned one male who remained mounted for 20 min and carried out six copulations, each lasting from 1 to 3 min.

Some reports of copulations have stated that the female flattens her spines so as not to hurt the male's soft belly (Degerbøl 1943, Stieve 1948, Burton 1965); however, in the few copulations I have observed and in the photographs taken by Haarløv (1943) and Skiba (shown in Herter 1965a) the female has remained bristling fiercely, although this may be due to an awareness of the observer. The long penis of the male may help him distance himself somewhat from the female's spines but presumably he simply tolerates any discomfort! Herter (1965a) reported that in the long-eared hedgehog *Hemiechinus auritus*, because the exit of the penis sheath is unusually far forward, the male stands in a more upright posture, on his hind legs, holding on to the rear of the female's back with his paws and tucking his head down towards the rump of the female.

There is no truth in the old story, promulgated by Aristotle, that hedgehogs copulate belly to belly, with the female lying on her back! There are no recent

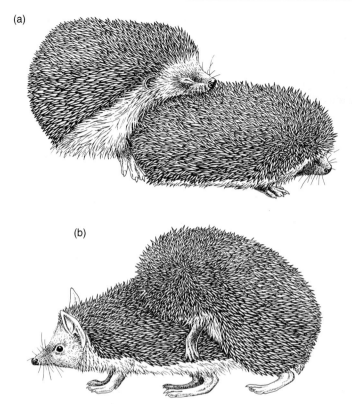

(a)

(b)

FIG. 8.7   *Position during copulation of (a) European hedgehogs (Erina-ceus) and (b) long-eared hedgehogs (Hemiechinus). Note the more upright position of the male* Hemiechinus *owing to the more anterior opening of the penis sheath. Sources: based on Morris (1983) and Herter (1965b).*

records of any species of hedgehog using anything other than conventional rear-mounting (Fig. 8.7)!

In the wild, the pair separate shortly after mating and the male does not subsequently guard, associate with or provide for the female, and takes no part in the rearing of young. Even when confined in captivity, the female will try to chase away any males when birth is imminent (Herter 1968). Ranson (1941) warned that males should not be kept together with females that have young and Prakash (1960) reported that a male *Hemiechinus collaris*, left together with a female giving birth, attacked and ate one of the babies even before it was fully born!

Olfactory communication during courtship

It seems certain that odours play an important part in hedgehog pre-mating behaviour. Males are clearly attracted to females in oestrus (possibly by odours from vaginal secretions), and there are many opportunities for scent-mediated communication during the courtship ritual, but there are few precise data. However, observations of *Erinaceus* and *Hemiechinus* species have revealed the apparent deployment of odour cues in several parts of the hedgehog's courtship (Poduschka 1969, 1977a,b, Poduschka & Poduschka 1986b). For example, males would squeeze their hind legs together, arch their backs convexly and use a sideways rocking motion to mark the ground with a whitish secretion from the tip of the partially unsheathed penis. The secretion smelled unlike urine or the normal body odour of a non-breeding hedgehog, but no details of the substance or its gland of origin are known. During courtship, the female would frequently pass over these scent marks and may have been marked with this secretion during mounting attempts. This scent-marking behaviour was reported to be especially frequent in *Paraechinus* and *Atelerix* species (Poduschka & Poduschka 1986b).

The Poduschkas also described a variety of other behaviour patterns during courtship which may relate to the use of odour cues. These seemed to be particularly well developed in *Hemiechinus* and included sniffing at the partner, crawling under the neck or belly of the partner, licking of the genitalia, perineal 'printing' (often in conjunction with urine) by the male, and rubbing the snout along the flank of the partner. They speculated that such snout-rubbing might distribute scent from possible glandular fields on the lips and mouth-corners (Poduschka 1977a, Poduschka & Poduschka 1986b; see Chapter 2). In captive studies of *Atelerix albiventris*, Herter (1965a) noted that defecation and urination, almost always by the male (but in eight out of 15 cases also by the female), occurred when animals were first introduced, just prior to sexual behaviour. Such behaviour may have been a result of being placed in each other's cages, although a sexual function is possible. Sebaceous gland secretions which lubricate the rectum during defecation and procto-deal glands may well produce an odour that could alter in response to changes in physiological state (Chapter 2).

Despite some speculation, no releaser pheromones (specific odour cues which elicit a particular behavioural response) have been found in hedgehogs, although observations of oestrous cycle synchrony in isolated groups of females (Poduschka 1977, Poduschka & Poduschka 1986b) could indicate that primer pheromones may operate in some contexts.

Sounds during courtship

The audible puffing and snorting sounds usually made by hedgehogs during courtship have already been described, but Gregory (1975), working in Kenya (Africa), recorded vocalizations, audible to humans up to 30 m away, made by mature male *Atelerix albiventris* exclusively during, or as a prelude to, courtship. The curious bird-like vocalization consisted of repeated squeaks that varied greatly from a pure sound (almost a whistle), with pure harmonic structure (frequencies between 2·4 and 4·8 kHz), to a coarse squawk. One sequence lasting 70 s, consisted of 124 pulses of 100–1000 ms, in 40 batches of up to nine pulses each. Technical limitations precluded the recording of possible ultrasonic components to the sounds. Gregory, although aware that none of the many other observers of European hedgehogs had heard courtship calling, was intrigued by Vesey-Fitzgerald's (1973) description of a courtship call by the male hedgehog (*E. europaeus*) as 'three short quick whistles and then a longer flatter one', and a quote from Shakespeare's *Macbeth*, 'Thrice, and once the hedgepig whin'd'. Frustratingly there are no records of this serenade in European studies of captive *A. albiventris*, but Herter (1965a) mentioned that the female snorted in a similar way to the European hedgehog.

Despite hundreds of hours observing European hedgehogs in the field, I have only once heard a true vocalization from courting hedgehogs. This was a very loud 'quacking', audible from at least 50 m (Chapter 2), interspersed with the usual snorting and repeated several times, seemingly by the female. The pair were large mature animals, and an examination revealed no abnormalities other than an infection in one of the female's eyes.

Sexual relationships

Many questions remain about the processes and functions of hedgehog courtship. Both sexes will court with several different partners; for example one female *Erinaceus europaeus* was courted by a *minimum* of seven different males in a 14-night period in August (Reeve & Morris 1986). However, these data showing promiscuous courtship behaviour do not necessarily mean that a female will be mated by several different males—only five of the 76 observed courtships were seen to result in copulation! Although a female might be inseminated by more than one male in one oestrous period, it is not known whether this does occur naturally. Competition among males is a feature common to many accounts of courtship. Rook (1959) reported up to four males competing for one female, and the copulation observed by Degerbøl (1943) was intruded upon by a male which started a fight lasting about 2 h, the female having meanwhile departed! The arduous courtship ritual allows plenty of time for a female to judge her suitor and less vigorous males may be displaced. The female may thus benefit from the competitive exclusion of 'weaker' males, and should multiple matings occur before a vaginal plug has formed, sperm competition may be possible. Even though ovulation is spontaneous, the prolonged courtship may prime the female, somehow maximizing her receptivity (see my earlier comments on pseudopregnancy). Poduschka (1969) speculated that this might be a function of the male's scent deposits.

Post-copulation mate-guarding has never been reported from any field study, possibly because a male hedgehog can spend his time more 'profitably' (in terms of reproductive 'fitness') by mating with other females (Kristiansson 1984). Also many matings do not result in pregnancy (Deanesly 1934), and a male would thus risk a waste of effort guarding a 'dud'! Furthermore, if a vaginal plug is formed shortly after copulation (see earlier) then mate-guarding by the male should be unnecessary.

PREGNANCY AND BIRTH

Although hedgehogs are rather inefficient at getting pregnant in the first place, prenatal mortality seems low. In a total of 53 pregnant European hedgehogs examined by Deanesly (1934) and Morris (1961), although some contained resorbing embryos, 234 of the 242 implanted embryos were healthy, indicating a post-implantation mortality of only 3·3%. Deanesly (1934) observed that the average number of foetuses closely matched the average number of ova ovulated, indicating a high fertilization and implantation success rate. Pre-implantation embryos also seem to migrate between the uterine horns, balancing the number of placental sites in each horn.

Most studies of European hedgehogs settle for a gestation length in the range of 35 ± 4 days, although some reports exceed 40 days (e.g. 5–6 weeks, Herter 1965b). The variation in the reported gestation length swamps any possible species differences: e.g. *Atelerix albiventris*, 35–37 days (Brodie *et al.* 1982), *A. frontalis* 35–40 days (Smithers 1983, Van der Colf 1987), *A. algirus*, 30–48 days (Hufnagl 1972), *Hemiechinus* spp., 35–42 days (Roberts 1977) and 30–32 days (Zherebtzova 1982). Much of this variation may result from inadequate information (mating is rarely witnessed), but gestation might be prolonged in some cases by periods of torpor in response to adverse environmental conditions. Although this is known to happen in some bats, it is unconfirmed in hedgehogs (Herter 1972, Racey 1981, Morris 1988a).

The chorioallantoic placenta of hedgehogs is discoidal and haemochorial (i.e. blood sinuses form in contact with the chorionic membrane), a form typical of insectivores but also found in rats, guinea pigs and humans (Versluys 1975, Heap & Flint 1984). In hedgehogs a highly vascular yolk-sac placenta (choriovitelline), also haemochorial, is formed early in pregnancy and a vestige of it persists to term (Morris 1960).

While the embryo is small (about 1·5–2·5 cm) it nestles in a cup-shaped placenta, but this spreads and flattens as the embryo grows. Eventually the placenta forms a thin discoid plate, attached to the uterus by the central part of its convex surface, with the embryo attached to the concave side (Owen 1868). The embryological development of *E. concolor* is summarized in Table 8.2.

Although females may show mammary gland development and gain weight during pregnancy, it is not easy to diagnose pregnancy in a living female. Palpation of the abdomen is impossible under normal circumstances, but if the hedgehog is anaesthetized, it is apparently possible, after considerable practice, to displace the bladder (which is easily mistaken for an embyro) and palpate the uterus (Edwards 1957).

Litter size

Litter size varies greatly, and though it may be tempting to suggest species differences from the published records, few of them are based on a sample size

TABLE 8.2 *The embryological development of the hedgehog* Erinaceus concolor.

Estimated age (days)	Crown-rump length (mm)		Description of embryo
	Mean	Range	
—	—	—	Primitive streak
—	—	—	First somites (1–7)
15	5	—	Fore and hind limb buds distinct, tail bud, 4 branchial bars present, olfactory placode and eye lens plate depressed below surface, otic vesicle closed, development of brain vesicles at rostral end
17	7·5	6–9	Eyes pigmented, handplate present, nostrils form narrow slits, hemispheres of telencephalon are prominent at rostral end, vesicula lentis is closed and separated from ectoderm, caudal somites marked, tail bud longer
20	11	9–13	Handplate indented, follicles of tactile hairs present on upper lip, marked pinna, follicles of spines present, cartilage skeleton in limb develops, tendons and ligaments undifferentiated
22	15	–19	Follicles of hairs present all over, toes separated, palate fused, pinna covers half of auditory meatus, ossification begins, differentiation of tendons and ligaments
25	22	20-	Eyelids fused, reposition of umbilical hernia with intestinal loops confined to abdominal cavity, rudimentary claws form and skin folds start to appear
29	33	32–34	Skin thicker and more wrinkled, striated muscle fibres form
32	42	–43	Tactile hairs on upper lip emerged, claws become more pointed. Resembles new-born
35	55	45–60	New-born. Weight 12–16 g, white spine tips emerge from skin of back

Weight was not considered a reliable guide to stage of embryological development.
Source: based on Štěrba (1977).

sufficient to inspire confidence. Nevertheless, there may be a trend towards smaller litters in desert species (Wroot 1984b).

In Britain, four or five young is the average litter size for the European hedgehog. Deanesly (1934) noted that up to 10 ova were released during oestrus. In a review of 53 pregnancies, Morris (1961) reported an average prenatal litter size of 4·6. The average number of early nestlings is around 4·4 (30 litters, range 2–6; Morris 1977). In New Zealand a modal litter size of five

(16 litters, range 2–6) was recorded by Parkes (1975). In Scandinavia and northern Europe, litters may tend to be slightly larger: in Sweden, average 5·2 (range 1–11, 85 litters; Kristiansson 1984); in Germany, average seven (range 2–10; Herter 1956, 1965b), and in Moscow 4–8 (five litters; Adolf 1966). Possibly litter size varies with climate (Chapter 9).

The eastern European hedgehog *E. concolor* has an average prenatal litter size of five or six (range 4–8) according to Vasilenko (1988) whose samples covered several sites and a wide range of climates, around the Black Sea coast and Caucasus.

Long-eared hedgehogs (*H. auritus*) have anything up to seven young per litter (Herter 1956, Schoenfeld & Yom-Tov 1985, Poduschka & Poduschka 1986b). In Pakistan, *H. megalotis* commonly bear litters of five or six (Roberts 1977). In the deserts of Rajasthan *H. collaris* would seem to have smaller litters, usually around two or three (range 1–4) (Prakash 1960), but another female from the same region bore six young (Gupta & Sharma 1961).

In the Rajasthan deserts *P. micropus* may give birth to only one or two young (Prakash 1960), but litters of five have been recorded in captives from this region (Gupta & Sharma 1961) and from the lower Indus valley (Walton & Walton 1973). Roberts (1977) suggested a typical litter size of three or four for *P. hypomelas*, but there are few data and one captive female from Baluchistan gave birth to six. A litter of four nestlings has been reported from the region east of the Caspian Sea (Ognev 1928). For *P. aethiopicus* litter sizes of two to five have been observed (Eisentraut 1952, Petter 1954, Herter 1956).

In Libya the Algerian hedgehog (*A. algirus*) has litters of from three to seven (Hufnagl 1972), but on the Pityusic Islands (near Spain) only two or three young per summer were recorded, even though the hedgehogs do not have to hibernate (Alcover 1984). Herter (1956) cited an observation by Siépi (1907) of a litter of two in southern France. In *A. albiventris*, the number of young is generally held to be around two to four irrespective of the region of origin (e.g. Asdell 1964, Meritt 1981, Lienhardt 1982, Happold 1987). More detailed data are available from 59 captive-bred litters (Brodie *et al.* 1982). Litter size averaged three (range one–six) with eight litters of one, 14 of two, 11 of three, six of four, nine of five and four of six nestlings.

In the southern African hedgehog (*A. frontalis*), average litter size is four (range one–nine; Smithers 1983); a figure in line with the ranges cited by Asdell (1964) and Meritt (1981). Larger litters, up to eight or nine, are not unusual (Jacobsen 1982, Kok & van Ee 1989).

Birth

Near the time of birth the female is very sensitive to disturbance and may abandon, kill or even eat the neonates if human observers are present. Workers usually avoid intrusions at this time, hence there are few data. Aberrant behaviour, especially of the mother, is very likely in observations of captive births—a point well illustrated by the loss, by Brodie *et al.* (1982), of

47 out of 59 litters of captive-bred *A. albiventris* (in only three litters did all survive). Similarly, Poduschka & Poduschka (1986b), who carefully tried to avoid disturbance, reported a perinatal mortality of almost 42% in captive long-eared hedgehogs (*H. auritus*).

I have yet to witness the birth of a hedgehog, and there are few published accounts. The following summary of events is based mainly upon an account of *E. europaeus* in the wild cited by Herter (1965b), and two first-hand accounts of captive births, one of *P. micropus* (Gupta & Sharma 1961) and another of *H. collaris* (Prakash 1955a). Under natural conditions, the expectant mother will construct a large breeding nest or burrow (Chapter 5). During birth, the female may rest on her side or lie on her belly with forepaws extended and hind legs raised, or stand with her hind legs apart. The genital region is licked at intervals and the female strains and trembles during contractions which last several seconds. The babies may be born either head-first or rear-first, the spines usually do not protrude at this stage and pose no obstacle to the birth (see later), but in any case the baby is enclosed by the amnion. The birth of the whole litter may last anything from a few minutes to several hours, and the mother may move about between births. Each baby is born enveloped in the birth membranes complete with placenta and the mother turns and quickly eats these, meanwhile licking the baby clean. Each youngster is tenderly grasped in the mother's mouth and placed by or underneath her belly until the delivery is complete.

Both observations of captive animals ended in the mother eating the young or in them being removed to avoid further carnage. The birth in the wild cited by Herter mentioned that the female places the young on her belly and they begin to suckle within a few minutes of delivery. However, I have found no other reports of such a feeding posture. Meritt (1981) observed the suckling of young *A. albiventris* with babies lying in a belly-upwards position under the mother's flanks. I have seen a mother *E. europaeus* lying on her side to suckle babies a week or more old, the same position reported for *P. micropus* by Walton & Walton (1973). Both positions have been recorded for *Hemiechinus*, and as the young grow the female may 'sit'—supported by the relatively long front legs of this species—a posture never observed in *Erinaceus* (Poduschka & Poduschka 1986b). Baby hedgehogs may encourage milk flow from the nipple by kneading around it with the front paws, and they rock backwards and forwards rhythmically while feeding (Poduschka 1969) although this was not observed in *P. micropus* or *H. collaris* by Walton & Walton (1973).

The mother remains with the young in the nest for the first 24 h (Herter 1956), but later will forage normally at night, and return to feed the young by day. As mentioned before, the males play no part in rearing the young and, if confined with the female and her brood, may make a snack out of them (Ranson 1941, Prakash 1955b)! The mother stimulates the nestlings to urinate and defecate by licking their genitalia, and lapping up the excretions (Eisentraut 1952, Poduschka & Poduschka 1986b, Stocker 1987).

THE DEVELOPMENT AND GROWTH
OF THE YOUNG

Newly born baby hedgehogs of all species look very similar. At birth they are
pink and hairless, with eyelids sealed tight and each ear pinna folded down to
seal the ear opening. They seem to have no spines, but in fact 100 or so
unpigmented spines lie buried in the skin of the back—the position of each is
marked by a small surface pimple. At birth, the skin is 'pumped-up' with fluid
and looks taut and bloated but it rapidly 'deflates', so that within an hour or so
the spines begin to emerge from the pimples on the back. It may take up to 24
h for the full length of the spines to be exposed. Once deflated, the skin is soft,
loose and wrinkly. Sometimes the spines may already protrude slightly at
birth in European hedgehogs (Herter 1965b) and *Hemiechinus* (Poduschka &
Poduschka 1986b) with the degree of protrusion depending on the duration of
the birth and the maturity of the baby.

Hedgehogs are attentive mothers if left undisturbed. After the first 5 days
they are less likely to eat or abandon the young and, if disturbed, will usually
try to move them to a new nest instead. The mother carries young babies in
her mouth, but larger young are grabbed by a mouthful of their spiny skin and
dragged along (Burton 1969).

For most species, size and weight measurements of new-born babies are
rare. Many workers prefer not to risk the rejection and death of the young that
can result from handling them. The size of the neonates depends both on
species and the number of young per litter; there may also be considerable
size-disparity among litter-mates, a feature common in insectivores
(Poduschka & Poduschka 1986b). New-born European hedgehogs average
around 70 mm (±about 15 mm) long and weigh anything from 8 to 25 g
depending on the number in the litter (Herter 1965b, Burton 1969, Versluys
1975, Morris 1977). In Russia, Adolf (1966) reported a rather low average of
10·1g and 56·4 mm body length.

Information about the neonates of other genera is scantier. *Atelerix
albiventris* weigh from around 5 to 11 g (Meritt 1981, Brodie *et al.* 1982,
Lienhardt 1982) and for *A. frontalis* Jacobsen (1982) reported an average
weight of 10·75 g (range 9·5–12 g) and a body length of 52·6 mm (range 51–53
mm) in one litter of six. A similar body length (47–54 mm) has been reported
for *P. micropus* and *P. aethiopicus*, with a bodyweight of 8–9 g (Eisentraut
1952, Prakash 1955). Neonate *H. auritus* weigh about 8–11 g and range from
50 to 61 mm in body length (Herter 1965b, Walton & Walton 1973,
Schoenfeld & Yom-Tov 1985).

When dry, the first white spines are bristly and sharp. Although more
flexible and insubstantial than the next generation of spines, they are not really
soft (as sometimes described) and are of real defensive value. The young,
though physically immature, can drag themselves actively about the nest and
search for a nipple by raising themselves up on their front legs and wagging
their heads from side-to-side, puffing and panting (Burton 1969). If a baby
finds itself separated from its mother it will emit a series of shrill piping calls

(Chapter 2), which stimulate the mother to retrieve it. Straying babies are retrieved until they are about 4 weeks old (Poduschka & Poduschka 1986b) and the mother may energetically defend her young by hissing and biting (Herter 1965b, Walton & Walton 1973, Brodie *et al*. 1982). Young nestlings are at first unable to roll-up in defence. If disturbed they will call and, with sharp 'huffing' noises, jerk their bodies upwards to jab their spines into the intruder. This might sound rather ineffectual and is amusing to watch, but I have found that it is quite difficult not to flinch as they do this to your hand! This bucking or 'boxing' is likely to be a better defence against predators than that possessed by most other nestling mammals, but is unlikely to stop a determined predator.

The first spines are distinctively unlike later spines (Chapter 2). They have no narrow 'neck' close to the skin, are weakly rooted and have a flattened biconcave (hour glass-shaped) cross-section (Versluys 1975, Poduschka & Poduschka 1986b). In *Erinaceus* these spines are about 7 mm long (range 6·1–8·5 mm, Versluys 1975), in *Atelerix* 4·9–5·5 mm (Jacobsen 1982) and in *Hemiechinus* around 8 mm (Herter 1956, Prakash 1960, Poduschka 1969). In keeping with the long spines of adult *Paraechinus*, the young also have longer first spines (8–10 mm) than the other genera (Eisentraut 1952). They reach 4–5 mm in 24 h, but may grow to 9–11 mm by the end of the first week (Gupta & Sharma 1961). All species have a bare 'parting' which runs from the centre of the brow, down the line of the backbone to the rump, a legacy of the bilateral embryological development of the *orbicularis* muscle (Chapter 2). This parting rapidly grows over with spines in *Hemiechinus* spp. but remains discernible on the crown in the other genera (Corbet 1988), although it is a rather weak feature in adult *Erinaceus* (Poduschka & Poduschka 1986b) (Chapter 1). In *Erinaceus*, the second generation of stouter pigmented spines, which began development before birth (Štěrba 1976), begin to emerge among the first spines about 36–60 h after birth (see Fig. 8.8), match their length at

FIG. 8.8   *A nestling European hedgehog (about 1 week old) showing the first brown spines starting to grow through.*

about 2 weeks and largely obscure them at 15–20 days. At 12–15 mm long, these spines are smaller than the adult spines but otherwise identical. The first spines remain among the second coat until the youngster is a month or more old, and are then gradually shed (Herter 1956, 1968, Morris 1983). Reports of white spines hardening and becoming pigmented are untrue. The second generation of spines is moulted after independence (from about 6 weeks) and are replaced by a flush of longer adult spines which may project up to 1 cm beyond the second generation coat (Poduschka 1969).

All hedgehog babies are altricial at birth, but grow rapidly. The timing varies somewhat, but all the species follow a similar developmental process. From early days, the youngsters are able to 'frown', that is to protect their faces by pulling down their forehead spines, and to curl their bodies somewhat. In *Erinaceus* erection of the spines starts at about 1 week old (Herter 1965a), but develops progressively. The spines start bristling on the forehead at 6 days old, on the flanks at 8 days and on the rest of the back at 9 days (Lindemann 1951).

At around 2 weeks old, the babies begin to roll-up more effectively, although their body proportions still prevent them from rolling-up tightly. Assessments of rolling-up ability are somewhat subjective, but young *Hemiechinus* are precociously able to roll-up partially at only 3 or 4 days. This is odd because other features (eye-opening and fur growth) develop more slowly than in *Erinaceus* (Poduschka & Poduschka 1986b).

In most hedgehogs the eyes and ears open at around 2 weeks and the babies become more mobile. Hair growth starts on the snout, and whiskers are well developed by the end of the first week (Versluys 1975). The rate of growth, length and density of fur varies from species to species (Poduschka & Poduschka 1986b), but there is usually a covering of short fur in animals 2 or 3 weeks old. Meritt (1981) noted some abdominal hair development in *A. albiventris* only 1 day old. At 3–4 weeks the babies begin to lose their blunt-nosed appearance and look more like small adults. They become more exploratory and venture outside the nest (Plate 17). They can now roll-up tightly. Their milk teeth have started to erupt and they may investigate or eat solid food. From now until they are weaned at 5–6 weeks, they will accompany their mother on foraging trips, calling if separated. Eisentraut's (1952) data suggest that *Paraechinus* takes longer to reach the weaning stage than other genera; suckling finally ended on day 58. Young hedgehogs do not play as such, but in captivity have been observed to crawl under and over each other, as if scent marking, and both sexes may indulge in mock sexual mounting (Herter 1956, Burton 1969, Poduschka 1969).

Little is known of the physiology of young hedgehogs, but thermoregulation seems to be poorly developed in *Erinaceus* under 2 weeks old, and is not fully developed until 27–31 days (Walhovd 1981). Babies of the desert hedgehog *P. aethiopicus* apparently did not match the thermoregulatory capacity of an adult until they were capable of independent feeding at 44 days old (Eisentraut 1952)

TABLE 8.3   *The age (days) at which hedgehogs of four genera reach selected developmental stages in selected studies.*

	Erinaceus	Paraechinus	Hemiechinus	Atelerix
Partial rolling-up	11[d]	12[b]	3–4[m]	14–16[i]
Eyes open	12[m] 14–18[d]	21[e] 22[b]	>16[m]	12–18[l] 14–16[gik] 18–24[h]
Body fur growth	14[j]	17[b]	c. 21[m]	17[i]
1st explore outside nest	19–24[d]	18[b]	20–21[m]	—
1st teeth erupt	20–21[adf]	—	—	18[i]
Complete rolling-up	28[c]	29[b]	—	—
Samples solid food	21[c] 23[d]	44[b]	21–28[d] 25[m]	21[jl] 24[g]
Fully weaned	38–44[c] 42[d]	58[d]	40[m]	c. 40[il]

— indicates no data or estimates too imprecise.
[a]Sometimes as early as 12 days (Burton 1969).
Source: Eisentraut (1952)[b], Edwards (1957)[c], Herter (1956, 1965a,b)[d], Gupta & Sharma (1961)[e], Adolf (1966)[f], Merrit (1981)[g], Brodie *et al.* (1982)[h], Lienhardt (1982)[i], Morris (1983)[j], Smithers (1983)[k], Gregory (1985)[l], Poduschka & Poduschka (1986b)[m].

Overall species differences in the rate of development of young hedgehogs seem minor, but remember that data are from assessments (often subjective) of the variable performance of only a few litters reared in captive conditions (Table 8.3).

Herter's studies of captive *Erinaceus* have shown that they can double their birthweight at 7 days, and achieve six times their birthweight by 3 weeks. As they begin to find their own food individual disparities increase. They usually weigh around 200–235 g (about 10 times birthweight) at around 40 days. Morris (1988a) commented that an average female, being the main source of food until this stage, will have raised about 1 kg of progeny, more than her own bodyweight! During weaning, growth may slacken slightly (Morris 1970) but subsequent growth remains rapid. To survive hibernation, animals must more than double their bodyweight at weaning. Even the small animals in Adolf's (1966) study, weighing an average of only 124 g at 40 days, achieved 450 g at 3 months old. Schoenfeld & Yom-Tov (1985) reported that a pair of 14-day-old *H. auritus* weighed an average of 65 g, roughly eight times their birthweight.

One litter of five *A. albiventris* grew very rapidly. They weighed 25 g at 7 days, 50 g at 13 days, 110–120 g at 28 days and after 40 days were weaned at 170–195 g, roughly 30 times their birthweight (Lienhardt 1982). A graph of one individual's growth presented by Meritt (1981) showed slower growth and a weight of a little over 90 g at 28 days, roughly 10 times the birthweight. Brodie *et al.* (1982) found that the young grew slowly at first, gaining only 1–2 g day^{-1} for the first 9 or 10 days, 4–5 g day^{-1} for 'the next few weeks', and then 7–9 g day^{-1} until they reached over 200 g at maturity (61–68 days).

A litter of eight *A. frontalis* grew rapidly to achieve a weaning weight of around 200 g at 40 days (Kok & van Ee 1989). After weaning, these obviously well-fed hedgehogs achieved prehibernation weights of 658 ± 109 g (males) and 560 ± 65 g (females) 5 months later, rather high for a species typically about 400 g when adult!

A study of three baby *P. aethiopicus* (Eisentraut 1952) showed initial slow growth (1·7 g day^{-1}), reaching just over 80 g at 6 weeks; about nine times the birthweight. But as solids were included in their diets they grew more rapidly (roughly 3 g day^{-1}) and doubled their weight to 160 g during the next 3 weeks. Observations by Walton & Walton (1973) of one litter of four *P. micropus* suggest that newly weaned young have reached about half their adult length, and one-third of their adult weight.

Judging by the rate of epiphyseal fusion in the bones of the forelimb (Morris 1971), European hedgehogs may continue to grow until around 18 months old. Tentative data from road casualties suggest that maximum body size may be reached at age 2–3 (Dickman 1988).

Lactation

Hedgehogs normally have four or five pairs of nipples (Chapter 2, Fig. 2.5). The mammary tissue is poorly developed in prepubertal animals and females that have not yet bred at the beginning of the season. During pregnancy, mammary gland development starts around the nipples, but by the end of gestation joins to form two continuous strips of tissue 19 cm long and 1·5–3·5 cm wide. During lactation, further glandular development occurs and the mammary tissue becomes thicker and more solid. After lactation the mammary tissue gradually regresses to its original condition at the start of the season (Deansely 1934).

The number of nipples does vary between species, usually five pairs in *Erinaceus* (Owen 1868, Grassé 1955, Firbas & Poduschka 1971) and *Hemiechinus* (Niethammer 1973), but more often four pairs in *Paraechinus* (Eisentraut 1952). Meritt (1981) reported that *A. albiventris* have two pairs of nipples on the chest, but a variable number on the abdomen. In all species there may be an additional or missing nipple on one side or the other, but not all nipple-like structures are genuine nipples! Firbas & Poduschka (1971) noted that nipple-like warty papillae, bearing vibrissae, were sometimes found along the line of the nipples anterior to the forelimbs.

Suckling hedgehogs, like many mammals, receive maternal antibodies in the milk that confer passive immunity against pathogens previously encountered by the mother. Morris (1959, 1960) demonstrated that *Brucella abortus* antibodies were mainly received post-natally in the mother's milk (transmission via the placenta was minimal). At first, the level of antibodies in the milk was similar to that in the maternal blood, but it declined by about 75% after 4–6 days. However, the antibody level in the blood of suckling young was at most only 3% of the maternal blood level. Versluys (1975) reviewed these and later studies (e.g. Morris & Steel 1964) which suggested that some

TABLE 8.4 *Basic nutritional analysis of the milk of the hedgehog and selected species.*

Species	Water	Fat	Carbohydrate	Protein	Minerals
Hedgehog	79·4	10·1	2·0	7·2	2·3
Domestic species					
Goat	87·14	4·09	4·20	3·71	0·78
Sheep	79·50	9·00	5·80	4·7	1·00
Cow	87	3·7	4·8	3·3	0·72
Dog	75·50	11·8	3·25	8·65	0·80
Cat	82·35	4·95	4·9	7·15	0·65
Rat	72·5	12·6	3·3	9·2	1·4
Rabbit	69·50	10·45	1·95	15·54	2·56
Humans	87·0	4·0	6·5	1·3	0·2

Values are per cent by weight.
Source: Ben Shaul (1962).

antibodies could pass through the intestine of the suckling hedgehogs throughout lactation (up to 41 days), a remarkably long period for this kind of intestinal permeability!

Little is known of the nutritional composition of the milk. An analysis of *E. europaeus* milk by Ben Shaul (1962) is shown in Table 8.4 but the data must be considered tentative as there was no indication of sample size, or the stage of lactation when the sample was taken. In other species, milk composition is known to change greatly at various stages of the lactation period. As mentioned in Chapter 3, cow's milk is unsuitable for rearing young orphan hedgehogs and it is clearly deficient in fat and protein. Stocker (1987,1988) advocated the use of goat's milk colostrum, or goat's milk, presumably because it is less rich in lactose and is the next most available option in Britain. Just for fun I have included data for some other domestic species which might be persuaded to yield milk for hedgehog rearing! If you think some are improbable, I have seen a photograph of a cat suckling a litter of three hedgehogs (*New Scientist*, 28 October 1982, page 253)!

Independence and sexual maturity

Newly independent youngsters, aged around 6 weeks, must disperse, establish themselves in a new area and gain enough weight to survive the hibernation period. They do not associate with their mother or their siblings, and generally do not tolerate company. This is a testing time and many may suffer accidents, illness or predation. For late litters there may be little time to build up fat reserves and many youngsters fail to reach good condition.

At this time in Britain, youngsters may be found wandering about, sometimes in such a poor state that many die despite feeding and care. As a very rough guide, before hibernation, youngsters need to weigh over 450 g in

Britain, and about 700 g in continental Europe (Poduschka & Saupe 1981, Morris 1984, also Chapter 6), and any that are close to or under these targets would benefit from being offered a meal of meaty pet food (Chapter 3). The provision of a suitable nesting site may, if it is accepted, also help the youngster over this difficult period. Animals that are obviously ill should be seen by a vet.

The age of sexual maturity in the wild is difficult to ascertain reliably. For male *E. europaeus* it was estimated at not less than 9 months old (Allanson 1934), although captive animals could mature about 2 months earlier. Similarly, Deanesly (1934) noted that even though it was possible for captive-reared females to become fertile during their first summer, it would be unlikely to happen in the wild in Britain. Edwards (1957) considered that hedgehogs could not breed in the season of their birth unless made to breed in the winter and Herter (1956) gave the age of sexual maturity at 9–11 months.

Sexual mounting in captive *E. concolor* in central Europe has been observed at 6·5–7 months, but this may not necessarily indicate maturity (Poduschka 1969). Poduschka also reported a captive female who bore a litter at 6·5 months, right in the middle of winter! This highlights the profound effects of captivity. Captive long-eared hedgehogs (*Hemiechinus*) have also been known to become sexually active at about 6·5 months old, but this is almost certainly advanced in comparison with wild animals (Poduschka 1969). The youngest animal to father a litter was just over 7 months old (Poduschka & Poduschka 1986b).

Female *A. frontalis* can become sexually mature within a year of their birth, and one captive-reared animal produced young at 13 months of age (Kok & van Ee 1989). Estimates of age of maturity for captive *A. albiventris* vary from around 5·5 months to as early as 61–88 days for both sexes (Herter 1965b, 1971, Brodie *et al.* 1982, Lienhardt 1982). This is earlier than recorded for other hedgehog species and may reflect the fact that they were taken from populations that bred all the year round. Oddly, captive females in Brodie's study had rather short reproductive lives of no more than 2 years, but one wild-caught female remained sexually active for 33 months.

Probably, most hedgehog species are capable of sexual maturity within about 6 months of birth when in captivity, but in seasonally breeding wild populations they would be unlikely to reproduce in the season of their birth.

CHAPTER 9

Demography, Disease and Death

A LL wild mammals suffer death or debilitation from a diversity of natural and human causes. The catalogue of parasites, diseases, predators and other causes of death can all too easily create an impression of a disease-riddled species that is virtually doomed! However, unless records of death and disease are combined with demographic studies, one can only guess at the effects of such factors on populations. In hedgehogs (all species) there are hardly any combined data of this kind, a fact to bear in mind while reading the many popular claims of serious threats to hedgehogs, such as deaths from road traffic and pesticides.

DEMOGRAPHIC STUDIES

In simple terms, demography is the study of a population defined by its likelihood of genetic exchange; genetically defined populations of a species are separate 'demes'. A good demographic study would gather data on population size and distribution, sex ratio, age structure, age-specific fertility rates and age-specific death rates. For in-depth analyses, one would also require details of significant diseases and causes of death, plus information about the ecological/behavioural factors affecting reproductive performance. Such data can be used to model population change under varying circumstances but to obtain more than a small fraction of this information is very difficult, even in studies of humans who can *tell* you their life history! One confounding factor is the rapidity with which population variables may change, and there is a great need for longer-term studies (covering several generations) to disclose the multivariate dynamics of population change. Short studies provide only a 'snap shot', and because there are 'good' and 'bad' years for reproduction, mortality etc., their findings may differ greatly.

TABLE 9.1 *A summary of age-determination methods used in hedgehog studies.*

Ageing method	Useable on live animals?	Useable in the field?	Absolute or Relative	Usual range of age-group discrimination	Notes
Appearance of genitalia/nipples	Yes	Yes	R	Only separates juvenile/adult	Subjective. Seasonally variable. Limited reliability
Coat length/colour	Yes	Unlikely	R	Up to adult	Subjective, needs good light and large sample. Individually variable and unreliable
Second spines remain in coat	Yes	Yes	R	Up to 2–3 months	Individually very variable
Bodyweight	Yes	Yes	R	Up to adult	Individually very variable
Tooth eruption	Yes	Yes	R	Up to adult	Anaesthetic usually needed if live. Individually variable
Epiphyseal fusion	Yes	No	R	Up to 18 months	Anaesthesia and X-ray equipment needed. Some variability but mostly reliable
Bone length measures	No	No	R	Up to adult	Individually variable, probably more reliable than bodyweight measures
Tooth wear	Unlikely	No	R	From adult	Individuals/populations may vary. Precise measures required. Limited reliability
Eye lens weight	No	No	R	All ages	Needs very fresh material, reliable once calibrated
Periosteal lines	No	No	A	All ages	Some subjectivity, prehibernation animals cannot be separated. Only suitable in populations which hibernate/aestivate
Condition of internal reproductive organs	No	No	R	Only separates juvenile/adult	May distinguish newly mature from animals which have bred previously (esp. females)

Relative methods allow animals to be ranked according to age. Once calibrated with known-aged animals the age-scale produced can be quite precise. Absolute methods give a direct measure of age.

How old is that hedgehog?

Because hedgehogs will never tell you their birthday, various methods have been used to determine their age (usually *Erinaceus*). All have limitations; therefore age-estimates should preferably be based on a consensus of several features (see Table 9.1 for a summary of methods).

Bodyweight is individually and seasonally variable to the extent that it is useful only in distinguishing first season young from older animals. Nevertheless, weight generally increases with age, possibly peaking at 3 years (Dickman 1988), and can therefore help to verify other measures of age. Bone lengths (more reliable than measures of limbs and body length on live animals) can provide a growth scale, which although subject to considerable individual variation, will not fluctuate seasonally.

Newly independent youngsters are sometimes distinguishable by the uneven size of their spines. The moult of second generation spines (one third the length of adult spines) is usually before the first hibernation but, in late litters, could be delayed until spring (Poduschka 1969). Kratochvíl (1975) noted age-related changes in the colour and length of fur, but considerable individual variation means that this subjective method must be considered unreliable.

The timing of tooth eruption varies and by itself is a poor guide to age, although unerupted teeth are a sure sign of a youngster. The last (third) molar erupts within a few weeks of independence in *Erinaceus* and at around 9 weeks in *Atelerix albiventris*, with the second premolar being replaced at about 3 months (Gregory 1976). In *Erinaceus* the milk teeth are gradually replaced until the animal is about 3 or 4 months old. The full adult dentition is usually in place by the end of the first year of life (Morris 1983).

Age-estimates based on tooth wear have been used in several studies of *Erinaceus* (Brockie 1958, Škoudlín 1976 1981, Vasilenko 1988), *Atelerix albiventris* (Gregory 1976) and *A. algirus* (Kahmann & Vesmanis 1977). An age-scale is deduced by categorizing the progressive wear of enamel (or reduction in cusp height, Fig. 9.1) into stages which correspond to age-classes. Although variations in enamel hardness and dietary differences can confound the assumption that tooth wear always occurs at a comparable rate, this method does provide a useful age-ranking for the adult population.

Eye lenses increase in dry weight throughout life, providing a useful index of relative age. However, in his evaluation of several age-determination methods, Morris (1969, 1970, 1971) judged this method to be unsuitable for most field studies, partly because of the requirement for freshly dead material. Morris adapted two age-determination methods for use on hedgehogs which have since been adopted by most studies.

Periosteal growth lines: during the hibernation period, bone deposition in the periosteum slows, or even stops and there are alterations in the hedgehog's calcium metabolism. Such seasonal changes produce 'growth lines', analogous to tree rings, visible in stained sections of certain bones such as the lower jaw (Fig. 9.2). The method has been used in several studies of hedgehogs (e.g.

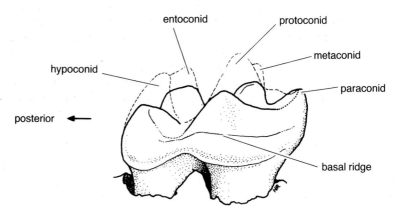

FIG. 9.1 *The lower right first molar (outside view) of the European hedgehog. Cusp height declines markedly with age; the dashed line indicates heights at 2–3 months, the solid line at 18–24 months. In older animals the tooth may wear down to the basal ridge. Source: based on Brockie (1958), cusp labelling after Butler (1948). Illustration by the author.*

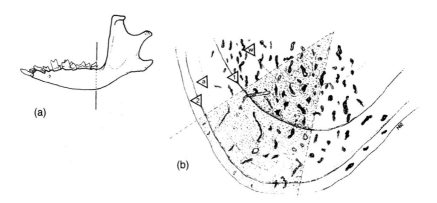

FIG. 9.2 *Age determination of European hedgehogs using periosteal growth lines. (a) A transverse section of the lower jaw is made in the region of the last molar. (b) Growth lines are visible in the stained section when viewed under a microscope. Detail of a sector from the lower edge of the jaw section shows a weaning line (w), an accessory line (a) representing a period of physiological stress, and two winter lines (1 and 2). This animal died in its third summer. Illustration by the author.*

Kristoffersson 1971, Kratochvíl 1975, Dickman 1988) and other species, including hares (*Lepus capensis*) (Frylestam & von Schantz 1977). However, the method cannot be used for live animals and requires tedious histological methods. Furthermore, accessory lines may be formed during periods of physiological stress such as weaning, pregnancy or illness (Morris 1970, Frylestam & von Schantz 1977) which may lead workers to propose differing assessments of the age of the same jaw section (Love & Reeve, unpublished data). Nevertheless, this method is the only direct means of absolute age-determination available and seems fairly reliable (Morris 1971, Dickman 1988) although further checks with animals of known age are needed.

Epiphyseal fusion: during long bone growth, the epiphyseal cartilages (areas of bone formation, near each end of the bone) remain unossified (Fig. 9.3). As bone growth slows, each epiphyseal cartilage progressively ossifies until the

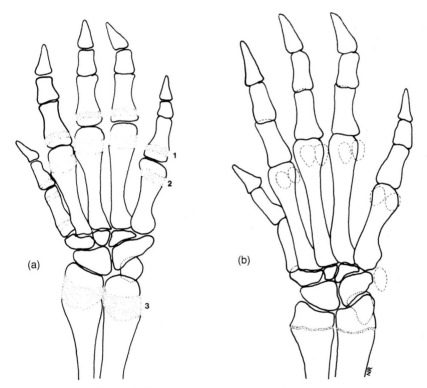

(a)

(b)

FIG. 9.3   *Epiphyseal fusion in the hedgehog forefoot. (a) A very young animal aged 2–3 months (recently weaned). Note the distinct, wide epiphyseal cartilages (stippled) in the phalanges (1), metacarpals (2) and forearm bones (3). (b) A mature animal aged over 18 months. Only the epiphyses of the forearm bones remain incompletely fused. Sesamoid bones (almost invisible in the very young) are well calcified and easily visible on X-ray plates. Illustration by the author.*

bone becomes solidly fused. X-ray radiographs of hedgehog forelimbs have revealed a staged process of epiphyseal fusion, allowing the relative ages of animals (living or dead) up to about 18 months to be determined (Morris 1971). Although X-ray equipment is usually needed (e.g. a low-powered dental unit), and the method is little use for animals over 18 months, it is excellent for separating younger animals into age-categories and has been used in various studies (e.g. Reeve 1981, Dickman 1988).

Population studies and survivorship

The sex ratio of hedgehogs captured in field studies often shows a predominance of males. Early in the season and during the rut, adult males are more active than females and thus more likely to be caught (or to become a road casualty). The 3:2 male:female ratio of *individuals* in my mark–recapture study (Reeve 1981), probably arose because widely ranging males from surrounding areas were also included in the catch. For theoretical reasons the sex ratio is most unlikely to be more than slightly uneven and Kristiansson's (1990) long-term study revealed an overall 1:1 sex ratio in all age groups. However, Ranson's (1941) report of a predominance of males in nestling hedgehogs is intriguing.

In Britain, Morris (1977) recorded a perinatal mortality rate of about 5% and surmised that slightly over 19% of surviving new-born hedgehogs may die before they are weaned. Thus an average litter of four may lose one baby, although this takes no account of whole litters lost without record. Morris also found evidence to suggest that mortality was higher in larger litters.

In both Britain and Sweden, average life-expectancy at weaning is about 2 years (Morris 1969, Kristiansson 1981a). In New Zealand, animals that have survived to their first breeding season have an average life-expectancy of a further 2 years (Parkes 1975). The maximum lifespan of *Erinaceus* spp. in the wild seems to be about 6–8 years (Morris 1969, Kristoffersson 1971, Kratoch-víl 1975, Parkes 1975, Škoudlín 1981), although none was older than 5 years in Kristiansson's study. The maximum recorded lifespan in captivity is 10 years (Burton 1969), an age never confirmed in the wild.

In Revingeby (southern Sweden), Kristiansson (1981a, 1984, 1990) carried out a valuable 8-season study of *E. europaeus*. For the first 3 seasons, the age-structure indicated a stable or decreasing population (few juveniles), but during the next three seasons the number of juveniles increased and the population roughly doubled its initial size. In the final 2 years, the number of juveniles fell once more, signalling a population decline. There was some evidence of a delayed relationship between high population density and a subsequent decline in recruitment—the delay was prolonged because, in Sweden, females do not breed until their second year. Such relationships cannot be confirmed without even longer studies. During this time, the annual production of independent surviving young per female averaged from 1·33 to 4·13 (estimated from the ratio of juveniles to adult females in the population). Annual mortality estimates varied greatly but averaged 34% in juveniles and

47% in adults and subadults (young non-breeding adults). Road mortality (see later) accounted for most summer losses, averaging around 12% of the subadult/adult population in each year (range 3–22%), much less (0–6%) in the juveniles. Winter losses accounted for most mortality and averaged 33% for subadults/adults (range 26–43%), and 33% for juveniles (range 6–94%). Although such figures also reflect emigration, winter losses of subadults and adults (but not juveniles) were correlated with severe winter cold. In England, Morris (1988a, 1991) reported a 60–70% mortality of juveniles in their first year and an adult mortality rate of about 30% per year—comparable to estimates of winter mortality in southern Germany at 70–80% for juveniles and 20–40% for adults (Esser 1984 and Obermaier 1985, studies cited by Hoeck 1987). In Denmark, however, Walhovd (1990) found that, during a 6-year period, an average of 69% of independent young marked in the autumn were recaptured the following spring and claimed that previous studies overrated winter mortality.

In the Czech Republic, Škoudlín (1981) found an average annual adult mortality rate of about 23% for *E. europaeus* and about 27% for *E. concolor*. A tendency for a slightly higher average mortality in the eastern species (none was older than 5 years) was also observed by Kratochvíl (1975) who nevertheless also recorded individuals aged 7 years in both species.

In Bavaria (Germany), after one of the coldest winters of the century (ground temperatures commonly reached $-20°C$, minimum $-35°C$), hedgehog (*E. europaeus*) road casualty counts in spring 1985 were 36% less than in the previous year (Reichholf 1986). Nevertheless, Reichholf argued that this decrease was not especially different from the wide fluctuations (-25 to $+37\%$) recorded in previous spring counts (1978–1984) and instead drew attention to the evident effectiveness of hibernation in resisting such severe cold.

Kristiansson (1984, 1990) found no sex difference in age-specific survival rates. He compared his survivorship data with that obtained by Morris (1969) in England and by Brockie (1974a) in New Zealand (Fig. 9.4). Survival rates in New Zealand, for all ages, seem greater than those in either Britain or Sweden. The harsh Scandinavian winters appear to be responsible for even lower rates of adult survival than in Britain. Parkes (1975) recorded winter losses of only around 20% in New Zealand. The general pattern is one of severe juvenile mortality, with fairly good annual survival rates for adults aged between 1 and 3 or 4 years, after which the annual rate of survival falls rapidly. Škoudlín (1981) found that only 4·4% of 213 *E. europaeus* and 3·5% of 162 *E. concolor* survived to the age of 6.

If European hedgehogs in the different climates of Sweden and Britain have differing age-specific life-expectancies, then one would predict adaptive differences in reproductive strategies. Kristiansson (1981a) suggested that females in Sweden (with shorter reproductive lives and only producing one litter per season) ought to invest in larger litters than those in Britain. He compared the distribution of 'litter size' (reported numbers of non-neonate nestlings) in Sweden with similar data from Britain (Morris 1977). Not only

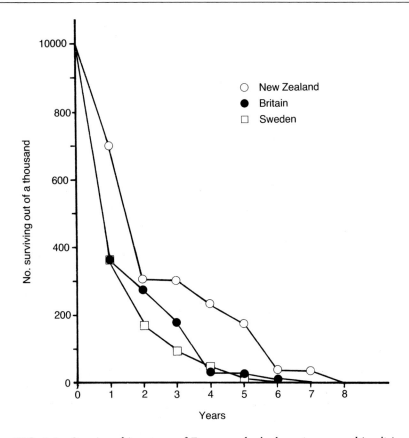

FIG. 9.4 *Survivorship curves of European hedgehogs (sexes combined) in New Zealand, Britain and Sweden. Source: Kristiansson (1984).*

was average litter size higher in Sweden (5·2) than in Britain (3·7), but also the range of litter size (up to 11) was much greater (Fig. 9.5). Such glimpses of possible life-history differences in this widely distributed species raise fascinating questions. Sadly no comparable data have been published for any of the other 13 or so species.

Game-keepers' records over many years can provide a long-term data set which may reflect population fluctuations. Such data, however, are limited by the fact that trapping effort is usually unquantified. In Britain, Jefferies & Pendlebury (1968) found that between 1943 and 1965, many fewer hedgehogs were killed annually on a Hampshire estate (8–23 per 1000 acres year^{-1}) than on an estate in Hertfordshire (25–40 per 1000 acres year^{-1}). Such a consistent difference may reflect either different trapping efforts, or a genuine difference in population density. Similarly, peak catches (roughly double the usual number) around 1946 and 1959 in Hertfordshire, and 1957 in Hampshire, can only hint at population increases. Overall, there seems to be a downward

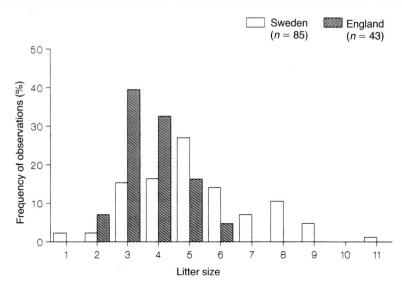

FIG. 9.5 *Frequency distribution of observed litter size (young at least 2 weeks old) of European hedgehogs from England and Sweden. Source: Morris (1977) and Kristiansson (1981a).*

trend in the average number of hedgehogs killed on Britain's game estates (Fig. 9.6), a trend also indicated by data collected prior to 1961 (Tapper 1992). The decline probably resulted from a reduced trapping effort as keepers shifted towards hand-rearing of pheasants and partridges. Furthermore, as a consequence of the 1981 Wildlife and Countryside Act, some estates no longer report hedgehog casualties. The declining catch might also indicate a actual reduction in hedgehog population, possibly as a result of changing farming practice (Tapper 1992).

So, are hedgehogs declining? Unfortunately, we have no clear answer. In Britain estimates of hedgehog population density vary: 0.23–0.25 ha^{-1} (rural Oxfordshire; Doncaster 1992), 0.33 ha^{-1} (traditionally managed farmland, Isle of Wight; Morris 1988b) 0.83 ha^{-1} (suburban golf course, West London; Reeve 1981). In New Zealand, recorded densities are generally higher, up to 2.5 ha^{-1} in summer (pasture and pine plantations, North Island; Parkes 1975). But without a long time-series of comparable records, we cannot make any solid judgements about the status of hedgehogs and how it may be changing. Populations fluctuate considerably (e.g. Reichholf 1986, Kristiansson 1990) and there is little information about the specific effects of either natural or human-related factors. Despite problems such as habitat destruction, pollutants and death on the roads, the evidence so far seems to suggest that hedgehogs do well around villages and in suburban environments, and may even benefit (on balance) from a degree of proximity to humans. The issue of deaths from road traffic is discussed in more detail later.

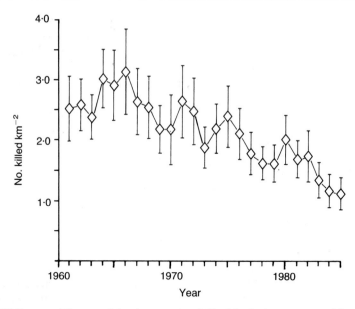

FIG. 9.6 *The trend in the average kill of hedgehogs reported by game-keepers in Britain 1961–1985. Source: Tapper (1992).*

MALENTITIES AND MISFORTUNE

Hedgehogs, like other mammals, suffer from a wide range of parasitic infestations, fungal, bacterial and viral diseases, tumours and injuries. Nor are they spared death by predation, although their spiny defences reduce the risk. In Britain and northern Europe, the winter period of food shortage and cold is probably the most significant direct cause of death (Morris 1977), although parasites and disease may reduce winter survival. Late in the active season, underweight youngsters are commonly found to be heavily parasitized and ill. These would not survive without human help. Advice on the care of European hedgehogs is given in Stocker (1987) and a booklet by the BHPS (1987), and Stocker (1991) has produced a code of practice for those helping sick and injured wildlife. Veterinary reviews are available for the European hedgehog: e.g. in German—Poduschka & Saupe 1981, Saupe & Poduschka 1985; in English—Gregory 1985, Stocker 1992. See Appendix 1 for a summary of treatments recommended in the literature. The diseases and parasites of the central African hedgehog (*Atelerix albiventris*) were reviewed by Gregory (1981b). The research literature for other species is scanty.

External parasites

Hedgehogs may harbour fleas, ticks, mites and fungal infections of the skin, but lice have never been found on any hedgehog species.

Fleas

In Europe, hedgehogs (*Erinaceus* spp.) are notorious for their heavy infestations with these blood-sucking insects. There are many reported flea counts. In Sweden, Brinck & Löfqvist (1973) recovered 49 714 fleas from 385 hedgehogs (a gross average of 129 each), but infestation rates varied from year to year, seasonally and also between the various age–sex categories. Morris (1983) reported up to 500 per animal and Versluys (1975) cited an instance in which 828 and 932 fleas were found on two youngsters. Stocker (1987) reported an average count of 100 but found at least 1100 on one animal. However, the hedgehog's reputation of being extraordinarily flea-ridden (everybody 'knows' it!) is a bit of an exaggeration, and I have often found hedgehogs with very few fleas. The average of 100 or so fleas per animal is not unusual for a wild mammal of this size! I believe that the hedgehog's reputation as a 'flea-bag' is reinforced by several circumstances: (i) sickly and heavily infested hedgehogs may be lethargic and/or active by day and are thus more noticeable, (ii) fleas stranded on dead hedgehogs will conspicuously spring towards an approaching warm body, (iii) the hedgehog's sparse fur makes the fleas particularly easy to see and (iv) when a live hedgehog is approached, the bristling movement of the banded spines creates an impression of a seething infestation.

It is commonly said that hedgehogs cannot groom their spines. This is untrue! They can scratch and rake through their spines using the long claws of the hind feet (Dimelow 1963a; see Chapter 2) and can reach most of their body with their tongue, as demonstrated during self-anointing (Chapter 7). In any case the fleas are more abundant on the hairy parts of the body (Smith 1968). Nevertheless, it is undeniable that hedgehogs are usually dirty and pay little attention to personal hygiene. Hedgehogs generally seem to ignore their fleas, and do not remove attached ticks even when these are in easy reach. However, severe ectoparasite infestations may cause irritation and even anaemia (Versluys 1975). One popular suggestion, that hedgehogs have some kind of mutual symbiosis with their fleas, is rubbish! Hedgehogs thrive in New Zealand with no hedgehog fleas (Brockie 1958) and fleas are potential vectors of debilitating diseases and parasites. Little is known about fleas as vectors of disease in hedgehogs, but flea-borne diseases in other animals include tularemia, plague and other *Pasteurella* spp., brucellosis, trypanosomiasis, and tapeworms, e.g. in dogs and cats (Chandler & Read 1961).

Fleas require careful identification using several anatomical features, but the hedgehog flea *Archaeopsylla erinacei* (family Pulicidae) may be superficially recognized by its genal ctenidium (Fig. 9.7) which has only two (sometimes three) spines on each side. In cat and dog fleas (*Ctenocephalides* spp.) the moustache-like genal ctenidium has eight or nine spines. There are no genal ctenidial spines in the rat fleas *Xenopsylla* spp. and *Nosopsyllus* spp.—both of which have been found on hedgehogs (Chandler & Read 1961, Mehl 1972, Brinck & Löfqvist 1973).

Archaeopsylla erinacei can tolerate the hedgehog's hibernation period and reproduces only in the nest of a breeding female. The female flea enlarges as it

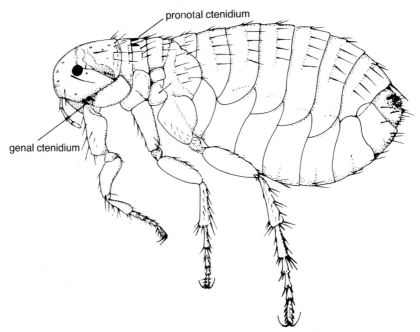

FIG. 9.7 *A female hedgehog flea* Archaeopsylla erinacei *(family Pulicidae), 2.5 mm long. Note the two spines of the genal ctenidium. The pronotal ctenidium is not well developed and as few as two spines may be present. Specimen from Britain drawn with additional reference to Mehl (1972). Illustration by the author.*

distends with eggs; the smallest and largest mean sizes for samples of female fleas collected by Brinck & Löfqvist (1973) were 2·50 and 2·89 mm long, respectively. Hedgehog flea larvae are 2–5 mm long, maggot-like and transluscent white with reddish gut contents. They live in the nest and scavenge detritus. The flea pupae hatch promptly in response to movement, which usually signals an approaching host. Although prolonged in some species, the pupal stage of hedgehog fleas is brief so that the nestlings are colonized. When independent, the juveniles rapidly spread the young fleas throughout the population. Newly emerged fleas are abundant on all animals in the late summer and autumn (Brinck & Löfqvist 1973, Versluys 1975). Hedgehogs sometimes have a brownish slime on their spines that is apparently produced by the fleas, which for some unknown reason are not fully digesting their blood meals (Morris 1983). Apart from attracting blowflies (see below) the slime seems harmless. An idea worth testing is that the bloody slime is produced when the flea larvae are in the nests. Brinck & Löfqvist (1973) noted that the rate of defecation of rabbit fleas (*Spilopsyllus cuniculi*) increased dramatically when breeding to provide food for the larvae.

In Britain, hedgehogs are commonly blamed as the source of infestation of pets and humans, a topic frequently debated by the public and considered in the veterinary literature (Baker 1985, Keymer *et al.* 1991). Pro-hedgehog lobbyists (e.g. Stocker 1987) have claimed that hedgehog fleas never infest pets, people or their homes, whereas many doting owners will never concede that the parasites on their pet may have a source other than hedgehogs!

Although *A. erinacei* **is** host-specific to hedgehogs, occasional transfers to other species may occur 'by mistake'. The disturbance of nest material could trigger the hatching of pupae, and the colonization of any mammal within range. Thus hedgehog fleas may turn up on many species (including humans and house-pets) but they *do not breed and cannot persist* although they occasionally do bite (Morris 1983, Keymer *et al.* 1991). Records of occasional hosts for hedgehog fleas include: polecats (*Mustela putorius*), brown rats (*Rattus norvegicus*), red foxes (*Vulpes vulpes*), badgers (*Meles meles*), domestic dogs (*Canis familiaris*) and humans (Mehl 1972, Bork *et al.* 1987). One case of hedgehog fleas biting humans (presumably the only available host) was reported by Pomykal (1985) during an extraordinary infestation of a Czech storehouse. Bork *et al.* (1987) also reported hedgehog fleas biting a human, via a dog that had been in contact with hedgehogs.

On the other hand, fleas from other species can infest hedgehogs, presumably temporarily. For European hedgehogs the list includes human fleas (*Pulex irritans*), rat fleas (*Nosopsyllus fasciatus*), dog fleas (*Ctenocephalides canis*) and cat fleas (*Ctenocephalides felis*) as well as the fleas of shrews, moles and various other small wild mammals (Smith 1968, Mehl 1972, Saupe & Poduschka 1985). However, of 51 719 fleas collected from European hedgehogs by Brinck & Löfqvist (1973) and Morris (1983), 99.98% were *A. erinacei*.

A subspecies (*A. erinacei maura*) is found on European hedgehogs in Spain and on the Algerian hedgehog (*Atelerix algirus*) in northern Africa, the Balearic and Pityusic islands. However, the European hedgehogs on Corsica and Sardinia have the nominal form *A. erinacei erinacei* (Beaucournu & Alcover 1984). The flea of the Chinese hedgehog (*Erinaceus amurensis*) has been identified as *A. sinensis* (Mehl 1972).

No specific flea is found on central African hedgehogs (*Atelerix albiventris*). Around Nairobi, Gregory (1981b) reported small numbers of fleas, *Ctenocephalides felis strongylus* (also on animals from the Ivory coast) and 'sticktight fleas' (*Echidnophaga gallinacea*) which can form clusters on domestic chickens (Table 9.2). The latter species was found once by Pearse (1929) in a study of seven hedgehogs in Nigeria. Pearse also found *Ctenocephalides canis*, *Synosternus pallidus* and *Xenopsylla cheopis*, all in small numbers. Again in Nigeria, Okaeme & Osakwe (1985) recorded *Ctenocephalides crataepus* on 36% of hedgehogs. In Algeria, Beaucournu & Kowalski (1985) recorded *Echidnophaga gallinacea* for the Algerian hedgehog (*Atelerix algirus*).

There are few data for other hedgehog species. Abdullah & Hassan (1987) reported a *Pulex irritans* (the human flea) on one long-eared hedgehog (*Hemiechinus auritus*) in northern Iraq. In Israel, Schoenfeld & Yom-Tov (1985) found *A. erinacei* on both *Hemiechinus auritus* and *Erinaceus concolor*.

TABLE 9.2   *Ectoparasites found on central African hedgehogs* (Atelerix albiventris) *from Nairobi.*

Species	Positive cases		Number parasites/animal	
	%	n	Mean	Range
Fleas				
Ctenocephalides felis plus *Echidnophaga gallinacea*	33	39	3	1–16
Mites				
Caparinia erinacei	72	68	—	—
Notoedres oudemansi (lesions)	6·5	140	—	—
Rodentopus sciuri	46	43	—	—
Ticks				
Haemaphysalis leachi plus *Rhipicephalus simus*	35	68	6	1–16

n = number of animals examined.
Source: Gregory (1981b).

Ticks

Both ticks and mites are arachnids (order Acarina) and are common ectoparasites of hedgehogs. By far the most usual tick to be found on European hedgehogs is *Ixodes hexagonus* (Fig. 9.8) although it is not very host-specific (Blackmore & Owen 1968, Liebisch & Walter 1986, Matuschka *et al.* 1990b). The sheep tick (*I. ricinus*) also known as the 'castor bean' tick is also occasionally found on hedgehogs in Britain, Norway and continental Europe (Thompson 1936, Mehl 1972, Versluys 1975). *Ixodes trianguliceps* has also been recorded (Walter 1981).

I have found various sizes of tick to be commonly attached to the flanks, underside (especially in the ano-genital region) and behind the ears, but they may occur anywhere on the body. The larvae are small, slow-moving and orange–brown (BHPS 1987). When fully engorged, the oval blue–grey body of a large adult tick may approach 1 cm in length and present an alarming sight, especially if several are clustered together. However, a tick will detach when satiated—probably in a nest. One study of an abandoned breeding nest (Thompson 1936) found 72 adult *I. hexagonus*, 314 nymphs and 412 larvae! More usually the number of ticks in a nest is in single figures. Thompson noted that, unlike *I. ricinus*, *I. hexagonus* never copulates on the host's body and that females are found mainly on the hedgehogs whereas the males are more commonly found in the nests. Laboratory experiments have suggested that subadult *I. hexagonus* and *I. ricinus* tend to detach from hedgehogs around midnight (Matuschka *et al.* 1990a,b). They would thus disperse outside the nests because, contrary to claims by the study authors, hedgehogs almost never return to their nests for naps during the night (Chapter 7).

Other ticks found on European hedgehogs (*Erinaceus* spp.) include *Dermacentor reticulatus*, *D. sinicus*, *Haemaphysalis concinna*, *H. punctata*, *H.*

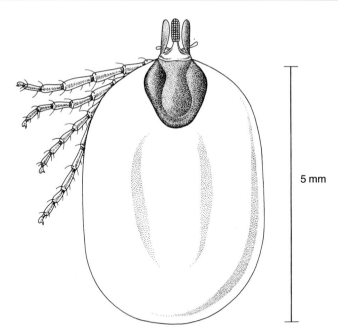

5 mm

FIG. 9.8   *The hedgehog tick*, Ixodes hexagonus, *dorsal view of a partially engorged individual: the commonest species of tick to be found on the European hedgehog.*

numidiana, Rhipicephalus bursa, R. sanguineus (Smith 1968). *Haemaphysalis erinacei* was found on hedgehogs in southern Italy (Bari-Puglia province; Morel & Sobrero 1976). In New Zealand the cattle tick *Haemaphysalis bispinosus* is the only tick found on hedgehogs (Smith 1968), and infestation rates are low. In Russia, *Dermacentor* spp. may spread red-water fever (caused by the blood sporozoan *Babesia ninensis*) and in Israel *Rhipicephalus bursa* reputedly transmits leptospirosis and maybe 'Q fever'—see below (Versluys 1975).

In Israel, Schoenfeld & Yom-Tov (1985) found *Rhipicephalus sanguineus* on 45% of 45 hedgehogs (*Erinaceus concolor*) examined, up to 20 ticks per animal. These ticks were also found on 25% of 40 long-eared hedgehogs (*Hemiechinus auritus*) but each had only one or two ticks. They suggested that the higher incidence of ticks in *Erinaceus* may reflect the use of foliage-lined nests, rather than the bare burrows of *Hemiechinus* (who also sand-bathed often).

In northern Iraq, Abdullah & Hassan (1987) reported heavy infestations of long-eared hedgehogs (*Hemiechinus auritus*) with ixodid ticks (*Boophilus annulatus, Rhipicephalus sanguineus, Haemaphysalis erinacei, Hyalomma detritum*) known to be vectors of serious disease in animals and humans.

Maheshwari (1986) examined 126 Indian long-eared hedgehogs (*Hemiechinus collaris*) and found *Rhipicephalus sanguineus* on 74% of females (yielding

63% of ticks collected). Fewer males were infested; 60% yielded 37% of the ticks. The heaviest infestations were in winter, the lowest in the monsoon. Although males, females, nymphs and larvae were collected from both sexes, female hedgehogs carried a higher overall percentage of nymphs.

Around Nairobi, Gregory (1981b) found a few *Haemaphysalis leachi* (common on cattle, dogs and small carnivores) and *Rhipicephalus simus* on central African hedgehogs (*Atelerix albiventris*) (Table 9.2). Easton (1979) recorded *H. leachi* from a hedgehog in Tanzania. In Nigeria, Pearse (1929) found ticks (*H. leachi, Amblyomma variegatum* and *Rhipicephalus sanguineus*) on all seven hedgehogs examined, but infestation rates were low, an average of 3·5 ticks per animal. Also in Nigeria, Okaeme & Osakwe (1985) reported these same three ixodid ticks, respectively on 23, 14 and 18% of animals, and pointed out that the latter two were implicated as vectors in the transmission of the sporozoan *Babesia* ('piroplasmosis') to domestic ruminants. *Amblyomma nuttali* (usually associated with reptiles) was found on 47% of 32 hedgehogs from the Ivory coast (Gregory 1981b). In Sudan, hedgehogs (*Atelerix albiventris*) were found with adult ticks *Haemaphysalis spinulosa* and *Rhipicephalus simus* (Hussein & Mustafa 1985). In Zimbabwe, Hoogstraal & Wassef (1983) described *Haemaphysalis norvali* (a new species of the *H. spinulosa* group) from a southern African hedgehog (*Atelerix frontalis*).

In Britain, tick infestations rarely warrant treatment, but I have occasionally seen large clusters (over 50) on some individuals in the field, especially on the neck behind the ears. Stocker (1987) treated a youngster weakened by its burden of 153 ticks! In such situations anaemia can result (Burgisser 1983). Although unconfirmed in hedgehogs, 'tick paralysis', probably caused by the neurotoxic saliva of gravid female ticks (including Ixodidae) attached to the neck (Chandler & Read 1961), might account for some cases of paralysis.

Mites

The most serious mites affecting hedgehogs are the mange and itch mites of the sub-order Sarcoptoidea. This includes both the sarcoptid mites which tunnel right into the skin and the psoroptid mites which cause crusting and surface skin lesions. These mites are generally tiny (under 0·5 mm long) and whitish, with short stumpy legs. Diagnosis is by microscopic examination of skin scrapings which may reveal adult mites, larvae and eggs. Symptoms of infestation include scaly, encrusted skin lesions, 'cauliflower ears', hair loss and sometimes even spine loss. In severe cases the animal is weakened, often hypothermic, unable to roll-up properly and may be blinded. The lesions may become infected or maggoty (see 'myiasis' below).

The psoroptid mite *Caparinia tripilis* (Fig. 9.9) commonly causes mange in hedgehogs from Europe and New Zealand, but does not affect humans. In Britain, this mite rarely causes severe mange, although in Germany fatal infestations have been reported (Morris & English 1973, Brockie 1974b, Gerson & Boever 1983, Gregory 1985, Keymer *et al.* 1991). In New Zealand infestations are particularly common and severe, and the mites may burrow into the skin. Parkes (1975) found *C. tripilis* infestations on 20% of hedgehogs

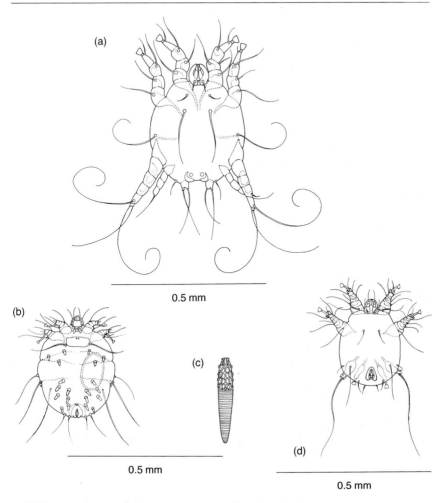

FIG. 9.9   *Some of the parasitic mites found on hedgehogs. (a)* Caparinia tripilis, *(b)* Sarcoptes *spp., (c)* Demodex erinacei, *(d)* Notoedres *spp. (See text for details.)*

examined. In a larger study, Brockie (1974b) examined 180 hedgehogs from Wellington and found 42% with *Caparinia* infestations. He found that debilitating infestations could develop in only 3 months, and that infestation could reduce the chances of winter survival by as much as 50%! The mites could also help to spread ringworm (see below); the fungus has been isolated from their droppings. The high density of hedgehogs in New Zealand could be a factor in explaining the high incidence of mange mite infestations. Brockie (1974b) pointed out that severe mange had not been reported before the 1950s, and suggested that mange may limit hedgehog populations at high densities. In New Zealand, the sarcoptid mite *Notoedres muris* may also be present in mixed infestations with *C. tripilis*. Records of numerous other mites include *Hirstionyssus* sp. and others of the families Ascaidae, Laelaptidae, Oribatulidae, Galumnidae and Ceratozetidae (studies cited by Smith 1968 and Brockie 1974b).

Other sarcoptic mites infesting European hedgehogs include *Sarcoptes* spp. (Saupe & Poduschka 1985). There are also records of notoedric mange mites (Gregory 1981b) and *Notoedres cati* (Fig. 9.9) can cause ear infestations exactly as found in domestic cats, with symptoms ranging from inflammation to disorientation and fits (Versluys 1975, Saupe & Poduschka 1985, Stocker 1987). A fatal case of sarcoptic mange (not precisely identified) was reported for a hedgehog (*Erinaceus concolor*) in Israel (Tadmor & Rauchbach 1972) and at least three similar cases have been identified in Britain (Versluys 1975).

The hair follicles of hedgehogs are commonly inhabited by *Demodex erinacei* (suborder Trombidiformes, family Demodicidae) which have elongated worm-like bodies and stumpy three-segmented legs (Fig. 9.9). A similar species (*Demodex folliculorum*) discreetly infests the hair follicles of most humans, especially on the face, but usually causes no symptoms at all. Other *Demodex* spp. are found on many wild and domestic mammals. Follicular (demodectic) mange has been reported in the European hedgehog in Britain (Stocker 1987).

Also reported from European hedgehogs, or their nests, are the mesostigmatid mites *Eulaelaps stabularis, Haemogamasus pontiger, H. nidi* and *Androlaelaps fahrenholzi*—which may be found on a variety of hosts (Morris & English 1969, Mehl 1972).

Spine loss after unspecified mange mite infestations of both *Erinaceus concolor* and captive *Hemiechinus auritus* has been reported (Poduschka 1986). One *Hemiechinus* lost almost all the spines only on its right side; the left side was normal and the boundary followed a neat median line down the animal's back! Poduschka suggested that some kind of neurological phenomenon might be involved.

Gregory (1981a) found three mite species on central African hedgehogs (*Atelerix albiventris*) around Nairobi. *Caparinia erinacei*, also found on the southern African hedgehog (*A. frontalis*), was common (Plate 19), as was *Rodentopus sciuri* (Hypoderidae) in the hair follicles. Infestations were of low pathogenicity. In contrast the sarcoptid mite *Notoedres oudemansi* although much less common (Table 9.2), caused a debilitating and fatal mange in all the cases encountered (all hedgehogs were males). The lesions (often complicated by myiasis, see below) were mainly on the hairy skin, especially the flanks. Because the animals became conspicuously day-active this affliction is probably over-represented in the sample.

The mesostigmatid mite *Androlaelaps casalis* was found on central African hedgehogs from the Ivory Coast, but unlike those from Nairobi, only one animal bore *Caparinia erinacei* and *Notoedres* was not found (Gregory 1981b). In Nigeria, Okaeme & Osakwe (1985) recorded the mange mite *Sarcoptes scabiei* on 3·6% of animals examined but without skin scrapings it will have been under-recorded. *Sarcoptes scabiei*, in one of its many forms, causes 'scabies' in humans.

The larval stages of the pentastomid *Armillifer armillatus* have been recorded in hedgehogs, presumably *Erinaceus* sp. (Wallach & Boever 1983). Pentastomes are strange endoparasitic mites in which the adults resemble a parasitic worm, with segment-like divisions of the body. The larvae more closely resemble conventional mites and while adults may live in the host's respiratory passages, the larvae live free or encyst in the viscera (Chandler & Read 1961). Pentastomes may show up on X-rays, but no effective treatment has been reported other than surgery (Wallach & Boever 1983).

Fly-strike (myiasis)

This is a common and distressing affliction. Flies lay clusters of eggs on the hedgehogs, near wounds or other skin lesions, around the eyes, ears, nose, anus or genitalia (especially of young or debilitated animals). The resulting maggot infestations can rapidly kill. I have several times had to clear fly eggs or maggots from severely ill youngsters that I have cared for, and also from the wounds of otherwise healthy hedgehogs.

In the central African hedgehog (*Atelerix albiventris*), Gregory (1981a,b) reported that skin lesions from mange and dog bites could lead to blowfly maggot infestations (*Hemipyrellia fernandica*). The same species also attacks the southern African hedgehog (*A. frontalis*). In Europe, genus *Lucilia* sp. is a common cause of myiasis (Saupe & Poduschka 1985).

Fungal infections

Ringworm

The identification of ringworm fungi (dermatophytes) is complicated and their nomenclature muddled. The ascomycete species *Trichophyton mentagrophytes* is in fact a 'complex' of several specific forms, including the hedgehog ringworm *T. erinacei* (= *T. mentagrophytes* var. *erinacei*), and its sexual form is sufficiently distinct to have been named as a separate organism, *Arthroderma benhamiae*—which has European and African forms (Chermette 1987). Many hedgehogs with ringworm show no visible symptoms, but severe infections can cause the skin to become powdery, very cracked and crusty, especially on the face which may get rather bald. In long-standing infections the ears become thickened, dry and crusty, and may crumble at the edges. Hedgehog ringworm is only mildly pathogenic; even quite severely infected hedgehogs show little sign of skin irritation and gain weight normally (Morris & English 1969, 1973). Scaling skin may also have other causes (e.g. mite infestations) and thus ringworm should be confirmed by culturing skin scrapings or hair samples on agar plates; e.g. at 28°C on Sabouraud's agar. As a general guide, *T. erinacei* cultures can be distinguished by a white, finely textured appearance, a bright lemon-yellow (sometimes greenish) staining of the agar and absence of the urease enzyme. The urease test (hydrolysis of a 3% solution of urea) is rapidly positive in *T. mentagrophytes* (Chermette 1987). Few of the many fungi recorded from hedgehog skin could be considered more than incidentals and only the non-pathogenic *Trichophyton terrestre* seems to be a true resident of European hedgehogs (Smith 1968).

Ringworm affects a substantial proportion of European hedgehogs (*Erinaceus europaeus*) in Britain and New Zealand where average infection rates are about 20–25% and 47%, respectively (Morris & English 1969). Direct transmission may occur from mother to infant and on contact during fights and courtships—which may explain why most infections occur on the head. English & Morris (1969) found that the ringworm fungus loses viability in the soil or in wet conditions, but remains viable in a dry nest lining for at least a year. The fungus was cultured from the linings of 23% of the 60 nests examined. Hedgehogs do sometimes use each other's nests (Reeve & Morris 1985), hence ringworm transmission via the nests is a possibility.

In Britain, animals from one urban area (Bushy Park, West London) had a particularly high incidence of ringworm (about 44%) (Morris & English 1969). This may reflect a dense population, as found in New Zealand, but there was no evidence of the mite *Caparinia tripilis* acting as a vector of this fungus in Britain. The higher incidence among males (25%), twice that of females (12·3%), is possibly because males have a higher number of 'social' interactions—they certainly use more nests (Chapter 5). Also, older animals had a higher incidence than youngsters. The infection survives hibernation, and no infected hedgehog is known to have recovered (Morris & English 1969, 1973).

Gregory & English (1975) were the first to record positive cultures for ringworm (*Arthroderma benhamiae*), affecting about 10% of wild central African hedgehogs (*Atelerix albiventris*) from around Nairobi (Kenya). In captivity the incidence rose to 33%. Animals of all ages and both sexes were affected. Mite infestations (*Notoedres* and *Caparinia*, see earlier) were also found but were evidently unrelated to the incidence of ringworm.

In Israel, Kuttin *et al.* (1977) reported a hedgehog (probably *Erinaceus concolor*) with severe sarcoptic mange (*Sarcoptes scabiei*) complicated by ringworm (*T. erinacei*) combined with two other fungi *Alternaria* and *Helmintosporium* spp. Also in Israel, Schoenfeld & Yom-Tov (1985) reported fungal infections of *Erinaceus concolor*, which were not identified but supposed to be *T. erinacei*.

Ringworm fungi (genera *Microsporum* or *Trichophyton*) are often quite host-specific, as in the case of human ringworm, but people are also susceptible to ringworm from domestic animals as well as rats and mice. Some of the *Microsporum gypseum* group can be caught from soil (English 1967).

In Britain and continental Europe, hedgehog ringworm has also been isolated from various carnivores (especially dogs), wild mice and rats, and occasionally humans. The latter have usually been infected via their dogs which have been in contact with hedgehogs, or (more rarely) from directly handling hedgehogs (Eddowes 1898, English *et al.* 1962, English 1967, Morris & English 1973, Simpson 1974, Gregory & English 1975, Bourdeau *et al.* 1987). Contact with hedgehog nest material is another potential route of infection (English & Morris 1969). In humans, a rapidly spreading, intensely itching, eczema-like scaling of the skin occurs, which may sometimes also affect the nail bed and thicken the nail. The ringworm, probably often misdiagnosed as eczema, may be complicated by secondary bacterial (staphylococcal) infections.

Other fungal infections

Smith (1968) noted that *Candida albicans* ('thrush') inhabited the guts of over 87% of European hedgehogs in New Zealand. It can cause chronic diarrhoea although the animals are frequently asymptomatic (Versluys 1975). Gregory (1985) cited a study by English *et al.* (1975) in which *C. albicans* had invaded the footpads of a European hedgehog. Other yeast-like fungi isolated from hedgehogs include other *Candida* spp., various *Rhodotorula* spp. and *Torulopsis famata*, all of which seem to be non-pathogenic.

Gregory *et al.* (1976) reported that 11% of 140 central African hedgehogs (*Atelerix albiventris*) from Nairobi bore skin growths associated with a yeast-like fungal infection. A further 12 cases of the disease developed in captivity. Regional lymph nodes were also affected but the disease did not spread to the viscera. This transmissible disease was sometimes associated with trauma, such as injuries during fights in which the males bit at the spines of others. This may explain the larger number of growths on the lips and palate among males. Gregory (1981b) reported that Karstad had observed a rise in the prevalence of this disease to about 50% of the population in 1973, following which the hedgehog population sharply declined and was still at a low level in 1980.

In England, hedgehogs have been found suffering from nodular lesions in the lungs from which *Emmonsia* (= *Chrysosporium*) *crescens* (causing 'adiaspiromycosis') has been isolated. Although this disease may be important in some small mammal populations, its significance in hedgehogs is unknown (Smith 1968).

Histoplasmosis, caused by an intracellular fungus *Histoplasma capsulatum*, was once isolated from a hedgehog and a rat in Abruzzo (Italy) (Mantovani *et al.* 1972). The inhaled spores cause calcareous nodules to form in the lungs, with resulting diffuse clinical symptoms.

Internal parasites

Numerous parasitic worms (helminths) have been described from hedgehogs of several species. In European hedgehogs, lungworm infestations are so common that some authors (e.g. Schicht 1982a,b, Saupe & Poduschka 1985, BHPS 1987) have suggested that any hedgehog taken in from the wild should be routinely treated with anthelmintic drugs (see Appendix 1 for a summary of helminth species and treatments). The eggs or larvae of many parasites (Fig. 9.10) may be extracted from faeces by flotation in saturated salt solution (sodium chloride), or sedimentation in tap water that has been allowed to stand, although various other methods may be used (Barutzki *et al.* 1984, BHPS 1987, Frank 1988) and faecal diagnosis kits are commercially available

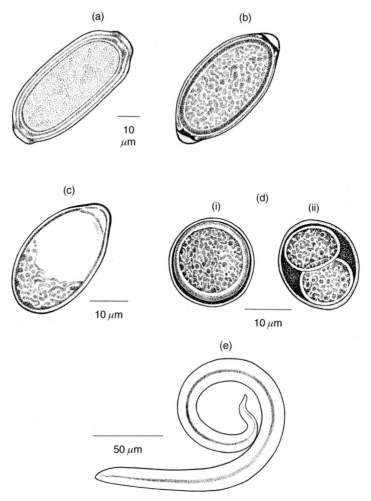

FIG. 9.10 *Some eggs and larvae of endoparasites commonly found in the faeces of European hedgehogs. (a)* Capillaria aerophila *egg, (b)* Capillaria *sp. egg, (c)* Brachylaemus erinacei *egg, (d) oocysts of* Isospora rastegaivae *(i) unsporulated, (ii) sporulated, (e) first-stage larva of* Crenosoma striatum.

(e.g. Ovassay, Pitman-Moore). *Crenosoma* infestations of the lungs are detectable by Baermann's funnel extraction of first-stage larvae from the faeces (Versluys 1975). Cestode (tapeworm) segments in the faeces may be visible to the unaided eye. Of course, parasites of prey species can turn up in faecal samples, for example the round primary cysts of the earthworm parasite *Monocystis* could confuse one looking for the eggs of genuine hedgehog endoparasites (Frank 1988).

Trematodes

European hedgehogs may have infestations of *Brachylaemus erinacei*, an intestinal fluke around 5–10 mm long and 1–2 mm across which may occasionally also invade the bile duct. The infective stages (metacercariae) are carried by snails. In faecal samples from hedgehogs, the small eggs (30–35 µm by 17–21 µm) are easy to miss; they are asymmetrically ovoid, appear lidded and each contains a miracidium (Koch 1981, Schicht 1982a,b, Saupe & Poduschka 1985, Frank 1988). In severe cases, *Brachylaemus* infestation can cause lethal haemorrhagic enteritis—as many as 2516 adult flukes have been found in one small intestine (Versluys 1975). In Norfolk (UK), *Brachylaemus* was found in only 2·7% of 74 hedgehog autopsies (Keymer *et al.* 1991). Most German studies have also indicated a generally low incidence. Timme (1980) recorded only one *Brachylaemus* infestation in 410 hedgehogs examined (see also Table 9.3). However, Barutzki *et al.*(1984) noted that previous studies (Schütze 1980, 1983) had found regional variation in the incidence of intestinal flukes: 1% in Mittelhessen and Taunus, but as high as 80% in Berlin. This may partly reflect the distribution of the snail intermediate host. Barutzki *et al.* also commented that faecal analysis, especially if sedimentation is not used, probably underestimates the true incidence of *Brachylaemus*.

Other trematodes that have been found in hedgehogs (*Erinaceus*) include *Agamodistomum pusillum* which may be found subcutaneously and in the mesenteries (Smith 1968) and *Euparyphium melis* (length 3·5–11 mm), carried by slugs and amphibia. In serious cases *Euparyphium* can cause haemorrhagic enteritis (Versluys 1975). *Dollfusinus frontalis* (family Brachylaemidae) has been found in the frontal and nasal sinuses of European hedgehogs in France and Italy. Its intermediate hosts include land snails (*Trochoidea* spp.). When the snail is eaten, infective metacercariae migrate directly from the hedgehog's mouth to the nasal cavities (Mas-Coma & Montoliu 1987). The same trematode was recorded for the Algerian hedgehog (*Atelerix algirus*) in the Pityusic Islands (Spain) (Mas-Coma & Feliu 1984). There are no records of trematodes from the Central African hedgehog (*Atelerix albiventris*) (Gregory 1981b).

Cestodes

The infective stages of the hymenolepid tapeworm *Rodentolepis erinacei* (previously placed in the genera *Hymenolepis* or *Vampirolepis*) develop in arthropods (insects, myriapods and others). Adult tapeworms may reach 34–84 mm (Versluys 1975). The hedgehog may lose weight and get diarrhoea. Whitish segments (proglottids) around 1 mm long and 3 mm wide, singly or in chains, may be visible on or beside the faeces. Eggs may also be detected by flotation of faeces. Judging from faecal analyses, this cestode is not common in German hedgehogs (Table 9.3), but *R. erinacei* was found in 3·7% of 127 hedgehogs examined in Bavaria (Germany) by Laubmeier (1985). In Britain, *R. erinacei* was found in only one of 39 (Boag 1988) and in one of 74 hedgehogs examined (Keymer *et al.* 1991).

TABLE 9.3　　*Results of two German endoparasite surveys of faecal samples from European hedgehogs* (Erinaceus europaeus).

	Bauer & Stoye (1984)		Barutzki et al. (1984)	
	% incidence overall	Range of annual % values	% incidence overall	Range of annual % values
Eggs of *Capillaria* spp.	61·8	(45·2–86·7)	43·4	(25·1–66·1)
Larvae of *Crenosoma striatum*	45·2	(32·8–78·3)	27·4	(7·0–46·5)
Eggs of *Brachylaemus erinacei*	1·6	(0·0–6·6)	1·9[a]	(0·0–4·8)
Rodentolepis spp.	0·1	(2 occurrences)	0·0	(Not found)
Oocysts of *Isospora* spp.	13·3	(9·4–16·0)	18·4[b]	(5·7–40·9)

Bauer & Stoye (1984) examined 1849 faeces over 7 years. Barutzki *et al.* (1984) examined 643 faeces from underweight hedgehogs (<700 g) found in winter over 3 years; 55–79% bore endoparasites of some kind.
[a]Probably underestimated.
[b]*Isospora rastegaivae* only, negative for other coccidia.

Other cestodes recorded from the European hedgehog include *Davainea parva, Staphylocystis bacillaris, Oochoristica erinacei* and *Raillietina voluta*, all found in the intestine. Plerocercoids (spargana) of *Spirometra erinacei* and *Spirometra mansoni* (in the Korean hedgehog *Erinaceus amurensis koreensis*) have been found in subcutaneous infestations (Smith 1968; species names have been updated, A. Jones, pers. comm.). Maskar (1953) found larval cysts (tetrathyridia) of the dog tapeworm (*Mesocestoides lineatus*) in *E. europaeus*, and infected dogs by feeding hedgehogs to them. *Mesocestoides* larvae were also found in various organs of 35% of 90 hedgehogs examined in Italy (Macchioni 1967). No cestodes have been found in New Zealand hedgehogs (Smith 1968).

Gregory (1981b) found cestode cysts in very large numbers in the liver and mesentery of the central African hedgehog (*Atelerix albiventris*) but these were not implicated as a cause of death or debility (Table 9.4). Cestode records for this species include *Oochoristica herpestis*—found in five out of seven animals from Nigeria (Pearse 1930) and *Raillietina voluta* (Linstow 1904). Mas-Coma & Feliu (1984) cited a record of *Oochoristica erinacei* in the Algerian hedgehog (*Atelerix algirus*) by Meggitt (1920). In long-eared hedgehogs (*Hemiechinus auritus*) *Mathevotaenia skrjabini* has been recorded (Khalil & Abdul-Salam 1985).

Nematodes

Of all parasitic diseases, nematode infections of the lungs are probably the most frequently fatal disease in hedgehogs (*Erinaceus* spp.) in Europe and New Zealand. The most common lungworms are of the genera *Crenosoma* and *Capillaria* which can fill the trachea and bronchi (Edwards 1957, Brockie 1958, Timme 1980, Saupe & Poduschka 1985, Boag 1988).

Crenosoma striatum is specific to hedgehogs and produces dry coughing, breathing difficulties and weight loss. Majeed *et al.* (1989) noted that adults and larvae were found in the lumina of the bronchi, bronchioles and alveolar ducts rather than the bronchial or tracheal epithelium. A marked thickening of the bronchioles and consolidation of the lung tissue may be seen (Boag 1988) and secondary bacterial infections (e.g. *Bordetella bronchiseptica*) are common (see below). Adult female worms are 0.3 mm across and around 12–13 mm long; males are half that size. Transparent first instar larvae (300 μm long) are passed out with the faeces (Saupe 1976, Carlson 1981, Saupe & Poduschka 1985, Frank 1988). The life cycle of *Crenosoma*, with its molluscan intermediate hosts, is shown in Fig. 9.11, but its occurrence in nestlings suggests that direct transmission is also possible (Majeed *et al.* 1989).

In European hedgehogs, similar symptoms are produced by lung infestations of the *Capillaria aerophila* species group, which may occur in mixed infestations with *Crenosoma*. Adult *Capillaria* (10–13 μm long) with encysted ova may be found in the tracheal, bronchial and bronchiolar epithelium, and varying degrees of inflammation may result (Majeed & Cooper 1984, Frank 1988, Majeed *et al.* 1989). The brown eggs (easily mis-identified as trichurid eggs) are oval (60–75 μm long) with a polar plug at each end, and are found intermittently in the faeces (Saupe & Poduschka 1985). However, Majeed *et al.* (1989) found that faecal analysis alone failed to detect up to a third of histologically confirmed *Capillaria* infestations and was even less reliable in detecting *Crenosoma* infestations. *Capillaria* transmission may be direct or earthworms may act as an intermediate host, possibly indicating that more than one *Capillaria* species is involved (Majeed *et al.* 1989). Earthworms might also concentrate the eggs (Poduschka & Saupe 1981). Experiments have shown that carabid beetles are also potential vectors of certain *Capillaria* species (Thiele 1977). Once eaten by the hedgehog, the nematode eggs develop into infective larvae or adults, penetrate the intestinal wall and migrate to the lungs (Majeed *et al.* 1989).

In Germany, Timme (1980) found that 39% of hedgehogs (410 examined) had respiratory tract infestations with *Crenosoma* or *Capillaria*, and over half of those had both (see also Table 9.3). In Britain, Majeed *et al.* (1989) found that 66% of hedgehogs (53 examined) had lungworm infestations, 14 (40%) had *Crenosoma* only, five (14%) *Capillaria* only and 16 (46%) had both. They noted that males and females suffered equally, but the incidence increased with age. Of 20 nestlings, four (20%) contained *Crenosoma* and two (10%) had *Capillaria*. Adults had an 80–90% incidence of lungworm infestation! Laubmeier (1985) found *Crenosoma* in 52% and *Capillaria aerophila* in 15–41% (depending on region) of hedgehogs examined from Glonn (Bavaria, Germany). Boag (1988) found *Crenosoma* in 44% of 39 hedgehogs from northern Britain and found up to 23 per animal (average 2–12); another species, possibly *Capillaria tenuis*, was also found.

Capillaria erinacei, and at least one other *Capillaria* sp. with smaller eggs (50–60 μm), may infest the gut (Saupe & Poduschka 1985, Frank 1988). The unnamed species was denoted *C. ovoreticulata* by Laubmeier (1985). The

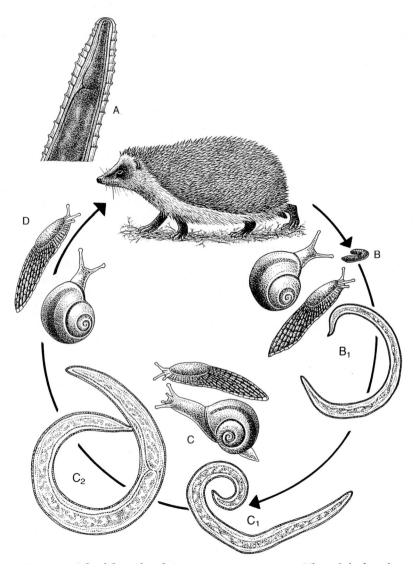

FIG. 9.11   *The life-cycle of Crenosoma striatum. A. The adult females inhabit the bronchi of the hedgehog. They viviparously produce first instar larvae (300 μm long) which are coughed-up, swallowed and pass through the gut. B. From the faeces, the larvae (B₁) infect slugs and snails by penetration of the foot. C. In the foot of the mollusc, ecdysis to the second instar (C₁) is followed 3 weeks later by the third instar infective stage (C₂). D. The hedgehogs are re-infected when the slugs and snails are eaten as food; 21 days later the worms are mature and larvae are again found in the faeces. Source: based on Saupe (1976). Drawings not to scale.*

reported infestation rates of intestinal *Capillaria* vary greatly: in Germany, 74% (Laubmeier 1985) and 12% (Timme 1980), in Britain, 79% (Boag 1988) but Majeed *et al.* (1989) found intestinal *Capillaria* to be rare. Boag found an average of 110–835 worms per hedgehog, but over 2000 worms were recorded in each of two animals, and neither showed any ill effects! The life cycle follows much the same plan as the *Capillaria aerophila* group. Symptoms may be vague but in severe cases (often young animals) severe diarrhoea, lethargy, emaciation and death can result. *Capillaria erinacei* (probably = *C. exigua*) has also been reported in the Algerian hedgehog (*Atelerix algirus*) (Mas-Coma & Feliu 1984).

Stomach worms (*Physaloptera dispar* [= *P. clausa* sensu Seurat, 1917]) and oesophageal worms (*Gongylonema* spp), of the order Spirurida, are found in several hedgehog species which are infected by eating insects (intermediate hosts). *Physaloptera* females can be 25 mm long (Linstow 1904), the males may reach 17 mm. The thick-walled oval eggs (70–75 μm across and containing embryonated larvae) can be extracted by flotation from the faeces. *Physaloptera dispar* occurs in European hedgehogs (*Erinaceus europaeus*) (e.g. Saupe & Poduschka 1985), but especially heavy infestations have been reported for the Algerian hedgehog (*Atelerix algirus*) in the Pityusic Islands (Spain) and northern Africa (Mas-Coma & Feliu 1984). *Physaloptera* is also common in the central African hedgehog (*Atelerix albiventris*) in Nigeria (Pearse 1930, Okaeme & Osakwe 1988) and in Kenya, where as many as 129 per stomach have been recorded (Gregory 1981b; see Tables 9.4 and 9.5)! In India, Maheshwari & Jain (1981) found larval cysts of *Physaloptera* in the liver of a long-eared hedgehog (*Hemiechinus collaris*).

TABLE 9.4 *Helminth parasites found in central African hedgehogs* (Atelerix albiventris) *from Nairobi.*

Species	Positive cases		No. parasites/animal		Site
	%	n	Mean	Range	
Cestoda					
Mesocestoides sp. larvae	13	57	Hundreds		Abdominal viscera
Adult Hymenolepids (?)	4	48	15	11–20	Small intestine
Nematoda					
Spirura gastrophila	19	48	5	1–16	Oesophagus lining
Physaloptera dispar	77	53	18	1–129	Stomach
Rictularia sp.	8	48	4	1–11	Small intestine
Acanthocephala					
Moniliformis cestodiformis	75	47	10	1–109	—

n = number of animals examined.
Source: Gregory (1981b).

TABLE 9.5   *The helminth parasites found by complete dissections of 45 central African hedgehogs (*Atelerix albiventris*) from the Kainji Lake area of Nigeria.*

Parasite species	No. hedgehogs infected	Location
Ascarops dentata[b]	7 (16%)	Stomach
Ascarops strongylina[b]	5 (11%)	Stomach
Gongylonema pulchrum[ab]	4 (9%)	Stomach
Macrocanthorhynchus hirudinaceus	11 (24%)	Oesophagus, stomach, intestine
Mesocestoides sp.	6 (13%)	Oesophagus, stomach
Nochtia atelerixia	4 (9%)	Intestine
Physocephalus sexalatus[b]	3 (7%)	Stomach
Physaloptera dispar[a]	11 (24%)	Stomach, intestine
Setaria sp.	1 (2%)	Oesophagus, stomach

Twenty-six animals contained endoparasites (between 1 and 30 individuals per hedgehog). Three animals bore unidentified cysts and one had a single subcutaneous filarial worm.
[a]Potential accidental transfer to humans.
[b]Potential accidental transfer to domestic ruminants.
Source: Okaeme & Osakwe (1988).

Oesophageal worms, such as *Gongylonema mucronatum* and *G. neoplasticum* (found in European hedgehogs) can reach 6–12 cm long and about 2 mm across), but despite their size seldom cause serious symptoms. They infest the mucosa of the oesophagus and have a similar life cycle to the stomach worms (Saupe & Poduschka 1985). Various *Gongylonema* species have also been reported from Algerian and eastern European hedgehogs (Mas-Coma & Feliu 1984) and central African hedgehogs (Okaeme & Osakwe 1988; see Table 9.5).

In Kuwait, Khalil & Abdul-Salam (1985) found spiruroid-type larval cysts in the mesenteries of long-eared hedgehogs (*Hemiechinus auritus*) and reported two new species of nematode: *Seuratum kuwaitensis* (the female up to 35 mm long) in the intestine and *Spirura auriti* (around 10 mm long) in the stomach.

Reports of *Trichinella* seem patchy, Orlandi (1972) examined 247 hedgehogs and found no evidence of *Trichinella spiralis* infection but Fameree *et al.* (1981), working in an area where infection was apparently widespread amongst wild mammals, found larvae in the muscles of European hedgehogs. Infection may occur from eating carrion, but carrion-feeding carabid beetles commonly carry *Trichinella* in their guts and probably provide an indirect infection route (Thiele 1977). Numerous other nematodes have been reported to infest European hedgehogs including ascarids and *Strongyloides* sp. (Smith 1968, Versluys 1975, Ruempler 1982). In central African hedgehogs (*Atelerix albiventris*) records have included a new species, *Trichuris mettami*, from the gut 'caecum' (in fact hedgehogs have no caecum) (Baylis 1935), and the larval form of *Porrocaecum* sp. were reported by Gregory (1981b). *Rictularia aethechini* has been reported from the southern African hedgehog (*Atelerix frontalis*) (Gregory 1981b) and *Erinaceus* (Smith 1968). Mas-Coma & Feliu (1984) listed additional helminth records for the Algerian hedgehog (*Atelerix algirus*) in Spain and northern Africa.

Acanthocephala

Acanthocephalan worms (thorny-headed worms) found in the intestines of hedgehogs (*Erinaceus* spp.) have included *Moniliformis erinacei, M. major*, various *Prosthenorchis* spp. and *Echinorhynchus rosai* (may be a synonym of *Prosthorhynchus cylindraeus*) which has been known to cause ulceration of the colon. *Echinorhynchus amphipachus* (a species of dubious validity) has been found in the mesentery (Smith 1968, Versluys 1975). Insects are the probable intermediate hosts. Versluys (1975) reported that *Prosthenorchis* spp. harboured by hedgehogs in zoological collections could be spread by crickets to other mammal species, causing considerable damage. Severe infestations may damage the intestinal mucosa, resulting in diarrhoea and emaciation. Acanthocephalan eggs are identifiable by sedimentation from faecal samples (Saupe & Poduschka 1985).

In the central African hedgehog (*Atelerix albiventris*) Gregory (1981b) commonly found *Moniliformis cestodiformis* (Table 9.4), which may grow to 115 mm long (Linstow 1904). Although Gregory found as many as 109 in one gut, the hedgehog seemed to show no ill effects!

Moniliformis moniliformis, which also infests rodents, has been found in Algerian hedgehogs (*Atelerix algirus*) from northern Africa and the Pityusic Islands (Mas-Coma & Feliu 1984), and in both *Erinaceus concolor* and *Hemiechinus auritus* in Israel (Schoenfeld & Yom-Tov 1985).

Protozoa

Coccidia

Coccidiosis is common in European hedgehogs but is usually asymptomatic. Occasional severe symptoms include poor appetite, emaciation, lethargy, haemorrhagic diarrhoea and death. Infections may be detected by the presence of oocysts in flotation extractions of faeces (Saupe & Poduschka 1985). Oocysts of *Isospora rastegaivae* are roundish and around 20 µm across (Frank 1988), and after sporulation contain two distinct round bodies (sporocysts). The oocysts of *Eimeria* spp. are oval and contain four sporocysts. In *I. rastegaivae*, probably the most important species in European hedgehogs, infection of the gut lining (mainly 30–45 cm below the stomach) occurs at around 8 days after the direct ingestion of infective stages (sporulated oocysts) which have matured (by sporogony) in the environment (Matuschka 1984, Saupe & Poduschka 1985). In Germany, studies have revealed coccidia in 13–15% of hedgehogs examined (Barutzki *et al.* 1984, Laubmeier 1985).

Other coccidia found in European hedgehogs include *Isospora erinacei, I. schmaltzi, Eimeria perardi, E. ostertagia* and *Yakimovella erinacei*; the distinctive oocysts of the latter have eight sporocysts containing many sporozoites (Versluys 1975).

Other protozoa

Hedgehogs are susceptible to toxoplasmosis and captives may become infected by eating raw meat (Smith 1968, Versluys 1975, Ruempler 1982). In Tuscany (Italy), Zardi *et al.* (1980) detected *Toxoplasma gondii* in 28.5% of European hedgehogs examined. Although *T. gondii* affects both hedgehogs and humans, only those eating raw hedgehogs would be at risk!

Microcysts of *Sarcocystis* spp. were found in the skeletal muscle of 7% of 57 central African hedgehogs (*Atelerix albiventris*) from Nairobi (Gregory 1981b), although no protozoa were found in blood smears of 24 hedgehogs.

Pearse (1930) isolated 'hexamitoids', flagellate protozoa (family Hexamitidae, which includes the genus *Giardia*), in 20% of the intestines of hedgehogs (*Atelerix albiventris*) examined in Nigeria. Hedgehogs have been experimentally infected with the haemoflagellates *Trypanosoma gambiense* and *T. vivax* although there is no evidence of natural infections (Smith 1968, Versluys 1975).

Elbihari *et al.* (1984) failed to implicate desert hedgehogs (*Paraechinus aethiopicus*) in the spread of the haemoflagellate causing cutaneous leishmaniasis in Saudi Arabia.

Bacterial diseases

Leptospirosis

Leptospirosis is an economically important disease caused by the bacterium *Leptospira interrogans*. It is transmitted by urine and affects a wide range of wild and domestic animals as well as humans (Weil's disease). Leptospires are highly adapted to their adopted hosts and more than 160 serovars (serological varieties) have been identified. These have been grouped into about 18 serogroups (Hathaway 1981) on the basis of their immunological characteristics; each serogroup is named after its most typical member. Many species, including hedgehogs, may act as 'maintenance hosts' which form reservoirs of particular serovars in the wild. Within its maintenance host the leptospire typically causes only subclinical pathogenic effects, but it may be severely pathogenic in accidental hosts (such as domestic cattle and humans)— although a relatively high infective dose may be necessary (Hathaway 1981). Although hedgehogs, once mature, are very susceptible to several serovars of leptospire (Table 9.6), clinical signs of infection are seldom apparent.

Serovar *bratislava* (of the Australis serogroup) has been found in hedgehogs from former Czechoslovakia, Poland and Russia. In Britain it is the only serovar that has been isolated from wild hedgehogs (Broom & Coughlan 1960, Twigg *et al.* 1968, Salt & Little 1977, Karaseva *et al.* 1979, Little *et al.* 1981). In agreement with previous studies, Hathaway *et al.* (1983) noted that

TABLE 9.6 *Leptospires that have been recovered from hedgehogs.*

Leptospira interrogans Serogroup	*Serovar*	*Country and hedgehog species*[a]
Australis	*bratislava*	Romania[c] Belgium[b] Hungary[c] CIS[b] Italy[b] Poland[c] Czechoslovakia[c] UK[b] Denmark[b] East Germany[b?].
	australis	Italy[b] Bulgaria[c] Israel[c]
Autumnalis	*erinacei-auriti*	CIS[d] Bulgaria[c]
Ballum	*ballum*	Israel[c] Italy[b] New Zealand[b]
Bataviae	*bataviae*	Bulgaria[c] Poland[c]
Canicola	*canicola*	Israel[cd]
Cynopteri	—	Sudan[e]
Grippotyphosa	*grippotyphosa*	Poland[c] Israel[d]
Hebdomadis	*mini (swajizak)*	Israel[c]
	saxkoebing	Italy[b] Denmark[b]
	sejroe	Poland[c] Czechoslovakia[c] Denmark[b]
	polonica	Poland[c]
Ictero-haemorrhagiae	*ictero-haemorrhagiae*	Poland[c] Denmark[b] Italy[b] Sudan[e]
Javanica	*sorex-jalna*	Poland[c]Czechoslovakia[c] Netherlands[b] UK[b]
	poi	CIS[b] Denmark[b] East Germany[b?]
Pomona	*pomona*	Czechoslovakia[c] Denmark[b]
Pyrogenes	—	Sudan[e]

[a]Species re-named to be consistent with Corbet (1988).
[b]*Erinaceus europaeus*, [c]*E. concolor*, [d]*Hemiechinus auritus*, [e]*Atelerix albiventris*.
Source: mainly Smith (1968), with additions from Horsch *et al.* (1970), Salt & Little (1977), Hathaway *et al.* (1983), Sebek *et al.* (1989).

the hedgehog is the only identified free-living maintenance host for serovar *bratislava* in England, Wales and Northern Ireland, and hedgehogs were considered to be the probable source of sporadic infections in domestic species. Intriguingly, Karaseva *et al.* (1979) in a field study in the Yaroslavl region (Russia) found that the titres of antibodies (Australis serogroup) peaked in the spring (coinciding with the rut) and fell thereafter.

In New Zealand, European hedgehogs, along with various rodents, constitute important reservoirs of serovar *ballum* (serogroup Ballum), although infection is restricted almost entirely to sexually mature animals (Hathaway 1981). In New Zealand, Webster (1957) found hedgehogs to be very susceptible to experimental innoculation with serovar *pomona* (serogroup Pomona) from sheep. Leptospires of a wide range of serological types have been isolated from wild hedgehogs in various countries (Table 9.6). When reported, the incidence of infection in hedgehogs seems quite high. In Israel, a 31% incidence of leptospires was reported (serogroups Canicola, Grippotyphosa, Ballum and serovar *mini*—of serogroup Hebdomadis) and one Hungarian study revealed that 36% of hedgehogs examined (presumably *E. concolor*) were infected with various leptospires—principally the Australis serogroup (studies cited by Broom and Coughlan 1960, Ruempler 1982).

Salmonella

As hedgehogs feed on carrion and carrion-eating insects such as maggots and carabid beetles, the presence of *Salmonella* in their guts is no surprise. These, and other, enteric bacteria are probably normal members of the gut flora but can cause illness if the hedgehog is stressed, fed an abnormal diet (e.g. cow's milk; Stocker 1987), or if the community of gut bacteria is unbalanced by antibiotic treatment. *Salmonella enteriditis* can certainly be pathogenic to wild hedgehogs (Keymer *et al.* 1991). *Salmonella* spp. are the main bacteria causing enteritis and may also cause septicaemia (Timme 1980, Saupe & Poduschka 1985; Table 9.7). Humans and livestock are also commonly affected and *Salmonella* infections in wild animals such as hedgehogs are a potential health risk, especially for handlers of such animals (Wallach & Boever 1983, Mayer & Weiss 1985, Keymer *et al.* 1991).

In Norfolk (UK), Keymer *et al.* (1991) found a 19% incidence of *S. enteriditis* phage type 11 (a strain particularly associated with hedgehogs in the region) in a sample of 74 hedgehogs. This is very roughly comparable with the 25% incidence suggested by Smith (1968) and the 12% (sample 410: Timme 1980) and 17% (sample 637: Mayer and Weiss 1985) found in Germany. *Salmonella enteriditis* is by far the commonest species found in British and German hedgehogs, although other salmonellae have also been isolated, e.g. *S. brancaster* (Taylor 1968) and *S. typhimurium* (Mayer and Weiss 1985, Keymer *et al.* 1991). However, in New Zealand, Smith (1968) noted that *S. typhimurium* was the main species (39·4% incidence).

In Italy, Andreani & Cardini (1969) isolated salmonellae from 14·7% of 34 hedgehogs examined. They identified *S. thompson* and *S. edmonton* to add to previous records of *S. stanleyville* and *S. enteriditis*. In Sicily *S. dublin*, *S.*

TABLE 9.7   *Bacterial diseases which were judged to be the cause of death of 76 European hedgehogs (19% of the 410 deaths recorded) in a German study.*

Organism	No. of hedgehogs affected (% of 76 total)
Salmonella spp.	49 (64%)
Escherichia coli	16 (21%)
Proteus sp. (??)	3 (4%)
Pasteurella multocida	3 (4%)
Yersinia pseudotuberculosis	2 (3%)
Streptococci	3 (4%)

Source: Timme (1980).

parathyphi and *S. typhimurium* have also been isolated. In Greece, Tomopolous (1970) found strains *adastua, miami, bispeberg, halle, kisarewe* and *carro*—all new records for Greece and for hedgehogs. *Salmonella sofia* has also been isolated from European hedgehogs (Smith 1968).

Algerian hedgehogs (*Atelerix algirus*) from northern Africa yielded 14 *Salmonella* species; 40% of the hedgehogs examined were infected. *Arizona* sp. has also been found in these hedgehogs (Smith 1968).

Other bacteria

Bordetella bronchiseptica is a contagious respiratory infection common in many species. In European hedgehogs (not in New Zealand) it is often associated with tracheitis, catarrhal rhinitis, profuse nasal discharge and may lead to broncho-pneumonia (Hulse & Edwards 1937, Edwards 1957, Wallach & Boever 1983, Saupe & Poduschka 1985). It often occurs in conjunction with lungworm infestations (Matthiese & Kunstyr 1974, Gregory 1985, Keymer *et al.* 1991) (see above).

Tularemia, *Francisella* (= *Pasteurella*) *tularensis* (so-called 'rabbit-fever'), is mainly a disease of rabbits and rodents, but may be spread by ticks to many other mammals and seriously affects humans. In hedgehogs it causes septicaemia with an enlarged spleen and multiple necrotic foci in the spleen and liver. The hedgehog is one of the natural hosts of the disease in the CIS (Versluys 1975). Arata *et al.* (1973) found serological evidence of a recent tularemia infection in a hedgehog in Iran.

Various types of tuberculosis (*Mycobacterium* spp.), or 'TB' have been reported in hedgehogs. Although bovine TB (*M. bovis*) has been recorded (Smith 1968), there have been no reported spontaneous infections in wild hedgehogs (Little *et al.* 1982). Hedgehogs are not significant reservoirs of *M. bovis* and are less susceptible than rabbits or guinea pigs. Experimental infections with *M. bovis* (strain AF117/79) have produced only persistent low-level, low-pathogenicity infections. The variable and sometimes low body temperatures of hedgehogs may make them unsuitable hosts—*M. bovis* cultures grow very slowly at 34°C (Thorns *et al.* 1982, Thorns & Morris 1983). Avian TB (*M. avium*) has occasionally been isolated from wild hedgehogs in Britain (e.g. Matthews & McDiarmid 1977).

One bizarre case of TB was a captive hedgehog in the USA, previously kept in an aquarium, which died from a systemic *M. marinum* infection, a disease of salt-water fish that occasionally affects humans, especially aquarists (Tappe *et al.* 1983).

European hedgehogs can be experimentally infected with *Mycobacterium leprae*, which causes leprosy in humans (McDougal *et al.* 1979).

Other potentially pathogenic bacteria which have been isolated from hedgehogs include *Escherichia* spp. (including *E. coli* types 078 and 055), four species of *Proteus, Clostridium perfringens, Pseudomonas* spp. (Smith 1968) and various streptococci, all of which may be found alone or as secondary infections (Saupe & Poduschka 1985). *Pseudomonas* spp. may be part of a normal intestinal flora but can also cause abscesses (Wallach & Boever 1983) and *Pseudomonas* infection was the probable cause of death of one captive central African hedgehog kept in cool conditions (Gregory 1981b).

Smith (1968) reported *Pasteurella multocida* and *Haemophilus* sp. as pathogens of the respiratory tract and mentioned that *Pasteurella* spp. were common in wild hedgehogs in New Zealand. In Britain, Edwards (1957) found that *Pasteurella* spp. (and haemolytic streptococci) could be readily isolated from the upper respiratory tract, but caused only secondary infections. In Germany, Timme (1980) found *P. multocida* to be a rather minor cause of death (Table 9.7) and Burgisser (1983) agreed that pasteurellosis was generally rare. In central African hedgehogs (*Atelerix albiventris*) Gregory (1981b) recorded *Pasteurella* in granular skin growths associated with a yeast-like fungal infection (see above).

Smith (1968) also reviewed studies of New Zealand hedgehogs which revealed a high incidence of *Staphylococcus aureus* occurring in the nostrils (40% of animals), faeces (55%) and on the skin (68%). A high level of host-specificity is indicated because of the 118 staphylococcal strains isolated, over 86% were penicillin-resistant, possibly because of their co-existence with the ringworm fungus which apparently produces a penicillin-like substance (Smith 1968).

Other bacteria isolated from hedgehogs include the following. *Corynebacterium pyogenes* and *C. pseudotuberculosis* were isolated from purulent areas of the lungs of a central African hedgehog (*Atelerix albiventris*) which died in Detroit Zoo (McAllister & Keahey 1971). In Norway, a cow and three calves were killed by 'botulism' (*Clostridium botulinum* type C(β)) the source of which was traced to a dead hedgehog (containing high levels of toxin) in the feed container (Ektvedt & Hanssen 1974).

Pseudotuberculosis, *Yersinia* (= *Pasteurella*) *pseudotuberculosis*, affects a number of species worldwide (including humans) and has also been reported in hedgehogs (Timme 1980, Wallach & Boever 1983, Saupe & Poduschka 1985, Keymer *et al.* 1991). *Listeria monocytogenes* (serotype I) has been isolated from a wild European hedgehog (André 1966) but it is unlikely to be diagnosed in living animals (Versluys 1975).

Rickettsiae, Chlamydiae and Mycoplasmas

Rickettsiae and chlamydiae are tiny gram negative bacteria that are obligate intracellular parasites. Q (Query) fever, a tick-borne rickettsial disease (*Coxiella burnetti*) causes an influenza-like illness in cattle, which is more severe in sheep and goats. Humans may become infected via inhalation of dust or droplets contaminated by rickettsiae from faeces, urine or milk—symptoms include a cough, fever and chest pains (Jawetz *et al.* 1989). It has been reported in *Erinaceus* and other hedgehogs including *Hemiechinus auritus* (Giroud *et al.* 1959, Smith 1968, Wallach & Boever 1983). In Israel, rickettsiae of the spotted fever group have been isolated from ticks from hedgehogs, dogs and sheep (Gross & Hadani 1984). In France, Giroud *et al.* (1959) referred to an ancient belief that hedgehogs have an occult ability to cause abortion in bovines. Their findings were interpreted by Smith (1968) as

able to tackle adult hedgehogs (Barrett-Hamilton 1911, Knight 1962, Morris 1988a). Nestlings could be vulnerable to other ground carnivores such as stoats (*Mustela erminea*) or weasels (*Mustela nivalis*) as well as rats. Poduschka (1971) reported that brown rats (*Rattus norvegicus*) invaded the burrows of hibernating hedgehogs, and in one case attacked and wounded the occupant. Rats were also mentioned as possible predators by Barrett-Hamilton (1911). Morris (1988a) included tawny owls (*Strix aluco*) in his list of potential predators and Uttendorfer (cited by Kingdon 1974) found hedgehog spines in 134 pellets out of 102 000 pellets from central European birds of prey. Hedgehogs active by day may be pecked at by crows, magpies or other scavengers and a weak hedgehog could easily be killed.

Roberts (1977) reviewed the predators of hedgehogs in Pakistan. Grey mongooses (*Herpestes edwardsi*) may kill hedgehogs (*Hemiechinus collaris*) and hedgehog remains have been found in the stomachs of jackals (*Canis aureus*) and foxes (*Vulpes* spp.). Jackals, like the fox in Europe, are reputed to urinate on hedgehogs to unroll them before seizing them by the face. However, Roberts supposed that foxes and jackals were probably quick enough to kill a hedgehog before it could roll up. In Baluchistan, the Afghan hedgehog (*Hemiechinus auritus megalotis*) may be taken by hill foxes (*Vulpes vulpes griffithi*) and rock-horned owls (*Bubo bubo turcomanus*)—owl pellets composed largely of hegehog spines have been found in nests of this species. Indian pale hedgehogs (*Paraechinus micropus*) are probably also eaten by foxes and grey mongooses, and Brandt's hedgehog (*Paraechinus hypomelas*) by foxes, jackals and rock-horned owls. In Algeria, desert hedgehogs (*Paraechinus aethiopicus*) are also eaten by jackals (Sellami *et al.* 1989).

The hedgehogs of central and southern Africa (*Atelerix albiventris* and *A. frontalis*) are vulnerable to the long talons of the Verreaux's eagle owl (*Bubo lacteus*) and hedgehog remains are commonly found in their regurgitated pellets (Kingdon 1974, Smithers 1983, Happold 1987). Kingdon also mentioned that scraps of spiny skin are sometimes found hung on trees—possibly by shrikes. Dog bites can be a problem for hedgehogs in Kenya (Gregory 1976). However, hedgehogs do get their revenge sometimes! Smithers (1983) described how a lion was seen to bat a southern African hedgehog around with its paws, get pricked and eventually leave it unharmed 'in disgust'!

Injuries and accidental death

Hedgehogs commonly have minor wounds on the flanks, face or limbs. Because these parts are effectively defended during predator attack, the wounds probably result from minor accidents or from fights with other hedgehogs. Males apparently have four times the injury rate of females (Reeve 1981) but the reasons for this are unclear. Maybe males are injured when courting aggressive females, or perhaps males fight amongst themselves more commonly than behavioural observations have suggested (Chapter 7), or the wider-ranging behaviour of males could expose them to more risks.

Sometimes severe wounds may be found. Some, on the undersurface and limbs, may have been caused by broken glass or other sharp objects, whereas others, on the flanks and spiny skin, seem to be either from predators (e.g. dog bites) or mowers, strimmers, garden spades or forks, and so on. In Germany, Timme (1980) reported that 1·7% of 410 hedgehog corpses examined had apparently died of some kind of injury. Bonfires can also cause serious injury. In Britain, Dickman (1988) found 1·8% of 109 corpses examined to have died from burns.

Because of their shock-absorbing spiny coat, hedgehogs seem unafraid of falling and they often tumble into drains (which should be covered), cattle grids, and other hazards such as garden ponds and become trapped. Although competent swimmers and climbers, hedgehogs may not escape unless a suitable ramp is provided, preferably 20 cm wide and no steeper than 30 degrees from the horizontal (Stocker 1987). My tame hedgehog Emily once wedged herself so tightly into a drain that it took a couple of hours to get her out! Hedgehogs are thus very prone to becoming trapped or entangled in various ways. Les Stocker (pers comm.) wrote 'Other than unavoidable road traffic accidents and milk, I think the most common human-related causes of death are hedgehogs getting tangled in cricket and tennis nets, plastic ring binders and falling down uncovered drains.' Hedgehogs also commonly get food containers (yoghurt pots, cans, etc.) stuck on their heads while scavenging from human refuse.

Death on the roads

It is commonly believed that hedgehogs are particularly at risk of being killed by cars because of their habit of freezing as danger approaches. However, running is also risky as it increases the chance of crossing the wheel-paths of vehicles (Morris 1983) and it is notable that some very fast and agile animals, such as rabbits and cats, are also frequently killed by road traffic. In Hampshire (Britain), Davies (1957) found that the four commonest mammal road casualties were (in rank order): rabbits, brown rats, hedgehogs and grey squirrels. In New Zealand, Brockie (1960) found that hedgehogs accounted for over 84% of all road deaths of mammals and birds, but a later study (Morris 1989) reported that introduced possums (*Trichosurus vulpecula*) were the commonest road casualty. It is clear that the hedgehog's vulnerability to road mortality is far from unique!

Although the number of hedgehogs killed on the roads is distressingly high, it might simply reflect the presence of a substantial, thriving population! There are few data on which to base an evaluation of the population effects of road mortality. Most studies of road mortality in European hedgehogs have shown a similar general pattern: most casualties among males occur early in the season and during the rut, and most of the female deaths occur late in the season—probably *after* they have reproduced (e.g. Göransson *et al.* 1976). Kristiansson (1990) pointed out that this pattern of mortality was unlikely to be a principal influence on hedgehog populations (climate and food availability are probably more important in Sweden) unless mortality particularly affected breeding females in a small population. In my study of suburban hedgehogs in Britain, road deaths accounted for about 18% of known deaths in the active season (Reeve 1981). In Revinge (southern Sweden), Göransson *et al.* (1976) reckoned that road kills accounted for about 17–22% of the estimated population of 23–27 hedgehogs (1972–1975). Road kills accounted for four (33%) of the 12 known deaths occurring in 30 hedgehogs translocated by Doncaster (1992) into Wytham Wood (Oxfordshire).

Studies that assess road mortality without relating it to a concurrent population study cannot answer questions about the demographic role of road mortality. However, Morris & Morris (1988) argued that road casualty rates could provide useful relative estimates of population differences between regions or seasonal/yearly changes in hedgehog numbers—despite the many variables affecting carcass persistence and observer reliability, such as traffic density, speed of travel and the weather. Road casualty studies have consistently indicated that European hedgehog populations seem to be highest around areas of human habitation (Davies 1957, Massey 1972, Göransson *et al.* 1976, Berthoud 1980, Morris & Morris 1988). A good example is a 5-year study by Reichholf & Esser (1981) who found 729 hedgehog corpses along a 150 km stretch of road between Munich and Passau (Germany). The route was driven 480 times, mainly (424) during the weekend to coincide with periods of peak traffic flow. The highest casualty rates were in June and October. The average corpse count was 1 km^{-1} $year^{-1}$, but more were found (5–5·3 km^{-1} $year^{-1}$) in small villages or on the outskirts of larger ones. Fewer corpses (0·4 km^{-1} $year^{-1}$) were found in the centres of large villages (over 1 km across) and 0·6 km^{-1} $year^{-1}$ were found in agricultural or woodland areas, but around rural settlements 2·0 km^{-1} $year^{-1}$ were found. Reichholf (1984) noted a disproportionately high road mortality of juveniles around villages in late autumn.

A 2-month (January–February) summer study in New Zealand, discovered 636 dead hedgehogs in 7479 km of road travel: a gross average of 0·085 km^{-1} (Morris & Morris 1988). There were huge regional variations in road casualty rates which corresponded well with previous studies (e.g. Brockie 1960) and the known distribution of hedgehogs (Brockie 1975). The casualty counts peaked in suburban and horticultural areas and (for the 2 months of the study) averaged 0·11 km^{-1} (range 0–0·58 km^{-1}) on North Island (for the same months Brockie recorded 0·372 km^{-1}), and 0·053 km^{-1} (range 0–0·08 km^{-1}) on South Island. In Britain, where there are 10 times as many cars as in New Zealand, the lower casualty rate suggests a less dense population. In the equivalent season (July/August), the authors drove 3171 km of roads in Britain and found an average casualty rate of 0·041 km^{-1} (range 0·03–0·06 km^{-1}). Again there were long stretches of road without hedgehogs (Somerset levels, Exmoor, arable land in eastern England) but noticeable clumping in villages and suburban areas. These counts may be compared with a 1952–1953 study (Davies 1957) when there were far fewer cars in Britain. The counts for July/August, a peak time for hedgehog casualties, were only 0·01 km^{-1}, and over two years the months April–

November showed an average annual death toll of 0.0074 km^{-1} (1.2 per 100 miles), very low by today's standards.

In Denmark, surveys have indicated an annual road-death toll of around 70 000 to 100 000 hedgehogs, about 1% of all vertebrate casualties (Morris 1983). The annual death toll of hedgehogs on Britain's 320 000 km of roads has also been estimated at 100 000 (Stocker 1987, Barnes 1989)—equivalent to 0.3 km^{-1}. This is twice the 0.16 km^{-1} rate that would be obtained by extrapolating Morris & Morris' (1988) July/August data over the 8 months of the active year, but is close to the equivalent average mortality rate found in New Zealand (0.34 km^{-1} over 8 months). However, in Norfolk (UK) Keymer *et al.* (1991) reported a much higher average mortality rate of 1.28 km^{-1} year^{-1} (highest 2.04 km^{-1} in 1979, lowest 0.52 km^{-1} in 1984) along a 29-km stretch of fairly busy B road. Such figures resemble those from Germany where Reichholf & Esser (1981) reported an overall figure of 1 km^{-1} year^{-1} (exceeding 5 km^{-1} year^{-1} in some built-up places), and from southern Sweden where 4 years of daily counts along a 16·5-km stretch of road between Lund and Revinge revealed an average death toll of 1.67 km^{-1} year^{-1} (Göransson *et al.* 1976). Similarly, in northern Spain, Garnica & Robles (1986) found an average death toll of 1.71 km^{-1} (between May and October) along an 8·2-km road which passed through suburban, agricultural and oak woodland areas. They cited a French study (Waetcher 1979) which found a lower casualty rate of 0.88 km^{-1}.

The only data I have found relating to other hedgehog species are from Gregory (1976) who reported 34 central African hedgehog (*Atelerix albiventris*) casualties in 1 year on a 10-km stretch of road near Nairobi. On the Ivory Coast only one dead hedgehog was seen during 25 000 km of driving. Smithers (1983) mentioned that the southern African hedgehog (*A. frontalis*) was commonly killed on the roads, for example in the Bulawayo district of Zimbabwe, especially after first rains in October.

Death by poisoning

Hedgehogs have a reputation for immunity to toxins. Their relative resistance to snake venom and noxious defensive substances produced by their prey has already been mentioned in Chapter 3. Hedgehogs appear untroubled by bee or wasp stings, even an injection of 72 mg of bee venom produces no clinical symptoms (Versluys 1975). A 4-mg dose of cantharidine (produced by meloid beetles) does not trouble a hedgehog although it would kill an 80-kg human; 100 mg is needed to kill a 700-g hedgehog (Versluys 1975). Hedgehogs are also reported to tolerate 7000 times as much toxin from tetanus bacteria (*Clostridium tetani*) as humans, and 70 times as much diphtheria toxin (from *Corynebacterium diphtheriae*) as a guinea pig of the same size (Burton 1969, Versluys 1975). Hedgehogs are also relatively resistant to chloroform (Herter 1965b, Burton 1969). Ognev (1928) claimed, somewhat improbably, that arsenic, 'corrosive sublimate' (presumably mercuric chloride, $HgCl_2$), cantharidine and opium have 'no effect whatsoever' on hedgehogs and that hydrocyanic acid kills them 'relatively slowly'. Strychnine, however, kills rapidly.

Such reports have contributed to a damaging misconception that hedgehogs are relatively untroubled by the many toxic substances in their environment. In fact, no one knows how many deaths may result from the effects of environmental pollutants such as heavy metals (e.g. mercury, lead and cadmium) or the herbicides and pesticides in common use by farmers and gardeners. There is very little formal evidence to suggest that hedgehogs die from the consumption of toxic baits or invertebrates affected by pesticides, but the evidence available is really an inadequate basis on which to form opinions. Toxic effects are not always obvious and may cause subtle sub-lethal behavioural changes, reduced fecundity, poor growth, impaired disease resistance, and other physiological changes which damage performance. Toxicological experiments would therefore also need to include long-term ecological assessments; there have been none.

European hedgehogs may be affected by metaldehyde, a molluscicide commonly used against slugs, but it is quickly broken down in the stomach to acetaldehyde (= ethanal)—a substance that may be naturally present (at low levels) in the body. This, and the need for fresh material, can make precise analysis difficult (Keymer *et al.* 1991). The degree to which hedgehogs are affected, and whether the poisoned bait is eaten directly or indirectly (via poisoned slugs) is unclear (Schicht 1982a,b, Morris 1983, Gregory 1985, Saupe & Poduschka 1985, Stocker 1987). Blue-dyed vomit or faeces probably indicates the direct consumption of slug pellets or rat poison (warfarin) (BHPS 1987). Stocker (pers comm.) stated that in his experience, 'metaldehyde poisoning can show in hedgehogs as increased hypersensitivity and excitability' and support for the view that metaldehyde causes significant mortality was provided by Keymer *et al.* (1991) who diagnosed methaldehyde poisoning in three of 35 autopsied animals. In two the stomach contents contained over 40 mg kg^{-1} of acetaldehyde and, in the third, 80 mg kg^{-1} was found in the liver. Lower levels, probably sublethal at under 20 mg kg^{-1}, were found in the stomachs of four other hedgehogs and in the kidneys of two. Keymer *et al.* considered it likely that slug pellets had been directly consumed—in which case only 5 g of pellets would have provided a poten-tially lethal dose.

The range of pollutants to which hedgehogs may be exposed can be revealed by post-mortem analyses. Saupe & Poduschka (1985) cited a study by Berthoud (1981) who, in Switzerland, found various pollutants in the livers of 100 hedgehogs, including HCB (hexachlorobenzene—a grain disinfectant and plasticizer), HCH (hexachlorocyclohexane—an insecticide; gamma HCH is 'lindane'), HCE (heptachlorepoxide—an insecticide), dieldrin (an insecticide), DDE (dichlorodiphenyldichloroethane—a breakdown product of DDT) and PCBs (polychlorinated biphenyls—in declining use mainly as coolants and plasticizers) as well as heavy metals (lead, mercury and cad-mium). Work is currently under way in Britain to measure the burdens of pollutants, especially heavy metals, in wild hedgehogs (R. Shore, pers. comm.).

In Britain, Jefferies & Pendlebury (1968) found no discernible relationship between the population fluctuations of hedgehogs or other mammals and the expected effects of organochlorine seed dressings introduced in 1956; peak mammal/bird deaths were attributed to them in 1959–1960. Indeed, the hedgehog population was apparently at a peak in 1959–1961 in one Hertford-shire estate.

Although the data are inadequate, it is most improbable that hedgehogs have remained unaffected, either directly or indirectly, by the widespread use of pesticides, herbicides and other environmental pollutants such as heavy metals. The common-sense answer would be to press for measures to reduce the number and quantity of 'eco-toxins', either known or suspected, that enter the environment, making it unnecessary to conduct toxicological trials of our wildlife species.

CHAPTER 10

Hedgehogs and Humans

H EDGEHOGS occupy a prominent role in the folklore of many countries. The old stories are often strange amalgams of fact and mythology and many were chronicled in the writings of Pliny or Aristotle. The hedgehog-related customs and beliefs of the past make colourful reading and have been well described in the popular literature. The stories about hedgehogs suckling cows, eating poultry or their eggs, fighting snakes and collecting apples by impaling them on their spiny backs, have already been discussed in Chapter 3.

In Britain, from 1566 to 1863 hedgehogs were, without any real justification, designated a pest species with a bounty on their heads (see also Chapter 3). Today they are partially protected under Schedule 6 of the 1981 Wildlife and Countryside Act (amended in 1987). The Act makes it illegal to trap or collect hedgehogs from the field, or kill them by certain specified methods without a licence. See Cooper (1991) for a summary of the Act as it relates to mammals. In practice, the 1981 Act is unwieldy and may be difficult to enforce; Morris (1983) described it as a 'complex hotch-potch'! Anyone who works with hedgehogs, or who may catch them when trapping for other species, should read the Act carefully and seek guidance on its interpretation. Whatever legal protection is afforded to hedgehogs by the 1981 Act, the 1911 Protection of Animals Act has little to offer. Stocker (1987) told of an unsuccessful attempt to use the 1911 Act to prosecute a man who, in 1986, had wantonly beaten a hedgehog to death with a broom handle! In most of Europe and Scandinavia the hedgehog, along with most other wildlife, is legally protected, with a heavy fine or imprisonment for any unlicensed person who is found catching or keeping hedgehogs (Versluys 1975, Poduschka & Saupe 1981).

Hedgehogs have been used by humans in many ways, not least as food. Most people will proclaim (with gruesome glee) that gypsies eat hedgehogs, but in fact hedgehogs have featured in the diet of a good many other peoples. 'Hyrchouns' were a delicacy on the menu of a feast in Britain in 1425, and were commonly eaten throughout Europe (Barrett-Hamilton 1911, Burton

1969). Hedgehogs (*Atelerix algirus*) have been eaten on the Balearic Islands since the middle of the 18th century (Corbet 1988). A traditional Mallorcan recipe for stuffed hedgehog ('*Eriçó farcit*') may be found in Molenaar (1988):

> Skin, clean and soak hedgehog overnight in salt water. Drain, wipe dry. Mix day-old bread with eggs, some chopped celery and parsley, season with fresh black pepper, grated nutmeg, pinch of saffron, chopped fresh basil, salt. Stuff and sew up hedgehog. Rub with lard, salt and pepper. Placed in greased oven-proof dish, bake in moderate oven for about 45 minutes or until tender. Baste often, add a little stock if necessary. Stir ground almonds with milk into a thickish sauce. Add cinnamon and lemon peel, bring to a boil. Pour over hedgehog just before serving.

In Nigeria, Okaeme & Osakwe (1988) reported that hedgehogs (*Atelerix albiventris*) are widely eaten as bush meat and Sellami *et al.* (1989) mentioned that desert hedgehogs (*Paraechinus aethiopicus*) are hunted and eaten in Algeria.

Harrison Matthews (1952) related some of ways in which a hedgehog might be prepared for the table:

> The classic way of cooking a hedgehog is to gut and stuff it with sage and onion, sew it up, and plaster it over with clay; then suspend it over the fire with a length of twisted worsted as a roasting jack, and when the clay cracks it is done. But this is not the best way because although the spines come away with the clay when it is broken open, the smaller hairs are not completely removed. It is better to singe the prickles and hairs off in the fire after gutting the animal, and then to scrape it with a very sharp knife before roasting it without clay. Another method is to gut and skin the animal, wash it well, and simmer it with seasoning in a little water for several hours; when cold the whole sets to a jelly, and the 'pudding' can be cut into slices like pressed meat; this is very good.

Burton (1969) also cited sources which suggested that the well-known 'gypsy method' of baking in clay was not currently favoured, at least by gypsies in Britain who apparently prefer to cut and singe away the spines and hair before spitting the animal over a fire. Barrett-Hamilton (1911) cited Jones (1910) who gave instructions for broiling hedgehogs; apparently they are best in the autumn when fat for hibernation. Stocker (1987) described an account by John Chaplin of the gypsy hedgehog hunter who trampled through the brambles with his hobnailed boots to find the nest of the 'hotchipig'.

Although hedgehogs are eaten by gypsies, they are not merely regarded as food but hold a special place in gypsy lore:

> In contrast to all other animals and birds, the hedgehog is both supremely edible and given high status

(Okely 1983)

Okely's analysis of the symbolism associated with various animals is revealing. A central concept is the symbolic separation between the inside and the outside of the body. Animals such as rats, mice, dogs, foxes and especially cats are considered to be *mochadi* (a term which encompasses concepts of uncleaniness or immorality) partly because they lick their bodies, taking hair and bodily dirt into their mouths. Gypsies are disgusted by *gorgios* (non-gypsies) who will stroke dogs and cats, allow them into their homes and even permit themselves to be licked by their pets! In contrast, hedgehogs are highly respected as creatures of *Moshto* (the god of life) and eating them, ideally in a special shared meal, is reputed to counteract poisons such as deadly nightshade and provide a symbolic antidote to any *mochadi* substance or pollution from contact with *gorgios*. The rigid spines of the hedgehog provide a protective casing for the 'inner body', and they must be singed off in a cleansing fire before the animal may be eaten (see above). The hedgehog is referred to in Romani as *hotchi-witchi*, a thing which must be burned. Hedgehogs with young are not killed for food and during the breeding season males are reputed to taste bad. Among *gorgios* hedgehogs are seldom taken seriously, they are considered inedible and commonly have a reputation for stealing eggs, milk and fruit. Unlike domestic livestock, hedgehogs are not bred by *gorgios* for food and unlike rabbits and hares are also unwanted by *gorgios*; accusations of stealing *gorgio* produce would, if anything, enhance their reputation amongst gypsies. Living as they do on the fringes of *gorgio* society, there is a fundamental bond between the gypsy and the hedgehog which is also known as the '*pal* of the *bor*' (brother of the hedge). The hedgehog is symbolically linked with the gypsies' better self—the self which is not involved in the deception of *gorgios* (Okely 1983).

Okely (1983) also drew attention to a gypsy distinction between 'pig-faced' and 'dog-faced' hedgehogs in some parts of Europe. As discussed in Chapter 1, this is unlikely to be a reference to the subtly different face shape in the two European hedgehog species which requires skull measurements to verify. The white chest-patch of the eastern European hedgehog (*Erinaceus concolor*) would be a much more obvious method of distinction. Apparently one gypsy group will condemn another for not distinguishing between the two types and for eating the 'dog-faced' hedgehog. It is thus more likely that the association with dogs, considered to be *mochadi*, is simply a way of insulting another gypsy group. Herter (1965b) pointed out that the 'pig' and 'dog' distinction is made by countryfolk even in regions where only one species occurs.

A belief in the medicinal power of the hedgehog is not exclusive to gypsy lore. Herter (1965b) quoted a translation of writings by Konrad of Megenberg in 1349 or 1350:

> the flesh of the hedgehog is wholesome for the stomach and strengthens the same. Likewise it hath a power of drying and relieving the stomach. It deals with the water of dropsy and is of great help to such as are inclined to the sickness called elephantiasis.

Morris (1983) gave an account of Topsel's writings in 1658 which included various 'medical' uses of hedgehogs and their body parts. These included treatments for boils, leprosy, colic, balding, urinary stones and the enhancement of night-vision. Burton (1969) noted that a hedgehog buried under a building was reputed to bring good luck. According to Pliny, hedgehogs can be used to foretell the weather; if they crawl quickly away from the open field into their holes, this indicates a change of wind and approaching rainy weather (Poduschka & Poduschka 1972). Some early texts are bizarrely fanciful: the Poduschkas quoted (in translation) a passage from the bestiary of Albertus Magnus:

> The hedgehog, called Ericinus and Erinaceus, or, as some will have it, Cyrogrillus, is very rough and prickly, with hard, sharp spines. For the philosophers assert that, although these animals are of a cold complexion, many superfluities collect in them, which are transformed into such spines and hard prickles. The hedgehog, which lives in its lair in the ground, indicates when storms of wind are coming. It makes three or four exits to its lair or dwelling and when it senses that the wind is going to blow from a certain direction, it closes the corresponding hole. It is an exception to all other four-legged beasts in having its genitals internally like a bird. For this reason it is often unchaste. It is also said that it has two anal holes, through which its waste matters pass, contrary to the nature of all other animals. The hedgehog mates in an upright position on account of the sharpness of its prickles.

In Scotland the name *crainneag* and in Ireland *grainneog* is associated with an ugly old woman (translator's note, Herter 1965b) or a witch in animal form that sucked milk from cows, bewitched them and dried up their milk (Stocker 1987).

In eastern Africa, the hedgehog (*Atelerix albiventris*) is also surrounded by many superstitions. The skin or spines may be used as fertility charms and, in Karamoja and Teso, a hedgehog's skin placed on the seed before sowing is believed to ensure a good harvest. Bumper harvests are said to result if a hedgehog's skin is burnt in the cotton fields (Kingdon 1974). The ancient Chinese of He Bei Province are reputed to have regarded their hedgehogs as sacred (Stocker 1987).

The dried, prickly skins of hedgehogs, nailed onto boards, were used by the Romans to 'card' wool. Similarly, the skins were used to dress flax and hemp, and as clothes brushes in medieval Europe (Herter 1965b). Burton (1969) mentioned that some coachmen tied a hedgehog's skin to the pole of a carriage to prevent a lazy horse leaning against it, and that a hedgehog skin tied to a calf's muzzle enforced its weaning. Hedgehog skins were sometimes fixed to the top rails of orchard gates to deter small boys (Morris 1983). Hedgehogs have also been kept as useful domestic pets. Burton (1969) told us of a Mr Sample of Northumberland (UK), who in 1799 kept a hedgehog as a 'turn-spit' which performed as well as a dog and answered to the name of Tom! Hedgehogs, fed on kitchen scraps, were also kept in cellars to eat the cockroaches and other pests (Stocker 1987).

Although the nature of hedgehogs has been variously portrayed, they have always been intriguing, mysterious and comical. The imagery of hedgehogs is commonly used in all kinds of crafts and literature. Numerous literary references to hedgehogs are listed in *The Oxford English Dictionary* (1989): few are complimentary but the sagacity of the hedgehog is praised by one Greek who wrote:

> The fox knows many things—the hedgehog one *big* one.
>
> (Archilochus, c.650 B.C., in:
> *The Oxford Dictionary of Quotations*, 1979)

In an account of the *Prophecies of Merlin* by Geoffrey of Monmouth (c. 1100–1155) there are intriguing allegorical references to hedgehog:

> A Hedgehog loaded with apples shall re-build the town and, attracted by the smell of these apples, birds will flock there from many different forests. The Hedgehog shall add a huge palace and then wall it round with six hundred towers.
> The Hedgehog will hide its apples inside Winchester and will construct hidden passages under the earth.
>
> (Translation by Thorpe 1966)

As already mentioned in Chapters 2 and 8, Shakespeare (1564–1616) referred to the cry of the hedgehog (*Macbeth*, Act 4 Scene 1)

> Witch 1: *Thrice the brindled cat hath mew'd.*
> Witch 2: *Thrice, and once the hedgepig whin'd.*

This is ambiguous, the repetition of thrice may signal agreement about the cat's calls or relate to the hedgehog. It is thus unclear whether the hedgehog was said to have whined once or four times. If the latter is true, one explanation for avoiding the use of the number 'four' is the suggestion that even numbers were considered inappropriate in the context of magic (Muir 1962).

In *The Tempest* (Act 2, Scene 2, line 10) Caliban referred to the hedgehog's habit of bristling when disturbed.

Hedgehogs are portrayed rather negatively in Act 2, Scene 3 of *A Midsummer Night's Dream*, where 'Thorny hedgehogs' are included with snakes, newts, blindworms, spiders, black beetles, worms and snails, in a list of nasty creatures. In Act 1, Scene 2 (line 102) of *King Richard III*, Anne refers to Richard of Gloucester as a hedgehog, a derogation of his badge (a white boar or hog). 'Hedgehog' was a term used for people who showed no regard for the feelings of others; furthermore the hedgehog's shape was likened to that of a hunchback (Adams 1974).

> Anne: *Thou wast provokèd by thy bloody mind*
> *That never dream'st on aught but butcheries:*
> *Didst thou not kill this King?*
> Richard: *I grant ye—yea.*
> Anne: *Dost grant me, hedgehog? Then, God grant me too*
> *Thou mayst be damnèd for that wicked deed!*
> *O, he was gentle, mild and virtuous.*

Further examples of the use of 'hedgehog' 'hedgehoggy' or 'hedgehogginess', to describe people who are externally repellant or difficult to get on with, are given in *The Oxford English Dictionary* (1989). Similarly in Germany, Herter (1968) commented that the hedgehog is considered unsocial and, although hedgehogs are generally well-liked and considered amusing, the term *Schweinigel* (swine hedgehog) is considered a big insult.

In Lewis Caroll's *Alice's Adventures in Wonderland* (published in 1865), hedgehogs were used as reluctant balls in the Red Queen's game of croquet; flamingos were used as the mallets! Hedgehogs also appear as heraldic 'charges' (figures on the field of the shield). A token penny from Birmingham in 1793 portrayed a heraldic shield with five hedgehogs, and in the 17th century, Thomas Martin of Southwark emblazoned a hedgehog on his coins (Stocker 1987).

The imagery of hedgehogs is such that many things have been named after or associated with them. In his review of 'hedgehogabilia', Stocker (1987) mentioned the warship HMS Urchin (an old name for a hedgehog, see Appendix 2); its emblem depicted a hedgehog. *The Oxford English Dictionary* (1989) noted the use of the term by the German army during the Second World War to describe a fortified position 'bristling' with guns, and 'the hedgehog'—an anti-submarine weapon which fired a salvo of 24 depth charges. 'Hedgehog' has also been used to describe many other spiny or bristling plants, animals, natural and unnatural forms, including hedgehog cactus (genus *Echinocactus*), hedgehog gooseberry, hedgehog fruit (*Echinocarpus australis*), hedgehog parsley (*Caucalis daucoides*), hedgehog wheat (*Triticum compactum*), hedgehog fungus (*Hydnum repandum*), hedgehog shell (*Murex erinaceus*), sea hedgehog (a fish, genus *Diodon*), hedgehog crystal (sodium urate crystals found in urine) and the hedgehog converter which was an old type of transformer in which the wire core assumed a bristling appearance (*The Oxford English Dictionary* 1989).

Once killed as vermin, and still regarded as such by some, hedgehogs are now more often valued as beneficial consumers of invertebrate pests in gardens, farms and horticultural areas. In Britain the popularity of hedgehogs was given a powerful boost by the publication in 1905 of *The Tale of Mrs. Tiggy-winkle* by Beatrix Potter, in which a hedgehog was portrayed as an endearing country washer-woman! Since then, the image of the hedgehog in childrens' stories, as toys and as symbols of benign wildlife have continued from strength-to-strength.

These days hedgehogs have acquired a huge popular following with a massive demand for hedgehog paraphernalia (Herter 1965b, Burton 1969, Morris 1983, Stocker 1987), and a hedgehog is the symbol of the Mammal Society UK.

Living in towns and cities insulates most people from contact with the natural world, but the hedgehog can survive—and even thrive—alongside humans. Millions of people are really fond of the hedgehogs that visit their gardens and feel proud to have been 'chosen' as they watch 'their' hedgehog bumbling about the patio and flower borders! For many the experience of contact with a truly wild mammal engenders a feeling of rapport and respect for other organisms and their needs. An animal that stimulates such fundamental feelings is a powerful ally in the struggle to get humans to take more interest in the quality of the natural environment and their own ecology!

APPENDIX 1:

Veterinary Information on the Treatment of Parasites and Diseases

REFER to Chapter 9 for information on the parasites and diseases mentioned below. Although certain treatments are outlined in this Appendix, anyone intending to care for an ailing hedgehog should *always* get professional veterinary advice from the outset. This is for the benefit of the carer as well as the animal itself; some afflictions (e.g. *Salmonella* infections) may seriously affect humans, and carers should be meticulously hygienic when housing and handling hedgehogs. The Wildlife Hospital Trust (Appendix 3) has published a code of practice for the rescue, treatment, rehabilitation and release of sick and injured wildlife (Stocker 1991) and a guide to medications used to treat a very wide range of hedgehog ailments (Stocker 1992). Please note that no drug is specifically licensed for use on hedgehogs, the brands cited are those mentioned in the literature (or their nearest current equivalent)—other brands may also be appropriate. *Drug treatments, especially injections, should only be administered by veterinary surgeons or those trained in the correct procedures.* During care, a balanced *artificial* diet with roughage is essential (Chapter 3) and multivitamin therapy may be very beneficial. Avoid natural prey which may be the intermediate hosts of parasites.

EXAMINATION AND INJECTION TECHNIQUE

With practice, a hedgehog can be unrolled (see Chapter 2) but only very superficial examination is possible without anaesthesia (see below).

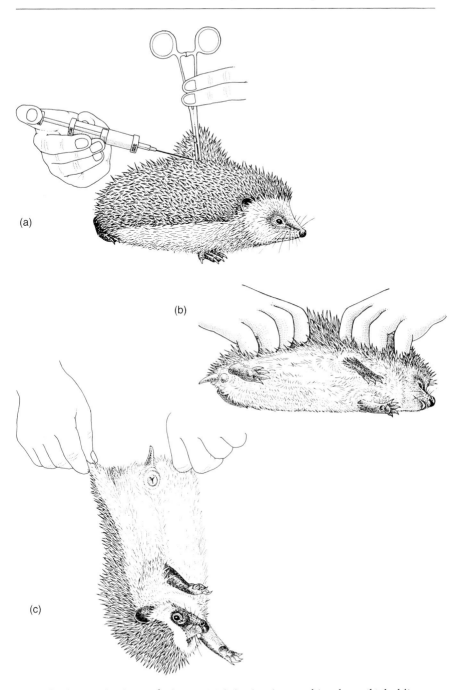

FIG. A1 *Injection techniques. (a) injecting into a skin pleat, (b) holding animal down by its spiny skin for injection into the skin of the flank, (c) Gregory's head-down position (see text for details).*

For subcutaneous injections, use forceps to grasp a *small* fold of the spiny skin (e.g. over the hind quarters) and inject into the connective tissue at the base of the 'pleat' formed, with the needle parallel to the animal's body (Poduschka & Saupe 1981, Schicht 1982a,b; Fig. A1a). Alternatively, a skin fold may be raised by pulling upwards on a spine. A common fault is to inject too deeply in the mistaken belief that the musculature is separate from the skin of the back (Kramm 1979). Another, possibly somewhat traumatic, option is to inject into the flank while a helper—wearing gloves and taking a firm grasp of the hedgehog's spiny skin—holds the animal down on the bench (Ruempler 1982; Fig. A1b). Intramuscular injections should be in the thigh and not in the skin muscles of the back.

Gregory (1985) described how a hedgehog could be held by the hind legs and suspended head-down, a position which allows even intraperitoneal injections (Fig. A1c; see also page 42).

ANAESTHESIA

Inhalation anaesthesia using bromochlorotrifluoroethane (Halothane, Hoechst, May and Baker) is widely recommended, especially for short-term anaesthesia; methoxyfluorane Metofane (Pitman-Moore and Janssen) is also mentioned (Poduschka & Saupe 1981, Ruempler 1982, Saupe & Poduschka 1985). Stocker (1992) also used isoflurane (Abbott Laboratories) at 1–3% in oxygen. Ether and chloroform should never be used for anaesthesia (Poduschka & Saupe 1981).

Subcutaneous injection of xylazine (Rompun, Bayer, UK) at 3 mg kg^{-1} bodyweight usually produces relaxation and sedation (BHPS 1987). For more profound and prolonged anaesthesia, Poduschka & Saupe (1981) recommended subcutaneous ketamine hydrochloride (e.g. Ketaset, C-Vet; Vetalar, Parke Davis) at around 10–20 mg kg^{-1} bodyweight. However, this may not produce good muscle relaxation (M. Sealey pers. comm.) and Schicht (1982a,b) reported variable success. Intramuscular injection of medetomidine (Domitor, SmithKline Beecham) at 100 ml kg^{-1} bodyweight (0·25 ml for deeper anaesthesia), reversible with atipamezole (Antisedan, SmithKline Beecham), was also used by Stocker (1992) for anaesthesia and as a sedative to treat stress, poisoning or convulsions (see below).

Subcutaneous injection of fentanyl/fluanisone (Hypnorm, Crown, Janssen) at a dose rate of 1–2 ml kg^{-1} bodyweight is another alternative (Poduschka & Kieliger 1972), and smaller doses (0·5 ml kg^{-1} bodyweight) may be sufficient for treatment of wounds and other minor work (Maggs 1985).

Gregory (1985) advocated intraperitoneal sodium pentobarbitone (25 mg kg^{-1} bodyweight) and Rousselot (1979) noted that glucocorticoid levels, which in any case may increase by up to 20 times during handling (presumably a stress response), rose less using this method than with intraperitoneal ketamine or inhaled anaesthetics (ether, fluothane and nitrous oxide).

Gregory (1985) suggested trying alphaxalone/alphadolone (Saffan, Glaxovet) injected intramuscularly at 15 mg kg^{-1} bodyweight. Edwards (1957) used the vein over the hock to administer chloral hydrate.

Stocker (1987) reported that post-operative recovery was enhanced by the use of analgesics and recommended subcutaneous buprenorphine (e.g. the human preparation Temgesic, Reckitt and Colman), maximum dose 0·012 mg kg^{-1}. This apparently provided pain relief for up to 12 h without the depressed respiration associated with the relatively short-lived effects of morphine or pethidine. For other analgesics see Stocker (1992).

ECTOPARASITES

Ticks and fleas

Treatment of ectoparasite infestations is rarely necessary unless an animal must be taken into care. Ticks detach when engorged and regular changes of bedding ensure that they will not persist on captives. Clumsy attempts to pull the ticks off may detach their mouthparts which remain in the skin to fester— although Saupe & Poduschka (1985) claimed this to be rare. If removal of ticks is really necessary, use forceps to grip the body of the attached tick (as close as possible to the host's skin) and a gentle but firm sideways pull usually removes the whole tick (M. Sealey pers. comm.). A dab of anaesthetic ether may help to incapacitate the ticks (Stocker 1992). A rather messy way to remove ticks of all sizes is to apply glycerine, petroleum jelly, etc. to the ticks which will begin to detach when their spiracles become clogged.

Pyrethrum-based flea-powders for house pets can be suitable for topical use on hedgehogs but some may have toxic side effects, e.g. permethrin may be harmful, even fatal to hedgehogs (Morris 1985b). Avoid using aerosol sprays because the noise can badly stress a hedgehog. Wallach & Boever (1983) suggested using Vapona (Shell) impregnated strips in the cage (in accordance with the manufacturer's space recommendations) to eliminate fleas or ticks.

Dipping can be very effective against all fleas, ticks and mites (see below), although very weak or hypothermic animals should not be dipped. Frank (1988) suggested the use of the pyrethroid insecticide flumethrin, available as a sheep dip (Bayticol, Bayer UK). Widely recommended was an aqueous solution (0·7 g litre^{-1}) of bromocyclen (Alugan concentrate, Hoechst) but this is now withdrawn in the UK (Gregory 1985; Saupe & Poduschka 1985, Poduschka 1986, BHPS 1987, Stocker 1987). If a dip is used, wetting must be thorough and the animal must dry naturally in a warm area. Care should be taken with some dips which may irritate the eyes and other sensitive areas. A possible alternative is a single topical application of fenthion, available as a 2% solution in paraffin (Tiguvon, Bayer UK) which may be dripped on to the animal's back; 5–20 mg kg^{-1} bodyweight (Schein & Hamel 1983). Fenthion (an organophosphorus substance) is absorbed systemically, kills blood-feeding ectoparasites within 24 h and is effective for four weeks. It is thus suitable for prophylactic use before releasing animals after treatment (Saupe & Poduschka 1985). However, fenthion should not be used in conjunction with other organophosphorus based drugs (e.g. anthelmintics such as levamisole or diethylcarbamazine citrate).

Mites

Mange mite infestations may be treated with various acaricidal creams and ointments usually indicated for mange in dogs (Gerson & Boever 1983). Bromocyclen dips are no longer recommended (see above). Stocker (1992) suggested oral or subcutaneous administration of ivermectin (Ivomec injection for cattle, MSD Agvet) 0·02 ml kg^{-1} bodyweight. Ivermectin would also be effective against ear infestations of *Notoedres cati* which otherwise would require repeated treatments (probably with anaesthesia) with acaricidal ear drops, e.g. Gac eardrops (Arnolds) containing gammabenzene hexachloride (M. Sealey, pers. comm.). Saupe & Poduschka (1985) recommended the thorough removal of debris from the ears and drops containing benzyl benzoate and hexachlorocyclohexane.

Myiasis

All fly eggs and maggots must be removed, but this is difficult if maggots have penetrated the flesh, or are inside the eyelids, ears or other orifices. For eye infestations, careful manual removal is required. Maggots can be made to crawl out of ears by dripping in 30% alcohol; 3% peroxide may be used for wounds (Saupe & Poduschka 1985). A hairdryer, used gently to heat and dry the skin, can encourage maggots to evacuate a wound. Negasunt powder (Bayer, UK), an organophosphorus compound that also inhibits bacterial growth, may be used to kill any remaining maggots (Stocker 1987). Stocker (1992) advocated the topical use of Battle Fly and Maggot Paste combined with an ivermectin injection (as for mites). One positive aspect of myiasis is that it effectively cleans necrotic (dead) tissue from wounds which, once cleared of maggots, can then heal rapidly (Thomas 1985). Antiseptic washing and antibiotics may help to guard against bacterial infections, e.g. amoxycillin-based preparations such as Synulox (Beecham) 50 mg kg^{-1} bodyweight, intramuscular or subcutaneous injection (Stocker 1992).

RINGWORM

Griseofulvin is widely used to treat hedgehog ringworm (Saupe & Poduschka 1985, Stocker 1987, 1992), e.g. Fulcin or Grisovin (Pitman-Moore). Saupe & Poduschka recommended oral griseofulvin at a dose of 30 mg kg^{-1} bodyweight (4 times the dose mentioned in Stocker 1992) with the additional use of vitamin A, plus local topical applications, e.g. Surolan (Janssen) or benzulda-zic acid (Defungit, Hoechst). Both humans and dogs are susceptible to hedgehog ringworm (Chaper 9). In humans the infection may subside spontaneously but will respond to treatment with oral griseofulvin (Simpson 1974) and topical applications of fungicidal creams may be effective. A dog with severe dermatitis on the head (a mixed infection of *Trichophyton mentagrophytes* and *T. erinacei*) was cured by local application of enilcona-zole (Imaverol, Janssen) for 1 month (Bourdeau *et al.* 1987).

ENDOPARASITES

Although some authors have recommended that hedgehogs taken into care should be routinely treated to clear endoparasitic helminth infestations (e.g. Poduschka & Saupe 1981), weak animals may not survive combined treat-ments such as dips for ectoparasites and/or injections of anthelmintic drugs (Kramm 1979). Table A1 shows the principal helminths of European hedge-hogs and a summary of the diverse treatments reported. For general treatment against endoparasites, Stocker (1992) used either oral febendazole (Panacur paste, Hoechst), or ivermectin (Ivomec, MSD Agvet) 0.02 ml kg^{-1} body-weight injected subcutaneously or delivered orally.

Infestations of oesophageal, stomach and intestinal nematodes may be treated in much the same way as lungworms (Saupe & Poduschka 1985, Frank 1988, Stocker 1992). For intestinal *Capillaria* infestations, Laubmeier (1985) advocated a single subcutaneous injection of ivermectin. The eggs of all the *Capillaria* are very tough, may resist disinfection and are easily spread to other hedgehogs in captivity (Saupe & Poduschka 1985). Because the eggs and larvae of lungworms and intestinal nematodes may episodically reappear in the faeces, treatments should usually be repeated after 2–3 weeks.

COCCIDIOSIS

Poduschka & Kieliger (1972) recommended treatment of coccidiosis with oral sulphonamides (100 mg kg^{-1} bodyweight daily for 5 days) and vitamin supplements. Subcutaneous sulphadimidine may be used at a dose rate of 100–200 mg kg^{-1} bodyweight on 3 successive days (Gregory 1985); oral adminis-tration is also possible (e.g. Sulphamezathine, Pitman-Moore). Frank (1988) advocated tetracycline to control secondary bacterial infections (Codrinal, Hoechst: 60 mg kg^{-1} bodyweight for 3 days). Sulfadimethoxine, a long-acting and rapidly absorbed derivative of sulphadiazine (e.g. Madribon Roche: a human drug) may be used: two drops in food twice daily for 5 days with a repeat treatment after a 5-day interval (Poduschka & Saupe 1981, Frank 1988). Sulphaguanidine is not absorbed by the gut and may be a better alternative (BHPS 1987).

TABLE A1 *The principal helminth parasites of the European hedgehog (Erinaceus europaeus) and a summary of their treatment.*

Parasite	Site	Transmission	Treatment summary
Trematoda			
Brachylaemus erinacei	Intestine and bile ducts	Via slugs and snails	Single oral dose praziquantel (Droncit, Bayer) 20 mg kg^{-1} bw or niclosamide (Yomesan, Bayer) 200 mg kg^{-1} bw or mebendazole (Mebenvet or Telmin KH, Janssen) 100 mg kg^{-1} bw daily for 5 days in food (half dose for animals under 500 g)
Cestoda			
Rodentolepis erinacei	Intestine	Via arthropods	Single dose of niclosamide or praziquantel (as above)
Mesocestoides spp.	Mesentery and liver (cysts)	Via arthropods and dogs	None necessary
Nematoda			
Crenosoma striatum	Lungs	Via slugs and snails	Oral mebendazole (as above), or levamisole HCl 1% injected sc 10 mg kg^{-1} bw (e.g. Nilvern 7.5%, Pitman-Moore—needs diluting) repeated after 48 h (also available for oral administration as Nilzan) or oral febantel (e.g. Bayverm, Bayer) 50–100 mg kg^{-1} bw for 5 days, or oral febendazole (e.g. Panacur paste, Hoechst) 5 mg daily for 5 days or 25 mg once and repeated after 3 weeks, or ivermectin (Ivomec, MSD Agvet) oral or injected sc 0.02 ml kg^{-1} bw. Repeat treatments if larvae/eggs in faeces after 2–3 weeks (presence may be episodic). See also text
Capillaria aerophila	Lungs	Direct or via earthworms	
Physaloptera dispar	Oesophagus	?Direct	Levamisole (as above) probably effective but can also combine with oral piperazine (Poduschka & Kieliger 1972) e.g. Piperazine citrate (Arnolds)
Capillaria spp.	Intestine	?	As for lung worms
Acanthocephala			
Moniliformis and other genera	Intestine and mesentery	?Via insects	Oral praziquantel (25 mg kg^{-1} bw), or levamisole, or mebendazole (as above) (Frank 1988)

bw = bodyweight; sc = subcutaneous.   Source: based on Gregory (1985) and additional sources (see text)

BACTERIAL INFECTIONS

Whenever possible, pathogenic bacteria should be identified by culture and tested to establish the most appropriate antibacterial treatment. The over-use of antibiotics encourages resistance in pathogens, hence purely prophylactic treatments should usually be avoided, e.g. as advocated by Poduschka & Kieliger (1972) to prevent possible salmonellosis in captives. Furthermore, some antibiotics may have unknown toxic effects (especially aminoglycosides which are ototoxic and nephrotoxic in some animals) and the hedgehog's gut flora might be unnecessarily disturbed.

Leptospirosis

Wallach & Boever (1983) suggested treatment with antibiotics such as streptomycin (although this is toxic in many animals) or tetracyclines, which are normally safer. Many other antibiotics would probably also be suitable, e.g. Synulox (SmithKline Beecham), see above.

Salmonella

Salmonellae are commonly present in the guts of hedgehogs (studies typically show a 12–25% incidence; Chapter 9) but suspected infections should be confirmed by faecal culture to determine the strain and most appropriate antibiotic treatment.

Treatments suggested in the literature include ampicillin (2–7 mg kg^{-1} bodyweight) daily for up to 3 days or oxytetracycline (50 mg kg^{-1} bodyweight) daily (BHPS 1987). Mayer & Weiss (1985) tested 10 antibacterial agents and found neomycin, streptomycin and chloramphenicol suitable for controlling *S. enteriditis*, while ampicillin was the most effective against *S. typhimurium*. Gentamicin resistance was found in about 5% of isolates of both strains.

Chloramphenicol is a valuable bacteriostatic drug but its use should be restricted. Schicht (1982a,b) recommended 14 daily intramuscular injections of 30 mg kg^{-1} bodyweight or 50 mg kg^{-1} bodyweight orally. Saupe & Poduschka (1985) used oral chloromycetin at 50 mg kg^{-1} bodyweight for 5–8 days (e.g. Palmitate suspension, Parke Davis). For subcutaneous and intramuscular injections of chloromycetin succinate, Stocker (1992) recommended a dosage of 40 mg kg^{-1} bodyweight.

Animals with enteritis and diarrhoea can dehydrate rapidly, and fluid replacement therapy (e.g. subcutaneous isotonic saline) is widely recommended. Kaolin-based preparations may help to bind the faeces; powdered charcoal was recommended by Poduschka & Kieliger (1972).

Other Bacteria

Suggested treatments for *Bordetella bronchiseptica* include sulphonamides or oxytetracycline at 50 mg kg^{-1} bodyweight daily (Schicht 1982a,b). Bronchosecretolytics (e.g. Bisolvon, Boehringer) may also be helpful (Saupe & Poduschka 1985).

Over 118 strains of staphylococci have been isolated from hedgehogs and over 86% were penicillin-resistant (Smith 1968). Nevertheless, many staphylococcal strains are susceptible to tetracyclines and streptomycin (Versluys 1975), and clavulanate-potentiated amoxycillin (Synulox, SmithKline Beecham) can often be used to overcome penicillin-resistance.

Wallach & Boever (1983) suggested treatment of tularemia (*Francisella (= Pasteurella) tularensis*) with oral tetracyclines, which are also effective against rickettsias and chlamydias. Mycoplasmas, although resistant to penicillins, are susceptible to tetracyclines and erythromycins (Jawetz *et al.* 1989).

WOUNDS

Wounds should be cleaned with antiseptic solution, e.g. centrimide (Savlon, ICI) and carefully inspected for fly eggs or maggots (see above). Necrotic tissue should be removed; Stocker (1987) recommended Dermisol Multi-cleanse Solution (SmithKline Beecham). Antibiotic treatment (oral or topical applications) may control or prevent bacterial infections. Burns can be treated with Betaisodona (Mundipharma, Limburg) or Actovegin Gel 20% (Hormon-Chemie, Munich) (Saupe & Poduschka 1985); fluid replacement therapy may also be indicated. Broken bones, a common result of road traffic accidents, may be immobilized with splints or plaster casts but in practice intramedullary pinning is preferable. In hedgehogs, pre- and post-operative antibiotic cover is essential.

POISONING

Versluys (1975) noted the difficulty of diagnosing poisoning by insecticides, rodenticides and molluscicides. For metaldehyde poisoning she recommended using an emetic (apomorphine) and charcoal, as well as anaesthesia and an intraperitoneal drip of calcium gluconate to combat liver damage. She suggested injecting atropine to help counteract the effects of cholinesterase blockers (malathion, carbaryl and others) and warned against administering milk or oils. Rodenticides such as strychnine may be counteracted with anaesthesia (see above and Stocker (1992) for more recommended sedatives). Emetics and diphenylthiocarbazone (around 70 mg orally) may be used to counteract the acidosis caused by thallium. For warfarin and pindone, Versluys recommended the use of emetics and vitamin K.

APPENDIX 2:

Names for Hedgehogs in Various Languages

THIS rather *ad hoc* 'dictionary' of words for hedgehog in several languages (some transcribed into the Roman alphabet) might be useful to those perusing the international literature and entertaining for the curious. The affinities of the terms for hedgehog in some European languages are discussed by the translator in Herter (1965b, page 24); several local names used in east Africa are listed in Kingdon (1974). For regional country names in Britain see Barrett-Hamilton (1911), Burton (1969) and *The Oxford English Dictionary* (1989).

Latin:	*erinaceus* (Pliny the younger), *ericius* (Varro), *echinus* (Horatius Flaccus).
Norwegian:	*piggsvin* or *pinnsvin*
Finnish:	*siili*
Danish:	*pindsvin*
Swedish:	*igelkott*
German:	*igel*
Dutch:	*egel*
Africaanse:	*krimpvarkie*
French:	*hérisson* (medieval; *ireçon*)
Anglosaxon:	*igil* may be contracted to *yl* (or *il*)
English:	*urchin* (derived from the Norman *ircheoun* or *herichun* used from about 1340, pre-dating *hedgehog* which has been in use at least since 1450)[a] also *hedge-pig*, *hedgehock*, etc.
Gaelic:	*crainneag*
Welsh:	*draenog*
Irish:	*grainneog*
Cornish:	*sort*

Romany
(Gypsy):   *hotchi-witchi* or '*pal* of the *bor*' (Okely 1983)
Italian: *riccio*
Spanish: *erizo*
Catalan: *eriçó*
Basque: *sagaroi*
Portuguese: *ouriço*
Russian: *ëzh* (= *Yozh* forms the root for various Slavonic forms [b])
Polish: *jez*
Greek: *skandzóhoiros*
Hebrew: *kipod*
Arabic: *qunfud*
Kiswahili: *kalunguyeye* (Kingdon 1974)
Persian/Urdu: *kharpusht*
Hindi: *aik parkar ka jangli chuha* (means 'a spiky kind of mouse')
Gujurati: *kantu waru prani* ('animal with thorns')
Punjabi: *kandiala* or *kanderala* ('thorned animal')
Kashmiri: *chagagroo* (informal transcription)
Bengali: *kata chua* ('spiky mouse')
Chinese: *ci-wei* (pinyin transcription, sounds like *tse-wai*; means 'needle animal')
Manchurian: *senge* (Ognev 1928)

[a]Dates from Burton (1969).
[b]See Herter (1965b, translator's note, page 24) also Ognev (1928) who gives names from many parts of the former Soviet Union.

Useful Contact Addresses in Britain

British Hedgehog Preservation Society
   Knowbury House
   Knowbury
   Ludlow
   Shropshire SY8 3LQ.

Her Majesty's Stationery Office
   HMSO Bookshop,
   49, High Holborn,
   London, WC1V 6HB.

The Mammal Society
   Conservation Office,
   Zoology Department,
   The University,
   Bristol, BS8 1UG

People's Dispensary for Sick Animals
   Whitechapel Way,
   Priorslee,
   Telford,
   Shropshire, TF2 9QP.

Royal Society for the Prevention of Cruelty to Animals,
   Causeway,
   Horsham,
   Sussex RH12 1HG.

Wildlife Hospital Trust
   Aston Road,
   Haddenham,
   Aylesbury,
   Buckinghamshire, HP17 8AF.

References

Abdullah, I.A. & Hassan, I.S. (1987) Ectoparasites of the long-eared hedge-hog *Hemiechinus auritus* Gmelin, in Ninevah district, Iraq. *J. Biol. Sci. Res.* **18**: 43–52.

Adams, R. (ed.) (1974) *Richard III* by William Shakespeare. London: Macmillan.

Adolf, T.A. (1966) [The biology of reproduction of the common hedgehog (*Erinaceus europaeus*).] *Zool. Zh.* **45**: 1108–1111. (In Russian with English summary.)

Åkesson, B. (1972) Fat metabolism II. Fatty acid composition of adipose tissue. *Acta physiol. scand. suppl.* **380**: 54–61.

Alcover, J.A. (1984) Mammals of the Pityusic Islands. *Monographie Biol.* **52**: 455–467.

Al-Khalili, A.D. (1990) New records and a review of the mammalian fauna of the State of Bahrain, Arabian Gulf. *J. Arid Environ.* **19**: 95–103.

Allanson, M. (1934) The reproductive process of certain mammals VII. Seasonal variation in the reproductive organs of the male hedgehog. *Phil. Trans. Roy. Soc. Lond.* (B) **223**: 277–303.

Allanson, M. & Deanesly, R. (1935) The reaction of anoestrus hedgehogs to experimental conditions. *Proc. Roy. Soc. Lond.* (B) **116**: 170–185.

André, P. (1966) Isolement de *Listeria monocytogenes* chez un hérisson. *Société Française de Microbiologie: Annls Inst. Pasteur* **111**: 225–226.

Andreani, E. & Cardini, G. (1969) Il riccio (*Erinaceus europaeus*) quale portatore di salmonelle—Indagini preliminari. *Atti Soc. Ital. Sci. Vet.* **33**: 1024–1026.

Arata, A., Chmasa, M., Farhang-Azad, A., Mescerjakova, I., Neronov & Saidi, S. (1973) First detection of Tularemia in domestic and wild mammals in Iran. *Bull. World Health Organisation* **49**: 597–603. (Abstract seen only.)

Arnanz, E. & Machin, C. (1987) Structure and ultrastructure of the hedgehog ovary in the active state and in hibernation. *Folia Morphol. (Prague)* **35**: 366–373 + unpaginated plates 1–7.

Asawa, S.C. & Mathur, R.S. (1981) Quantitative evaluation of the endocrine glands of *Hemiechinus auritus collaris* (Gray) during the reproductive cycle. *Acta. anat.* **111**: 259–267.

Asawa, S.C. & Mathur, R.S. (1986) Influence of annual cycle on the acid phosphatase activity in certain endocrine glands of hedgehog *Hemiechinus auritus collaris* (Gray). *Uttar Pradesh J. Zool.* **6**: 207–214.

Asdell, S.A. (1964) *Patterns of Mammalian Reproduction*, 2nd edn. Ithaca, New York: Cornell University Press.

Attié, C. (1990) Emission sonores chez le Hérisson européen *Erinaceus europaeus*, et signification comportmentale. *Mammalia* **54**: 3–12.

Baker, K.P. (1985) Hedgehog information wanted. *Vet. Rec.* **June 15**: 648

Barnes, S. (1989) Year of the hedgehog. *The Times* **May 30**.

Barquin, E., Nogales, M. & Wildpret, W. (1986) Intervención de vertebrados en la diseminación de plantas vasculares en Inagua, Gran Canaria (Islas Canarias). *Vieraea* **16**: 263–272.

Barrett-Hamilton, G.E.H. (1911) Erinaceidae. In *A History of British Mammals, vol.* 2, G.E.H. Barrett-Hamilton & M.A.C. Hinton (eds.), pp. 45–75. London: Gurney & Jackson.

Barutzki, D., Schmid, K. & Heine, J. (1984) Untersuchungen über das Vorkommen von Endoparasiten beim Igel. *Berl. Münch. Tierärz. Wschr.* **97**: 215–218.

Batzri-Izraeli, R., Kelly, J.B., Glendenning, K.K., Masterton, R.B. & Wollberg, Z. (1990) Auditory cortex of the long-eared hedgehog (*Hemiechinus auritus*). I. Boundaries and frequency representations. *Brain Behav. Evol.* **36**: 237–248.

Bauchot, R. & Stephan, H. (1966) Données nouvelles sur l'encéphalisation des insectivores et les prosimiens. *Mammalia* **30**: 160–196.

Bauer, C. & Stoye, M. (1984) Ergebnisse parasitologischer Kotuntersuchungen von Equiden, Hunden, Katzen und Igeln der Jahre 1974 bis 1983. *Berl. Münch. Tierärz. Wschr.* **91**: 255–258.

Baylis, H.A (1935) Four new species of nematodes *Ann. Mag. Nat. Hist. S.10.* **16**: 370–382.

Beaucournu, J.C. & Alcover, J.A. (1984) Siphonaptera from small terrestrial mammals in the Pityusic Islands. *Monographie Biol.* **52**: 377–392.

Beaucournu, J.C. & Kowalski, K. (1985) New data on the fleas (*Insecta, Siphonaptera*) of Algeria. *Bull. Soc. Pathol. Exotique* **78**: 378–392.

Bennett, E.T. (1832) Characters of two new species of hedgehog (*Erinaceus* L.) from the Himalaya mountains. *Proc. Zool. Soc. Lond.* 123–124.

Ben Shaul, D.M. (1962) The composition of milk of wild animals. *Int. Zoo Ybk.* **4**: 333–342

Berthoud, G. (1978) Note préliminaire sur les déplacements du hérisson Européen (*Erinaceus europaeus* L.). *Terre Vie* **32**: 73–82.

Berthoud, G. (1980) Le hérisson (*Erinaceus europaeus* L.) et la route. *Rev. Ecol. (Terre Vie)* **34**: 361–372.

Berthoud, G. (1982) L'activité du hérisson Européen (*Erinaceus europaeus* L.), *Rev. Ecol. (Terre Vie)* **36**: 3–14.

BHPS—see British Hedgehog Preservation Society

Bibikov, D.I. (1956) [Biological observations on the long-eared hedgehog, *Erinaceus europaeus*, as a reservoir of leptospirae.] *Zool. Zh.* **35**: 1059–1063. (In Russian.)

Bidwai, P.P. & Bawa, S.R. (1981) Correlative study of the ultrastructure and the physiology of the seasonal regression of the epididymal epithelium in the hedgehog *Paraechinus micropus*. *Andrologia* **13**: 20–32.

Biörck, G., Johansson, B.W. & Schmidt, H. (1956a) Reactions of hedgehogs, hibernating and non-hibernating, to the inhalation of oxygen, carbon dioxide and nitrogen. *Acta physiol. scand.* **37**: 71–83.

Biörck, G., Johansson, B.W. & Veige, S. (1956b) Some laboratory data on hedgehogs, hibernating and non-hibernating. *Acta physiol. scand.* **37**: 281–294.

Biswas, B. & Ghose, R.K. (1970) Taxonomic notes on the Indian pale hedgehog *Paraechinus* Troussart, with descriptions of a new species and subspecies. *Mammalia* **34**: 467–477.

Blackmore, D.K. & Owen, D.G. (1968) Ectoparasites in British wild rodents. *Symp. Zool. Soc. Lond.* **24**: 197–220.

Blewett, D. (1979) You can't keep a good hedgehog away from home. *Sunday Express* **August 12**.

Boag, B. (1988) The prevalence of helminth parasites from the hedgehog *Erinaceus europaeus* in Great Britain. *J. Zool. Lond.* **214**: 379–382.

Boitani, L. & Reggiani, G. (1984) Movements and activity patterns of hedgehogs *Erinaceus europaeus* in Mediterranean coastal habitats. *Z. Säugetierk.* **49**: 193–206.

Bork, K., Honomichl, K. & Hoede, N. (1987) [Flea bites caused by *Archaeopsylla erinacei*, the hedgehog flea.] *Häutärtz* **38**:, 690–692. (In German, English abstract seen only.)

Bourdeau, P., Chermette, R. & Bussieras, S. (1987) Formes rares de dermatomycoses des carnivores, IIIe cas: dermatite localisée du chien due à une infection mixte par *Trichophyton mentagrophytes* et *Trichophyton erinacei*. *Le Point Vétérinaire* **19**: 619–625.

Boys Smith, J. S. (1967) Behaviour of a hedgehog *Erinaceus europaeus*. *J. Zool.* **153**: 564–566.

Bretagnolle, V. & Attié, C. (1989) Variabilité morphologique dans une population de hérissons de l'ouest de la France. *Mammalia* **53**: 85–96

Bretting, H. (1972) Die Bestimmung der Riechschwellen bei Igeln (*Erinaceus europaeus* L.) für einige Fettsäuren. *Z. Säugetierk.* **37**: 286–311.

Bridges, C.D.B. & Quilliam, T.A. (1973) Visual pigments of men, moles and hedgehogs. *Vision Res.* **13**: 2417–2421.

Brinck, P. & Löfqvist, J. (1973) The hedgehog *Erinaceus europaeus* and its flea *Archaeopsylla erinacei*. *Zoon. suppl.* **1**: 97–103.

British Hedgehog Preservation Society (1987) *Know your Hedgehog: Treating Sick Hedgehogs.* Ludlow, Shropshire, UK: British Hedgehog Preservation Society.

Brockie, R.E. (1958) The ecology of the hedgehog (*Erinaceus europaeus* L.) in

Wellington, New Zealand. M.Sc. Thesis. Victoria University of Wellington. (Extracts seen only.)

Brockie, R.E. (1959) Observations on the food of the hedgehog (*Erinaceus europaeus* L.) in New Zealand. *N. Z. J. Sci.* **2:** 121–136.

Brockie, R.E. (1960) Road mortality of the hedgehog in New Zealand. *Proc. Zool. Soc. Lond.* **134:** 505–508.

Brockie, R.E. (1964) Dental abnormalities in European and New Zealand hedgehogs. *Nature* **202:** 1355–1356.

Brockie, R.E. (1974a) Studies of the hedgehog (*Erinaceus europaeus*) in New Zealand. Ph.D. Thesis. Victoria University of Wellington. (Extracts seen only.)

Brockie, R.E. (1974b) The hedgehog mange mite *Caparinia tripilis*, in New Zealand. *N. Z. Vet. J.* **22:** 243–247.

Brockie, R.E. (1975) Distribution and abundance of the hedgehog (*Erinaceus europaeus*) in New Zealand, 1869–1973. *N. Z. J. Zool.* **2:** 445–462

Brockie, R.E. (1976) Self-anointing by wild hedgehogs (*Erinaceus europaeus*) in New Zealand. *Anim. Behav.* **24:** 68–71.

Brodie, E D. (1977) Hedgehogs use toad venom in their own defence. *Nature* **268:** 627–628.

Brodie, E.D. III, Brodie, E.D. Jr. & Johnson, J.A. (1982) Breeding the African hedgehog *Atelerix pruneri* in captivity. *Int. Zoo Ybk* **22:** 195–197

Brooksby, J.B. (1968) Wild animals and the epizootiology of foot and mouth disease. *Symp. Zool. Soc. Lond.* **24:** 1–11.

Broom J.C. & Coughlan, J.D. (1960) *Leptospira bratislava* isolated from a hedgehog in Scotland. *Lancet* **June 18:** 1326–1327.

Brown, R.E. & Macdonald, D.W. (eds.) (1985) *Social Odours in Mammals, Vol. 1.* Oxford: Clarendon Press.

Burgisser, H. (1983) Compte-rendu sur les maladies des animaux sauvages de 1975–1982. *Schweiz. Arch. Tierheilk.* **125:** 519–527.

Burt, W.H. (1943) Territoriality and home range concepts as applied to mammals. *J. Mammal.* **24:** 346–352.

Burton, J.A. & Pearson, B. (1987) *Collins Guide to the Rare Mammals of the World.* London: Collins.

Burton, M. (1957) Hedgehog self-anointing. *Proc. Zool. Soc. Lond.* **129:** 452–453.

Burton, M. (1965) Hedgehog's double wedding. *Illustr. Lond. News* **June 12**.

Burton, M. (1969) *The Hedgehog.* London: André Deutsch.

Butler, P.M. (1948) On the evolution of the skull and teeth in the Erinaceidae, with special reference to fossil material in the British Museum. *Proc. Zool. Soc. Lond.* **118:** 446–500.

Butler, P.M. (1978) Insectivora and Chiroptera: Family Erinaceidae. In *Evolution of African Mammals*, V.J. Maglio & H.B.S. Cooke (eds.), pp. 56–68. Cambridge Massachusetts: Harvard University Press.

Butler, P.M. (1980) The giant erinaceid insectivore, *Deinogalerix* Freudenthal, from the upper miocene of Gargano, Italy. *Scripta Geol.* **57:** 1–72.

Butler, P.M. (1988) The phylogeny of the insectivores. In *The Phylogeny and Classification of the Tetrapods, Vol. 2, Mammals*, M.J. Benton (ed.), pp. 117–142. Oxford: Clarendon Press.

Campbell, P.A. (1973a) The feeding behaviour of the European hedgehog (*Erinaceus europaeus* L.) in a New Zealand pasture. Ph.D. Thesis, University of Canterbury, New Zealand.

Campbell, P.A. (1973b) The feeding behaviour of the hedgehog (*Erinaceus europaeus* L.) in pasture land in New Zealand. *Proc. N.Z. Ecol. Soc.* **20**: 35–40.

Campbell, P.A. (1975) Feeding rhythms of caged hedgehogs (*Erinaceus europaeus* L.). *Proc. N.Z. Ecol. Soc.* **22**: 14–18.

Camus, L. & Gley, E. (1901) Sur les variations de poids des hérissons. *C. R. Soc. Biol. Paris* **53**: 1019–1020.

Carlier, E.W. (1893a) Contributions to the histology of the hedgehog (*Erinaceus europaeus*): part I. The alimentary canal. *J. Anat. Physiol.* **27**: 85–107 + plates IV,V,VI.

Carlier, E.W. (1893b) Contributions to the histology of the hedgehog (*Erinaceus europaeus*): part IV. The lymphatic glands. *J. Anat. Physiol.* **27**: 354–360 + plate XXI.

Carlier, E.W. (1893c) Contributions to the histology of the hedgehog (*Erinaceus europaeus*): part III. The skin. *J. Anat. Physiol.* **27**: 169–178 + plate XI.

Carlier, E.W. (1893d) Contributions to the histology of the hedgehog (*Erinaceus europaeus*): part V. The so-called hibernating gland. *J. Anat. Physiol.* **27**: 508–518 + plates XXVI, XXVII.

Carlier, E.W. (1896) On the pancreas of the hedgehog during hibernation. *J. Anat. Physiol.* **30**: 334–346.

Carlier, E.W. & Lovatt-Evans, C.A. (1903) A chemical study of the hibernating gland of the hedgehog, together with the changes it undergoes during winter sleep. *J. Anat. Physiol.* **38**: 15–31.

Carlson, A. (1981) Diagnose unde Therapie der Parasitosen der Igel. *Prakt. Tierärzt* **62** (**suppl.**): 73–75.

Caroll, L. (1865) *Alice's Adventures in Wonderland*, Puffin Classics edn. (1946). London: Penguin Books.

Castex, C. & Hoo-Paris R. (1987) Régulation des sécrétions du pancréas endocrine (insuline et glucagon), au cours du cycle létharie-réveil périodique du mammifère hibernant. *Diabete Metab.* (Paris) **13**: 176–181.

Causey, O.R., Kemp, G.E., Hamdy Madbouly, M. & David-West, T.S. (1970) Congo virus from domestic livestock, African hedgehog and arthropods in Nigeria. *Amer. J. Trop. Med. Hygiene* **19**: 846–850.

Chandler, A.C. & Read, C.P. (1961) *Introduction to Parasitology*. 10th edn. Chichester: John Wiley.

Chandra, H. (1985) The hedgehog, *Hemiechinus auritus* Gray, a potential predator of acridids. *Plant Protect. Bull. India* **37**: 27–28. (Abstract only seen.)

Chang Hsiang-Tung (1936) An auditory reflex of the hedgehog. *Chinese J. Physiol.* **10**: 119–124.

Chard, J.S.R. (1936) *British Animal Tracks.* London: Pearson.

Chermette, R. (1987) Identification des dermatophytes appartenant au complexe d'espèces *Trichophyton mentagrophytes. Le Point Veterinaire* **19**: 628–629.

Clausen, G. & Storesund, A. (1971) Electrolyte distribution and renal function in the hibernating hedgehog. *Acta physiol. scand.* **83**: 4–12.

Clemens, E.T. (1980) The digestive tract: an insectivore, prosimian and advanced primate. In *Comparative Physiology: Primitive Mammals*, K. Schmidt-Nielson, L. Bolis & C.R. Taylor (eds.), pp. 90–99. Cambridge: Cambridge University Press.

Coles, A. (1983) Feeding hedgehogs. *Br. Hedgehog Preserv. Soc. Newsl.* **2**: 6.

Cooper, E.M. (1991) British mammals and the law. In *Handbook of British Mammals*, G.B. Corbet & S. Harris (eds.), 2nd edn., pp. 24–34. Oxford: Blackwell.

Corbet, G.B. (1971) Family Erinaceidae. In *The Mammals of Africa: an Identification Manual*, J. Meester & H.W. Setzer (eds.), pp. 1–3. Washington D.C.: Smithsonian Institution Press.

Corbet, G.B. (1988) The family Erinaceidae: a synthesis of its taxonomy, phylogeny, ecology and zoogeography. *Mamm. Rev.* **18**: 117–172.

Corcoran, C.J. (1967) A case report. *Vet. Rev.* **18**: 73.

Cott, H.B. (1951) The palatability of the eggs of birds: illustrated by experiments on the food preferences of the hedgehog *Erinaceus europaeus. Proc. Zool. Soc. Lond.* **121**: 1–42.

Crompton, A.W., Taylor, C.R. & Jagger, J.A. (1978) Evolution of homeothermy in mammals. *Nature* **272**: 333–336.

Davies, J.L. (1957) A hedgehog road mortality index. *Proc. Zool Soc. Lond.* **128**: 593–608.

Dawson, T.J. & Grant, T.R (1980) Metabolic capabilities of monotremes and the evolution of homeothermy. In *Comparative Physiology: Primitive Mammals*, K. Schmidt-Nielson, L. Bolis & C.R. Taylor (eds.), pp. 140–147. Cambridge: Cambridge University Press.

Deag, J.M. (1980) *Social Behaviour in Animals*, London: Edward Arnold.

Deanesly, R. (1934) The reproductive processes of certain mammals VI. The reproductive cycle of the female hedgehog. *Phil. Trans. Roy. Soc. Lond. (B)* **223**: 239–276.

Degerbøl, M. (1943) Pairing and pairing fights of the hedgehog (*Erinaceus europaeus* L.). *Vidensk. Medd. Dansk naturh. Foren.* **106**: 427–430.

de Kretser, D.M. (1984) The testis. In *Reproduction in Mammals: 3. Hormonal Control of Reproduction*, 2nd edn., C.R. Austin & R.V. Short (eds.), pp. 76–90. Cambridge: Cambridge University Press.

Delany, M.J. (1989) The zoogeography of the mammal fauna of the southern Arabia. *Mamm. Rev.* **19**: 133–152.

Delany, M.J. & Farook, S.M.S (1989) The small mammals of a coastal gravel plain in the Sultanate of Oman. *J. Zool. Lond.* **218**: 319–321.

de Wit, C.A. & Westrom, B.R. (1987a) Venom resistance in the hedgehog *Erinaceus europaeus:* purification and identification of macroglobulin inhibitors as plasma anti-hemorrhagic factors. *Toxicon* **25**: 315–324.

de Wit, C.A. & Westrom, B.R. (1987b) Purification and characterization of alpha-2, alpha-2-beta and beta macroglobulin inhibitors in the hedgehog *Erinaceus europaeus:* beta macroglobulin identified as the plasma antihemorrhagic factor. *Toxicon* **25**: 1209–1220.

Dickman, C.R. (1988) Age-related dietary change in the European hedgehog, *Erinaceus europaeus. J. Zool. Lond.* **215**: 1–14.

Dimelow, E.J. (1963a) The behaviour of the hedgehog (*Erinaceus europaeus* L.) in the routine of life in captivity. *Proc. Zool. Soc. Lond.* **141**: 281–289.

Dimelow, E.J. (1963b) Observations on the feeding of the hedgehog (*Erinaceus europaeus* L.). *Proc. Zool. Soc. Lond.* **141**: 291–309.

Dmi'el, R. & Schwartz, M. (1984) Hibernation patterns and energy expenditure in hedgehogs from semi-arid and temperate habitats. *J. Comp. Physiol. B*, **155**: 117–123.

Doncaster, C.P. (1992) Testing the role of intraguild predation in regulating hedgehog populations. *Proc. Roy. Soc. Lond. B*, **249**: 113–117.

Dowie, M. (1987) Rural hedgehogs—many questions to answer. *Game Conserv. Ann. Rev.* **18**: 126–129.

Dowie, M. (1988) Radio-tracking hedgehogs. *Game Conserv. Ann. Rev.* **19**: 122–124.

Duker, G., Sjöquist, P.-O., Svensson, O., Wohlfart, B. & Johansson, B.W. (1986) Hypothermic effects on cardiac action potentials: differences between a hibernator, hedgehog, and a nonhibernator, guinea pig. In *Living in the Cold. Physiological and Biochemical Adaptations*, H.C. Heller, X.J. Musacchia & L.C.H. Wang (eds.), pp. 565–572. New York: Elsevier.

Dunstone, N. (1993) *The Mink.* London: T & A. D. Poyser.

Dutourné, B. & Saboureau, M. (1983) An endocrine and histophysiological study of the testicular annual cycle in the hedgehog (*Erinaceus europaeus* L.). *Gen. Comp. Endocrinol.* **50**: 324–332.

Easton, E.R. (1979) Observations on the distribution of the hedgehog (*Erinaceus albiventris*) in Tanzania. *Afr. J. Ecol.* **17**: 175–176.

Eddowes, A. (1898) A case of ringworm contracted from a hedgehog. *Trans. Derm. Soc. Great Britain and Ireland* **4**: 32–35.

Edwards, B.A. & Munday, K.A. (1969) The function of brown fat in the hedgehog (*Erinaceus europaeus*). *Comp. Biochem. Physiol.* **30**: 1029–1036.

Edwards, J.T.G. (1957) The European hedgehog (*Erinaceus europaeus* L.). In *The UFAW Handbook on the Care and Management of Laboratory Animals* 2nd edn., A.N. Worden & W. Lane-Petter (eds.), pp. 450–460. Edinburgh: Churchill Livingstone.

Eisenberg, J.F. (1980) Biological strategies of living conservative mammals. In *Comparative Physiology: Primitive Mammals*, K. Schmidt-Nielson, L. Bolis & C.R. Taylor (eds.), pp. 13–30. Cambridge: Cambridge University Press.

Eisenberg, J.F. (1981) *The Mammalian Radiations: an Analysis of Trends in*

Evolution, Adaptation, and Behavior, Chicago: University of Chicago Press.

Eisentraut, M. (1952) Contribution a l'étude biologique de *Paraechinus aethiopicus* Ehrenb. *Mammalia* **16**: 232–252.

Eklund, B., Senturia, J.B. & Johansson, B.W. (1972) Electrocardiogram. *Acta physiol. scand. suppl.* **380**: 28–30

Ektvedt, R. & Hanssen, I. (1974) [Outbreak of botulism in cattle.] *Norsk Veterinaer Tidsskrift* **86**: 286–290. (In Norwegian, English abstract seen only.)

Elbihari, S., Kawasmeh, Z.A. & Al Naiem, A.H. (1984) Possible reservoir host(s) of zoonotic cutaneous leishmaniasis in Al-Hassa oasis, Saudi Arabia. *Ann. Trop. Med. Parasitol.* **78**: 543–545.

Eliassen, E. (1961) Changes of blood volume in the pre-hibernating and deep-hibernating hedgehog. *Nature* **192**: 1047–1049.

El Omari B., Lacroix, A. & Saboureau, M. (1989) Daily and seasonal variations in plasma LH and testosterone concentrations in the adult male hedgehog, *Erinaceus europaeus*. *J. Reprod. Fert.* **86**: 145–156.

English, M.P (1967) Ringworm in wild mammals. *J. Zool. Lond.* **153**: 556–561.

English, M.P. & Morris, P.A. (1969) *Trichophyton mentagrophytes* var. *erinacei* in hedgehog nests. *Sabouraudia* **7**: 118–121.

English, M.P., Evans, C.D., Hewitt, M. & Warin, R.P. (1962) Hedgehog ringworm. *Br. Med. J.* **1**: 149–151.

Ewer, R.F. (1973) *The Carnivores*. London: Weidenfeld & Nicolson.

Fameree, L., Cotteleer, C. & Abbeele, O. van den (1981) Epidemiological and sanitary implication of sylvatic trichinelliasis in Belgium. Collated results for 1979–1981. *Schweiz. Archiv Teirheilk.* **124**: 401–412.

Firbas, W. & Poduschka, W. (1971) Beitrag zur Kenntnis des Zitzen des Igels, *Erinaceus europaeus* Linne, 175., *Saugetierk. Mitteil.* **19**: 39–44.

Forssberg, A. & Sarajas, H.S.S. (1955) Studies on the metabolism of ^{14}C-labelled glucose in awake and hibernating hedgehogs. *Ann. Acad. Sci. fenn. A.IV Biol.* **28**: 1–8.

Fowler, P.A. (1988) Seasonal endocrine cycles in the European hedgehog (*Erinaceus europaeus*). *J. Reprod. Fert.* **84**: 259–272.

Fowler, P.A. & Racey, P.A. (1987) Relationship between body and testis temperatures in the hedgehog, *Erinaceus europaeus*, during hibernation and sexual reactivation. *J. Reprod. Fert.* **81**: 567–574.

Fowler, P.A. & Racey, P.A. (1990a) Effect of melatonin administration and long day-length on endocrine cycles in the hedgehog *Erinaceus europaeus*. *J. Pineal Res.* **8**: 193–204.

Fowler, P.A. & Racey, P.A. (1990b) Daily and seasonal cycles of body temperature and aspects of heterothermy in the hedgehog *Erinaceus europaeus*. *J. Comp. Physiol. B* **160**: 299–307.

Frank, W. (1988) Parasiten des Igels. *Mikrocosmos* **77**: 73–80.

Frye, F. & Dutra, F. (1973) Squamous cell carcinoma of the feet of an Indian hedgehog. *J. Wildl. Diseases* **9**: 249–250.

Frylestam, B. & von Schantz, T. (1977) Age determination of European hares based on periosteal growth lines. *Mamm. Rev.* **7**: 151–154.

Garnica, R. & Robles, L. (1986) Seguimento de la mortalidad de erizos, *Erinaceus europaeus*, producida por vehículos en una carretera de poca circulacíon. *Misc. Zool* **10**: 406–408.

Geisler, M. & Gropp, A. (1967) Chromosome polymorphism in the European hedgehog, *Erinaceus europaeus* (Insectivora). *Nature* **214**: 396–397.

Geoffrey of Monmouth (c. 1136)—see Thorpe, L. (1966).

Gerson, L. & Boever, W.J. (1983) Acariasis (*Caparinia* sp.) in hedgehogs (*Erinaceus* spp): diagnosis and treatment. *J. Zool. An. Med.* **14**: 17–19.

Giacometti, S., Scherini, E. & Bernocchi, G. (1989) Seasonal changes in the nucleoli of Purkinje cells of the hedgehog cerebellum. *Brain Res.* **488**: 365–368

Giagia, E.B. & Ondrias, J.C. (1980) Karyological analysis of eastern European hedgehog *Erinaceus concolor* (Mammalia, Insectivora) in Greece. *Mammalia* **44**: 59–71.

Gillies, A.C., Ellison, G.T.H. & Skinner, J.D. (1991) The effect of seasonal food restriction on activity, metabolism and torpor in the South African hedgehog (*Atelerix frontalis*). *J. Zool. Lond.* **223**: 117–130.

Girardier, L. (1983) Brown fat: an energy dissipating tissue. In *Mammalian Thermogenesis*, L. Girardier & M.J. Stock (eds.), pp. 50–98. London: Chapman & Hall.

Giroud, P., Le Gac, P., Dumas, N. & Colas-Belcour, J. (1959) Le hérisson *Erinaceus europaeus*, réservoir de rickettsies ou de néo-rickettsies et même d'agents du group de l'avortement des ovins. *Bull. Soc. Pathol. Exotique* **52**: 726–730.

Göransson, G., Karlsson, J. & Lingren, A. (1976) Igelkotten och biltrafiken. *Fauna och Flora* (Stockholm) **71**: 1–6.

Gould, E. & Eisenberg, J.F. (1966) Notes on the biology of the Tenrecidae. *J. Mammal.* **47**: 660–686.

Goyal, R.P. & Mathur, R. S. (1974) Anatomic, histologic and certain enzymatic studies on the male genital organs of *Hemiechinus auritus collaris* (Gray), the Indian long eared hedgehog. *Acta Zool.* **55**: 47–58.

Grassé, P.-P. (ed.) (1955) *Traite de Zoologie Anatomie Systematique, Vol. 17 Mammalia, Fasc.IIA.* Paris: Masson.

Green, R.E., Hawell, J. & Johnson, T.H. (1987) Identification of predators of wader eggs from egg remains. *Bird Study* **34**: 87–91.

Gregory, M.W. (1975) Observations on vocalisation in the central African hedgehog *Erinaceus albiventris*, including a courtship call. *Mammalia* **39**: 1–7.

Gregory, M.W. (1976) Notes on the Central African hedgehog *Erinaceus albiventris* in the Nairobi area. *E. Afr. Wildl. J.* **14**: 177–179.

Gregory, M.W. (1981a) Mites of the hedgehog *Erinaceus albiventris* Wagner in Kenya: observations on the prevalence and pathogenicity of *Notoedres oudemansi* Fain, *Caparinia erinacei* Fain, and *Rodentopus sciuri* Fain. *Parasitology* **82**: 149–157.

Gregory, M.W. (1981b) Diseases and parasites of the Central African hedgehog *Erinaceus albiventris* Wagner. *Zool. Beitr.* **27**: 205–213.

Gregory, M.W. (1985) Hedgehogs. In *B.S.A.V.A. Manual of Exotic Pets*, J. Cooper, M.F. Hutchinson, O.F. Jackson & R.J. Maurice (eds.), pp. 54–58. Cheltenham: British Small Animal Veterinary Association.

Gregory, M.W. & English, M.P (1975) *Arthroderma benhamiae* infection in the central African hedgehog, *Erinaceus albiventris*, and a report of a human case. *Mycopathologica* **55**: 143–147.

Gregory, M.W., Karstad, L., Frank, H. & Rutherford, D.M (1976) An enzootic 'growth' of Kenya hedgehogs: preliminary observations. In *Wildlife Diseases*, L.A. Page (ed.), pp. 661–673. New York: Plenum Press.

Gross, E.M. & Hadani, A. (1984) The occurrence of the brown dog tick, *Rhipicephalus sanguineus* (Latr. 1806), a possible vector of the spotted fever group rickettsiae, on sheep in the Negev region of Israel. *Trans. Roy. Soc. Trop. Med. Hygiene* **78**: 139–140. (Abstract seen only.)

Grosshans, W. (1983) Zur Nahrung des Igels (*Erinaceus europaeus* L. 1758). Untersuchungen von Magen-Darminhalten schleswig-holsteinischer Igel. *Zool. Anz. Jena* **211**: 364–384.

Gunderson, H.L. (1976) *Mammalogy*. New York: McGraw-Hill.

Günther, M. & Schaefer, H.E. (1983) Nachweis von Zytomegalie-Viren in der submandibulären Speicheldrüse europäischer und algerischer Igel (*Erinaceus europaeus* und *Aethechinus algirus*). Ein neuer Aspekt der Selbstbespeichelung. *Z. Säugetierk* **48**: 316–320.

Gupta, B.B. & Sharma, H.L. (1961) Birth and early development of Indian hedgehogs. *J. Mammal.* **42**: 398–399.

Gustato, G., Alfieri, G. & Iuliano, A. (1984) Indagine su un 'puzzle'. Alcuni data sull'autosputo in *Erinaceus europaeus* (Insectivora). *Boll. Soc. Natur. Napoli* **93**: 131–141.

Haarløv, N. (1943) Die Kopulation der Igel. *Vidensk. Medd. Dansk. naturh. Foren.* **106**: 431–433.

Happold, D.C.D. (1969) The mammalian fauna of some jebels in the northern Sudan. *J. Zool. Lond.* **157**: 133–145.

Happold, D.C.D. (1987) *The Mammals of Nigeria*. Oxford: Oxford University Press.

Harrison, D.L. & Bates, P.J.J. (1985) An unusual dental anatomy in an African hedgehog (*Erinaceus albiventris* Wagner, 1841) (Insectivora: Erinaceidae). *Mammalia* **49**: 432–434.

Harrison Matthews, L. (1952) *British Mammals*. London: Collins.

Harrison Matthews, L. (1969) *The Life of Mammals I*. London: Weidenfeld & Nicolson.

Hathaway, S.C. (1981) Leptospirosis in New Zealand: an ecological view. *N.Z. vet. J.* **29**: 109–112.

Hathaway, S.C., Little, T.W.A., Stevens, A.E., Ellis, W.A. & Morgan, J. (1983) Serovar identification of leptospires of the Australis serogroup isolated from free-living and domestic species in the United Kingdom. *Res. Vet. Sci.* **35**: 64–68.

Haynes, L. (1989) Hibernating hedgehogs amplify their brains' weak signals. *New Scientist* **October 28:** 31.

Heap, R.B. & Flint, A.P.F. (1984) Pregnancy. In *Reproduction in Mammals: 3. Hormonal Control of Reproduction,* 2nd edn., C.R. Austin & R.V. Short (eds.), pp. 153–194. Cambridge: Cambridge University Press.

Heglund, N.C. (1980) Mechanics of locomotion in primitive and advanced mammals. In *Comparative Physiology: Primitive Mammals.* K. Schmidt-Nielson, L. Bolis & C.R. Taylor (eds.), pp. 213–219. Cambridge: Cambridge University Press.

Herter, K. (1934) Körpertemperatur und Aktivität beim Igel. *Z. vergl. Physiol.* **20:** 511–544.

Herter, K. (1956) Das Verhalten der Insektivoren. *Handb. Zool.* **8:** chapter 10.

Herter, K. (1964) Gefangenschaftsbeobachtungen an einem Algerischen Igel (*Aethechinus algirus,* Duvernoy und Lereboullet). *Zool. Beitr.* **10:** 189–225.

Herter, K. (1965a) Über das Paarungsverhalten der Igel. *Stzgb. Gesellsch. Naturforsch. Freunde Berlin* **5:** 57–77.

Herter, K. (1965b) *Hedgehogs, a Comprehensive Study.* Phoenix House.

Herter, K. (1968) The Insectivores. In *Grzimek's Animal Life Encyclopedia,* B. Grzimek (ed.), pp. 176–257. New York: Van Nostrand Reinhold.

Herter, K. (1971) Gefangenschaftsbeobachtungen an Mittleafrikanischen Igeln (*Atelerix pruneri* (Wagner)). *Zool. Beitr.* **17:** 337–370.

Herter, K. (1972) Die Schweizer Igel-Station und beobachtungen über die entwicklung von *Erinaceus europaeus* L. *Zool. Beitr.* **18:** 467–474.

Himms-Hagen, J. (1983) Thyroid hormones and thermogenesis. In *Mammalian Thermogenesis,* L. Girardier & M.J. Stock (eds.), pp. 141–177. Chapman & Hall.

Hoeck, H.N. (1987) Hedgehog mortality during hibernation. *J. Zool. Lond.* **213:** 755–757.

Holz, H. (1978) Studien an europäischer Igeln. *Z. zool. Syst. Evolut.-forsch.* **16:** 148–165.

Hoogstraal, H. & Wassef, H.Y. (1983) Notes on African *Haemaphysalis* ticks XV. *H.(Rhipistoma) norvali* sp.N., a hedgehog parasite of the *H.(R.) spinulosa* group in Zimbabwe (Acarina: Ixodidae). *Onderstepoort J. Vet. Res.* **50:** 183–189.

Hoo-Paris, R. & Sutter, B. Ch. J. (1980) Role of glucose and catecholamines in the regulation of insulin secretion in the hibernating hedgehog (*Erinaceus europaeus*) during arousal. *Gen. Comp. Endocrinol.* **41:** 62–65.

Hoo-Paris, R., Hamsany, M., Sutter, B.Ch.J., Assan, R. & Boillot, J. (1982) Plasma glucose and glucagon concentrations in the hibernating hedgehog. *Gen. Comp. Endocrinol.* **46:** 246–254.

Hoo-Paris, R., Hamsany, M., Sutter, B.Ch.J., Assan, R. & Boillot, J. (1984a) In vitro β cell response to glucose in the hibernating hedgehog: comparison with the homeothermic hedgehog and the rat. *Comp. Biochem. Physiol.* **78A:** 559–563.

Hoo-Paris, R., Castex, Ch. & Sutter, B.Ch.J. (1984b) Alanine-turnover and conversion to glucose of alanine in the hibernating, arousing and active hedgehog (*Erinaceus europaeus*). *Comp. Biochem. Physiol.* **78A**: 159–161.

Horsch, F., Klockmann, J., Janetzky, B., Drechsler, H. & Lobnitz, P. (1970) [A leptospirosis survey in wild animals.] *Monats. Veterinärmed.* **25**: 634–639. (In German, English abstract seen only.)

Horwitz, B.A., Kott, K.S., Hamilton, J.S. & Moore, B.J. (1986) Regulation of brown fat thermogenesis in hibernators. In *Living in the Cold. Physiological and Biochemical Adaptations*, H.C. Heller, X.J. Musacchia & L.C.H. Wang (eds.), pp. 101–108. New York: Elsevier.

Hubalek, Z. (1987) Geographic distribution of Bhanja virus. *Folia Parasitol. (Prague)* **34**: 77–86.

Hübner, R., Maddalena, T. & Poduschka, W. (1991) The karyotype of the Middle-African hedgehog *Atelerix albiventris* Wagner, 1841 and its cytotaxonomical relationships to other Erinaceinae (Insectivora: Erinaceidae). *Genetica* **83**: 243–246.

Hufnagl, E. (1972) *Libyan Mammals*, Harrow: The Oleander Press.

Hulse, E.C. & Edwards, J.T. (1937) Foot-and-mouth disease in hibernating hedgehogs. *J. Comp. Path. Therapeutics* **50**: 421–430.

Hussein, H.S. & Mustafa, B.E. (1985) *Haemaphysalis spinulosa* and *Rhipicephalus simus* (Acari: Ixodidae): seasonal abundance of immature stages and host range in the Shambat area, Sudan. *J. Med. Entomol.* **22**: 72–77.

Inkovaara, P. & Suomalainen, P. (1973) Studies on the physiology of the hibernating hedgehog 18. On the leucocyte counts in the hedgehog's intestine and lungs. *Ann. Acad. Sci. fenn. A,IV Biol.* **200**: 1–21.

Jacobsen, N.H.G. (1982) A note of mating and neonate development of the South African hedgehog (*Erinaceus frontalis*), *Säugetierk. Mitt.* **30**: 199–200.

Jawetz, E., Melnick, J.L., Adelberg, E.A., Brooks, G.F., Butel, J.S. & Ornston, L.N. (1989) *Medical Microbiology*. 18th edn. London: Prentice Hall International.

Jefferies, D.J. & Pendlebury, J.B. (1968) Population fluctuations of stoats, weasels and hedgehogs in recent years. *J. Zool. Lond.* **156**: 513–549.

Jennings, A.R. (1968) Tumours of free-living wild mammals and birds. *Symp. Zool. Soc. Lond.* **24**: 273–287.

Jewell, P.A. (1966) The concept of home range in mammals. *Symp. Zool. Soc. Lond.* **18**: 85–109.

Johansson, B.G. & Johansson, B.W. (1972) Fat metabolism I. Plasma lipids and lipoproteins. *Acta physiol. scand. suppl.* **380**: 49–53.

Johansson, B.W. & Senturia, J.B. (1972a) Blood gases. *Acta physiol. scand. suppl.* **380**: 36–39.

Johansson, B.W. & Senturia, J.B. (1972b) Nitrogen metabolism: serum variables. *Acta physiol. scand. suppl.* **380**: 40–42.

Kahmann, H. & Vesmanis, I. (1977) Zur Kenntnis des Wanderigels (*Erinaceus algirus* Lereboullet, 1842) auf der Insel Formentera (Pityusen) und im nordafrikanischen Verbreitungsgebiet. *Spixiana* **1**: 105–135.

Kanwar, K.C., Singh, A. & Verma, R. (1980) Seasonal reproductive fluctuations in Indian male hedgehog *Hemiechinus auritus* Collaris. *Res. Bull. Punjab Univ. Sci.* **31:** 77–86.

Karaseva, E.V., Gotfrid, A.B. & Dubinina, N.V. (1979) [The way of life of European hedgehogs (*Erinaceus europaeus*) and their role in the natural focus of leptospirosis in the Yaroslavl district by the observations over marked individuals.] *Zool. Zh.* **58:** 705–715. (In Russian with English summary.)

Kayser, Ch. (1961) *The Physiology of Natural Hibernation*. Oxford: Pergamon Press.

Keymer, I.F., Gibson, E.A. & Reynolds, D.J. (1991) Zoonoses and other findings in hedgehogs (*Erinaceus europaeus*): a survey of mortality and review of the literature. *Vet. Rec.* **128:** 245–249.

Khalil, L.F. & Abdul-Salam, J. (1985) Helminth parasites of the hedgehog, *Hemiechinus auritus* in Kuwait. *J. Univ. Kuwait (Sci.)* **12:** 113–126.

Kingdon, J. (1974) *East African Mammals Vol II A (Insectivores and Bats)*. London: Academic Press.

Kirkebö, A. (1968) Cardiovascular investigations on hedgehogs during arousal from the hibernation state. *Acta physiol. scand.* **73:** 394–406.

Knight, M. (1962) *Animals of Britain No.3: Hedgehogs*. London: A Sunday Times Book Publication.

Koch, J. (1981) Worm control in hedgehogs (*Erinaceus europaeus*) brief report. *Vet. Med. Rev.* **2:** 150–151.

Kock, D. (1980) Distribution of hedgehogs in Tunisia corrected. *Afr. Small Mammal Newsl.* **5:** 1–6.

Kock, N. (1985) Hedgehog information. *Vet. Rec.* **117:** 136.

Kok, O.B. & Van Ee, C.A. (1989) Die versorging en ontwikkeling van Suid Afrikaanse krimpvarkies in aanhouding. *S. Afr. J. Wildl. Res.* **19:** 89–91.

Kramm, C., Sattrup, G., Baumann, R. & Bartels, H. (1975) Respiratory function of blood in hibernating and non-hibernating hedgehogs. *Respir. Physiol.* **25:** 311–318.

Kramm, H. (1979) Zur Injectionstechnik am Igel. Neue Untersuchungen der Hautmuskulatur des Igels. *Prakt. Tierärzt* **60:** 320–330.

Kratochvíl, J. (1975) [On knowledge of the hedgehog of the genus Erinaceus in the C.S.S.R.] *Zool. Listy* **24:** 297–312. (In Russian, seen only in translation.)

Krebs, J.R & Davies, N.B. (1984) *Behavioural Ecology: an Evolutionary Approach*, 2nd edn. Oxford: Blackwell Scientific Publications.

Krebs, J.R and Davies, N.B. (1987) *An Introduction to Behavioural Ecology*, 2nd edn. Oxford: Blackwell Scientific Publications.

Krishna, D. (1956) Hedgehogs of the desert of Rajasthan. Part 2. Food and feeding habits. *J. Bombay Nat. Hist. Soc.* **53:** 362–366.

Krishna, D. & Prakash, I. (1955) Hedgehogs of the desert of Rajasthan. Part 1. Fossorial habits and distribution. *J. Bombay Nat. Hist. Soc.* **53:** 38–43.

Kristiansson, H. (1981a) Young production of European hedgehog in Sweden and Britain. *Acta Theriol.* **26:** 504–507.

Kristiansson, H. (1981b) Distribution of the European hedgehog (*Erinaceus europaeus* L.) in Sweden and Finland. *Ann. Zool. Fenn.* **18**: 115–119.

Kristiansson, H. (1984) Ecology of a hedgehog (*Erinaceus europaeus*) population in southern Sweden. Ph.D. Thesis, University of Lund, Sweden.

Kristiansson, H. (1990) Population variables and causes of mortality in a hedgehog population (*Erinaceus europaeus*) population in southern Sweden. *J. Zool. Lond.* **220**: 391–404.

Kristiansson, H. & Erlinge, S. (1977) Rörelser och aktivitetsområde hos igelkotten. *Fauna och Flora* **4**: 149–155.

Kristoffersson, R. (1961) Hibernation of the hedgehog (*Erinaceus europaeus*). The ATP and O-phosphate levels in blood and various tissues of hibernating and non-hibernating animals. *Ann. Acad. Sci. fenn. A,IV, Biol.* **50**: 1–45.

Kristoffersson, R. (1964) An apparatus for recording general activity of hedgehogs. *Ann. Acad. Sci. fenn. A,IV, Biol.* **79**: 2–8.

Kristoffersson, R. (1965) Hibernation in the hedgehog (*Erinaceus europaeus*). Blood urea levels after known length of continuous hypothermia and in certain phases of spontaneous arousals and entries into hypothermia. *Ann. Acad. Sci. fenn. A,IV, Biologica* **96**: 1–8.

Kristoffersson, R. (1971) A note on the age distribution of hedgehogs in Finland. *Ann. Zool. Fenn.* **8**: 554–557.

Kristoffersson, R. & Soivio, A. (1964a) Hibernation of the hedgehog (*Erinaceus europaeus* L.). The periodicity of hibernation of undisturbed animals during the winter in a constant ambient temperature. *Ann. Acad. Sci. fenn. A,IV, Biol.* **80**: 1–22.

Kristoffersson, R. & Soivio, A. (1964b) Hibernation of the hedgehog. Changes of respiratory pattern, heart rate, and body temperature in response to gradually decreasing or increasing ambient temperature. *Ann. Acad. Sci. fenn. A,IV, Biol.* **82**: 1–17.

Kristoffersson, R. & Soivio, A. (1964c) Studies on the periodicity of hibernation in the hedgehog (*Erinaceus europaeus* L.). I. A comparison of induced hypothermia in constant ambient temperatures of 4.5 and 10°C. *Ann. Zool. Fenn.* **1**: 370–372.

Kristoffersson, R. & Soivio, A. (1964d) Studies on the periodicity of hibernation in the hedgehog II. Changes of respiratory rhythm, heart rate and body temperature at the onset of spontaneous and induced arousals. *Ann. Zool. Fenn.* **4**: 595–597.

Kristoffersson, R. & Soivio, A. (1967) A comparative long-term study of hibernation in Finnish and German hedgehogs in a constant ambient temperature. *Ann. Acad. Sci. fenn. A,IV, Biol.* **122**: 1–11.

Kristoffersson, R. & Suomalainen, P. (1964) Studies on the physiology of the hibernating hedgehog. 2. Changes of body weight of hibernating and non-hibernating animals. *Ann. Acad. Sci. fenn. A,IV, Biol.* **79**: 1–11.

Kristoffersson, R., Soivio, A. & Terhivuo, J. (1977) The distribution of the hedgehog (*Erinaceus europaeus* L.) in Finland in 1975. *Ann. Acad. Sci. fenn. A,IV, Biol.* **209**: 1–6.

Křivanec, K., Kopecký, J., Tomková, E. & Grubhoffer, L. (1988) Isolation of TBE virus from the tick *Ixodes hexagonus*. *Folia Parasitol. (Prague)* **35**: 273–276.

Kruuk, H. (1964) Predators and anti-predator behaviour of black-headed gull (*Larus ridibundus* L.). *Behav. Suppl.* **11**: 1–129.

Kumar, A. & Pandey, S.D. (1990) Classification of the follicle population based on oocyte diameter and number of granulosa cells in the ovary of large-eared hedgehogs, *Hemiechinus auritus* Gmelin. *Acta Physiol. Hung.* **76**: 165–173.

Kuttin, E.S., Beemer, A.M. & Gerson, U. (1976) A dermatitis in a hedgehog associated with *Sarcoptes scabei* and fungi. *Mykosen* **20**: 51–53.

Lancum, F.H. (1951) *Wild Mammals and the Land*. London: Ministry of Agriculture Fisheries and Food, Bulletin No. 150., H.M.S.O.

Landsberg, L. & Young, J.B. (1983) Autonomic regulation of thermogenesis. In *Mammalian Thermogenesis*, L. Girardier & M.J. Stock (eds.), pp. 99–140. London: Chapman & Hall.

Lane Fox, R. (1989) Sex, drugs and other hedgehog hobbies. *Weekend Financial Times*, **XVIII**, November 11.

Laplaud, P.M., Saboureau, M., Beaubatie, L. & El-Omari, B. (1989) Seasonal variations of plasma lipids and lipoproteins in the hedgehog and animal model for lipoprotein metabolism in relation to plasma thyroxine and testosterone levels. *Biochim. Biophys. Acta* **1005**: 143–156.

Laubmeier, E. (1985) [Observations on the endoparasites of *Erinaceus europaeus* in the wild and hibernating in cages, and treatment with ivermectin.] Inaugural Thesis, Ludwig Maximilians Universität, München. (In German, English abstract seen only.)

Laukola, S. & Suomalainen, S. (1971) Studies on the physiology of the hibernating hedgehog 13. Circum-annual changes of triglyceride fatty acids in white and brown adipose tissue. *Ann. Acad. Sci. fenn. A,IV, Biol.* **180**: 1–11.

Lawrence, M.J. & Brown, R.W. (1973) *Mammals of Britain. Their Tracks, Trails and Signs*. London: Blandford Press.

Lescoat, D., Saboureau. M., Castaing, L. & Chambon, Y. (1985) The hedgehog uterus. *Acta. anat.* **122**: 29–34.

Leyhausen, P. (1963) The communal organisation of solitary mammals. *Symp. Zool. Soc. Lond.* **14**: 249–263.

Liebisch, A. & Walter, G. (1986) [Studies on ticks (Ixodidae) in domestic and wild animals in Germany: on the occurrence and biology of the hedgehog tick (*Ixodes hexagonus*) and the fox tick (*Ixodes canisuga*).] *Deutsche Tierärz. Wochenschr.* **93**: 447–450. (In German, English abstract seen only.)

Lienhardt, G. (1982) Beobachtungen zur Morphologie, Jugendentwicklung und zum Verhalten von Weißbauchigeln *Erinaceus albiventris* (*Atelerix pruneri* [Wagner 1841]) in Gefangenschaft. *Säugetierk. Mitt.* **30**: 251–259.

Lim Boo Liat (1967) Note on the food habits of *Ptilocercus lowii* (pentail tree shrew) and *Echinosorex gymnurus* (Raffles) (moonrat) in Malaya with remarks on 'ecological labelling' by parasite patterns. *J. Zool. Lond.* **152:** 375–379.

Lindemann, W. (1951) Zur Psychologie des Igels. *Z. Tierpsychol.* **8:** 224–251.

Linstow, V. (1904) Neue Helminthen aus Westafrika. *Centralblatt Bakteriol., Parasitenk., Infektionskr. Hygiene. Abt. 1 Originale* **36:** 379–383.

Little, T.W.A., Parker, B.N.J., Stevens, A.E., Hathaway, S.C. & Markson, L.M. (1981) Inapparent infection of sheep in Britain by leptospires of the Australis serogroup. *Res. Vet. Sci.* **31:** 386–387.

Little, T.W.A., Swan, C., Thompson, H.V. & Wilesmith, J.W. (1982) Bovine tuberculosis in domestic and wild mammals in an area of Dorset. III. The prevalence of tuberculosis in mammals other than badgers and cattle. *J. Hyg. Camb.* **89:** 225–234.

Liu, B., Wohlfart, B. & Johansson, B.W. (1990) Mechanical restitution at different temperatures in papillary muscles from rabbit, rat and hedgehog. *Cryobiology* **27:** 596–604.

Liu, B., Arlock, P., Wohlfart, B. & Johansson, B.W. (1991) Temperature effects on the Na and Ca currents in rat and hedgehog's ventricular muscle. *Cryobiology* **28:** 96–104.

Liu, Ch'eng-Chao (1937) Notes on the food of Chinese hedgehogs. *J. Mammal.* **18:** 355–357.

Lohiya, N.K. & Dixit, V.P. (1975) Sustained fertility in a non-scrotal mammal, the Indian hedgehog (*Hemiechinus auritus Collaris*) after CdCl$_2$ administration. *Acta anat.* **93:** 96–303.

Lopez-Mascaraque, L., De Carlos, J.A. & Valverde, F. (1986) Structure of the olfactory bulb of the hedgehog (*Erinaceus europaeus*): description of cell types in the granular layer. *J. Comp. Neurol.* **253:** 135–152.

Lyman, C.P. (1982) Why bother to hibernate?, Who is who among the hibernators? Entering hibernation, The hibernating state, Sensitivity to arousal, Mechanisms of arousal, Hibernation: some intrinsic factors, Hibernation: responses to external challenges, Recent theories of hibernation. In *Hibernation and Torpor in Mammals and Birds,* C.P. Lyman, J.S. Willis, A. Malan & L.C.H. Wang (eds.), pp. 1–91, 104–123, 172–205, 283–301. London: Academic Press.

Lyman, C.P. & O'Brien, R.C. (1986) Is brown fat necessary? In *Living in the Cold. Physiological and Biochemical Adaptations,* H.C. Heller, X.J. Musacchia & L.C.H. Wang (eds.), pp. 109–116. New York: Elsevier.

Macchioni, G. (1967) Infestione del riccio (*Erinaceus europaeus* L., 1758) da larve di *Mesocestoides lineatus* (Goeze, 1782) (Railliet, 1893). *Annali Fac. Med. Pisa* **19:** 325–339.

McAllister, H.A. & Keahey, K.K. (1971) Infection of a hedgehog (*Erinaceus albiventris*) by *Corynebacterium pseudotuberculosis. Vet. Rec.* **89:** 280.

McDiarmid, A. (1976) Some research needs in the zoonoses. In *Wildlife Disease,* L.A. Page (ed.), pp. 369–378. New York: Plenum.

Macdonald, D.W. (ed.) (1984) *Encyclopedia of Mammals Vol.II.* London: George Allen and Unwin.

Macdonald, D.W., Ball, F.G. & Hough, N.G. (1980) The evaluation of home range size and configuration using radio tracking data. In *A Handbook on Biotelemetry and Radio Tracking*, C.J. Amlaner & D.W. Macdonald (eds.), pp. 405–424. Oxford: Pergamon Press.

McDougal, A.C., Rees, R.J.W. & Lowe, C. (1979) Preliminary histopathological data on experimental *Mycobacterium leprae* infections in the hedgehog. *J. Med. Microbiol.* **12:** VII (abstract).

McLaughlan, J.D. & Henderson, W.M. (1947) The occurrence of foot-and-mouth disease in the hedgehog under natural conditions. *J. Hyg. Camb.* **45:** 474–479.

McNab, B.K. (1963) Bioenergetics and the determination of home range size. *Amer. Nat.* **XCVII** No. 894: 133–139.

Mace, G., Harvey, P. & Clutton-Brock, T. (1981) Brain size and ecology in small mammals. *J. Zool. Lond.* **193,** 333–354.

Machin, C. & Arnanz, E. (1989) Study of the testis in the active and hibernating hedgehog. *Folia Morphol. (Prague)* **37:** 172–178.

Maggs, M.J. (1985) Hedgehog information. *Vet. Rec.* **June 29:** 699.

Maheshwari, U.K. (1982) Some observations on reproduction of the Indian hedgehog (*Hemiechinus auritus collaris* Gray, 1830). *Säugetierk. Mitt.* **30:** 184–189.

Maheshwari, U.K. (1984) Food of the long eared hedgehog in Ravine near Agra. *Acta Theriol.* **29:** 133–137.

Maheshwari, U.K. (1986) Seasonal incidence of infection of *Rhipicephalus sanguineus* (Acarina) on Indian hedgehog *Hemiechinus auritus collaris* (Gray). *Indian J. Ecol.* **13:** 169–171.

Maheshwari, U.K. & Jain, S.P. (1981) On the occurrence of a helminth from an Indian hedgehog, *Hemiechinus auritus collaris* (Gray)—a new host record. *Vet. Res. J.* **4:** 151–156.

Majeed, S.K. & Cooper, J.E.(1984) Lesions associated with a *Capillaria* infestation in the European hedgehog (*Erinaceus europaeus*). *J. Comp. Path.* **94:** 625–628.

Majeed, S.K., Morris, P.A. & Cooper, J.E. (1989) Occurrence of the lungworms *Capillaria* and *Crenosoma* spp. in British hedgehogs (*Erinaceus europaeus*). *J. Comp. Path.* **100:** 27–36.

Malan, A. (1982) Respiration and acid-base state in hibernation. In *Hibernation and Torpor in Mammals and Birds*, C.P. Lyman, J.S. Willis, A. Malan & L.C.H. Wang (eds.), pp. 237–282. London: Academic Press.

Mallon, D.P. (1985) The mammals of the Mongolian People's Republic. *Mamm. Rev.* **15:** 71–102.

Mantovani, A., Morganti, L., Caporale, V., Gramenzi, F., Tonelli, E. & Cagnolaro, L. (1972) Ricerca di *Histoplasma capsulatum* in micromammiferi dell'Abruzzo. *Giorn. Malatt. Infett. Parass.* **24:** 461–462. (Abstract seen only.)

Marshall, F.H.A. (1911) The male generative cycle in the hedgehog; with experiments on the functional correlation between essential and accessory sexual organs. *J. Physiol.* **43:** 247–259.

Mas-Coma, S. & Feliu, C. (1984) Helminthfauna from small mammals (insectivores and rodents) on the Pityusic Islands. *Monographie Biol.* **52:** 469–525.

Mas-Coma, S. & Montoliu, I. (1987) The life cycle of *Dollfusinus frontalis*, a brachylaimid trematode of small mammals (Insectivora and Rodentia). *Int. J. Parasitol.* **17:** 1063–1079.

Maskar, U. (1953) Über die experimentell erzeugte Entwicklung des Hundebandwurmes (*Mesocestoides lineatus*) aus den Dithyridien von Huhn und Igel. *Schweiz. Archiv Tierheilk.* **95:** 188–193.

Massey, C.I. (1972) A study of hedgehog road mortality in the Scarborough district, 1966–1971. *Leeds Nat.* **922:** 103–105.

Matthews, P.R.J. & McDiarmid, A. (1977) *Mycobacterium avium* infection in freeliving hedgehogs (*Erinaceus europaeus*). *Res. Vet. Sci.* **22:** 388.

Matthiese, T. & Kunstyr, I. (1974) Lungenwurmbefall (*Crenosoma striatum*) beim Igel. *Berl. Münch. Tierärz. Wochenschr.* **87:** 479–480.

Mayer, H. & Weiss, H.E. (1985) Salmonellosis and salmonellae in hedgehogs. *Prakt. Tierärzt* **66:** 574–578.

Matuschka, F.-R. (1984) Endodyogeny in *Isospora rastegaievae* from the Eurasian hedgehog (*Erinaceus europaeus* L.). *Parasitology* **88:** 9–12 + 1 unpaginated plate.

Matuschka, F.-R., Richter, D., Fischer, P. & Spielman, A. (1990a) Time of repletion of subadult *Ixodes ricinus* ticks feeding on diverse hosts. *Parasitol. Res.* **76:** 540–544.

Matuschka, F.-R., Richter, D., Fischer, P. & Spielman, A. (1990b) Nocturnal detachment of the tick *Ixodes hexagonus* from nocturnally active hosts. *Med. Vet. Entomol.* **4:** 415–420.

Mehl, R. (1972) Lopper, flått og midd på piggsvin i Norge. *Fauna* **25:** 186–196.

Meritt, D.A. Jr. (1981) Husbandry reproduction and behavior of the West African hedgehog *Erinaceus albiventris* at Lincoln Park Zoo Chicago Illinois USA. *Int. Zoo Ybk* **21:** 128–131.

Meyer, G., Gonzalez-Hernandez, T., Carrillo-Padilla, F. & Ferres-Torres, R. (1989) Aggregations of granule cells in the basal forebrain islands of Calleja, golgi and cytoarchitectonic study in different mammals including man. *J. Comp. Neurol.* **284:** 405–428.

Middleton, A.D. (1935) Factors controlling the population of the partridge (*Perdix perdix*) in Great Britain. *Proc. Zool. Soc. Lond.* **105:** 795–815.

Molenaar, T (1988) *Discovering the Art of Mallorcan Cookery*. Palma de Mallorca: Moll.

Moors, P.J. (1979) Observations on the nesting habits of the European hedgehog in the Manawatu sand country, New Zealand. *N. Z. J. Zool.* **6:** 489–492.

Morel, C.P. & Sobrero, L. (1976) *Haemaphysalis erinacei* (Pavesi 1884) in Italia. *Atti Soc. Ital. Sci. Vet.* **30:** 605–606.

Morris, B. (1959) The transmission of passive immunity in an insectivore. *Nature* **184:** 1151.

Morris, B. (1960) The transmission of anti-*Brucella* agglutinins from the mother to the young in *Erinaceus europaeus*. *Proc. Roy. Soc. (B)* **152:** 137–141.

Morris, B. (1961) Some observations on the breeding season of the hedgehog and the rearing and handling of the young. *Proc. Zool. Soc. Lond.* **136:** 201–206.

Morris, B. (1967) The European hedgehog. In *The UFAW Handbook on the Care and Management of Laboratory Animals* 3rd edn., A.N. Worden & W. Lane-Petter (eds.), pp. 478–488. Edinburgh: Churchill Livingstone.

Morris, P.A. (1966) The hedgehog in London. *Lond. Nat.* **45:** 43–49.

Morris, P.A. (1969) Some aspects of the ecology of the hedgehog (*Erinaceus europaeus*). Ph.D. Thesis. University of London.

Morris, P.A (1970) A method for determining absolute age in the hedgehog. *J. Zool. Lond.* **161:** 277–281.

Morris, P.A (1971) Epiphyseal fusion in the forefoot as a means of age determination in the hedgehog (*Erinaceus europaeus*) *J. Zool. Lond.* **164:** 254–259.

Morris, P.A. (1973) Winter nests of the hedgehog (*Erinaceus europaeus* L.). *Oecologia* (Berl.) **11:** 299–313.

Morris, P.A. (1975) Studying hedgehogs. *Nat. Sci. Schools* **13:** 47–49.

Morris, P.A. (1977) Pre-weaning mortality in the hedgehog (*Erinaceus europaeus*). *J. Zool. Lond.* **182:** 162–167.

Morris, P.A. (1983) *Hedgehogs.* Weybridge: Whittet.

Morris, P.A. (1984) An estimate of the minimum body weight necessary for hedgehogs (*Erinaceus europaeus*) to survive hibernation. *J. Zool. Lond.* **203:** 291–294.

Morris, P.A. (1985a) The effects of supplementary feeding on movements of hedgehogs (*Erinaceus europaeus*). *Mamm. Rev.* **15:** 23–32.

Morris, P.A. (ed.) (1985b) Flea powder and hedgehogs. *Mamm. Soc. Newsl.* **61 January**.

Morris, P.A. (1986) Nightly movements of hedgehogs (*Erinaceus europaeus*) in forest edge habitat. *Mammalia* **50:** 395–398.

Morris, P.A. (1988a) *The Hedgehog.* Aylesbury: Shire Natural History.

Morris, P.A. (1988b) A study of home range and movements in the hedgehog (*Erinaceus europaeus*). *J. Zool. Lond.* **214:** 433–449.

Morris, P.A. (1989) Hedgehogs in New Zealand. *Mammalaction* **45:** 5.

Morris, P.A. (1991) Family Erinaceidae. In *The Handbook of British Mammals*, 3rd edn., G.B. Corbet & S. Harris (eds.), pp. 37–43. Oxford: Blackwell.

Morris, P.A. & English, M.P. (1969) *Trichophyton mentagrophytes* var. *erinacei* in British hedgehogs. *Sabouraudia* **7:** 122–128.

Morris, P.A. & English, M.P. (1973) Transmission and course of *Trichophyton erinacei* infections in British hedgehogs. *Sabouraudia* **11:** 42–47.

Morris, P.A. & Morris, M.J. (1988) Distribution and abundance of hedgehogs (*Erinaceus europaeus*) on New Zealand roads. *N. Z. J. Zool.* **15:** 491–498

Muir K. (ed.) (1962) *Macbeth. The Arden Shakespeare* 9th edn. London: Methuen and Harvard University Press.

Munshi, S. & Pandey, S.D. (1987) The oestrous cycle in the large-eared hedgehog, *Hemiechinus auritus* Gmelin. *Anim. Reprod. Sci.* **13:** 157–160.

Nicholls, D. & Locke, R. (1983) Cellular mechanisms of heat dissipation. In *Mammalian Thermogenesis*, L. Girardier & M.J. Stock (eds.), pp. 8–49. London: Chapman & Hall.

Nicoll, M.E & Rathbun, G.B. (1990) *African Insectivora and Elephant-Shrews: an Action Plan for their Conservation*, Gland, Switzerland: IUCN.

Nielsen, K.C. & Owman, C. (1972) Sympathetic nervous system II. Histochemistry. *Acta physiol. scand. suppl.* **380:** 106–112.

Niethammer, J. (1973) Zur Kenntnis der Igel (Erinaceidae) Afghanistans. *Z. Säugetierk.* **38:** 271–276.

Nowak, R.M. & Paradiso, J.L. (1983) *Walker's Mammals of the World* Vol. I. 4th edn. Baltimore: Johns Hopkins University Press.

Nowak, W. (1972) Zur Haltung von spätherbstlichen 'Igelkindern' (*Erinaceus europaeus*). *Z. Angew. Zool.* **59:** 285–288.

Nowak, W. (1977) Zur Haltung von untergewichtigen Herbstigeln (*Erinaceus* sp.) Eine Vergleichsstudie. *Z. Angew. Zool.* **64:** 101–103.

Obrtel, R. & Holišová V. (1981) The diet of hedgehogs in an urban environment. *Folia Zool.* **30:** 193–201.

Ognev, S.I. (1928) *Mammals of Eastern Europe and Northern Asia Vol. 1 Insectivora and Chiroptera*. Translation 1962, Israel Programme for Scientific Translations, Jerusalem.

Okaeme, A.N. & Osakwe, M.E. (1985) Ectoparasites of the African hedgehog *Atelerix albiventris* (Wagner) in the Kainji Lake area of Nigeria. *Afr. J. Ecol.* **23:** 167–169.

Okaeme, A.N. & Osakwe, M.E. (1988) Gastro intestinal helminths and food of the African hedgehog *Atelexia albiventris* (Wagna) in the Kainji Lake area of Nigeria. *Afr. J. Ecol.* **26:** 239–241.

Okely, J. (1983) *The Traveller-Gypsies*. Cambridge: Cambridge University Press.

Olsson, S.-O. R. (1972a) Dehydrogenases (LDH,MDH,G–6-PDH and alpha-GPDH) in the heart, liver, white and brown fat. *Acta physiol. scand. suppl.* **380:** 62–95.

Olsson, S.-O. R. (1972b) Ultrastructure of brown adipose tissue and myocardium. *Acta physiol. scand. suppl.* **380:** 117–130

Orlandi, V. (1972) [Trichinosis in the Ascoli Piceno Province of Italy.] *Atti Soc. Ital. Sci. Veter.* **26:** 482–484. (In Italian, English abstract seen only.)

Owen, R. (1868) *On the Anatomy of Vertebrates: Vol. 3 Mammals*. London: Longmans Green.

Owman, C. & von Studnitz, W. (1972) Sympathetic nervous system I. Metabolism. *Acta physiol. scand. suppl.* **380:** 96–105.

The Oxford Dictionary of Quotations (1979) 3rd edn. Oxford: Oxford University Press.

The Oxford English Dictionary (1989) 2nd edn. Oxford: Clarendon Press.

Packer, D.J. (1987) The influence of carotid arterial sounds on hearing sensitivity in mammals. *J. Zool. Lond.* **211:** 547–560.

Pandey, S.D. & Munshi, S. (1987) The genital system of the female large-eared hedgehog *Hemiechinus auritus* Gmelin. *Folia Biol. (Kraków)* **35**: 95–100 + unpaginated plates.

Pandolfi, M., Bjernstad, A. & Ericsson, H. (1972) Tissue activator of fibrinolysis in the hedgehog. *Acta physiol. scand. suppl.* **380**: 113–116.

Parkes, J. (1975) Some aspects of the biology of the hedgehog (*Erinaceus europaeus* L.) in the Manawatu, New Zealand. *N. Z. J. Zool.* **2**: 463–472.

Pearse, A.S. (1929) Ecology of the ectoparasites of Nigerian rodents and insectivores. *J. Mammal.* **10**: 229–239.

Pearse, A.S. (1930) The ecology of the internal parasites of Nigerian rodents and insectivores. *J. Elisha Mitchell Scient. Soc.* **45**: 221–238.

Petter, F. (1954) Nouvelle note biologique sur le hérisson du désert. *Mammalia* **18**: 220–221.

Philchagov, A.V. (1988) [Circadian activity and movement of hedgehogs based on individual tracking data.] *Biul. Moskovsk. Obsh. Ispyt. Prir. Otdel Biol.* **93**: 38–49. (In Russian with English summary.)

Pinatel, M.C., Durand, N. & Girod, C. (1970) Etude des variations de l'iodémie et de l'iode thryoïdien au cours du cycle annuel chez le hérisson (*Erinaceus europaeus* L.); comparaison avec l'histologie thyroïdienne. *C. R. Séances Soc. Biol. Ses Fil.* **164**: 1719–1722.

Placidi, L. (1957) Le hérisson (*Aethechinus algirus*) n'est pas réceptif au virus de Sanarelli (Myxome infectieux du Lapin). *Bull. L'academie Vet. de France* **30**: 281–283.

Poczopko, P. (1980) Relations of metabolic rate and body temperature. In *Comparative Physiology: Primitive Mammals*, K. Schmidt-Nielson, L. Bolis & C.R. Taylor (eds.), pp. 155–162. Cambridge: Cambridge University Press.

Poduschka, W. (1968) Über die Wahrnehmung von Ultraschall beim Igel, *Erinaceus europaeus roumanicus*. *Z. vergl. Physiol.* **61**: 420–426.

Poduschka, W. (1969) Ergänzungen zum Wissen über *Erinaceus e. roumanicus* und kritische Überlegungen zur bisherigen literatur über europäische Igel. *Z. Tierpsychol.* **26**: 761–804.

Poduschka, W. (1971) Einbeziehung von Bauen des Igels (*Erinaceus europaeus*) in die Wühltätigkeit von Wanderratten (*Rattus norvegicus*). *Säugetierk. Mitt.* **19**: 171–177.

Poduschka, W. (1977a) Das Paarungsvorspiel des Osteuropäischen Igels (*Erinaceus e. roumanicus*) und theoretische Überlegungen zum Problem männlicher Sexualpheromone. *Zool. Anz., Jena* **199**: 187–208.

Poduschka, W. (1977b) Insectivore communication. In *How Animals Communicate*, T.A. Sebeok (ed.), pp. 600–633. Bloomington: Indiana University Press.

Poduschka, W. (1979) Xerophthalmie bei einem Igel. *Kleinteir Praxis* **24**: 43–45.

Poduschka, W. (1981a) Starke Papillomatose bei einem Igel (*Erinaceus concolor roumanicus*). *Kleinteir Praxis* **26**: 379–380.

Poduschka, W. (1981b) Abnormes Sexualverhalten zusammengehaltener weiblicher *Hemiechinus auritus syriacus* (Insectivora: Erinaceinae). *Bijdr. Dierkd.* **51**: 81–88.

Poduschka, W. (1986) Halbseitiger Stachelverlust nach Milbenbefall bei *Hemiechinus auritus syriacus*, Wood 1876 (Insectivora:Erinaceinae). *Praktische Tierärzt* **67**: 804 & 807–808.

Poduschka, W. (1988) Ertser Beleg eines Albinos aus dem Verbreitungsgebiet des Weißbrustigels *Erinaceus concolor roumanicus* Barr-Hamilton, 1900. *Biol. Rundsch.* **26**: 217–219.

Poduschka, W. & Firbas, W. (1968) Das Selbstbespeicheln des Igels, *Erinaceus europaeus* Linné, 1758, steht in Beziehung zur Funktion des Jacobsonschen Organes. *Z. Säugertierk.* **33**: 160–172.

Poduschka, W. & Kieliger, F. (1972) Zur medizinischen Betreuung des Igels (*Erinaceus europaeus* und *Erinaceus europaeus roumanicus*). *Kleintier Praxis* **17**: 192–197.

Poduschka, W. & Poduschka, C. (1972) *Dearest Prickles. The Story of a Delightful Hedgehog Family*, London: Neville Spearman.

Poduschka, W. & Poduschka, C. (1983a) Klimateinflüsse auf Fruchtbarkeit, Wachstum und Verbreitung des Igels in Mittel- und Nordeuropa. *Sitzungsberichte Österr. Akad. Wissenschaften Mathem. -naturw. Kl.* **192**: 21–36.

Poduschka, W. & Poduschka, C. (1983b) Kreuzungsversuche an mitteleuropäischen Igeln (*Erinaceus concolor roumanicus* B.- Ham., 1900 × *Erinaceus europaeus* L., 1758). *Säugetierk. Mitt.* **31**: 1–12.

Poduschka, W. & Poduschka, C. (1986a) Zahnstein, Zahnfleischerkrankungen und Zahnanomalien bei Erinaceinen (Mammalia: Insectivora). *Z. Angew. Zool.* **73**: 231–243.

Poduschka, W. & Poduschka, C. (1986b) Fortpflanzung und Jungenentwicklung bei *Hemiechinus auritus* Fitzinger, 1866 (Insectivora: Erinaceinae). *Zool. Jb. Physiol.* **90**: 501–535.

Poduschka, W. & Saupe, E. (1981) *Das Igel Brevier*, Frankfurt a.M: Zoologische Gesellschaft.

Pomykal, J. (1985) A case of infestation of humans with fleas *Archaeopsylla erinacei* (Siphonaptera: Pulicidae). *Folia Parasitol. (Prague)* **32**: 348.

Poole, C. (1986) Osteomalacia in a young hedgehog. *Vet. Rec.* **June 21**: 707.

Potter, B. (1905) *The Tale of Mrs. Tiggy-winkle*. London: Frederick Warne.

Potter, J.M. (1987) Field notes. *Countryside* **25**: 718.

Prakash, I. (1955a) Notes on the desert hedgehog (*Hemiechinus auritus collaris* Gray). *J. Bombay Nat. Hist. Soc.* **52**: 921–922.

Prakash, I. (1955b) Cannibalism in hedgehogs. *J. Bombay Nat. Hist. Soc.* **52**: 922–923.

Prakash, I. (1959) Food of some Indian desert mammals. *J. Biol. Sci.* **2**: 100–109.

Prakash, I. (1960) Breeding of mammals in Rajasthan desert, India. *J. Mammal.* **41**: 386–389.

Proctor, E. (1949) Temperature changes in hibernating hedgehogs. *Nature* **163**: 108–109.

Racey, P.A. (1981) Environmental factors affecting the length of gestation in mammals. In *Environmental Factors in Mammal Reproduction*, D. Gilmore & B. Cook (eds.), pp. 199–213. London: Macmillan.

Räf, P.-O. (1988) Igelkotten och huggormen Fabelhäftiga försök i Skara på 1800-talet. *Svensk Veterinärtidning* 40: 615–617.

Ranson, R.M. (1941) New laboratory animals from wild species. Breeding a laboratory stock of hedgehogs (*Erinaceus europaeus* L.). *J. Hyg. Camb.* 41: 131–138.

Reeve, N.J. (1980) A simple and cheap radio tracking system for use on hedgehogs. In *A Handbook on Biotelemetry and Radio Tracking*, C.J. Amlaner & D.W. Macdonald (eds.), pp. 169–173. Oxford: Pergamon Press.

Reeve, N.J. (1981) A field study of the hedgehog (*Erinaceus europaeus*) with particular reference to movements and behaviour. Ph.D. Thesis, University of London.

Reeve, N.J. (1982) The home range of the hedgehog as revealed by a radio tracking study. *Symp. Zool. Soc. Lond.* 49, 207–230.

Reeve, N.J. & Morris P.A. (1985) Construction and use of summer nests by the hedgehog (*Erinaceus europaeus*). *Mammalia* 49: 187–194.

Reeve, N.J. & Morris P.A. (1986) Mating strategy in the hedgehog (*Erinaceus europaeus*). *J. Zool. Lond. (A)* 210: 613–644.

Reichholf, J. (1984) Über die Wirkung von Igelschutzzäunen im Siedlungsrandbereich. *Säugetierk. Mitt.* 31: 267.

Reichholf, J. (1986) Beeinflussen Perioden extremer Winterkälte die Überlebensrate des Igels *Erinaceus europaeus*. *Säugetierk. Mitt.* 33: 83–85.

Reichholf, J. & Esser, J. (1981) Daten sur Mortalität des Igels (*Erinaceus europaeus*) verursacht durch den Straßenverkehr. *Z. Säugertierk.* 46: 216–222.

Roberts, T.J. (1977) *The Mammals of Pakistan*. London: Ernest Benn.

Rook, D.A. (1959) Notes on the behaviour of hedgehogs in a suburban garden. *Lond. Nat.* 38: 30–32.

Rousselot, M. (1979) Étude du stress provoqué par divers anesthésiques chez le hérisson. Thesis, École Nationale Vétérinaire, Maisons-Alfort. (Abstract seen only.)

Rowe-Rowe, T. (1974) Daily and seasonal activity patterns of an African hedgehog. *Lammergeyer* 21: 34–36.

Ruempler, G. (1982) Insectivora. In *Handbook of Zoo Medicine*, H.G. Klos & E.M. Lang (eds.), pp. 312–316. New York: Van Nostrand Reinhold.

Ruprecht, A.L. (1972) Correlation structure of the skull dimensions in European hedgehogs. *Acta theriol.* XVII, 32: 419–442.

Saarikoski, P.-L. & Suomalainen, P. (1971) Studies on the physiology of the hibernating hedgehog 12. The glycogen content of the liver, heart, hindleg muscle and brown fat at different times of the year and in different phases of the hibernation cycle. *Ann. Acad. Sci. fenn. A.IV Biol.* 175: 1–7.

Saarikoski, P.-L. & Suomalainen, P. (1975) Studies on the physiology of the hibernating hedgehog 20. The changes in the adrenaline and noradrenaline level induced by seasons and hibernation cycle. *Ann. Acad. Sci. fenn. A.IV Biol.* 205: 1–9.

Saboureau, M. (1986) Hibernation in the hedgehog: influence of external and internal factors. In *Living in the Cold. Physiological and Biochemical Adaptations*, H.C. Heller, X.J. Musacchia & L.C.H. Wang (eds.), pp. 253–263. New York: Elsevier.

Saboureau, M. & Dutourné, B. (1981) The reproductive cycle in the male hedgehog (*Erinaceus europaeus* L.): a study of endocrine and exocrine testicular functions. *Reprod. Nutr. Dévelop.* **21**: 109–126.

Saboureau, M., Laurent, A.-M. & Boissin, J. (1982) Plasma testosterone binding protein capacity in relation to the annual testicular cycle in a hibernating mammal, the hedgehog (*Erinaceus europaeus* L.). *Gen. Comp. Endocrinol.* **47**: 59–63.

Saint Girons, M.C. (1969) Données sur la morphologie et la répartition de *Erinaceus europaeus* et *Erinaceus algirus*. *Mammalia* **33**: 206–218.

Salt, G.F.H. & Little, T.W.A. (1977) Leptospires isolated from wild mammals caught in the south west of England. *Res. Vet. Sci.* **22**: 126–127.

Sanchez-Toscano, F., Caminero, A.A., Machin, C. & Abella, G. (1989) Neuronal plasticity in the hedgehog supraoptic nucleus during hibernation. *Neuroscience* **31**: 543–550.

Sarajas, H.S.S. (1954) Observations on the electrocardiographic alterations in the hibernating hedgehog. *Acta physiol. scand.* **32**: 28–38.

Sarajas, H.S.S. (1967) Blood glucose studies in permanently cannulated hedgehogs during a bout of hibernation. *Ann. Acad. Sci. fenn. A.IV Biol.* **120**: 1–11.

Saupe, E. (1976) The hedgehog lungworm *Crenosoma striatum* (Zeder, 1800) and its control with tetramisole. *Vet. Med. Rev.* **1**: 91–96.

Saupe, E. & Poduschka, W. (1985) Igel. In *Krankheiten der Heimtiere*, K. Gabrisch & P. Zwart (eds.), pp. 75–96. Hanover: Schlütersche.

Saure, L. (1969) Histological studies on the sexual cycle of the male hedgehog (*Erinaceus europaeus* L.). *Aquilo, Ser. Zool.* **19**: 1–43.

Schein, E. & Hamel, D. (1983) Control of fleas in dogs, cats and hedgehogs with Tiguvon Spot-on. *Zentbl. Bakt. Mikrob. Hygiene, A* **256**: 271. (Abstract.)

Schicht, M. (1982a) *Der Igel als gelegentlicher patient in der Kleintierpraxis*, Beirat für Tierschutz und Tierhygiene der Hauptstadt der DDR Berlin. (Booklet.)

Schicht, M. (1982b) Der Igel als gelegentlicher patient in der Kleintierpraxis. *Monatshefte Vet.* **37**: 829–831.

Schoenfeld, M. & Yom-Tov, Y. (1985) The biology of two species of hedgehogs, *Erinaceus europaeus concolor* and *Hemiechinus auritus aegyptius*, in Israel. *Mammalia* **49**: 339–355.

Searle, J.B. & Erskine, I. (1985) Evidence for a widespread karyotypic race of hedgehog (*Erinaceus europaeus*) in Britain. *J. Zool. Lond.* **206**: 276–278.

Sebek, Z., Sixl, W., Reinthaler, F., Valová, M., Schneeweiss, W., Stünzner, D. & Mascher, F. (1989) Results of serological examination for leptospires of domestic and wild animals in the upper Nile province (Sudan). *J. Hygiene, Epidemiol., Microbiol. Immunol.* **33**: 337–345.

Sellami, M., Belkacemi, H. & Sellami, S. (1989) Premier inventaire des mammiferes de la réserve naturelle de Mergueb (M'Sila, Algerie). *Mammalia* **53:** 116–121.

Senturia, J.B. & Johansson, B.W. (1972) Body and organ weights, body temperature. *Acta physiol. scand. suppl.* **380:** 21–27.

Senturia, J.B., Eklund, B. & Johansson, B.W. (1972) Blood ions. *Acta physiol. scand. suppl.* **380:** 31–35.

Sexton, D.B. (1989) The curse of Mrs Tiggywinkle. *BBC Wildl. Mag.* **June issue:** 402.

Shakespeare, W. (1564–1616) *The Complete Works of William Shakespeare*, 1947. London: Waverley.

Shehata, R. (1981) Para-vaginal and anal glands in the Egyptian hedgehog Hemiechinus auritus (Fischer, 1829). *Zool. Soc. Egypt. Bull.* (= *al-gam'iyyah al-Misriyyah li-'llm al-Hayawan*) **31:** 31–36.

Shepherd, A.J., Leman, P.A. & Swanepoel, R. (1989) Viremia and antibody response of small African and laboratory animals of Crimea–Congo haemorrhagic fever virus infection. *Amer. J. Trop. Med. Hygiene* **40:** 541–547.

Shilova-Krassova, S.A. (1952) [The food of the hedgehog (*Erinaceus europaeus*) in southern woodlands.] *Zool. Zh.* **31:** 944–947. (In Russian, seen only in translation.)

Shkolnik, A. (1980) Energy metabolism in hedgehogs. In *Comparative Physiology: Primitive Mammals*, K. Schmidt-Nielson, L. Bolis & C.R. Taylor (eds.), pp. 148–154. Cambridge: Cambridge University Press.

Short, R.V. (1984) Oestrus and menstrual cycles. In *Reproduction in Mammals: 3. Hormonal Control of Reproduction*, 2nd edn., C.R. Austin & R.V. Short (eds.), pp. 115–152. Cambridge: Cambridge University Press.

Shortridge, K.F. & Belyavin, G. (1973) Occurrence of canine adenovirus antibodies and non-specific inhibitors of haemagglutination in the sera of diverse animal species. *J. Comp. Path.* **83:** 181–189.

Simpson, D.I.H. (1968) Arboviruses and free-living wild animals. *Symp. Zool. Soc. Lond.* **24:** 13–28.

Simpson, J.R. (1974) Tinea barbae caused by *Trichophyton erinacei*. *Br. J. Dermatol.* **60:** 697–698.

Sixl, W., Batikova, M., Stunzner, D., Sekeyova, M., Sixl-Voigt, B. & Gresikova, M. (1973) Haemagglutination-inhibiting antibodies against arboviruses in animal sera collected in some regions of Austria. II. *Zentralblatt für Bakteriologie, Parasitenkunde, Infektionskrankeiten und Hygiene I*, Originale **224A:** 303–308.

Skoudlín, J. (1976) Zur Alterbestimmung bei *Erinaceus europaeus* und *Erinaceus concolor* (Insectivora: Erinaceidae). *Vest. cs. Spolec. zool.* **40:** 300–306.

Skoudlín, J. (1981) Age structure of Czechoslovak populations of *Erinaceus europaeus* and *Erinaceus concolor* (Insectivora: Erinaceidae). *Vest. cs. Spolec. zool.* **45:** 307–313.

Smith, J.M.B. (1968) Diseases of hedgehogs. *Vet. Bull.* **38:** 425–430.

Smithers. R.H.N. (1983) *Mammals of the Southern African Subregion*, Pretoria: University of Pretoria.

Smythe, R.H. (1967) Some more pages from an old diary. *Vet. Rev.* **18**: 35.

Soivio, A., Tähti, H. & Kristoffersson, R. (1968) Studies on the periodicity of hibernation in the hedgehog (*Erinaceus europaeus* L.) III. Hibernation in a constant ambient temperature of −5°C. *Ann. Zool. Fenn.* **5**: 224–226.

Sokolov, V.E., Shabadash, S.A. & Zelikina, T.I. (1982a) Some histochemical characteristics of the metabolism of the eccrine sweat glands of hedgehogs (*Erinaceus europaeus*) in the active state and during hibernation. *Dok. Biol. Sci.* **262**: 57–61. (Translated from *Dokl. Akad. Nauk. SSSR.*)

Sokolov, V.E., Shabadash, S.A. & Zelikina, T.I. (1982b) Cutaneous gland innervation of the hedgehog (*Erinaceus europaeus*) and its histochemical changes evoked by winter hibernation. *Dok. Biol. Sci.* **262**: 61–64. (Translated from *Dokl. Akad. Nauk. SSSR.*)

Stack, M.J., Higgins, R.J., Challoner, D.J. & Gregory, M.W. (1990) Herpesvirus in the liver of a hedgehog (*Erinaceus europaeus*). *Vet. Rec.* **127**: 620–621.

Štěrba, O. (1976) Zur Entstehung der Stacheln bei der Gattung *Erinaceus* (Mammalia, Insectivora). *Zool. Listy* **25**: 33–38 + unpaginated plate VI.

Štěrba, O. (1977) Prenatal development of central European insectivores. *Folia Zool.* **26**: 27–44.

Stieve, H. (1948) Zur Fortpflanzungsbiologie des Igels. *Verh. d. deut. Zoologen in Kiel*, 253–256.

Stocker, L. (1987) *The Complete Hedgehog*. London: Chatto & Windus.

Stocker, L. (1988) Artificial rearing of orphaned hedgehogs. *Proc. Symp. Assoc. Br. Wild Anim. Keep.* **13**: 45–50.

Stocker, L. (1991) *Code of Practice for the Rescue, Treatment, Rehabilitation and Release of Sick and Injured Wildlife*, Aylesbury: The Wildlife Hospital Trust.

Stocker, L. (1992) *Medication for Use in the Treatment of Hedgehogs*. Aylesbury: The Wildlife Hospital Trust.

Suomalainen, P. (1935) Über den Winterschlaf des Igels mit besonderer Berücksichtigung der enzymtätigkeit und des Bromstoffwechsels. *Ann. Acad. Sci. fenn. A.IV Biol.* **45**: 1–115.

Suomalainen, P. (1960) Stress and neurosecretion in the hibernating hedgehog. *Bull. Mus. Comp. Zool. (Harvard)* **124**: 271–283.

Suomalainen, P. & Rosokivi, V. (1973) Studies on the physiology of the hibernating hedgehog 17. The blood cell count at different times of the year and in different phases of the hibernation cycle. *Ann. Acad. Sci. fenn. A.IV Biol.* **198**: 1–8.

Suomalainen, P. & Saarikoski, P.-L. (1967) The content of non-esterified fatty acids and glycerol in the blood of the hedgehog during the hibernation period. *Experientia* **23**: 457–458.

Suomalainen, P. & Saarikoski, P.-L. (1971) Studies on the physiology of the hibernating hedgehog 14. Serum free fatty acid, glycerol and total lipid concentration at different times of the year and of the hibernating cycle. *Ann. Acad. Sci. fenn. A.IV Biol.* **184:** 1–6.

Suomalainen, P. & Suvanto, I. (1953) Studies on the physiology of the hibernating hedgehog 1. The body temperature. *Ann. Acad. Sci. fenn. A.IV Biol.* **20:** 1–20.

Suomalainen, P., Laukola, S. & Seppä, E. (1969) Studies on the physiology of the hibernating hedgehog 6. The serum and blood magnesium in relation to seasonal and hibernation cycles. *Ann. Acad. Sci. fenn. A.IV Biol.* **139:** 1–9.

Tadmor, A. & Rauchbach, K. (1972) Zum Vorkommen von Räude beim Igel; (*Erinaceus europaeus* (Linné)), Kurze Mitteilung. *Berl. Münch. Tierärz. Wochschr.* **11:** 214.

Tähti, H. (1975) Effects of changes in CO_2 and O_2 concentrations in inspired gas in respiration in the hibernating hedgehog (*Erinaceus europaeus* L.). *Ann. Zool. Fenn.* **12:** 183–187.

Tähti, H. (1978) Seasonal differences in O_2 consumption and respiratory quotient in a hibernator (*Erinaceus europaeus* L.). *Ann. Zool. Fenn.* **15:** 69–75.

Tähti, H. & Soivio A. (1975) Blood gas concentration, acid-base balance and blood pressure in hedgehogs in the active state and in hibernation with periodic respiration. *Ann. Zool. Fenn.* **12:** 188–192.

Tähti, H. & Soivio A. (1977) Respiratory and circulating differences between induced and spontaneous arousal in hibernating hedgehogs (*Erinaceus europaeus* L.). *Ann. Zool. Fenn.* **14:** 198–203.

Tan, R.J.S., Davey, G.P. & Smith, J.M.B. (1971) A strain of *Mycoplasma* from the short-eared European hedgehog (*Erinaceus europaeus*). *Res. Vet. Sci.* **12:** 390–391.

Tappe, J.P., Weitzman, I., Liu, S.-K., Dolensek, E.P. & Karp, D. (1983) Systemic *Mycobacterium marinum* infection in a European hedgehog. *J. Amer. Vet. Med. Assoc.* **183:** 1280–1281.

Tapper, S. (1992) *Game Heritage. An Ecological Review from Shooting and Gamekeeping Records*. Fordingbridge, UK: Game Conservancy.

Taylor, J. (1968) Salmonella in wild animals. *Symp. Zool. Soc. Lond.* **24:** 51–73.

Taylor, C.R. (1980) Evolution of mammalian homeothermy: a two-step process? In *Comparative Physiology: Primitive Mammals*, K. Schmidt-Nielson, L. Bolis & C.R. Taylor (eds.), pp. 100–111. Cambridge: Cambridge University Press.

Tennyson, A. (1809–1892) *The Poems of Tennyson*, C. Ricks, (ed.) (1969) *Longman's Annotated English Poets*. London: Longmans.

Teräväinen, T. & Saure, A. (1976) Changes in the testicular metabolism of dehydroepiandrosterone during the annual cycle of the hedgehog (*Erinaceus europaeus* L.). *Gen. Comp. Endocrinol.* **29:** 328–332.

Thiele, H.U. (1977) *Carabid Beetles in their Environments*. Berlin: Springer.

Thomas, E.A. (1985) Maggot control. *Vet. Rec.* **116:** 699.

Thompson, G.B. (1936) The parasites of British birds and mammals VII.

Records of Ixodoidea from hedgehogs and their nests. *Entomol. Monthly Mag.* **72**: 116-118.

Thorell, J., Johansson, B.W. & Senturia, J.B. (1972) Carbohydrate metabolism. *Acta physiol. scand. suppl.* **380**: 43–48.

Thorns, C.J. & Morris, J.A. (1983) The immune spectrum of *Mycobacterium bovis* infections in some mammalian species: a review. *Vet. Bull.* **53**: 543–550.

Thorns, C., Morris, J.A. & Little, T.W.A. (1982) A spectrum of immune responses and pathological conditions between certain animal species to experimental *Mycobacterium bovis* infection. *Br. J. exp. Path.* **63**: 562–572.

Thorpe, L. (translator) (1966) *The History of the Kings of Britain*, by Geoffrey of Monmouth (*c.* 1136). London: Penguin Books.

Timme, A. (1980) Krankheits- und Todesursachen beim Igel (*Erinaceus europaeus*). Sektionsfälle 1975 bis 1979. *Prakt. Tierärzt* **61**: 744, 746, 748.

Tomopolous D. (1970) [Research on zoonoses in Greece. Study of the occurrence of salmonellae in wild animals. I. Hedgehog.] *Scient. Ybk Aristotelean Univ. Thessaloniki*, **10**: 79–90. (In Greek, English abstract seen only.)

Trayhurn, P. & James, W.P.T. (1983) Thermogenesis and obesity. In *Mammalian Thermogenesis*, L. Girardier & M.J. Stock (eds.), pp. 234–258. London: Chapman & Hall.

Trevor-Deutsch, B. & Hackett, D.F. (1980) An evaluation of several grid trapping methods by comparison with radio telemetry in a home range study of the eastern chipmunk (*Tamias striatus* L.). In *A Handbook on Biotelemetry and Radio Tracking*, C.J. Amlaner & D.W. Macdonald (eds.), pp. 375–386. Oxford: Pergamon Press.

Twigg, G.I., Cuerden, C.M. & Hughes, D.M. (1968) Leptospirosis in small mammals. *Symp. Zool. Soc. Lond.* **24**: 75–98.

Uuspää, A.V.J. (1963a) The 5-hydroxytryptamine content of the brain and some other organs of the hedgehog (*Erinaceus europaeus*) during activity and hibernation. *Experientia* **19**: 156–159.

Uuspää, A.V.J. (1963b) Effects of hibernation on the noradrenaline and adrenaline contents of the adrenal glands in the hedgehog. *Ann. Med. exp. Biol. Fenn.* **41**: 349–354.

Valverde, F., Lopez-Mascaraque, L. & De Carlos, J.A. (1989) Structure of the nucleus olfactorius anterior of the hedgehog, *Erinaceus europaeus*. *J. Comp. Neurol.* **279**: 581–600.

Van der Colf, W. (1987) A rather prickly affair. *S. Afr. Panorama* **February**: 48–50.

Vasilenko, V.N. (1988) Age and sex structure in the white-chested hedgehog *Erinaceus concolor* (Martin) from the Caucasus. *Ékologiya (Sverdlosk)* **19**: 45–49.) (English translation in *Sov. J. Ecol*, July–August 1988: 220–223.)

Vaughan, T.A. (1986) *Mammalogy*, 3rd edn. Philadelphia: Saunders College Publishing.

Venables, L.S.V. & Venables U.M. (1972) Unusual hedgehog diet. *Nat. Wales* **13**: 56.

Versluys, S.D.W. (1975) Wel en wee van der egel. *Diergeneeskundig Memorandum* **22nd Year:** 235–301.

Vesmanis, I.E. (1979) Bemerkungen zur Verbreitung und Taxonomie von *Erinaceus a. algirus* Lereboullet 1842 und *Paraechinus aethiopicus deserti* Loche 1858. *Afr. Small Mammal News. Special* **1:** 1–14.

Vincent, J.F.V. & Owers, P. (1986) Mechanical design of hedgehog spines and porcupine quills. *J. Zool. Lond.*(A) **210:** 55–75.

Viret, J. (1938) Les érinacéidés actuels et fossiles. *Bull. Soc. Linnéen, Lyon* 7e Année, No. 5, 142–144.

Vizoso, A.D. & Thomas, W.E. (1981) Paramyxoviruses of the Morbilli group in the wild hedgehog, *Erinaceus europaeus. Br. J. exp. Pathol.* **62:** 79–86.

Voigt, D.R. & Tinline, R.R. (1980) Strategies for analyzing radio tracking data. In *A Handbook on Biotelemetry and Radio Tracking*, C.J. Amlaner & D.W. Macdonald (eds.), pp. 405–424. Oxford: Pergamon Press.

Walhovd, H. (1975) Winter activity of Danish hedgehogs in 1973/74, with information on the size of the animals observed and location of the recordings. *Nat. Jutland.* **18:** 53–61 (English version of *Flora og Fauna* **82:** 35–42).

Walhovd, H. (1978) The overwintering pattern of Danish hedgehogs in outdoor confinement, during three successive winters. *Nat. Jutland.* **20:** 273–284.

Walhovd, H. (1979) Partial arousals from hibernation in hedgehogs in outdoor hibernacula. *Oecologia (Berl.)* **40:** 141–153.

Walhovd, H. (1981) Body temperature relations in suckling hedgehogs *Erinaceus europaeus. Acta Theriol.* **26:** 499–503.

Walhovd, H. (1990) Records of young hedgehogs (*Erinaceus europaeus*) in a private garden. *Z. Säugetierk.* **55:** 289–297.

Walin, T.A., Soivio, A. & Kristoffersson, R. (1968) Histological changes in the reproductive system of female hedgehogs during the hibernation season. *Ann. Zool. Fenn.* **5:** 227–229.

Wallach, J.D. & Boever, W.J. (1983) *Diseases of Exotic Animals. Medical and Surgical Management.* Philadelphia: W.B. Saunders.

Walter, G. (1981) [The seasonal dynamics and biology of *Ixodes trianguliceps*, Birula 1895 (Ixodoidea, Ixodidiae) in northern Germany.] *Z. Ange. Entomol.* **92:** 433–440. (In German, English abstract seen only.)

Walton, G.M. & Walton, D.W. (1973) Notes on hedgehogs of the lower Indus valley. *Korean J. Zool.* **16:** 161–170.

Wang, L.C.H. (1982) Hibernation and the endocrines. In *Hibernation and Torpor in Mammals and Birds*, C.P. Lyman, J.S., Willis, A. Malan & L.C.H. Wang (eds.), pp. 206–236. London: Academic Press.

Webster, W.M (1957) Susceptibility of the hedgehog (*Erinaceus europaeus*) to infections with *Leptospira pomona. Nature* **180:** 1372.

Werner, R. & Riecke A. (1987) Role of adrenal steroids in the control of regulatory heat production: effect of an adrenocorticostatic agent in the hedgehog, guinea-pig, Syrian hamster and Cretan spiny mouse. *Gen. Comp. Endocrinol.* **66:** 35 (abstract.)

Werner, R. & Vens-Cappell, F. (1982) Pituitary-adrenal response to acute cold: effect of metopirone on regulatory heat production in hedgehogs *Erinaceus europaeus*. *Acta Endocrinol. Suppl.* **99**: 104–105.

Willis, J.S.W. (1982) The mystery of the periodic arousal, Intermediary metabolism in hibernation, Is there cold adaptation of metabolism in hibernators? In *Hibernation and Torpor in Mammals and Birds*, C.P. Lyman, J.S. Willis, A. Malan & L.C.H. Wang (eds.), pp. 92–103, 124–171. London: Academic Press.

Wodzicki, K.A. (1950) Hedgehog. *Bull. Dep. Sci. Ind. Res. Wellington* **98**: 55–64.

Wroot, A.J. (1984a) Feeding ecology of the European hedgehog, *Erinaceus europaeus*. Ph.D. Thesis, University of London.

Wroot, A.J. (1984b) Hedgehogs. In *The Encyclopedia of Mammals Vol 2*, D.W. Macdonald (ed.), pp. 750–757. London: George Allen & Unwin.

Wroot, A.J. (1985a) A quantitative method for estimating the amount of earthworm (*Lumbricus terrestris*) in animal diets. *Oikos* **44**: 239–242.

Wroot, A.J. (1985b) Foraging in the European hedgehog, *Erinaceus europaeus*. *Mamm. Rev.* **15**: 2 (abstract.)

Wysocki, C.J., Beauchamp, G.K., Reidinger, R.R. & Wellington, J.L. (1985) Access of large and nonvolatile molecules to the omeronasal organ of mammals during social and feeding behaviours. *J. Chem. Ecol.* **11**: 1147–1159.

Yalden, D.W. (1976) The food of the hedgehog in England. *Acta Theriol.* **21**: 401–424.

Yates, T.L. (1984) Insectivores, elephant shrews, tree shrews, and dermopterans. In *Orders and Families of Recent Mammals of the World*, S. Anderson & J.K. Jones (eds.), pp. 117–144. Chichester: John Wiley.

Yongshan, Y. & Ficin, S. (1987) Sister chromatid exchange points in the heterochromatin and euchromatin regions of Chinese hedgehog chromosomes. *Theor. Appl. Genet.* **73**: 469–475. (Abstract only seen.)

Zardi, C., Adorisio, E., Gradoni, L., Pozio, E. & Bettini, S. (1980) *Toxoplasma gondii* in wild mammals of a Mediterranean biotope of Tuscany, Italy. *Trans. Roy. Soc. Trop. Med. Hygiene* **74**: 409–410.

Zherebtzova, O.V. (1982) [Materials on biology of *Erinaceus (Hemiechinus) auritus* in Zaunguzskiye Karakumy.] *Zool. Zh.* **61**: 411–418. (In Russian with English summary.)

Species Index

Page numbers in parentheses refer to illustrations
† = extinct.

299

General Index

Page numbers in parentheses refer to illustrations.
Numbers in bold refer to a section about a particular subject.